World Economic and Financial Surveys

WORLD ECONOMIC OUTLOOK
October 2012

Coping with High Debt and Sluggish Growth

International Monetary Fund

Cover and Design: Luisa Menjivar and Jorge Salazar
Composition: Maryland Composition

Cataloging-in-Publication Data

World economic outlook (International Monetary Fund)
  World economic outlook : a survey by the staff of the International Monetary Fund. —
Washington, DC : International Monetary Fund, 1980–
  v. ; 28 cm. — (1981–1984: Occasional paper / International Monetary Fund, 0251-6365).
— (1986– : World economic and financial surveys, 0256-6877)

Semiannual. Some issues also have thematic titles.
Has occasional updates, 1984–

  1. Economic development — Periodicals. 2. Economic forecasting — Periodicals.
3. Economic policy — Periodicals. 4. International economic relations — Periodicals.
I. International Monetary Fund. II. Series: Occasional paper (International Monetary Fund).
III. Series: World economic and financial surveys.

HC10.80

ISBN 978-1-61635-389-6

Publication orders may be placed online, by fax, or through the mail:
International Monetary Fund, Publication Services
P.O. Box 92780, Washington, DC 20090, U.S.A.
Tel.: (202) 623-7430 Fax: (202) 623-7201
E-mail: publications@imf.org
www.imfbookstore.org
www.elibrary.imf.org

CONTENTS

Tables

Online Tables

Figures

A number of assumptions have been adopted for the projections presented in the *World Economic Outlook*. It has been assumed that real effective exchange rates remained constant at their average levels during July 30–August 27, 2012, except for the currencies participating in the European exchange rate mechanism II (ERM II), which are assumed to have remained constant in nominal terms relative to the euro; that established policies of national authorities will be maintained (for specific assumptions about fiscal and monetary policies for selected economies, see Box A1 in the Statistical Appendix); that the average price of oil will be $106.18 a barrel in 2012 and $105.10 a barrel in 2013 and will remain unchanged in real terms over the medium term; that the six-month London interbank offered rate (LIBOR) on U.S. dollar deposits will average 0.7 percent in 2012 and 0.6 percent in 2013; that the three-month euro deposit rate will average 0.6 percent in 2012 and 0.2 percent in 2013; and that the six-month Japanese yen deposit rate will yield on average 0.4 percent in 2012 and 0.3 percent in 2013. These are, of course, working hypotheses rather than forecasts, and the uncertainties surrounding them add to the margin of error that would in any event be involved in the projections. The estimates and projections are based on statistical information available through mid-September 2012.

The following conventions are used throughout the *World Economic Outlook:*

. . .   to indicate that data are not available or not applicable;

–   between years or months (for example, 2011–12 or January–June) to indicate the years or months covered, including the beginning and ending years or months;

/   between years or months (for example, 2011/12) to indicate a fiscal or financial year.

"Billion" means a thousand million; "trillion" means a thousand billion.

"Basis points" refer to hundredths of 1 percentage point (for example, 25 basis points are equivalent to ¼ of 1 percentage point).

For Cyprus, data reflect a passive scenario based on implementation of approved policies only. It is also assumed that the government will be able to roll over its debt and finance its deficit at a reasonable cost over the medium term and that banks will achieve adequate capitalization without government assistance.

Data for South Sudan are now included in the sub-Saharan Africa aggregates and classified under those for a country with fuel as the main source of export earnings. Sudan, which remains in the Middle East and North Africa region, is now classified as a country with nonfuel primary products as the main source of export earnings.

Data for San Marino are now included in the advanced economy classification.

As in the April 2012 *World Economic Outlook,* data for Syria are excluded for 2011 and later due to the uncertain political situation.

Starting with the October 2012 *World Economic Outlook,* the label for the Emerging and Developing Economies group is Emerging Market and Developing Economies. The member countries remain unchanged with the exception of South Sudan as a new member of the group.

If no source is listed on tables and figures, data are drawn from the World Economic Outlook (WEO) database.

When countries are not listed alphabetically, they are ordered on the basis of economic size.

Minor discrepancies between sums of constituent figures and totals reflect rounding.

As used in this report, the terms "country" and "economy" do not in all cases refer to a territorial entity that is a state as understood by international law and practice. As used here, the term also covers some territorial entities that are not states but for which statistical data are maintained on a separate and independent basis.

Composite data are provided for various groups of countries organized according to economic characteristics or region. Unless otherwise noted, country group composites represent calculations based on 90 percent or more of the weighted group data.

The boundaries, colors, denominations, and any other information shown on the maps do not imply, on the part of the International Monetary Fund, any judgment on the legal status of any territory or any endorsement or acceptance of such boundaries.

This version of the *World Economic Outlook* is available in full through the IMF eLibrary (www.elibrary. imf.org) and the IMF website (www.imf.org). Accompanying the publication on the IMF website is a larger compilation of data from the WEO database than is included in the report itself, including files containing the series most frequently requested by readers. These files may be downloaded for use in a variety of software packages.

The data appearing in the *World Economic Outlook* are compiled by the IMF staff at the time of the WEO exercises. The historical data and projections are based on the information gathered by the IMF country desk officers in the context of their missions to IMF member countries and through their ongoing analysis of the evolving situation in each country. Historical data are updated on a continual basis as more information becomes available, and structural breaks in data are often adjusted to produce smooth series with the use of splicing and other techniques. IMF staff estimates continue to serve as proxies for historical series when complete information is unavailable. As a result, WEO data can differ from other sources with official data, including the IMF's *International Financial Statistics*.

The WEO data and metadata provided are "as is" and "as available," and every effort is made to ensure, but not guarantee, their timeliness, accuracy, and completeness. When errors are discovered, there is a concerted effort to correct them as appropriate and feasible. Corrections and revisions made after publication are incorporated into the electronic editions available from the IMF eLibrary (www.elibrary.imf.org) and on the IMF website (www.imf.org). All substantive changes are listed in detail in the online tables of contents.

For details on the terms and conditions for usage of the WEO database, please refer to the IMF Copyright and Usage website, www.imf.org/external/terms.htm.

Inquiries about the content of the *World Economic Outlook* and the WEO database should be sent by mail, fax, or online forum (telephone inquiries cannot be accepted):

World Economic Studies Division

Research Department

International Monetary Fund

700 19th Street, N.W.

Washington, DC 20431, U.S.A.

Fax: (202) 623-6343

Online Forum: www.imf.org/weoforum

PREFACE

The analysis and projections contained in the *World Economic Outlook* are integral elements of the IMF's surveillance of economic developments and policies in its member countries, of developments in international financial markets, and of the global economic system. The survey of prospects and policies is the product of a comprehensive interdepartmental review of world economic developments, which draws primarily on information the IMF staff gathers through its consultations with member countries. These consultations are carried out in particular by the IMF's area departments—namely, the African Department, Asia and Pacific Department, European Department, Middle East and Central Asia Department, and Western Hemisphere Department—together with the Strategy, Policy, and Review Department; the Monetary and Capital Markets Department; and the Fiscal Affairs Department.

The analysis in this report was coordinated in the Research Department under the general direction of Olivier Blanchard, Economic Counsellor and Director of Research. The project was directed by Jörg Decressin, Deputy Director, Research Department, and by Thomas Helbling, Division Chief, Research Department.

The primary contributors to this report are Abdul Abiad, John Bluedorn, Rupa Duttagupta, Jaime Guajardo, Andrea Pescatori, Damiano Sandri, John Simon, and Petia Topalova. Other contributors include Ashvin Ahuja, Ali Alichi, Peter Allum, Derek Anderson, Michal Andrle, Samya Beidas-Strom, Olivier Blanchard, Stijn Claessens, Davide Furceri, Nick Gigineishvili, Benjamin Hunt, Joong Shik Kang, M. Ayhan Kose, Douglas Laxton, Daniel Leigh, Prakash Loungani, Junior Maih, Akito Matsumoto, Dimitre Milkov, Armando Morales, Malhar Nabar, Marina Rousset, Marco E. Terrones, and Kenichi Ueda.

Hites Ahir, Gavin Asdorian, Shan Chen, Angela Espiritu, Sinem Kilic Celik, Nadezhda Lepeshko, Murad Omoev, Ezgi O. Ozturk, Katherine Pan, Daniel Rivera-Greenwood, Jair Rodriguez, Marina Rousset, Min Kyu Song, and Bennet Voorhees provided research assistance. Kevin Clinton provided comments and suggestions. Tingyun Chen, Mahnaz Hemmati, Toh Kuan, Rajesh Nilawar, Emory Oakes, and Steve Zhang provided technical support. Skeeter Mathurin and Luke Lee were responsible for word processing. Linda Griffin Kean of the External Relations Department edited the manuscript and coordinated the production of the publication. External consultants Amrita Dasgupta, Aleksandr Gerasimov, Shamiso Mapondera, Nhu Nguyen, and Pavel Pimenov provided additional technical support.

The analysis has benefited from comments and suggestions by staff from other IMF departments, as well as by Executive Directors following their discussion of the report on September 14, 2012. However, both projections and policy considerations are those of the IMF staff and should not be attributed to Executive Directors or to their national authorities.

FOREWORD

The recovery continues, but it has weakened. In advanced economies, growth is now too low to make a substantial dent in unemployment. And in major emerging market economies, growth that had been strong earlier has also decreased. Relative to our April 2012 forecasts, our forecasts for 2013 growth have been revised from 2.0 percent down to 1.5 percent for advanced economies, and from 6.0 percent down to 5.6 percent for emerging market and developing economies.

The forces at work are, for the most part, familiar.

Those forces pulling growth down in advanced economies are fiscal consolidation and a still-weak financial system. In most countries, fiscal consolidation is proceeding according to plan. While this consolidation is needed, there is no question that it is weighing on demand, and the evidence increasingly suggests that, in the current environment, the fiscal multipliers are large. The financial system is still not functioning efficiently. In many countries, banks are still weak, and their positions are made worse by low growth. As a result, many borrowers still face tight borrowing conditions.

The main force pulling growth up is accommodative monetary policy. Central banks continue not only to maintain very low policy rates, but also to experiment with programs aimed at decreasing rates in particular markets, at helping particular categories of borrowers, or at helping financial intermediation in general.

More seems to be at work, however, than these mechanical forces—namely, a general feeling of uncertainty. Assessing the precise nature and effects of this uncertainty is essential, but it is not easy. Essential: If uncertainty could be decreased, the recovery could well turn out to be stronger than currently forecast. But not easy: Explicit indexes of uncertainty, such as the VIX in the United States or the VStoxx in Europe, remain at fairly low levels.[1] Uncertainty appears more diffuse, more Knightian in nature. Worries about the ability of European policymakers to control the euro crisis and worries about the failure to date of U.S. policymakers to agree on a fiscal plan surely play an important role, but one that is hard to nail down.

Low growth and uncertainty in advanced economies are affecting emerging market and developing economies, through both trade and financial channels, adding to homegrown weaknesses. As was the case in 2009, trade channels are surprisingly strong, with, for example, lower exports accounting for most of the decrease in growth in China. Alternative risk-off and risk-on episodes, triggered by progress and regress on policy action, especially in the euro area, are triggering volatile capital flows.

Turning to policy action, the main focus continues to be the euro area. Here, there has been a clear change in attitudes, and a new architecture is being put in place. The lessons of the past few years are now clear. Euro area countries can be hit by strong, country-specific, adverse shocks. Weak banks can considerably amplify the adverse effects of such shocks. And, if it looks like the sovereign itself might be in trouble, sovereign-bank interactions can further worsen the outcome.

Therefore a new architecture must aim at reducing the amplitude of the shocks in the first place— at putting in place a system of transfers to soften the effects of the shocks. That architecture must aim at moving the supervision, the resolution, and the recapitalization processes for banks to the euro area level. It must decrease the probability of default by sovereigns, and were default nevertheless to occur, it must decrease the effects on creditors and on the

---

[1]VIX = Chicago Board Options Exchange Market Volatility Index; VStoxx = Bloomberg's Euro Stoxx 50 Volatility Index.

financial system. It is good to see these issues being seriously explored and to see some of these mechanisms being slowly put together.

In the short term, however, more immediate measures are needed. Spain and Italy must follow through with adjustment plans that reestablish competitiveness and fiscal balance and maintain growth. To do so, they must be able to recapitalize their banks without adding to their sovereign debt. And they must be able to borrow at reasonable rates. Most of these pieces are falling into place, and if the complex puzzle can be rapidly completed, one can reasonably hope that the worst might be behind us.

If uncertainty is indeed behind the current slowdown, and if the adoption and implementation of these measures decrease uncertainty, things may turn out better than our forecasts, not only in Europe, but also in the rest of the world. I, for once, would be happy if our baseline forecasts turn out to be inaccurate—in this case, too pessimistic.

Olivier Blanchard
Economic Counsellor

EXECUTIVE SUMMARY

The recovery has suffered new setbacks, and uncertainty weighs heavily on the outlook. A key reason is that policies in the major advanced economies have not rebuilt confidence in medium-term prospects. Tail risks, such as those relating to the viability of the euro area or major U.S. fiscal policy mistakes, continue to preoccupy investors. The *World Economic Outlook* (WEO) forecast thus sees only a gradual strengthening of activity from the relatively disappointing pace of early 2012. Projected global growth, at 3.3 and 3.6 percent in 2012 and 2013, respectively, is weaker than in the July 2012 *WEO Update,* which was in turn lower than in the April 2012 WEO (Chapter 1). Output is expected to remain sluggish in advanced economies but still relatively solid in many emerging market and developing economies. Unemployment is likely to stay elevated in many parts of the world. And financial conditions will remain fragile, according to the October 2012 *Global Financial Stability Report* (GFSR). Chapter 2 discusses regional developments in detail.

The WEO forecast rests on two crucial policy assumptions. The first is that European policymakers—consistent with the GFSR's *baseline scenario*—will adopt policies that gradually ease financial conditions further in periphery economies. In this regard, the European Central Bank (ECB) has recently done its part. It is now up to national policymakers to move and activate the European Stability Mechanism (ESM), while articulating a credible path and beginning to implement measures to achieve a banking union and greater fiscal integration. The second assumption is that U.S. policymakers will prevent the drastic automatic tax increases and spending cutbacks (the "fiscal cliff") implied by existing budget law, raise the U.S. federal debt ceiling in a timely manner, and make good progress toward a comprehensive plan to restore fiscal sustainability. The WEO forecast could once again be disappointed on both accounts.

More generally, downside risks have increased and are considerable. The IMF staff's fan chart, which uses financial and commodity market data and analyst forecasts to gauge risks—suggests that there is now a 1 in 6 chance of global growth falling below 2 percent, which would be consistent with a recession in advanced economies and low growth in emerging market and developing economies. Ultimately, however, the WEO forecast rests on critical policy action in the euro area and the United States, and it is very difficult to estimate the probability that this action will materialize.

This juncture presents major difficulties for policymakers. In many advanced economies, injections of liquidity are having a positive impact on financial stability and output and employment, but the impact may be diminishing. Many governments have started in earnest to reduce excessive deficits, but because uncertainty is high, confidence is low, and financial sectors are weak, the significant fiscal achievements have been accompanied by disappointing growth or recessions. In emerging market and developing economies, policymakers are conscious of the need to rebuild fiscal and monetary policy space but are wondering how to calibrate policies in the face of major external downside risks.

An effective policy response in the major advanced economies is the key to improving prospects and inspiring more confidence about the future. In the short term, the main tasks are to rule out the tail risk scenarios and adopt concrete plans to bring down public debt over the medium term.

The crisis in the euro area remains the most obvious threat to the global outlook. The ECB has put in place a mechanism to improve the transmission of low policy rates to borrowing costs in the periphery, where investors' fears about the viability of the euro have pushed market rates to very high levels. The periphery economies need to continue to adjust. Governments must meet their commitment to make the euro area firewall more flexible. Specifically, the ESM must intervene in banking systems and provide support to sovereigns, while national leaders must work toward true economic and monetary union. This requires establishing a banking union with a unified financial stability framework and implementing measures toward fiscal integration, on the principle that more area-wide insurance must come with more area-wide control. Unless more action is taken soon, recent improvements in financial markets could prove fleeting. The WEO forecast may then be disappointed once again, and the euro area could slide into the October 2012 GFSR *weak policies* scenario. If, however, policy actions were to exceed WEO assumptions—for example, if euro area policymakers were to deliver a major down payment on the road to more integration, such as an area-wide bank resolution mechanism with a common fiscal backstop—real GDP growth could well be higher than projected, consistent with the October 2012 GFSR *complete policies* scenario.

Reducing the risks to the medium-term outlook presaged by the public debt overhang in the major advanced economies will require supportive monetary policies and appropriate structural reforms (Chapter 3), as well as careful fiscal policy. Good progress has already been made and planned fiscal consolidation is sizable for the near term, as discussed in the October 2012 *Fiscal Monitor*. U.S. legislators must soon remove the threat of the fiscal cliff and raise the debt ceiling—if they fail to do so, the U.S. economy could fall back into recession, with deleterious spillovers to the rest of the world. Furthermore, policymakers in the United States urgently need to specify strong medium-term fiscal plans. Those in Japan need to persevere with planned adjustments and specify new measures to halt and soon reverse the increase in the public-debt-to-GDP ratio.

More generally, policymakers need to specify realistic fiscal objectives and develop plans for contingencies. This means adopting structural or cyclically adjusted targets, or anchoring plans on measures and their estimated yields, rather than on nominal targets. Automatic stabilizers should be allowed to play freely. Also, should growth fall significantly short of WEO projections, countries with room to maneuver should smooth their planned adjustment

over 2013 and beyond. At the same time, declining inflation rates, growing slack, and sizable fiscal adjustment in the advanced economies argue for maintaining very accommodative monetary conditions, including unconventional measures because interest rates are near the zero lower bound.

So far, policymakers' record in meeting structural challenges has been mixed; therefore, further efforts are needed. Programs to relieve chronic household debt burdens, where these have been tried, have not been commensurate with the scale of the problem. Efforts to strengthen the regulatory framework for financial institutions and markets have been patchy, according to Chapter 3 of the October 2012 GFSR, with some success in rebuilding capital but less in lowering reliance on wholesale funding and containing incentives for excessive risk taking and regulatory arbitrage. In addition, in the euro area, the restructuring or resolution of weak financial institutions has advanced slowly and only in response to major market pressure—a more proactive, area-wide approach is urgently needed. Increases in statutory retirement ages have reduced the long-term path of pension outlays, but as health care spending continues to increase quickly, more measures will be needed to contain the growth of entitlements to a sustainable rate. Some countries, notably the economies of the euro area periphery, have introduced reforms to make labor markets more flexible. However, many economies need to take stronger action to help the long-term unemployed, including through improvements to job-search support and training.

In emerging market and developing economies, activity has been slowed by policy tightening in response to capacity constraints, weaker demand from advanced economies, and country-specific factors. Policy improvements have raised their resilience to shocks (Chapter 4). Since the crisis erupted in 2008, expansionary policies have buffered the negative impact of the weakness in advanced economy markets: fiscal deficits have typically been above precrisis levels, whereas real interest rates have been lower. Domestic credit has grown rapidly. Over the medium term, policymakers will need to ensure that they retain the ability to respond flexibly to shocks by maintaining a sound fiscal position and by keeping inflation and credit growth at moderate rates. In this respect, the policy tightening during 2011 was appropriate. Given the growing downside risks to external demand, central banks have appropriately paused or reversed some of the monetary policy tightening. Many have scope to do more to support demand if external downside risks threaten to materialize.

Global imbalances, and the associated vulnerabilities, have diminished, but there is still a need for more decisive policy action to address them. Within the euro area, current account imbalances—the large surpluses in Germany and the Netherlands and the deficits in most periphery economies—need to adjust further. At the global level, the current account positions of the United States, the euro area as a whole, and Japan are weaker than they would be with more sustainable fiscal policies—and the real effective exchange rates of the dollar, euro, and yen are stronger. In contrast, the current account positions of many Asian economies are undesirably strong and their exchange rates undesirably weak. In part, this reflects distortions that hold back consumption. But it also reflects the effect of large-scale official accumulation of foreign exchange.

In general, the policies required to lower current account imbalances and related vulnerabilities suit the interests of the economies concerned. More adjustment in external-deficit economies and more internal demand in external-surplus economies would contribute not only to a safer global economy but also to stronger growth for all. Many external-deficit economies need further fiscal adjustment and strengthened financial sector supervision and regulation. These efforts need to be complemented with structural measures, the details of which differ widely across the external-deficit advanced and emerging market economies but include labor and product market reform, improvements to governance and the business environment, and measures to boost private saving for retirement. The structural measures needed in external-surplus economies with undervalued exchange rates also vary by country but include boosting investment in Germany, reforming the social safety net in China to encourage consumption, and reducing the accumulation of official reserves in many emerging market economies, which would also help rein in high credit and asset price growth.

The global economy has deteriorated further since the release of the July 2012 *WEO Update,* and growth projections have been marked down (Table 1.1). Downside risks are now judged to be more elevated than in the April 2012 and September 2011 *World Economic Outlook* (WEO) reports. A key issue is whether the global economy is just hitting another bout of turbulence in what was always expected to be a slow and bumpy recovery or whether the current slowdown has a more lasting component. The answer depends on whether European and U.S. policymakers deal proactively with their major short-term economic challenges. The WEO forecast assumes that they do, and thus global activity is projected to reaccelerate in the course of 2012; if they do not, the forecast will likely be disappointed once again. For the medium term, important questions remain about how the global economy will operate in a world of high government debt and whether emerging market economies can maintain their strong expansion while shifting further from external to domestic sources of growth. The problem of high public debt existed before the Great Recession, because of population aging and growth in entitlement spending, but the crisis brought the need to address it forward from the long to the medium term.

Recent Developments

Indicators of activity and unemployment show increasing and broad-based economic sluggishness in the first half of 2012 and no significant improvement in the third quarter (Figure 1.1). Global manufacturing has slowed sharply. The euro area periphery has seen a marked decline in activity (Figure 1.2, panel 1), driven by financial difficulties evident in a sharp increase in sovereign rate spreads (Figure 1.2, panel 2). Activity has disappointed in other economies too, notably the United States and United Kingdom. Spillovers from advanced economies and homegrown difficulties have held

back activity in emerging market and developing economies. These spillovers have lowered commodity prices and weighed on activity in many commodity exporters (see the Special Feature).

The result of these developments is that growth has once again been weaker than projected, in significant part because the intensity of the euro area crisis has not abated as assumed in previous WEO projections. Other causes of disappointing growth include weak financial institutions and inadequate policies in key advanced economies. Furthermore, a significant part of the lower growth in emerging market and developing economies is related to domestic factors, notably constraints on the sustainability of the high pace of growth in these economies and building financial imbalances. In addition, IMF staff research suggests that fiscal cutbacks had larger-than-expected negative short-term multiplier effects on output, which may explain part of the growth shortfalls (Box 1.1).

The Crisis in the Euro Area Intensified

Notwithstanding policy action aimed at resolving it, the euro area crisis has deepened and new interventions have been necessary to prevent matters from deteriorating rapidly. As discussed in the October 2012 *Global Financial Stability Report* (GFSR), banks, insurers, and firms have swept spare liquidity from the periphery to the core of the euro area, causing Spanish sovereign spreads to hit record highs and Italian spreads to move up sharply too (Figure 1.2, panel 2). This was triggered by continued doubts about the capacity of countries in the periphery to deliver the required fiscal and structural adjustments, questions about the readiness of national institutions to implement euro-area-wide policies adequate to combat the crisis, and concerns about the readiness of the European Central Bank (ECB) and the European Financial Stability Facility/ European Stability Mechanism (EFSF/ESM) to respond if worst-case scenarios materialize.

Table 1.1. Overview of the *World Economic Outlook* Projections

(Percent change unless noted otherwise)

			Year over Year				Q4 over Q4		
			Projections		Difference from July 2012 WEO Update		Estimates	Projections	
	2010	2011	2012	2013	2012	2013	2011	2012	2013
World Output[1]	**5.1**	**3.8**	**3.3**	**3.6**	**−0.2**	**−0.3**	**3.2**	**3.0**	**4.0**
Advanced Economies	**3.0**	**1.6**	**1.3**	**1.5**	**−0.1**	**−0.3**	**1.3**	**1.1**	**2.1**
United States	2.4	1.8	2.2	2.1	0.1	−0.1	2.0	1.7	2.5
Euro Area	2.0	1.4	−0.4	0.2	−0.1	−0.5	0.7	−0.5	0.8
Germany	4.0	3.1	0.9	0.9	0.0	−0.5	1.9	0.9	1.4
France	1.7	1.7	0.1	0.4	−0.2	−0.5	1.2	0.0	0.8
Italy	1.8	0.4	−2.3	−0.7	−0.4	−0.4	−0.5	−2.3	0.0
Spain	−0.3	0.4	−1.5	−1.3	−0.1	−0.7	0.0	−2.3	0.2
Japan	4.5	−0.8	2.2	1.2	−0.2	−0.3	−0.6	1.6	2.1
United Kingdom	1.8	0.8	−0.4	1.1	−0.6	−0.3	0.6	0.0	1.2
Canada	3.2	2.4	1.9	2.0	−0.2	−0.2	2.2	1.7	2.2
Other Advanced Economies[2]	5.9	3.2	2.1	3.0	−0.4	−0.4	2.4	2.3	3.6
Newly Industrialized Asian Economies	8.5	4.0	2.1	3.6	−0.6	−0.6	3.0	3.2	3.5
Emerging Market and Developing Economies[3]	**7.4**	**6.2**	**5.3**	**5.6**	**−0.3**	**−0.2**	**5.7**	**5.5**	**6.2**
Central and Eastern Europe	4.6	5.3	2.0	2.6	0.1	−0.2	3.6	1.9	3.3
Commonwealth of Independent States	4.8	4.9	4.0	4.1	−0.1	0.0	4.3	2.9	4.8
Russia	4.3	4.3	3.7	3.8	−0.3	−0.1	4.6	2.5	4.8
Excluding Russia	6.0	6.2	4.7	4.8	0.2	0.2	. . .	. . .	. . .
Developing Asia	9.5	7.8	6.7	7.2	−0.4	−0.3	6.9	7.2	7.4
China	10.4	9.2	7.8	8.2	−0.2	−0.2	8.9	7.9	8.1
India	10.1	6.8	4.9	6.0	−1.3	−0.6	5.0	5.5	5.9
ASEAN-5[4]	7.0	4.5	5.4	5.8	0.0	−0.3	2.8	7.2	6.6
Latin America and the Caribbean	6.2	4.5	3.2	3.9	−0.2	−0.3	3.7	3.0	4.6
Brazil	7.5	2.7	1.5	4.0	−1.0	−0.7	1.4	2.9	3.8
Mexico	5.6	3.9	3.8	3.5	−0.1	−0.2	3.9	3.2	4.1
Middle East and North Africa	5.0	3.3	5.3	3.6	−0.2	0.0	. . .	. . .	. . .
Sub-Saharan Africa[5]	5.3	5.1	5.0	5.7	−0.1	0.0	. . .	. . .	. . .
South Africa	2.9	3.1	2.6	3.0	0.0	−0.3	2.6	2.7	3.3
Memorandum									
European Union	2.1	1.6	−0.2	0.5	−0.2	−0.5	0.8	−0.2	1.2
World Growth Based on Market Exchange Rates	4.1	2.8	2.6	2.9	−0.1	−0.3	2.3	2.2	3.3
World Trade Volume (goods and services)	**12.6**	**5.8**	**3.2**	**4.5**	**−0.6**	**−0.7**	. . .	. . .	. . .
Imports									
Advanced Economies	11.4	4.4	1.7	3.3	−0.2	−0.9	. . .	. . .	. . .
Emerging Market and Developing Economies	14.9	8.8	7.0	6.6	−0.8	−0.4	. . .	. . .	. . .
Exports									
Advanced Economies	12.0	5.3	2.2	3.6	−0.1	−0.7	. . .	. . .	. . .
Emerging Market and Developing Economies	13.7	6.5	4.0	5.7	−1.7	−0.5	. . .	. . .	. . .
Commodity Prices (U.S. dollars)									
Oil[6]	27.9	31.6	2.1	−1.0	4.2	6.5	20.8	3.7	−3.3
Nonfuel (average based on world commodity export weights)	26.3	17.8	−9.5	−2.9	2.6	1.4	−6.4	1.9	−5.4
Consumer Prices									
Advanced Economies	1.5	2.7	1.9	1.6	−0.1	0.0	2.8	1.7	1.7
Emerging Market and Developing Economies[3]	6.1	7.2	6.1	5.8	−0.2	0.2	6.5	5.6	5.3
London Interbank Offered Rate (percent)[7]									
On U.S. Dollar Deposits	0.5	0.5	0.7	0.6	−0.1	−0.2	. . .	. . .	. . .
On Euro Deposits	0.8	1.4	0.6	0.2	−0.1	−0.3	. . .	. . .	. . .
On Japanese Yen Deposits	0.4	0.3	0.4	0.3	0.0	−0.1	. . .	. . .	. . .

Note: Real effective exchange rates are assumed to remain constant at the levels prevailing during July 30–August 27, 2012. When economies are not listed alphabetically, they are ordered on the basis of economic size. The aggregated quarterly data are seasonally adjusted.

[1]The quarterly estimates and projections account for 90 percent of the world purchasing-power-parity weights.

[2]Excludes the G7 economies (Canada, France, Germany, Italy, Japan, United Kingdom, United States) and euro area countries.

[3]The quarterly estimates and projections account for approximately 80 percent of the emerging market and developing economies.

[4]Indonesia, Malaysia, Philippines, Thailand, and Vietnam.

[5]The current WEO projections include South Sudan. However, for sub-Saharan Africa, the forecast comparison with the July 2012 *WEO Update* does not include South Sudan because South Sudan was not included in the July projections. The World and Emerging Market and Developing Economies aggregates also are not directly comparable with the July 2012 *WEO Update* for the same reason, but South Sudan's weight in these aggregates is very small.

[6]Simple average of prices of U.K. Brent, Dubai, and West Texas Intermediate crude oil. The average price of oil in U.S. dollars a barrel was $104.01 in 2011; the assumed price-based on futures markets is $106.18 in 2012 and $105.10 in 2013.

[7]Six-month rate for the United States and Japan. Three-month rate for the euro area.

These concerns culminated in questions about the viability of the euro area and prompted a variety of actions from euro area policymakers. At the June 29, 2012, summit, euro area leaders committed to reconsidering the issue of the seniority of the ESM with respect to lending to Spain. In response to escalating problems, Spain subsequently agreed on a program with its European partners to support the restructuring of its banking sector, with financing of up to €100 billion. Also, leaders launched work on a banking union, which was followed up recently with a proposal by the European Commission to establish a single supervisory mechanism. Leaders agreed that, once established, such a mechanism would open the possibility for the ESM to take direct equity stakes in banks. This is critical because it will help break the adverse feedback loops between sovereigns and banks. Moreover, in early September, the ECB announced that it will consider (without ex ante limits) Outright Monetary Transactions (OMTs) under a macroeconomic adjustment or precautionary program with the EFSF/ESM. The transactions will cover government securities purchases, focused on the shorter part of the yield curve. Importantly, the ECB will accept the same treatment as private or other creditors with respect to bonds purchased through the OMT program.

The anticipation of these initiatives and their subsequent deployment set off a relief rally in financial markets, and the euro appreciated against the U.S. dollar and other major currencies. However, recent activity indicators have continued to languish, suggesting that weakness is spreading from the periphery to the whole of the euro area (Figure 1.3, panel 2). Even Germany has not been immune.

Output and Employment Weakened Again in the United States

The U.S. economy also has slowed. Revised national accounts data suggest that it came into 2012 with more momentum than initially estimated. However, real GDP growth then slowed to 1.7 percent in the second quarter, below the April WEO and July *WEO Update* projections. The labor market and consumption have failed to garner much strength. The persistent weakness has prompted another round

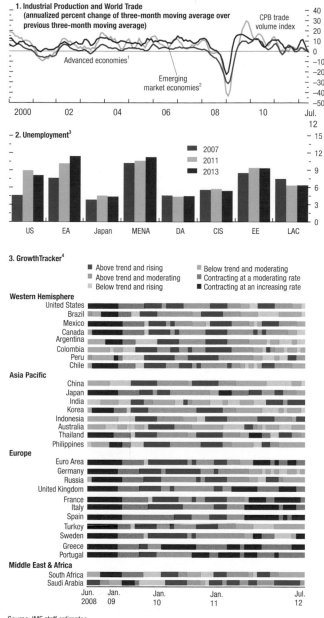

Figure 1.1. Global Indicators

The global manufacturing cycle has turned down again. Industrial production has slowed sharply in advanced and emerging market and developing economies and so has world trade. The deterioration is broad based. Unemployment in advanced economies remains appreciably above precrisis levels and is elevated in eastern Europe and the Middle East and North Africa.

Source: IMF staff estimates.
Note: US = United States; EA = euro area; CIS = Commonwealth of Independent States; DA = developing Asia; EE = emerging Europe; LAC = Latin America and the Caribbean; MENA = Middle East and North Africa.
[1]Australia, Canada, Czech Republic, Denmark, euro area, Hong Kong SAR, Israel, Japan, Korea, New Zealand, Norway, Singapore, Sweden, Switzerland, Taiwan Province of China, United Kingdom, and United States.
[2]Argentina, Brazil, Bulgaria, Chile, China, Colombia, Hungary, India, Indonesia, Latvia, Lithuania, Malaysia, Mexico, Pakistan, Peru, Philippines, Poland, Romania, Russia, South Africa, Thailand, Turkey, Ukraine, and Venezuela.
[3]Sub-Saharan Africa (SSA) is omitted due to data limitations.
[4]The Growth Tracker is described in Matheson (2011). Within regions, countries are listed by economic size.

Figure 1.2. Euro Area Developments

The crisis in the euro area has deepened. Activity is contracting, mainly due to deep cutbacks in production in the periphery economies, because financial and fiscal conditions are very tight. Sovereign issuers and banks in the periphery are struggling to attract foreign investors. Their sovereign debt spreads have risen appreciably, and their banks rely increasingly on the European Central Bank (ECB) for funding. As a result, they have cut back domestic credit.

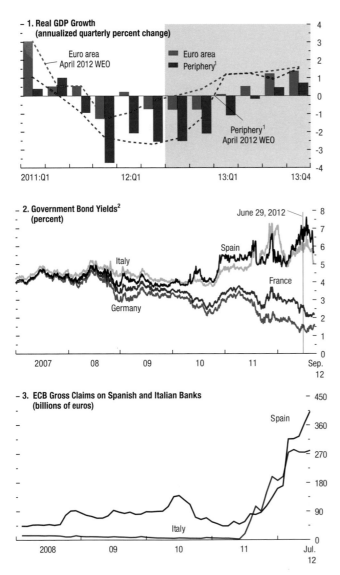

Sources: Bloomberg Financial Markets; national central banks; and IMF staff estimates.
[1]Greece, Ireland, Italy, Portugal, and Spain.
[2]Ten-year government bonds.

of policy stimulus by the Federal Reserve. Because of ongoing political gridlock, the fiscal cliff will not be addressed before the November elections. On the positive side, the housing market may be stabilizing, albeit at depressed levels, and private credit has continued to expand despite retrenchment in the U.S. market by EU banks.

Domestic Demand Continued to Lose Momentum in Key Emerging Market Economies

Policy tightening in response to capacity constraints and concerns about the potential for deteriorating bank loan portfolios, weaker demand from advanced economies, and country-specific factors slowed GDP growth in emerging market and developing economies from about 9 percent in late 2009 to about 5¼ percent recently. Indicators of manufacturing activity have been retreating for some time (Figure 1.3, panel 1). The IMF staff's Global Projection Model suggests that more than half of the downward revisions to real GDP growth in 2012 are rooted in domestic developments.

- Growth is estimated to have weakened appreciably in developing Asia, to less than 7 percent in the first half of 2012, as activity in China slowed sharply, owing to a tightening in credit conditions (in response to threats of a real estate bubble), a return to a more sustainable pace of public investment, and weaker external demand. India's activity suffered from waning business confidence amid slow approvals for new projects, sluggish structural reforms, policy rate hikes designed to rein in inflation, and flagging external demand.

- Real GDP growth also decelerated in Latin America to about 3 percent in the first half of 2012, largely due to Brazil. This reflects the impact of past policy tightening to contain inflation pressure and steps to moderate credit growth in some market segments—with increased drag recently from global factors.

- Emerging European economies, following a strong rebound from their credit crisis, have now been hit hard by slowing exports to the euro area, with real GDP growth coming close to a halt. In Turkey, the slowdown has been driven by domestic demand, on the heels of policy tightening and a decline in confidence. Unlike in 2008, however, generalized risk aversion toward the region is no longer a factor. Activity in Russia, which has benefited various economies in the region, has also lost some momentum recently.

Prospects Are for Sluggish and Bumpy Growth

Looking ahead, no significant improvement appears in the offing. The WEO forecast includes only a modest reacceleration of activity, which would be helped along by some reduction in uncertainty related to assumed policy reactions in the euro area and the United States, continued monetary accommodation, and gradually easier financial conditions. Healthy nonfinancial corporate balance sheets and steady or slowing deleveraging by banks and households will encourage the rebuilding of the capital stock and a gradual strengthening of durables consumption. In emerging market and developing economies, monetary and fiscal policy easing will strengthen output growth. However, if either of two critical assumptions about policy reactions fails to hold, global activity could deteriorate very sharply.

- The first assumption is that, consistent with the October 2012 GFSR *baseline scenario*, European policymakers take additional action to advance adjustment at national levels and integration at the euro area level (including timely establishment of a single supervisory mechanism). As a result, policy credibility and confidence improve gradually while strains remain from elevated funding costs and capital flight from the periphery to the core countries. If these policy actions are not taken, the WEO forecast may be disappointed once again and the area could slide into the GFSR's *weak policies* scenario, which is described in further detail below.
- The second assumption is that U.S. policymakers avoid the fiscal cliff and raise the debt ceiling, while making good progress toward a comprehensive plan to restore fiscal sustainability.

Fiscal Adjustment Will Continue but Not in Many Emerging Market Economies

Fiscal adjustment has been detracting from activity in various parts of the world and will continue

Figure 1.3. Current and Forward-Looking Growth Indicators

Purchasing managers' indices for the manufacturing sector do not yet point to a significant reacceleration of activity—they remain below the level of 50, indicating falling output. The deterioration is particularly pronounced in the periphery of the euro area. Investment in machinery and equipment has also weakened, especially in the euro area. Furthermore, the pace of stock building has moved into a lower gear. Consumption has shown greater resilience, especially in emerging market and developing economies. Somewhat lower oil prices may support consumption in the advanced economies. However, higher food prices will harm many households, especially in emerging market and developing economies.

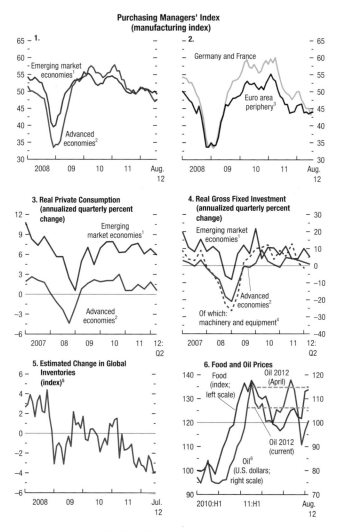

Sources: Haver Analytics; and IMF staff calculations.
Note: Not all economies are included in the regional aggregations. For some economies, monthly data are interpolated from quarterly series.
[1]Argentina, Brazil, Bulgaria, Chile, China, Colombia, Hungary, India, Indonesia, Latvia, Lithuania, Malaysia, Mexico, Peru, Philippines, Poland, Romania, Russia, South Africa, Thailand, Turkey, Ukraine, and Venezuela.
[2]Australia, Canada, Czech Republic, Denmark, euro area, Hong Kong SAR, Israel, Japan, Korea, New Zealand, Norway, Singapore, Sweden, Switzerland, Taiwan Province of China, United Kingdom, and United States.
[3]Greece, Ireland, Italy, and Spain.
[4]Purchasing-power-parity-weighted averages of metal products and machinery for the euro area, plants and equipment for Japan, plants and machinery for the United Kingdom, and equipment and software for the United States.
[5]Based on deviations from an estimated (cointegral) relationship between global industrial production and retail sales.
[6]U.S. dollars a barrel: simple average of spot prices of U.K. Brent, Dubai Fateh, and West Texas Intermediate crude oil. The dashed lines indicate projected oil price in April 2012 WEO and current WEO.

Figure 1.4. Fiscal Policies

In 2012, fiscal policy became more contractionary in the advanced economies. It became much less contractionary in the emerging market and developing economies, where the fiscal deficit is expected to be about 1½ percent of GDP—much lower than the 6 percent of GDP level projected for the advanced economies. However, before the crisis, emerging market and developing economies were running surpluses. Over the medium term, many should strengthen their fiscal positions to rebuild room for policy maneuvering. The main challenges with respect to deficit reduction lie, however, in the advanced economies, where public debt is in excess of 100 percent of GDP and rising.

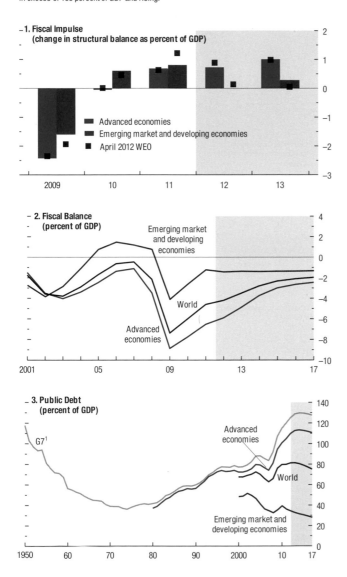

Source: IMF staff estimates.
[1]G7 comprises Canada, France, Germany, Italy, Japan, United Kingdom, and United States.

to do so over the forecast horizon in the advanced economies but not in the emerging market and developing economies. The October 2012 *Fiscal Monitor* discusses the trends.

In major advanced economies, general government structural balances are on course to tighten by about ¾ percent of GDP in 2012, which is about the same as in 2011 and in line with the April 2012 WEO projections (Figure 1.4, panel 1). In 2013, the tightening is projected to increase modestly to about 1 percent of GDP, but its composition across countries will be different (see Table A8 in the Statistical Appendix). In the euro area, much adjustment has already been implemented and the pace of tightening will diminish somewhat. In the United States, the budget outlook for 2013 is highly uncertain, given the large number of expiring tax provisions and the threat of automatic spending cuts and in the context of highly polarized politics. The fiscal cliff implies a tightening of more than 4 percent of GDP, but the WEO projection assumes that the outcome would be only a 1¼ percent of GDP reduction in the structural deficit, which is slightly more than in 2012, mainly on account of expiring stimulus measures, such as the payroll tax cut, and a decline in war-related spending. The budget outlook has also become uncertain in Japan, where a political impasse has delayed approval of budget funding for the remainder of the fiscal year ending in March 2013. Earthquake-related spending has lent support to growth in 2012 but will decline sharply in 2013. As a result, there will be a fiscal withdrawal of about ½ percent of GDP. This withdrawal could be much larger if the political impasse is not resolved soon.

In emerging market and developing economies, no significant fiscal consolidation is on tap for 2012–13, following a 1 percent of GDP improvement in structural balances during 2011 (Figure 1.4, panel 1). The general government deficit in these economies is expected to remain below 1½ percent of GDP, and public debt levels are expected to decline as a share of GDP, toward 30 percent. Fiscal prospects, however, vary across economies. Policy will be broadly neutral in China, India, and Turkey in 2012 and 2013. In Brazil, policy will be broadly neutral in 2012 and tighten somewhat in 2013. In Mexico, there will be a roughly 1 percent of GDP fiscal tightening in 2012, followed by a modest further fiscal withdrawal in 2013. Russia is loosening noticeably in 2012, but its stance is projected to become broadly neutral in 2013.

Monetary Policy Is Expected to Support Activity

Monetary policy has been easing and will remain very accommodative, according to market expectations (Figure 1.5, panel 1). The ECB recently launched its OMT program (see above) and broadened collateral requirements. The Federal Reserve recently announced that it would purchase mortgage-backed securities at a pace of $40 billion a month, consider additional asset purchases, and employ its other policy tools until economic conditions improve. It also extended its low-interest-rate guidance from late 2014 to mid-2015. Earlier, the Bank of England had expanded its quantitative easing program. Various advanced economies recently cut policy rates (Australia, Czech Republic, Israel, Korea) or postponed rate hikes. The Bank of Japan expects a roughly 5 percent of GDP monetary expansion during the coming year on account of its Asset Purchase Program and estimates that this would suffice to push inflation up to its 1 percent goal. It recently eased its monetary policy further by expanding its asset purchase program ceiling for government bonds.

The Bank of England launched some innovative measures. Under its Funding for Lending Scheme (FLS), banks and building societies will be able to borrow U.K. Treasury bills in exchange for less liquid collateral. Banks may borrow bills in an amount equal to 5 percent of their June 2012 stock of loans to the U.K. nonfinancial sector, plus any expansion of lending from that date until the end of 2013. Swap fees will be lower for banks that maintain or expand rather than cut their lending. These measures should encourage bank lending and ease access to wholesale credit by improving the quality of assets held by banks.

Emerging market and developing economies launched a variety of easing measures in response to softening activity and inflation. Many postponed anticipated tightening, and some cut policy rates, including Brazil, China, Colombia, Hungary, the

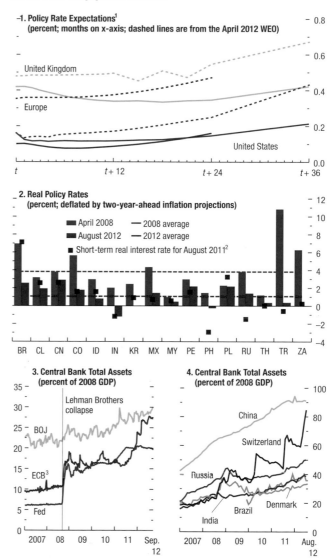

Figure 1.5. Monetary Policies

Expectations are for very accommodative monetary policies in the major advanced economies. Real interest rates are also low in many emerging market and developing economies, and several economies have cut their policy rates in the past six months. However, only a few economies implemented large cuts. Over the medium term, policy rates will have to be raised, but considering the downside risks to the outlook, many central banks can afford to hold steady now or ease further. In advanced economies, central bank balance sheets have expanded appreciably, but their size is not unusual compared with those of various emerging market economies.

1. Policy Rate Expectations[1]
   (percent; months on x-axis; dashed lines are from the April 2012 WEO)

2. Real Policy Rates
   (percent; deflated by two-year-ahead inflation projections)

- April 2008   — 2008 average
- August 2012   — 2012 average
- Short-term real interest rate for August 2011[2]

BR CL CN CO ID IN KR MX MY PE PH PL RU TH TR ZA

3. Central Bank Total Assets
   (percent of 2008 GDP)

4. Central Bank Total Assets
   (percent of 2008 GDP)

Sources: Bloomberg Financial Markets; and IMF staff estimates.
Note: BR = Brazil; CL = Chile; CN = China; CO = Colombia; ID = Indonesia; IN = India; KR = Korea; MX = Mexico; MY = Malaysia; PE = Peru; PH = Philippines; PL = Poland; RU = Russia; TH = Thailand; TR = Turkey; ZA = South Africa. BOJ = Bank of Japan; ECB = European Central Bank; Fed = Federal Reserve.
[1]Expectations are based on the federal funds rate for the United States, the sterling overnight interbank average rate for the United Kingdom, and the euro interbank offered forward rates for Europe; updated September 13, 2012.
[2]Bank Indonesia rate for Indonesia; the Central Bank of the Republic of Turkey's effective marginal funding cost estimated by IMF staff for Turkey.
[3]ECB calculations based on the Eurosystem's weekly financial statement.

Figure 1.6. Recent Financial Market Developments

Equity markets recently registered large losses and have been very volatile. Policy pronouncements have had large effects. Bank lending conditions are gradually easing from very tight levels in the United States but are continuing to tighten in the euro area. U.S. credit to households and nonfinancial firms is growing again; euro area credit remains in the doldrums, amid cutbacks in the periphery.

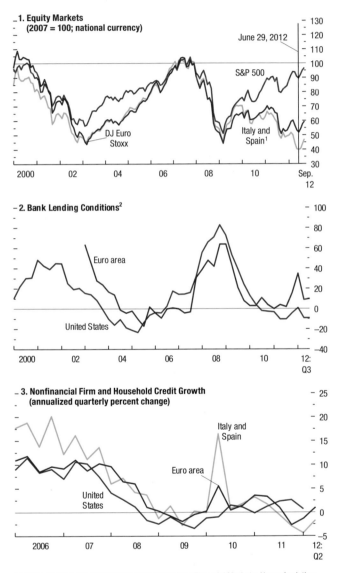

Sources: Bank of America/Merrill Lynch; Bloomberg Financial Markets; Haver Analytics; and IMF staff estimates.
[1]Weighted average of the Spanish IBEX and Italian FTSEMIB using September 13, 2012, market capitalizations.
[2]Percent of respondents describing lending standards as tightening "considerably" or "somewhat" minus those indicating standards as easing "considerably" or "somewhat" over the previous three months. Survey of changes to credit standards for loans or lines of credit to firms for the euro area; average of surveys on changes in credit standards for commercial and industrial and commercial real estate lending for the United States; diffusion index of "accommodative" minus "severe," Tankan (survey of lending attitudes of financial institutions) for Japan.

Philippines, and South Africa (Figure 1.5, panel 2). However, only Brazil cut aggressively, also easing macroprudential measures to further encourage lending. On the whole, real interest rates in many emerging market and developing economies are still relatively low and credit growth is high. For these reasons, many central banks have chosen to hold steady.

Financial Conditions Will Remain Very Fragile

Despite the summer 2012 market rally, financial vulnerabilities are higher than in the spring, according to the October 2012 GFSR. Confidence in the global financial system remains exceptionally fragile. Bank lending has remained sluggish across advanced economies (Figure 1.6, panels 2 and 3). U.S. credit standards have been easing modestly for some time, although not yet for residential real estate. In the euro area, by contrast, lending surveys point to a further tightening of standards and falling loan demand. Bank credit has contracted sharply in the periphery, and credit growth slowed to a crawl in the core economies amid large increases in periphery credit spreads.

Increased risk aversion has dampened capital flows to emerging markets (Figure 1.7, panel 1), although local-currency debt has continued to attract inflows throughout the euro area crisis. Concerns center on slowing domestic growth and heightened financial vulnerabilities. Sovereign and corporate spreads edged up (Figure 1.7, panel 2). Emerging market banks have been tightening lending standards in the face of rising nonperforming loans and worsening funding conditions (Figure 1.7, panel 4). Survey responses suggest that tightness in global funding markets played a major role in this regard. Indicators for loan demand are still expansionary in all major regions (Figure 1.7, panel 5). Credit growth itself fell off its very high pace but remains elevated in many economies.

Financial conditions are likely to remain very fragile over the near term because implementing a solution to the euro area crisis will take time and the U.S. debt ceiling and fiscal cliff raise concerns about the U.S. recovery. Bank lending in the advanced economies is expected to stay sluggish—much more so in the euro area, where the periphery will suffer further reductions in lending. Most emerging markets will likely experience volatile capital flows. In economies where credit growth has already slowed appreciably, such as China, credit is likely to rebound further as project approvals are fast-tracked; elsewhere, growth rates are likely to move sideways or decline. External funding conditions are likely to have a larger impact on credit developments in emerging Europe than in other emerging market economies.

Activity Is Forecast to Remain Tepid in Many Economies

The recovery is forecast to limp along in the major advanced economies, with growth remaining at a fairly healthy level in many emerging market and developing economies. Leading indicators do not point to a significant acceleration of activity, but financial conditions have recently improved in response to euro area policymakers' actions and easing by the Federal Reserve.

- In the euro area, real GDP is projected to decline by about ¾ percent (on an annualized basis) during the second half of 2012 (Figure 1.8, panel 2). With diminishing fiscal withdrawal and domestic and euro-area-wide policies supporting a further improvement in financial conditions later in 2013, real GDP is projected to stay flat in the first half of 2013 and expand by about 1 percent in the second half. The core economies are expected to see low but positive growth throughout 2012–13. Most periphery economies are likely to suffer a sharp contraction in 2012, constrained by tight fiscal policies and financial conditions, and to begin to recover only in 2013.
- In the United States, real GDP is projected to expand by about 1½ percent during the second half of 2012, rising to 2¾ percent later in 2013 (Figure 1.8, panel 1). Weak household balance sheets and confidence, relatively tight financial conditions, and continued fiscal consolidation stand in the way of stronger growth. In the very short term, the drought will also detract from output.
- In Japan, the pace of growth will diminish noticeably as post-earthquake reconstruction winds down.

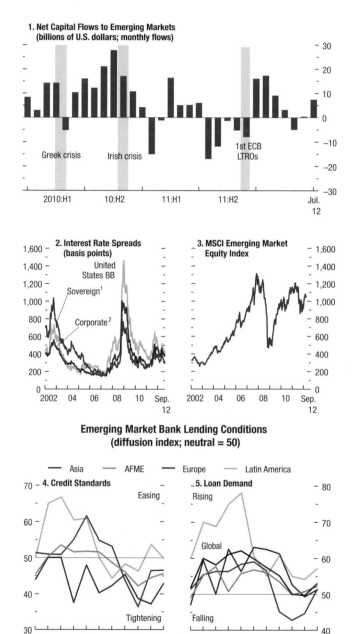

Figure 1.7. Emerging Market Conditions

Emerging markets suffered capital outflows until recently, their equity markets declined, and their risk spreads widened somewhat. Banks are tightening credit standards in the face of credit and asset price booms and reduced external funding. However, demand for loans continues to expand.

Sources: Bloomberg Financial Markets; Capital Data; EPFR Global; Haver Analytics; IIF Emerging Markets Bank Lending Survey; and IMF staff calculations.
Note: ECB = European Central Bank; LTROs = Longer-term refinancing operations; AFME = Africa and Middle East.
[1]JPMorgan EMBI Global Index spread.
[2]JPMorgan CEMBI Broad Index spread.

Figure 1.8. GDP Growth
(Half-over-half annualized percent change)

Real GDP growth is projected to move sideways or accelerate modestly in 2012. Activity is expected to continue to contract during 2013 in the periphery economies of the euro area. In emerging Asia and Latin America, the projected acceleration is mainly driven by China and Brazil, which have been easing their macroeconomic policies in response to weakening activity.

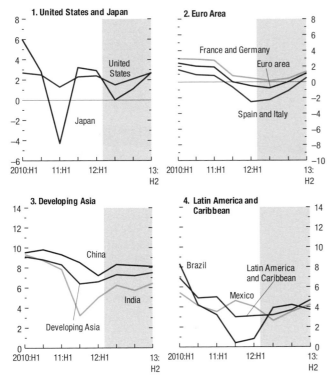

Source: IMF staff estimates.

Real GDP is forecast to stagnate in the second half of 2012 and grow by about 1 percent in the first half of 2013. Thereafter, growth is expected to accelerate further (Figure 1.8, panel 1).

Fundamentals remain strong in many economies that have not suffered a financial crisis, notably in many emerging market and developing economies. In these economies, high employment growth and solid consumption (Figure 1.3, panel 3) should continue to propel demand and, together with macroeconomic policy easing, support healthy investment and growth. However, growth rates are not projected to return to precrisis levels.

- In developing Asia, real GDP is forecast to accelerate to a 7¼ percent pace in the second half of 2012 (Figure 1.8, panel 3). The main driver will be China, where activity is expected to receive a boost from accelerated approval of public infrastructure projects. The outlook for India is unusually uncertain: For 2012, with weak growth in the first half and a continued investment slowdown, real GDP growth is projected to be 5 percent, but improvements in external conditions and confidence—helped by a variety of reforms announced very recently—are projected to raise real GDP growth to about 6 percent in 2013.

- In Latin America, real GDP growth is projected to be about 3¼ percent for the second half of 2012. It is then expected to accelerate to 4¾ percent in the course of the second half of 2013 (Figure 1.8, panel 4). The projected acceleration is strong for Brazil because of targeted fiscal measures aimed at boosting demand in the near term and monetary policy easing, including policy rate cuts equivalent to 500 basis points since August 2011. The pace of activity elsewhere is not forecast to pick up appreciably.

- In the central and eastern European (CEE) economies, improving financial conditions in the crisis-hit economies, somewhat stronger demand from the euro area, and the end of a boom-bust cycle in Turkey are expected to raise growth back to 4 percent later in 2013.

- Growth is projected to stay above 5 percent in sub-Saharan Africa (SSA) and above 4 percent in the Commonwealth of Independent States (see

Table 1.1). In both regions, still-high commodity prices and related projects are helping.

- In the Middle East and North Africa (MENA), activity in the oil importers will likely be held back by continued uncertainty associated with political and economic transition in the aftermath of the Arab Spring and weak terms of trade—real GDP growth is likely to slow to about 1¼ percent in 2012 and rebound moderately in 2013. Due largely to the recovery in Libya, the pace of overall growth among oil exporters will rise sharply in 2012, to above 6½ percent, and then return to about 3¾ percent in 2013.

Cyclical Indicators Point to Slack in Advanced Economies

Cyclical indicators point to ample slack in many advanced economies but to capacity constraints in a number of emerging market economies (Figure 1.9). WEO output gaps in the major advanced economies are large, varying from about 2½ percent of GDP in the euro area and Japan to 4 percent in the United States for 2012 (see Table A8 in the Statistical Appendix). These gaps are consistent with weak demand due to tight financial conditions and fiscal consolidation. By contrast, most emerging market and developing economies that were not hit by the crisis continue to operate above precrisis trends. However, their potential growth rates in recent years are judged to have been higher than indicated by the 1996–2006 precrisis average, and therefore WEO output gap estimates do not signal much overheating.

Amid sharply differing developments across advanced and emerging market and developing economies, the world unemployment rate is estimated to remain flat during 2012–13, near 6¼ percent (Figure 1.1, panel 2). Unemployment rates have on average declined below precrisis levels in emerging market and developing economies, but they remain elevated in advanced economies and are not expected to fall significantly during 2012–13.

- In the United States, the unemployment rate dropped from close to 10 percent in 2010 to about 8 percent lately, where it is expected to remain through 2013. However, a large part of

the decline is due to sluggish labor force expansion through 2011. In addition, more than 40 percent of those unemployed have been out of work for more than six months. In Europe, more than 1 in 10 labor force participants are projected to be unemployed through 2013; in Greece and Spain the ratio is 1 in 4 workers. More generally, almost half of all young labor force participants are without jobs in the periphery of the euro area. As in the United States, the number of long-term unemployed has also risen starkly, increasing the risk of hysteresis and skills atrophy.

- In emerging market and developing economies, the unemployment record varies widely. Rates are very high in economies that were hit by the crisis, such as in many of the CEE and a few CIS economies, but relatively low in most parts of developing Asia and Latin America. Unemployment rates are projected to remain high in the MENA region, mainly among the oil importers. These economies face a number of challenges, ranging from major political changes, to social needs related to rapidly expanding populations, to decreased revenues from tourism—all of which are weighing on employment prospects in the short term.

The slowdown in global activity and ample slack in many advanced economies have meant that inflation has fallen (Figure 1.10, panels 1 and 2). In advanced economies, lower commodity prices reduced headline inflation to about 1½ percent as of July 2012, down from more than 3 percent in late 2011. Core inflation has been steady at about 1½ percent. In emerging market and developing economies, headline inflation has declined by almost 2 percentage points, to slightly under 5½ percent, in the second quarter of 2012; core inflation too has declined, although to a lesser extent. The forecast is for further easing of inflation pressure in the advanced economies, with headline inflation moving to about 1¾ percent in 2013; in emerging market and developing economies, headline inflation is projected to move broadly sideways.

This inflation forecast assumes broadly unchanged commodity prices, but sharply rising food prices raise increasing concern (see the Special Feature and Box 1.5). Thus far, price pressures do not encompass all

Figure 1.9. Overheating Indicators for the G20 Economies

Domestic overheating indicators point to ample slack in the advanced economies—most indicators flash blue. By contrast, a number of yellow and red indicators for the emerging market and developing economies point to capacity constraints. External overheating indicators flash yellow or red for Japan and China—rather thanraising concerns, these are symptoms of an internal demand rebalancing process that has helped bring down global current account imbalances. However, in China, the rebalancing is overly reliant oninvestment. In Germany, which is the world's other major surplus economy, the rebalancing process is lagging. The red indicators for Turkey point to external vulnerabilities.Credit indicators point to excesses in many emerging market and developingeconomies. Other financial indicators are mostly reassuring about overheating, except for Brazil.

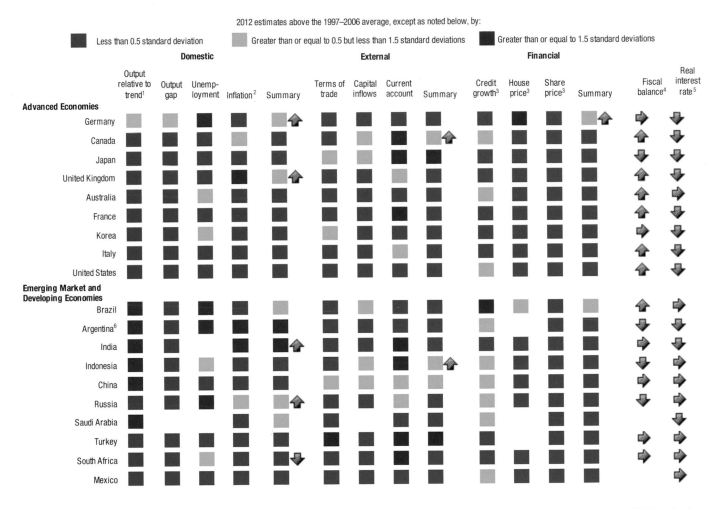

Sources: Australia Bureau of Statistics; Bank for International Settlements; CEIC China Database; Global Property Guide; Haver Analytics; IMF, Balance of Payments Statistics Database; IMF, International Financial Statistics Database; Organization for Economic Cooperation and Development; and IMF staff estimates.

Note: For each indicator, except as noted below, economies are assigned colors based on projected 2012values relative to theirprecrisis (1997–2006) average. Each indicator is scored as red = 2, yellow= 1, and blue = 0; summary scores are calculated as the sum of selected component scores divided by the maximum possible sum of those scores. Summary blocks are assigned red if thesummaryscore is greater than or equal to 0.66, yellow if greater than or equal to 0.33 but less than 0.66, and blue if less than 0.33. When data are missing, no color is assigned. Arrows up (down) indicate hotter (colder) conditions compared with the April 2012 WEO predicted values for 2012.

[1]Output more than 2.5 percent above the precrisis trend is indicated by red. Output less than 2.5percent below the trend is indicated by blue. Output within ±2.5 percent from the precrisis trend is indicated by yellow.

[2]For the following inflation-targeting economies, the target inflation rate was used instead of the 1997–2006 average in the calculation of the inflation indicator: Australia, Brazil, Canada, Indonesia, Korea, Mexico, South Africa, Turkey, United Kingdom. For the non-inflation-targeting economies, red was assigned if inflation is approximately 10 percent or higher, yellow if inflation is approximately 5 to 9 percent, and blue if inflation is less than 5 percent.

[3]The indicators for credit growth, house price growth, and share price growth refer to the latest2012 values relative to the 1997–2006 average of output growth.

[4]Arrows in the fiscal balance column represent the forecast change in the structural balance as apercent of GDP over the period 2011–12. An improvement of more than 0.5 percent of GDP is indicatedby an up arrow; a deterioration of more than 0.5 percent of GDP is indicated by a down arrow.

[5]Real policy interest rates below zero are identified by a down arrow; real interest rates above 3 percent are identified by an up arrow. Real policy interest rates are deflated by two-year-ahead inflation projections.

[6]Calculations are based on Argentina's official GDP data. The IMF has called on Argentina to adopt remedial measures to address the quality of the official GDP data. The IMF staff is also using alternative measures of GDP growth for macroeconomic surveillance, including data produced by private analysts, which have shown significantly lower real GDP growth than the official datasince 2008. The IMF staff's estimate of average provincial inflation is used as a measure of inflation and to deflate nominal variables.

major food crops, unlike in 2007–08. As discussed further below, monetary policy should not react to food-price-driven increases in headline inflation unless there are significant risks for second-round effects on wages. Governments may need to scale up targeted social safety net measures and implement other fiscal measures (such as reducing food taxes) where there is fiscal space to do so. Also, countries should avoid any restrictions on exports, which would exacerbate price increases and supply disruptions. Over the longer term, broader policy reforms are necessary to reduce global food price volatility.

The Outlook Has Become More Uncertain

Risks to the WEO forecast have risen appreciably and now appear more elevated than in the April 2012 and September 2011 WEO reports, whose policy assumptions and hence growth projections for advanced economies proved overly optimistic. Although standard risk metrics suggest that downside risks are much higher now than only a few months ago, upside risks appear higher too, although to a lesser extent. This may be a reflection of the fact that many market participants have a bimodal view of global prospects: the recovery could be set back if European and U.S. policymakers fail to live up to expectations, but it could also be stronger if they deliver on their commitments. The most pertinent near-term risks—escalation of the euro area crisis and fiscal policy failures in the United States—are quantified and discussed with the help of scenarios. In addition, this section considers a variety of medium- and long-term risks and scenarios.

Risks for a Serious Global Slowdown Are Alarmingly High

The WEO's standard fan chart suggests that uncertainty about the outlook has increased markedly (Figure 1.11, panel 1).[1] The WEO growth forecast is now 3.3 and 3.6 percent for 2012 and 2013, respectively, which is somewhat lower than in

[1]For details about the construction of the fan chart, including a discussion of the role of the risk factors, see Elekdag and Kannan (2009).

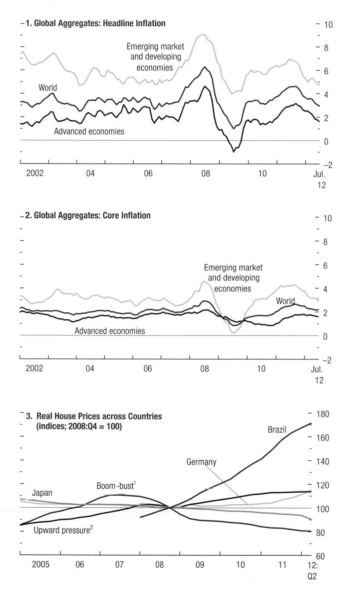

Figure 1.10. Global Inflation
(Twelve-month change in the consumer price index unless noted otherwise)

Headline inflation has declined everywhere, helped by lower commodity prices. In the emerging market and developing economies, core inflation has declined too. In advanced economies, it has remained stable around 1½ percent. House price developments increasingly diverge across economies. In various smaller advanced and a number of emerging market and developing economies, upward pressure remains, notwithstanding already high prices.

1. Global Aggregates: Headline Inflation

2. Global Aggregates: Core Inflation

3. Real House Prices across Countries
(indices; 2008:Q4 = 100)

Sources: Haver Analytics; and IMF staff calculations.
[1]Boom-bust countries: Bulgaria, Croatia, Cyprus, Czech Republic, Denmark, Estonia, Finland, France, Greece, Iceland, Ireland, Italy, Latvia, Lithuania, Malta, Netherlands, New Zealand, Poland, Russia, Slovak Republic, Slovenia, South Africa, Spain, Turkey, Ukraine, United Kingdom, United States.
[2]Upward pressure countries: Australia, Austria, Belgium, Canada, Colombia, China, Hong Kong SAR, Hungary, India, Israel, Malaysia, Norway, Philippines, Switzerland, Singapore, Serbia, Sweden, Uruguay.

Figure 1.11. Risks to the Global Outlook

Risks around the WEO projections have risen, consistent with market indicators, and remain tilted to the downside. The oil price and inflation indicators point to downside risks to growth, while S&P 500 options prices and the term spread suggest some upside risk.

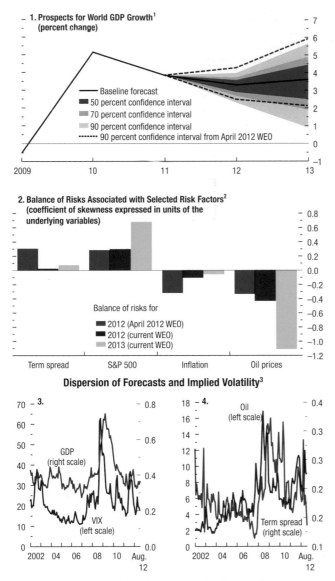

1. Prospects for World GDP Growth[1]
(percent change)

— Baseline forecast
■ 50 percent confidence interval
■ 70 percent confidence interval
■ 90 percent confidence interval
----- 90 percent confidence interval from April 2012 WEO

2. Balance of Risks Associated with Selected Risk Factors[2]
(coefficient of skewness expressed in units of the underlying variables)

Balance of risks for
■ 2012 (April 2012 WEO)
■ 2012 (current WEO)
■ 2013 (current WEO)

Term spread   S&P 500   Inflation   Oil prices

Dispersion of Forecasts and Implied Volatility[3]

3.
GDP (right scale)
VIX (left scale)
2002 04 06 08 10 Aug. 12

4.
Oil (left scale)
Term spread (right scale)
2002 04 06 08 10 Aug. 12

Sources: Bloomberg Financial Markets; Chicago Board Options Exchange; Consensus Economics; and IMF staff estimates.
[1]The fan chart shows the uncertainty around the WEO central forecast with 50, 70, and 90 percent confidence intervals. As shown, the 70 percent confidence interval includes the 50 percent interval, and the 90 percent confidence interval includes the 50 and 70 percent intervals. See Appendix 1.2 in the April 2009 *World Economic Outlook* for details.
[2]The values for inflation and oil price risks enter with the opposite sign, because they represent downside risks to growth.
[3]GDP measures the dispersion of GDP forecasts for the G7 economies (Canada, France, Germany, Italy, Japan, United Kingdom, United States), Brazil, China, India, and Mexico. VIX = Chicago Board Options Exchange S&P 500 Implied Volatility Index. Term spread measures the dispersion of term spreads implicit in interest rate forecasts for Germany, Japan, United Kingdom, and United States. Oil measures the dispersion of one-year-ahead oil price forecasts for West Texas Intermediate. Forecasts are from Consensus Economics surveys.

April 2012. The probability of global growth falling below 2 percent in 2013—which would be consistent with recession in advanced economies and a serious slowdown in emerging market and developing economies—has risen to about 17 percent, up from about 4 percent in April 2012 and 10 percent (for the one-year-ahead forecast) during the very uncertain setting of the September 2011 WEO.

The IMF staff's Global Projection Model (GPM) uses an entirely different methodology to gauge risk but confirms that risks for recession in advanced economies (entailing a serious slowdown in emerging market and developing economies) are alarmingly high (Figure 1.12, panel 1). For 2013, the GPM estimates suggest that recession probabilities are about 15 percent in the United States, above 25 percent in Japan, and above 80 percent in the euro area.

Risk Scenarios for the Short Term

As emphasized, immediate risks relate to the assumptions about the sovereign debt crisis in the euro area and about the U.S. budget, both of which could negatively affect growth prospects. Furthermore, oil prices could again provide a shock.

A further deepening of the euro area crisis

The euro area crisis could reintensify again. The OMT program will reduce risks from self-fulfilling market doubts related to the viability of the Economic and Monetary Union (EMU) most effectively if it is implemented decisively. However, serious risks remain outside this safety net—posed, for example, by rising social tensions and adjustment fatigue that raise doubts about adjustment in the periphery or by doubts about the commitment of others to more integration.

The downside scenario developed here uses the IMF staff's Global Integrated Monetary and Fiscal Model (GIMF) to consider the implications of an intensification of euro area sovereign and banking stress. Unlike in the WEO forecast and GFSR *baseline scenario*, European policymakers in this scenario do not strengthen their policies, as discussed in further detail in the *weak policies* scenario in the October 2012 GFSR. In this scenario, the forces of financial fragmentation increase and become entrenched, capital holes in banking systems expand, and the intra-euro-area capital account crisis increasingly spills outward. Within the GIMF, this scenario features the following shocks relative to the WEO forecast (Figure 1.13): lower credit, mainly in the periphery; higher sovereign risk premiums for the periphery; modestly lower premiums for the core sovereigns, which benefit from a flight to safety; an even larger fiscal consolidation in the periphery; and increases in corporate risk premiums for all (including non-European) advanced and emerging market economies. Capital flight from the euro area and emerging markets is assumed to benefit the United States, and its sovereign risk premium falls. Monetary policy is constrained at the zero interest rate floor in the advanced economies, and the assumption is that they do not proceed with additional unconventional easing. Emerging market economies, by contrast, are assumed to ease as growth and inflation fall, which considerably reduces the impact of the external shock on their economies.

In this scenario, output in the euro area core would fall by about 1¾ percent relative to the WEO projections within one year; in the periphery, the decline would be about 6 percent. Output losses in non-European economies would be about 1 to 1½ percent. Chapter 2 provides further details for the various regions.

Stronger-than-expected euro area policies

This second GIMF scenario assumes that national policymakers follow up the latest ECB actions with a more proactive approach toward domestic adjustment and EMU reforms. The details are discussed in the *complete policies* scenario in the October 2012 GFSR. This scenario requires regaining credibility through an unflinching commitment to implementing already agreed plans. Policymakers need to build political support for the necessary pooling of sovereignty that a more complete currency union entails. It envisages that they quickly introduce a road map for banking union and fiscal integration and deliver a major down payment. Examples of possible action include implementation of a bank resolution mechanism with common backstops or a pan-European deposit insurance guarantee plan (for both, concrete proposals still need to be spelled out) and concrete measures

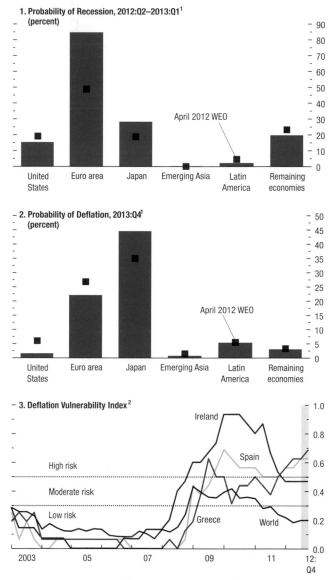

Figure 1.12. Recessions and Deflation Risks

Risks for a prolonged recession and for sustained deflation are elevated in the euro area, notably in periphery economies. The risk of deflation continues to be a problem in Japan. In other areas, the risks are minimal.

1. Probability of Recession, 2012:Q2–2013:Q1[1] (percent)

2. Probability of Deflation, 2013:Q4[1] (percent)

3. Deflation Vulnerability Index[2]

Source: IMF staff estimates.
[1]Emerging Asia: China, Hong Kong SAR, India, Indonesia, Korea, Malaysia, Philippines, Singapore, Taiwan Province of China, and Thailand; Latin America: Brazil, Chile, Colombia, Mexico, and Peru; remaining economies: Argentina, Australia, Bulgaria, Canada, Czech Republic, Denmark, Estonia, Israel, New Zealand, Norway, Russia, South Africa, Sweden, Switzerland, Turkey, United Kingdom, and Venezuela.
[2]For details on the construction of this indicator, see Kumar (2003) and Decressin and Laxton (2009). The indicator is expanded to include house prices.

Figure 1.13. Upside and Downside Scenarios
(Percent or percentage point deviation from WEO baseline)

The Global Integrated Monetary and Fiscal Model (GIMF) is used to consider a scenario in which policy is initially unable to prevent the intensification of euro area sovereign and banking stress as well as a scenario in which policy action quickly alleviates the current level of stress. The model contains two blocks of euro area countries, those with acute fiscal sustainability issues (referred to as "periphery") and those with less acute fiscal sustainability issues (referred to as "core").

The intensification-of-stress scenario (red bars) assumes that policymakers delay taking sufficient action to prevent a sharp intensification of financial stress. Consequently, deleveraging by euro area banks leads to a sharp credit contraction in periphery countries but milder contraction elsewhere. Credit in periphery countries falls €475 billion below the WEO baseline in 2013, while that in the core countries falls by €50 billion. Concerns about fiscal sustainability raise periphery sovereign spreads 350 basis points in 2013; however, subsequent policy action results in spreads falling thereafter and returning fully to baseline by 2016. The core countries' sovereign risk premium is assumed to decline by 50 basis points in 2013 as a flight to quality within the euro area occurs. Sovereigns in the periphery are forced into more front-loaded fiscal consolidation, averaging an additional 2 percentage points of GDP in 2013. Risk concerns are also assumed to spill over to all other regions, with corporate risk premiums rising by 50 basis points in advanced economies and 150 basis points in emerging market and developing economies in 2013. The capital flight is assumed to benefit the U.S. sovereign, with the risk premium falling by 50 basis points in 2013. Monetary policy is constrained at the zero interest rate floor in the G3 countries (euro area, Japan, United States), whereas elsewhere monetary policy eases to help offset the impact on market interest rates of rising risk premiums.

In the scenario in which policy is able to alleviate the stress (blue bars), credit in the euro area expands relative to the baseline and sovereign spreads decline. In the periphery countries, credit expands by roughly €225 billion relative to the baseline, and sovereign spreads decline by roughly 200 basis points in 2013. In other advanced economies, corporate spreads fall by 50 basis points in 2013, and in emerging markets, the decline is 100 basis points.

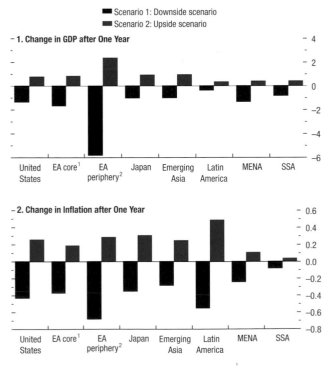

Source: GIMF simulations.
Note: EA = euro area; MENA = Middle East and North Africa; SSA = sub-Saharan Africa.
[1]Core countries are Austria, Belgium, Cyprus, Estonia, Finland, France, Germany, Luxembourg, Malta, Netherlands, Slovak Republic, and Slovenia.
[2]Periphery countries are Greece, Ireland, Italy, Portugal, and Spain.

toward fiscal integration. Under this scenario (Figure 1.13), the euro area begins to reintegrate as policy credibility is restored and capital flight reverses. Relative to the WEO forecast and the GFSR *baseline scenario*, credit expands by roughly €225 billion and sovereign spreads decline by about 200 basis points in 2013 in the periphery of the euro area. Economic growth resumes in the periphery and picks up in the core. In other advanced economies, corporate spreads fall by 50 basis points; in emerging market economies, by 100 basis points. Output would then be roughly ½ to 1 percent higher within one year in most other parts of the world.

The U.S. debt ceiling and fiscal cliff

The U.S. fiscal cliff could entail significantly more fiscal tightening (by about 3 percent of GDP) than assumed in the WEO projections. A recent *Spillover Report* (IMF, 2012e) finds that if this risk materializes and the sharp fiscal contraction is sustained, the U.S. economy could fall into a full-fledged recession. The global spillovers would be amplified through negative confidence effects, including, for example, a global drop in stock prices. The impact of hitting the debt ceiling is more difficult to model. Political delays before the previous deadline, in summer 2011, led credit rating agencies to downgrade the United States, and major market turmoil ensued. At this stage, markets appear to consider the fiscal cliff a tail risk, given that Congress has in the past eventually reached a compromise to resolve similar high-stakes situations. However, this implies that, should this risk actually materialize, there would be a great shock to confidence that would quickly spill over to financial markets in the rest of the world. Notice that risks for a sudden fiscal withdrawal are also present in Japan: however, if they materialize, they will probably have spillovers that are not as large as those from the U.S. fiscal cliff.

A renewed spike in oil prices

If either the euro area or U.S. downside scenario were to materialize, oil prices would likely fall substantially. But there is also an important risk that intensified geopolitical tensions could boost oil prices. The April 2012 WEO included a scenario featuring oil supply disruptions that showed that a 50 percent increase in oil prices due to less supply would lead to a 1 to 1½ percent decline in output in many parts of the world. The latest distribution of options prices for oil—which is skewed to the upside, implying a downside skew for the distribution of global growth—suggests that this scenario remains relevant for the global economy (Figure 1.11, panel 2).

Risk Scenarios for the Medium Term

A large number of risks and scenarios can be envisaged for the medium term. This section focuses on two specific risk scenarios and one general risk scenario that appear pertinent for policymakers at this juncture. The specific risk scenarios relate to large central bank balance sheets and high public debt—they are directly relevant for monetary and fiscal policy in the advanced economies. The general risk scenario is for globally lower growth over the medium term. This is akin to the experience following the shocks of the 1970s, but this time rooted in other shocks and policy failures—and, for the advanced economies, similar to the experience of Japan after the mid-1990s.

Risks related to swollen central bank balance sheets

The concern is that the vast acquisition of assets by central banks will ultimately mean a rise in the money supply and thus inflation (Figure 1.5, panel 3). However, as discussed in previous WEO reports, no technical reason indicates this would be inevitable. Central banks have more than enough tools to absorb the liquidity they create, including selling the assets they have bought, reverting to traditionally short maturities for refinancing, raising their deposit rates, and selling their own paper. Furthermore, in principle, central bank losses do not matter: their creditors are currency holders and reserve-holding banks; neither can demand to be paid with some other form of money.[2] The reality, however, may well be different. A national legislature may see such losses as a symptom that the central bank is operating outside its mandate,

which could be of concern if it led to efforts to limit the central bank's operational independence. A related concern is that economic agents may begin to doubt the capacity of central banks to fight inflation. Two scenarios come to mind:

- Public deficits and debt may run out of control, causing governments to lean on central banks to pursue more expansionary policies with a view to eroding the real value of the debt via inflation. Similarly, losses on holdings of euro area, Japanese, and U.S. (G3) government securities may cause emerging market economies' central banks or sovereign wealth funds to buy fewer G3 government assets, investing instead in better opportunities at home and triggering large depreciations of G3 currencies.
- Policymakers may falsely perceive central bank balance sheet losses to be damaging to their economies. Such perceptions may make central banks more hesitant to raise interest rates, because doing so would decrease the market value of their asset holdings. The mere appearance of such hesitation may lead private agents to expect an increase in inflation.

Risks related to high public debt levels

Public debt has reached very high levels, and if past experience is any guide, it will take many years to appreciably reduce it (see Chapter 3). Risks related to public debt have several aspects. First, when global output is at or above potential, high public debt may raise global real interest rates, crowding out capital and lowering output in the long term.[3] Second, the cost of debt service may lead to tax increases or cutbacks in infrastructure investment that lower supply. Third, high public debt in individual countries may raise their sovereign risk premiums, with a variety of consequences—from limited scope for countercyclical fiscal policies (as evidenced by the current problems in the euro area periphery) to high inflation or outright default in the case of very large increases in risk premiums.

Simulations with the GIMF suggest that an increase in public debt in the G3 economies of

---

[2]Central bank capital is, in many ways, an arbitrary number, as is well illustrated by the large balance sheets of central banks that intervene in foreign exchange markets (Figure 1.5, panel 4).

[3]See, for example, Elmendorf and Mankiw (1999) for a review of the literature and Kumar and Woo (2010) for some recent evidence.

about 40 percentage points of GDP raises real interest rates almost 40 basis points in the long term (Box 1.2). This simulation and discussion necessarily abstracts from the potential long-term benefits of fiscal stimulus. The 2009 stimulus, for example, was likely instrumental in averting a potential deflationary spiral and protracted period of exceedingly high unemployment, macroeconomic conditions that general equilibrium models such as the GIMF are not well suited to capture. Bearing this in mind, the simulation suggests that in the long term the higher debt lowers real GDP by about ¾ percent relative to a baseline without any increase in public debt. This is because of the direct effect of higher interest rates on investment and the indirect effect via higher taxes or lower government investment. The GIMF simulations indicate that within the G3 the negative effects would be larger, with output 1 percent below baseline projections. The loss of output over the medium term would be even larger if, for example, savings were to drop more than expected because of aging populations in the advanced economies or if the consumption patterns of emerging market economies with very high saving rates align more quickly than expected with those of advanced economies.

Scenarios that involve very high levels of debt and high real interest rates may not only result in lower growth but may also involve a higher risk of default when fiscal dynamics are perceived to be unstable. This combination of high debt and high real interest rates can lead to bad equilibriums, when doubt about the sustainability of fiscal positions drives interest rates to unsustainable levels.

Disappointing potential output and growing risk aversion

Looking beyond the near term, a concern is that output growth may disappoint in both advanced and emerging market economies, albeit for different reasons, and will precipitate a general flight to safety. As noted, growth outcomes have already disappointed repeatedly, including relative to the September 2011 and April 2012 WEO projections. These disappointments could be symptomatic of medium-term problems.

- In advanced economies that suffered from the financial crisis, prospects for employment remain dim, and many workers may ultimately drop out of the labor force. Banks are in the middle of an arduous process of lowering their leverage and strengthening their funding models. High public debt and, for some economies, external liabilities could mean new bouts of instability and generally low growth. Projections for these economies already incorporate marked-down estimates for potential output relative to precrisis trends, typically by 10 percent or more (Figure 1.14, panel 1). However, output could be lower still over the medium term.

- In response to forecast errors and policy changes, estimates for the medium-term output levels of emerging market economies have been marked down (relative to September 2011 estimates)—by about 3 percent for Brazil, 5 percent for China, and 10 percent for India, for example—and there may be more to come (Figure 1.14, panel 4). The April 2012 WEO already featured a downside scenario with weaker potential output in emerging Asian economies. Given recent disappointments elsewhere, this scenario is broadened to other emerging market economies. In fact, many emerging Asian and Latin American economies have seen growth above the 10-year precrisis average, and the IMF staff sees further scope for such high growth, as evidenced by WEO output gap estimates that point to slack (Figure 1.14, panel 1). The findings of Chapter 4 justify this optimism to some extent: there are indications of growing resilience on the part of emerging market and developing economies, mainly reflecting stronger policies. However, the chapter's findings suggest that less frequent adverse funding and terms-of-trade shocks have also played a role in these economies' recent strong performance, and the frequency of such shocks could increase again. Moreover, strong credit growth, which likely supported demand, cannot continue at the present pace without raising concerns about financial stability in many of these economies (Figure 1.14, panels 2 and 3). In short, there may be less cyclical slack and scope to grow over the medium term than suggested by IMF staff projections.

The scenario used to model lower potential output and the global macroeconomic implications is the IMF staff's Global Economy Model. Figure 1.15 shows the impact of downward revisions to medium-term output growth by about ½ percent in the United States, the euro area, and Latin America and by about 1 percent in Asia. Along the transition path to lower equilibrium output is a flight into the most liquid and safest assets—mainly cash—because of growing concern about prospects, and private and public risk premiums increase temporarily. In this scenario, global growth for 2013–16 is only about 2 to 3 percent, or 1½ to 2 percentage points below the baseline WEO forecast. The euro area and Japan would experience several years of stagnation or recession, whereas the United States would see positive but very modest growth. Eventually, advanced economies have some scope to ease monetary policy as the zero bound no longer binds, which helps support growth toward the very end of the WEO horizon and bring inflation back toward the baseline. Growth in emerging Asia would be closer to 5 to 6 percent, rather than 7 to 8 percent; in Latin America, it would be about 2½ percent rather than 4 percent as weaker global growth translates into significantly weaker demand for commodities. The price of oil falls by roughly 30 percent after three years, with prices for non-oil commodities falling by roughly 20 percent. These drops, in turn, lower growth in Africa and the Middle East. Developments in the real world could easily be much worse than the model suggests. The reason is that the model does not consider the social and political ramifications of rising unemployment; nor can it do justice to the adverse feedback loops between activity, banks, and sovereigns that can be triggered by unusually large shocks.

Policy Requirements

Five years after the onset of the Great Recession, the recovery remains tepid and bumpy, and prospects remain very uncertain. Unemployment is unacceptably high in most advanced economies, and workers in emerging market and developing economies face a chronic struggle to find formal employment. Aside from the legacies of the crisis, uncertainty itself is likely to weigh on output (Box 1.3).

Figure 1.14. Output in Emerging Market and Developing Economies

Output in emerging market and developing economies in Asia and Latin America is above precrisis trends, but WEO output gap estimates still see some slack. Amid disappointment relative to output projections, estimates for medium-term output have been lowered. For China and India, the reduction amounts to 5 to 10 percentage points by 2016; for all emerging market and developing economies, the reduction amounts to about 3½ percentage points. Buoyant activity in many emerging market and developing economies has been driven partly by better policies and partly by high credit growth and favorable terms-of-trade shocks. In many economies, the high credit growth will be difficult to sustain at present rates without weakening bank balance sheets. Also, future improvements in the terms of trade may be more limited. Thus, there are risks that medium-term output could surprise further on the downside.

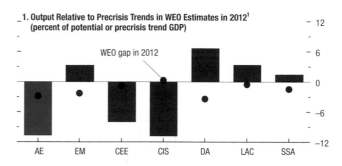

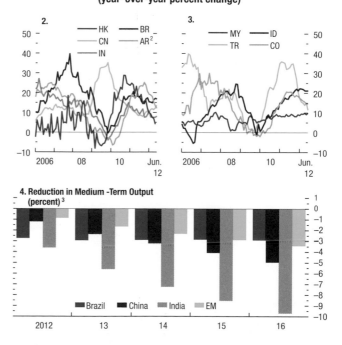

Sources: IMF, *International Financial Statistics;* and IMF staff estimates.
Note: AE = advanced economies; AR = Argentina; BR = Brazil; CEE = central and eastern Europe; CIS = Commonwealth of Independent States; CN = China; CO = Colombia; DA = developing Asia; EM = emerging market economies; HK = Hong Kong SAR; ID = Indonesia; IN = India; LAC = Latin America and the Caribbean; MY = Malaysia; SSA = sub-Saharan Africa; TR = Turkey.
[1]Precrisis trend is defined as the geometric average of real GDP level growth between 1996 and 2006.
[2]Nominal credit is deflated using the IMF staff's estimate of average provincial inflation.
[3]Relative to September 2011 WEO.

Figure 1.15. Lower Global Growth Scenario
(Percent or percentage point deviation from baseline)

This scenario uses the IMF's Global Economy Model to trace the global macroeconomic implications of slower potential growth and temporarily higher risk premiums. For the United States and the euro area, this scenario assumes that annual potential output growth is ½ percentage point below baseline over the WEO horizon, whereas for Japan, growth is ¼ percentage point below baseline. In emerging Asia, potential growth is assumed to be 1 percentage point lower than baseline. For Latin American and all remaining countries, it is assumed that potential growth is ½ percentage point below baseline. It takes until mid-2015 before it becomes clear that potential growth will be lower until end-2017. For advanced economies, this raises debt-sustainability concerns, and sovereign risk premiums rise by 50 basis points by 2016 before gradually returning to baseline. As sovereign risk premiums rise, advanced economies gradually tighten fiscal policy. The fiscal balance improves by 1 percent of GDP by 2016, and then gradually returns to baseline once the debt-to-GDP ratio declines and risk premiums moderate. In emerging market and developing economies, lower growth prospects raise concerns about the viability of some private investment, and corporate risk premiums rise, particularly in the tradable sector. In this sector, corporate risk premiums peak roughly 200 basis points above baseline in 2016 in emerging Asia and about 150 basis points above baseline in Latin America. In the G3 (euro area, Japan, United States), monetary policy is constrained by the zero bound on nominal policy interest rates. For the first few years, interest rates cannot ease at all relative to the baseline, and beyond that, there is only limited scope for easing.

GDP growth in all regions is well below the WEO baseline between 2013 and 2016, with global growth roughly 2 percentage points lower in 2015. Eventually, advanced economies have scope to ease monetary policy, which helps support growth toward the end of the WEO horizon and bring inflation back toward the baseline. Lower global growth translates into weaker demand for commodities, and the price of oil falls by roughly 30 percent after three years, with non-oil commodities falling by roughly 20 percent.

GDP Growth
(percentage points)

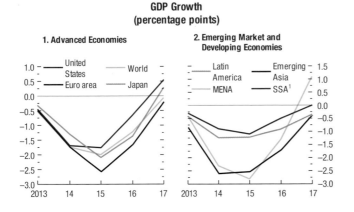

Inflation and Commodity Prices

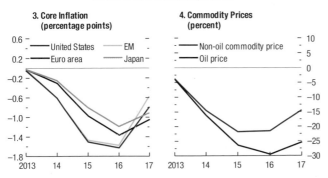

Source: IMF staff estimates.
Note: EM = emerging market and developing economies; MENA = Middle East and North Africa; SSA = sub-Saharan Africa.
[1]Excluding South Africa.

A basic challenge for policymakers is thus to move away from an incremental approach to policymaking and address the many downside risks to global activity with strong medium-term fiscal and structural reform programs in order to rebuild confidence. In the euro area, action is also needed to address the current crisis and, over the medium term, to complete the EMU. Only after substantial progress is made on these various fronts will confidence and demand strengthen durably in the major advanced economies. Investors will be reassured that public debt is a safe investment and that advanced economy central banks have scope to use monetary policy to maintain low inflation and forestall renewed bouts of financial instability. Policymakers in emerging market and developing economies will need to balance two priorities: rebuilding policy buffers so as to maintain hard-won increases in the resilience of their economies to shocks and supporting domestic activity in response to growing downside risks to external demand.

Addressing the Euro Area Crisis

Despite policy progress, the euro area crisis has deepened. Unless recent ECB actions are followed up with more proactive policies by others, the WEO forecast and GFSR *baseline scenario* may once again prove overly optimistic and the euro area could slide into the *weak policies* scenario, with deleterious consequences for the rest of the world.

Ensuring market confidence in the viability of the EMU will require robust action on multiple fronts. Sovereigns under stress must continue to adjust, and support for these countries and their banks needs to be provided via the EFSF and the ESM to relieve funding pressures and break the adverse feedback loops between sovereigns and banks. Meanwhile, the ECB's commitment to act on secondary markets via the OMT program is very important to address elevated risk premiums due to convertibility concerns, and monetary policy should be very accommodative to support demand. Anticrisis measures must be anchored by the vision of—as well as reasonably fast and tangible progress toward—a more complete monetary union.

- EU partners should support countries making adequate adjustment efforts but still subject to market pressure. While economies in the periphery must continue to adjust their fiscal balances at a pace they can bear, it is essential to ensure their access to funding at reasonable cost. Common resources can be channeled via the EFSF or the ESM—and countries in need should request those resources, with the goal of preserving or regaining market access.

- Direct equity injections into banks are key to cutting bank-sovereign loops in the near term. For this to happen, the ESM needs to be made operational as soon as possible, and a single supervisory mechanism—a precondition for the ESM to take a stake in banks—should be established quickly, following up on the European Commission's proposals to that effect. Viable banks should be recapitalized, but those that are nonviable should be resolved, in part to minimize fiscal costs.

- An integrated regulatory and supervisory structure—a banking union—is indispensable for the smooth functioning of integrated financial markets in the EMU. Such a union should rest on four pillars: common supervision, harmonized regulation, a pan-European deposit guarantee scheme, and a pan-European resolution mechanism with common backstops. The last two building blocks are critical, and proposals for them still need to be spelled out.

Fiscal integration would provide critical tools to support a banking union, improve fiscal discipline, and enhance adjustment to idiosyncratic shocks while preventing them from becoming systemic. The immediate priority is to establish a common fiscal backstop for a banking union anchored on a single supervisory mechanism. More generally, fiscal risk sharing is an integral component of common currency areas. However, mutual support needs to be complemented by stricter and more robustly enforced rules and greater coordination of national policies—including through swift approval and sensible implementation of the Fiscal Compact (at the country level). There are different ways to achieve ex ante risk sharing, but all approaches would benefit from a clear road map.

Rebuilding Room for Fiscal Policy Maneuvering

Fiscal adjustment has become necessary in many cases to strengthen confidence in sovereign balance sheets and in many other cases because the prospects for future potential output—and hence revenue growth—are substantially less promising than they were before 2008. Unless governments spell out how they intend to effect the necessary adjustment over the medium term, a cloud of uncertainty will continue to hang over the international economy, with downside risks for output and employment in the short term.

Fiscal adjustment should be gradual and sustained, where possible, supported by structural changes, as, inevitably, it weighs on weak demand. Developments suggest that short-term fiscal multipliers may have been larger than expected at the time of fiscal planning (Box 1.1). Research reported in previous issues of the WEO finds that fiscal multipliers have been close to 1 in a world in which many countries adjust together; the analysis here suggests that multipliers may recently have been larger than 1 (Box 1.1).[4] There are other reasons for avoiding abrupt adjustments: fiscal problems can be rooted in structural problems that take time to address, and sharp expenditure cutbacks or tax increases can set off vicious cycles of falling activity and rising debt ratios, ultimately undercutting political support for adjustment. The historical record for public debt reduction suggests that a gradual, sustained approach supported by structural changes offers the best chance for success within today's constraints (Chapter 3).

To build credibility, governments should commit to measures and medium-term targets that are actually under their control. They must clearly explain how they will react to such setbacks as unexpected slowdowns in activity or increases in funding costs. Except in economies facing acute financing constraints, automatic stabilizers should be allowed to operate freely. Budget forecasts must be based on realistic assumptions about the negative short-term impact of adjustment on output and employment. Similarly, projections for the evolution of debt

---

[4]See for example, chapter 3 of the October 2010 *World Economic Outlook*.

ratios should be based on realistic, not optimistic, assumptions about the growth of potential output and interest rates. In short, fiscal policy must be transparent, realistic, and predictable, and although geared toward medium-term objectives, it should be a stabilizing factor against short-term downturns or booms. Clear analogies can be drawn with the practice of successful monetary policy.

Among the advanced economies, planned fiscal adjustment is sizable over the near term. The main policy shortfalls, discussed in more detail in the October 2012 *Fiscal Monitor*, relate to the need for stronger commitment to a sound fiscal framework:

- To anchor market expectations, policymakers need to specify adequately detailed medium-term plans for lowering debt ratios, which must be backed by binding legislation or fiscal frameworks. Among large advanced economies, the United States lacks such a plan, and Japan's medium-term plan needs to be strengthened, notwithstanding the welcome legislative passage of the doubling of the consumption tax. U.S. authorities must now urgently deal with the debt ceiling and the fiscal cliff, which would severely affect growth in the short term; the Japanese authorities also need to quickly approve funding for this year's budget.

- Countries should go much further in reducing the growth of aging-related expenditures—an issue that they cannot avoid forever—because such reductions can greatly improve debt dynamics without detracting severely from demand in the short term.

- More countries need to define targets in structural or cyclically adjusted terms and prepare contingency plans for coping with shocks. The first line of defense against shocks should be automatic stabilizers and monetary policy, including unconventional support and measures to improve the transmission of already low policy rates to demand. But these efforts might not suffice. Should growth fall significantly short of WEO projections, countries with room to maneuver should smooth their planned adjustment over 2013 and beyond.

- Emerging market and developing economies typically have much lower public debt than do advanced economies and therefore less urgent need for fiscal adjustment, but they still should rebuild room for policy maneuvering. Deficits are appreciably larger than before 2008, even in countries that were not hit by the crisis. These countries have typically experienced a relatively quick recovery and are operating above precrisis trends. Therefore, now is an appropriate time for them to adopt fiscal consolidation to fully restore their flexibility to deal with unexpected adverse contingencies. They should leave the task of supporting demand in response to greater-than-expected external weakness to monetary policy.

Among the major emerging market economies, more effort is needed in India, Russia, and, over the medium term, Turkey. China, also slowing, is different for two reasons: first, the authorities are trying to rebalance economic growth toward consumption, which will require expanding social support programs, and second, less scope is available for credit growth because the economy is still digesting a large expansion of credit released in response to the Great Recession. Similarly, the major oil exporters are also increasing spending to address social challenges, which is helping to rebalance global demand. Over the medium term, however, these economies will need to bring spending growth down to more sustainable levels.

Supporting Adjustment with Liquidity

In many advanced economies, ample liquidity provision continues to be essential given the weakness of demand and the very protracted implementation periods for fiscal, financial, and structural adjustment. Prudential authorities must ensure that they control the risks that may be created by the extended period of low yields and exceptionally easy access to central bank funding. Easy credit provides incentives for excessive risk taking and also gives banks easy options for postponing desirable restructuring. Over time, very low interest rates may distort the efficient investment of savings, which is an underlying function of the financial system. Credible medium-term fiscal adjustment programs and banking system restructuring are extremely valuable supports to the monetary policy objective of keeping inflation expectations firmly anchored at a low rate while maintaining financial stability.

A widespread concern is that monetary stimulus is not reaching all markets evenly. Households and small companies struggle to obtain bank loans, whereas large corporations are paying record low rates in bond markets. In the euro area, bank lending is slumping in the periphery but still growing in Germany. Changes in borrower risk premiums in response to changes in economic conditions and tighter bank lending policies in response to strained capital and funding are playing important roles. However, large differences in financing conditions do not mean that monetary policy is not working. The actions taken by central banks have forestalled worse outcomes. In some euro area economies, such as France and Italy, credit has thus far fared better during the current recovery than during the post-1993 recovery, despite a much larger drop in output (Figure 1.16, panels 3–6). The same holds in comparison with U.S. credit after 1989 (Figure 1.16, panels 1 and 2). More generally, liquidity provision has prevented a collapse of the banking systems in the periphery economies.

Specific monetary policy requirements vary across economies. In many advanced economies, the stance should remain very accommodative, given that inflation expectations are well anchored, headline and core inflation are receding, and activity is typically well below potential. Policymakers should continue to help reduce risk premiums and improve the transmission of monetary policy to the real economy, with direct interventions in key asset markets or with measures to strengthen banks' incentives to lend, such as the Bank of England's FLS. The specific policy requirements for the major economies are the following:

- The Federal Reserve has recently adopted strong measures to ease monetary and financial conditions, consistent with high unemployment and headline inflation that is projected to drop below 2 percent. The traction of these and previous unconventional measures would be greatly enhanced if more progress were made in mortgage debt relief for overly burdened households and in the reform of the housing market.
- In the euro area, underlying inflation pressure is low—core inflation has been running about 1½ percent for some time, with tax and administrative price hikes contributing about ¼ to ½

Figure 1.16. Crisis Comparisons
(Index; years from crisis on x-axis)

Credit appears to be doing better after the Great Recession than after previous recessions associated with credit crises. For example, domestic credit in the United States has held up better than after 1989, notwithstanding a much sharper drop in output. The same holds for credit in France and Italy when compared with the European exchange rate mechanism (ERM) crisis, although real credit is now falling in Italy. In Spain, credit is doing less well, consistent with a larger drop in output. Overall, these output and credit developments suggest that low policy rates and unconventional measures have, thus far, helped avert a much deeper credit crunch. However, more action is needed to sustain and improve credit, especially in the euro area periphery.

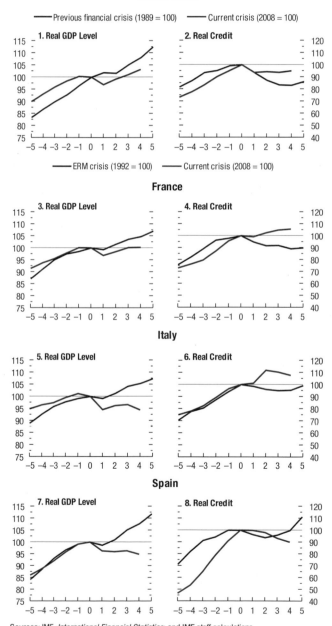

Sources: IMF, *International Financial Statistics*; and IMF staff calculations.
Note: Latest 2012 credit data are based on June 2012 levels.

percentage point. Headline inflation is forecast to decline to about 1½ percent during the course of 2013, and risks from domestic wages and profits are to the downside—the IMF staff's Global Projection Model suggests that the probability of falling prices is unusually high, reaching almost 25 percent (Figure 1.12, panel 2). This projection gives the ECB ample justification for keeping policy rates very low or cutting them further.

- In Japan, inflation is forecast to remain near zero in 2012 and 2013. The easing of monetary policy announced in September is welcome and should help support economic growth and an exit from deflation. However, further easing of monetary policy may be needed to accelerate achievement of the Bank of Japan's (BoJ's) inflation goal of 1 percent, supported by enhanced communication of the policy stance and framework. Any further easing by the BoJ could include purchasing Japanese government bonds with longer maturities, as well as selected private paper.

Among emerging market and developing economies, policy requirements differ, but many can afford to wait and see or to ease policy further because of downside risks to activity. Headline and core inflation are generally declining. The main reason for caution is that although credit growth rates have recently come down, they remain at fairly elevated levels (Figure 1.14, panels 2 and 3). Supervisory and macroprudential measures should be employed to counter any emerging credit bubbles, such as in real estate.

- In emerging Asia, headline and core inflation rates have been low or declining. In many economies, inflation is forecast to be close to 3 percent over the medium term. Credit has expanded rapidly in a number of these economies (China, India) and is still expanding quickly in some (Indonesia and, to a lesser extent, Malaysia); several have also seen booming real estate prices. Various economies' currencies are undervalued relative to medium-term fundamentals (China, Malaysia, Thailand). Considering this credit and exchange rate picture, these countries should wait and see or consider modest further easing of monetary policy stances and rely mainly on fiscal policy to support demand. Those with less fiscal space could proceed to more monetary easing, provided

macroprudential measures keep credit growth in check. Those with high inflation (India, Vietnam) cannot afford to loosen monetary policy unless they slow down domestic demand with more fiscal adjustment.

- In Latin America, many economies are forecast to operate with inflation near or below 5 percent in 2013, which is appreciably less than in 2011. High credit growth rates bear watching. Considering the downside risks to the global growth outlook, many central banks can afford to hold steady; if these risks materialize, they can reduce policy rates. High or rising real estate prices or growing household debt burdens, notably in Brazil, call for continued vigilence by policymakers. Central banks in economies with relatively high inflation (Argentina, Venezuela) will need to tighten further.

- Inflation rates are low or forecast to decline noticeably in many emerging European economies, typically to about 3 percent. There is therefore room for easing in various economies in response to very high unemployment rates and sluggish activity. Much higher and more volatile inflation in the CIS stands in the way of lower policy rates. The same holds for a number of economies in the MENA region and SSA.

Sharp increases in food prices present significant challenges for policymakers on many fronts (see the Special Feature). Regarding monetary policy, the concern is that the heavy weight of food in the consumption baskets of poorer households could trigger a push for higher wages and thus second-round effects on inflation. In this setting, monetary policymakers need to communicate that they will tighten policy if threats of second-round effects build. Until they do, however, central banks should not react to food prices, which would destabilize output and inflation over the medium term.[5]

Advancing Global Demand Rebalancing

The slowdown in global trade and activity has been accompanied by a marked narrowing of global

---

[5]For a detailed discussion, see Chapter 3 of the September 2011 *World Economic Outlook*.

imbalances, and this is projected to persist (Figure 1.17, panel 1).[6] As discussed in the April 2012 WEO and a recent IMF *Pilot External Sector Report* (IMF, 2012d), most of this narrowing reflects weaker domestic demand from crisis-stricken, external-deficit economies rather than stronger demand from external-surplus economies. But healthier adjustments have taken place—improvements in fiscal balances in external-deficit economies, resilient domestic demand in China, and more social spending by oil exporters—which are bringing down their large surpluses.

In the euro area, imbalances have narrowed but mainly because of lower demand in the deficit economies of the periphery; labor costs have adjusted relative to the core but this process has much further to go (Figure 1.18, panels 1–3). Adjustments in surplus economies toward stronger, domestic-demand-driven growth are at an early stage. External indicators for Germany, the main surplus country, suggest that its internal demand rebalancing process is less advanced than that of Japan or China (see Figure 1.9). Furthermore, major adjustment is still needed in the deficit economies, notably Greece and Portugal, to reduce their net foreign liabilities to 35 percent of GDP, the indicative guideline under the European Commission's Macroeconomic Imbalance Procedure (Figure 1.18, panel 4).

Despite recent improvements, global imbalances and the associated vulnerabilities are likely to remain well above desirable levels unless governments take additional, decisive action (IMF, 2012d). The current account positions of the G3 economies are all estimated to be weaker and their real effective exchange rates stronger than desirable because of unduly large fiscal deficits (Figure 1.17, panel 3). By contrast, in many Asian economies, including China, Korea, Malaysia, Singapore, and Thailand, current account positions are stronger and currencies weaker than they would be with a more desirable set of policies. Several of these economies have accumulated very high levels of official reserves or have internal distortions that hold back consumption (Figure 1.17, panel 4). Among the large economies of the euro area, policies

[6]Imbalances are current accounts that differ from those warranted by fundamentals and desirable policies.

Figure 1.17. Global Imbalances

Global current account balances narrowed sharply during the Great Recession and are not projected to widen again, except for the contribution of emerging Asia. Exchange rate developments since the onset of the crisis have been consistent with global demand rebalancing. However, the appreciation of external surplus currencies has stopped during the past eight months. IMF staff assessments suggest that current account balances remain larger than desirable in emerging Asia and weaker elsewhere. Sustained accumulation of international reserves in these economies is contributing to global current account imbalances and associated vulnerabilities that are larger than desirable.

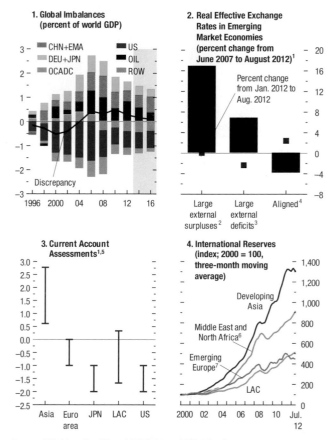

Sources: IMF, *International Financial Statistics,* and IMF staff estimates.
Note: CHN+EMA: China, Hong Kong SAR, Indonesia, Korea, Malaysia, Philippines, Singapore, Taiwan Province of China, and Thailand; DEU+ JPN: Germany and Japan; LAC: Latin America and the Caribbean; OCADC: Bulgaria, Croatia, Czech Republic, Estonia, Greece, Hungary, Ireland, Latvia, Lithuania, Poland, Portugal, Romania, Slovak Republic, Slovenia, Spain, Turkey, and United Kingdom; OIL: oil exporters; ROW: rest of the world; US: United States.
[1]Classifications are based on the IMF staff's *Pilot External Sector Report* (2012d), which covers Australia, Belgium, Brazil, Canada, China, euro area, France, Germany, Hong Kong SAR, India, Indonesia, Italy, Japan, Korea, Malaysia, Mexico, Netherlands, Poland, Russia, Saudi Arabia, Singapore, South Africa, Spain, Sweden, Switzerland, Thailand, Turkey, United Kingdom, and United States.
[2]These economies account for 12.3 percent of global GDP.
[3]These economies account for 7.3 percent of global GDP.
[4]These economies account for 4.8 percent of global GDP.
[5]Estimated differences between cyclically adjusted current accounts and those consistent with fundamentals and desirable policies (percent of GDP).
[6]Bahrain, Djibouti, Egypt, Iran, Jordan, Kuwait, Lebanon, Libya, Oman, Qatar, Saudi Arabia, Sudan, Syria, United Arab Emirates, and Yemen.
[7]Bulgaria, Croatia, Hungary, Latvia, Lithuania, Poland, Romania, and Turkey.

Figure 1.18. Euro Area Imbalances

Current account imbalances have also narrowed within the euro area, reflecting mainly a collapse of demand in the deficit economies in the periphery rather than stronger demand in surplus economies, such as Germany and the Netherlands. Since the onset of the crisis, unit labor costs have grown less in the deficit economies than in the surplus economies, but more adjustment will be needed. Reducing global and euro area current account imbalances will also require further policy changes. In external-deficit economies, these include reducing large fiscal deficits, slowing entitlement spending, and, within the euro area, reforming labor and product markets. In external-surplus economies, policies should improve social protection and remove a variety of distortions.

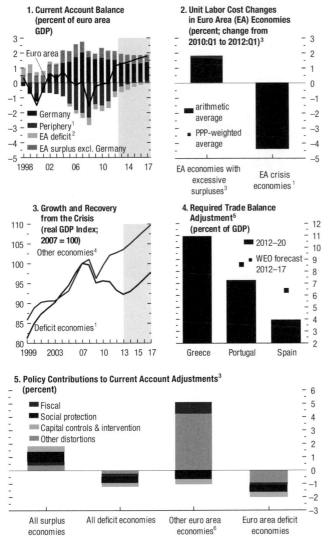

Sources: Eurostat; and IMF staff estimates.
Note: PPP = purchasing power parity.
[1]Greece, Ireland, Italy, Portugal, Spain.
[2]Excludes five periphery economies.
[3]Classifications based on the IMF Staff's *Pilot External Sector Report* (2012d), which covers Australia, Belgium, Brazil, Canada, China, euro area, France, Germany, Hong Kong SAR, India, Indonesia, Italy, Japan, Korea, Malaysia, Mexico, Netherlands, Poland, Russia, Saudi Arabia, Singapore, South Africa, Spain, Sweden, Switzerland, Thailand, Turkey, United Kingdom, and United States.
[4]Austria, Belgium, Finland, Germany, Luxembourg, and Netherlands.
[5]Required adjustment of the trade balance between 2012 and 2020 to lower net foreign liabilities to 35 percent of GDP by 2030, assuming that the nominal external interest rate is 3 percent and that the nominal GDP growth rate stays at the level projected for 2017.
[6]Germany, Netherlands.

that would result in stronger domestic demand for Germany and stronger competitiveness for France, Italy, and Spain would be beneficial.

It must be emphasized that the policies that would most effectively lower global imbalances and related vulnerabilities serve the self-interests of the countries concerned, even when considered purely from a domestic viewpoint (Figure 1.18, panel 5). Many external-deficit economies need strong medium-term fiscal adjustment programs—the need is urgent for the United States. In the euro area, much of the planned adjustment in the periphery economies would be warranted regardless of their external positions, and such fiscal efforts must be complemented with structural reforms to labor and product markets that help rebuild competitiveness. The requirements for emerging market economies with external surpluses and undervalued currencies are to cut back official reserve accumulation, adopt more market-determined exchange systems, and implement structural reforms, for example, to broaden the social safety net.

Improving Growth Prospects with Structural Policies

Structural problems shape much of the legacy of the Great Recession. They also contribute to wide global current account imbalances, which have exacerbated the crisis in the euro area. The impact on growth of reforms to alleviate these structural problems can be significant. In an upside policy scenario produced by the IMF staff for the G20 Mutual Assessment Process, most of the 2½ percent increase in global output is generated by reforms to labor and product markets and the beneficial spillovers via international trade (IMF, 2012e). Through confidence and wealth effects and by facilitating relative price adjustments, structural reforms can promote aggregate demand, particularly investment, over time. But these benefits are unlikely to accrue unless such reforms are supported with macroeconomic policies that lower uncertainty and improve confidence among investors.

Structural policies in crisis-hit economies

Household debt and bank restructuring: Although only a few countries have adopted effective household debt restructuring programs, others should consider following their lead. Programs in the United States got off to a sluggish start, but the recent expansion of the modification and refinancing programs is welcome. Further steps would help support a recovery of the housing market. These could include participation by government-sponsored enterprises in the principal reduction program, implementation of the administration's proposal to further expand refinancing, timely expansion of the program aimed at fostering conversion of foreclosed properties into rental units, and permitting mortgages to be modified in bankruptcy courts. Other economies suffering from housing market slumps may also benefit from policies to directly alleviate household debt.[7]

Progress in financial sector reform, which is critical to building a safer global economy, has been patchy. Chapter 3 of the October 2012 GFSR observes that a host of regulatory reforms are under way but that the structure of financial intermediation remains largely unchanged and vulnerable. Areas that require further attention from policymakers include a global-level discussion of the pros and cons of direct restrictions on business models, monitoring and a set of prudential standards for nonbank financial institutions that pose systemic risks, incentives for the use of simpler financial products, further progress on recovery and resolution planning for large institutions, and cross-border resolution. Crucially, none of the current or prospective reforms will be effective in the absence of enhanced supervision, incentives for the private sector to follow the reforms, and the political will to deliver progress.

Bank restructuring has advanced on a broader front. Many countries have adopted programs to strengthen bank balance sheets and to tide banks over during temporary liquidity difficulties. Capital bases have been strengthened: between 2008 and 2011, for example, large European and U.S. banks raised common-equity-to-asset ratios by about one-fifth and one-third, respectively. They also reduced their reliance on wholesale funding, although such

funding remains extensive in Europe. However, the worsening euro area crisis and weak global economy are posing increasingly severe banking difficulties. Prudential authorities must continue to push balance sheet repair and, where necessary, impose losses on bank stakeholders and force recapitalization. This may require the injection of public funds or the winding-up of weak institutions. In the periphery economies of the euro area, external support in the form of equity injections is critical to breaking the vicious feedback loops between deteriorating sovereigns and weakening banks.

Labor and product market reform: Progress has been uneven. A number of countries, especially in the euro area, are beginning to take action to improve the functioning of their labor markets, but there has been less action to tackle stubborn long-term unemployment or to reform the markets for products and, especially, for services.

Labor market reforms can boost employment in various ways. Reforms can lower hiring and firing costs or reduce minimum wages when they are high enough to undercut employment of the young or the less skilled. Such reforms are under way in Italy and Spain. Trilateral agreements between unions, employers, and their governments can be an important element of reform efforts by helping coordinate relative labor cost adjustment, which is essential for realigning competitiveness between deficit and surplus economies in the euro area. Unions and employers can also develop more flexible collective wage bargaining agreements, as they have done with much success in Germany. To the extent that large-scale wage cuts occur in deficit economies, households may need help to cope with their debt burdens, underscoring the significance of effective household debt restructuring programs. Active labor market policies can have very positive effects on employment by promoting better job matching and supporting education and vocational training for workers displaced by sector-specific shocks, such as the collapse of construction activity in Spain and the United States. Labor force participation can be buoyed by subsidies for jobs filled by the long-term unemployed or jobs created by small and medium-size firms, many of which are finding it hard to obtain credit.

---

[7]For a more in-depth discussion of issues related to household debt restructuring, see Chapter 3 of the April 2012 *World Economic Outlook.*

In various economies, especially in Europe, reform of the services sector should be accelerated, not least to help generate more employment over the medium term. Stronger competition and lower barriers to entry would help ensure that lower wages result in more job creation rather than higher profits for firms. The business environment in various euro area economies also needs to be improved by reducing procedures and costs that weigh on entrepreneurship and by streamlining bankruptcy proceedings to better defend property rights and facilitate exit of inefficient firms (Barkbu and others, 2012).

Structural reforms to facilitate global demand rebalancing

Structural reforms will be important in boosting growth and fostering global demand rebalancing while reducing associated vulnerabilities. In surplus countries such as China and Germany, reforms are needed to boost domestic demand; in deficit countries such as Brazil and India, they are needed to improve supply.

- In Germany, structural reforms will be needed to boost the relatively low level of investment and, more generally, increase potential growth from domestic sources. In the near term, the underlying strength in the labor market should foster a pickup in wages, inflation, and asset prices, and this should be seen as part of a natural rebalancing process within a currency union. By way of example, inflation in Germany and the Netherlands, the other major surplus economy in the euro area, would have to be about 3 to 4 percent to keep euro area inflation close to the ECB's target of "below but close to 2 percent," if inflation in Greece, Ireland, Italy, Portugal, and Spain

were kept around zero to 1 percent and inflation elsewhere remained in line with the ECB target. This underscores the importance of wage and spending adjustments in the surplus economies for the proper functioning of the EMU.

- Previous reports for China have stressed the need for better pension and health care support to lower precautionary saving and boost consumption. Progress is being made on these fronts, but the measures will take time to exert their effects on demand. Meanwhile, support for demand continues to come mainly from measures that support more investment. An obvious risk is that the quality of bank lending could be further lowered, adding to already ample capacity in the export sector or boosting already-high real estate prices.

- In India, there is an urgent need to reaccelerate infrastructure investment, especially in the energy sector, and to launch a new set of structural reforms, with a view to boosting business investment and removing supply bottlenecks. Structural reform also includes tax and spending reforms, in particular, reducing or eliminating subsidies, while protecting the poor. In this regard, the recent announcements with respect to easing restrictions on foreign direct investment in some sectors, privatizations, and lowering fuel subsidies are very welcome.

- Brazil's consumption boom has been a large component of its strong growth performance, and domestic saving and investment remain relatively low. Reforms could usefully focus on further developing the defined-contribution pillar of the pension system, streamlining the tax system, and developing long-term financial instruments.

Special Feature: Commodity Market Review

The first section of this special feature discusses developments in commodity prices, and the second confirms that fluctuations in demand have played a key role in the drop in prices during the second quarter of 2012. The important complementary role of supply developments is discussed for energy markets in the third section and for food markets in the fourth, as these contributed to sharp price increases during the third quarter of 2012. The special feature concludes with the outlook for commodity markets.

Price Developments during 2012

Broad developments

After a robust recovery during 2009–10, the IMF's Primary Commodities Price Index (PCPI) stayed essentially flat during 2011 and then fell during the second quarter of 2012, only to stage a comeback in the third quarter (Figure 1.SF.1). The PCPI is a weighted average of prices for 51 primary commodities, grouped into three main clusters—energy, industrial inputs (mainly base metals), and edibles (of which food is the main component—Table 1.SF.1). Among the three clusters, energy and base metal prices declined during the second quarter by nearly 30 and 20 percent, respectively, from their first quarter peaks. Although metal prices have leveled off during the third quarter, energy prices increased sharply once again, by about 13 percent (through August). Food prices remained broadly flat until mid-June, but have increased since then, by about 10 percent.

Energy prices

The prices of petroleum, natural gas, and coal together have a weight of nearly two-thirds in the PCPI; petroleum alone accounts for more than half of the index. The average petroleum spot price (APSP)—a simple average of the Brent, Dubai, and West Texas

Figure 1.SF.1. IMF Commodity Price Index
(2005 = 100)

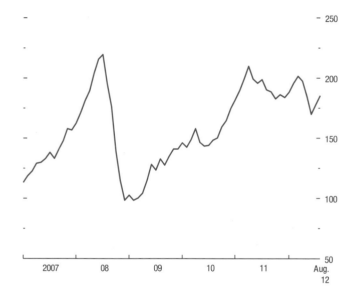

Source: IMF, Primary Commodity Price System.

The authors of this special feature are Samya Beidas-Strom, Joong Shik Kang, Prakash Loungani, Akito Matsumoto, and Marina Rousset. Daniel Rivera Greenwood and Min Kyu Song provided research assistance.

Table 1.SF.1. Indices of Market Prices for Nonfuel and Fuel Commodities, 2009–12

(2005 = 100, in U.S. dollar terms)[1]

Commodities	Weights	2009	2010	2011	2011:Q3	2011:Q4	2012:Q1	2012:Q2
Nonfuel Commodities	36.9	127.4	161.0	189.6	190.7	168.0	172.8	170.2
Food	16.7	134.0	149.4	178.8	179.1	163.8	168.8	171.0
Cereals	3.6	162.4	166.5	231.2	236.2	216.6	216.6	215.7
Wheat	1.7	146.6	146.7	207.4	207.0	183.5	182.9	176.4
Maize	1.0	168.2	189.0	296.5	307.3	273.5	282.2	274.4
Rice	0.6	204.8	180.9	191.7	201.4	207.6	192.9	209.0
Barley	0.3	135.0	166.6	217.9	221.8	221.7	226.7	247.1
Vegetable Oils and Protein Meals	4.4	154.0	170.4	209.1	209.6	189.7	202.5	216.7
Soybeans	1.2	169.7	172.5	217.0	223.2	193.4	209.1	234.9
Soybean Meal	0.8	174.6	161.0	184.1	188.7	161.6	181.0	221.0
Soybean Oil	0.4	158.8	186.6	245.2	247.9	225.1	235.2	233.0
Palm Oil	0.7	175.2	233.9	292.8	278.9	260.1	287.7	282.5
Fish Meal	0.2	168.7	233.7	204.1	191.3	184.7	176.0	204.6
Sunflower Oil	0.2	91.0	103.6	141.7	146.1	135.6	129.2	125.9
Olive Oil	0.3	63.6	57.5	55.6	55.6	54.4	52.5	51.8
Groundnuts	0.2	129.3	161.1	224.2	231.5	240.3	240.6	238.3
Rapeseed Oil	0.3	118.8	140.3	189.6	187.8	175.4	177.5	172.1
Meat	3.7	98.0	117.2	134.5	136.4	134.2	136.2	133.4
Beef	1.4	100.8	128.4	154.3	150.1	154.7	162.7	158.1
Lamb	0.3	91.3	90.5	92.7	94.0	88.0	77.7	62.0
Pork	1.1	82.4	110.0	131.6	142.1	129.1	125.7	123.5
Poultry	0.9	115.9	116.2	118.2	119.3	120.9	123.7	127.1
Seafood	3.2	113.7	135.9	132.8	119.6	102.9	109.8	111.8
Fish	2.5	121.2	151.3	145.5	128.4	107.3	116.4	119.2
Shrimp	0.7	84.7	75.9	83.4	85.4	85.9	83.9	82.9
Sugar	0.9	151.8	172.0	210.8	225.4	200.3	192.5	172.7
Free Markets	0.6	180.2	207.5	260.5	281.3	245.7	235.8	208.0
United States	0.1	115.5	147.4	178.3	184.8	178.6	162.7	144.3
European Union	0.2	86.0	85.0	88.1	88.4	86.5	86.3	87.0
Bananas	0.4	147.0	152.8	169.2	165.9	165.4	181.4	170.0
Oranges	0.5	107.9	122.1	105.8	123.3	97.9	91.5	100.2
Beverages	1.8	154.4	176.2	205.5	207.9	184.6	175.2	162.7
Coffee	0.9	131.5	165.4	231.0	231.1	212.3	200.0	179.7
Other Milds	0.5	123.8	170.0	239.0	238.6	216.1	194.8	160.2
Robusta	0.3	144.5	157.6	217.3	218.3	205.9	208.8	213.0
Cocoa Beans	0.7	187.4	202.7	192.8	196.5	159.9	151.6	143.4
Tea	0.3	145.1	146.4	160.0	165.8	160.5	157.0	157.6
Agricultural Raw Materials[2]	7.7	94.1	125.4	153.8	153.2	135.1	135.8	136.9
Timber[2]	3.4	101.5	101.6	111.4	116.4	111.4	105.4	109.6
Hardwood	1.2	128.9	132.7	159.1	169.9	158.9	150.5	148.7
Logs[2]	0.4	141.4	137.6	193.2	220.0	202.3	184.6	178.6
Sawed[2]	0.8	123.5	130.6	144.5	148.5	140.2	135.8	135.9
Softwood	2.2	86.4	84.5	85.0	86.8	85.2	80.4	88.0
Logs[2]	0.4	75.3	77.9	82.6	80.9	79.2	79.8	77.6
Sawed[2]	1.8	88.6	85.8	85.5	88.0	86.4	80.5	90.1
Cotton	0.7	113.7	187.7	280.2	229.6	187.8	182.1	163.6
Wool	0.5	115.1	152.9	234.2	243.2	212.9	240.5	218.7
Fine	0.2	114.9	151.0	241.7	247.7	213.2	226.5	200.0
Coarse	0.3	115.2	154.6	227.9	239.4	212.6	252.2	234.3
Rubber	0.5	128.0	243.3	320.8	309.9	240.1	256.5	239.1
Hides	2.6	68.4	109.6	125.0	130.8	115.1	117.8	128.0
Metals	10.7	136.5	202.3	229.7	233.1	195.4	205.4	194.2
Copper	2.8	140.5	205.0	240.0	244.3	204.3	226.4	214.1
Aluminum	3.9	87.8	114.3	126.3	126.3	110.2	114.8	104.1

SPECIAL FEATURE

Table 1.SF.1. *(concluded)*

Commodities	Weights	2009	2010	2011	2011:Q3	2011:Q4	2012:Q1	2012:Q2
Iron Ore	1.3	284.6	521.9	596.9	625.7	500.9	504.5	496.3
Tin	0.2	184.2	275.8	352.7	333.9	282.3	310.6	278.3
Nickel	1.1	99.3	147.6	155.0	149.1	124.4	133.0	116.1
Zinc	0.6	120.1	156.5	159.0	161.1	138.1	146.9	139.7
Lead	0.2	176.5	220.5	246.4	251.8	204.5	214.8	202.7
Uranium	0.5	167.1	164.6	201.3	185.5	188.2	185.8	183.8
Energy	63.1	116.8	147.1	193.8	193.6	193.9	208.3	192.3
Spot Crude[3]	53.6	116.2	148.5	195.9	194.3	194.4	211.9	193.9
Natural Gas	6.9	109.6	113.3	154.3	165.4	172.6	170.9	178.0
Russian in Germany	3.2	149.7	139.0	179.1	188.3	204.2	208.8	212.5
Indonesian in Japan	1.9	106.5	133.4	221.2	245.4	253.8	249.3	271.5
U.S., Domestic Market	1.9	44.5	49.5	45.1	46.5	37.6	27.7	25.7
Coal	2.6	148.8	206.0	253.7	253.3	238.2	233.8	198.3
Australian, Export Markets	2.1	151.0	207.8	254.0	253.3	239.7	235.3	197.2
South African, Export Markets	0.5	140.2	198.5	252.5	253.4	232.0	228.0	202.9

Source: IMF, Primary Commodity Price System.

[1]Weights are based on 2002–04 average world export earnings.

[2]Provisional.

[3]Average petroleum spot price. Average of U.K. Brent, Dubai Fateh, and West Texas Intermediate, equally weighted.

Intermediate (WTI) crude oil varieties—increased from a low of $35 a barrel in late 2008 to a high of $120 a barrel in March 2012. Since then, oil prices declined during the second quarter only to climb back during the third, albeit with some volatility. Implied volatility remained moderate when compared with the spikes after the Libyan revolution in 2011 but picked up during the summer months (Figure 1.SF.2).

Metal and food prices

These two components comprise the remaining third of the PCPI, each receiving a similar weight. After a strong rally earlier in 2012, base metal prices declined in tandem with petroleum prices—albeit less sharply—during the second quarter and have leveled off somewhat during the third quarter (Figure 1.SF.3). After remaining broadly flat for much of the year, food prices started to pick up strongly in mid-June. Grain and soybean prices rose, offsetting the weakness in seafood, sugar, and vegetable oil prices. Implied volatility also rose significantly (Figure 1.SF.4).

Economic Activity and Commodity Prices

A tight link with demand

Fluctuations in economic activity and in the outlook are the primary determinants of short-term commodity price movements, with some caveats.

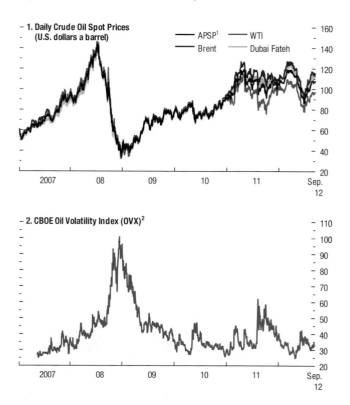

Figure 1.SF.2. Oil Prices and Volatility

Sources: Bloomberg, L.P.; and IMF staff calculations.
Note: As of September 11, 2012.
[1]Average petroleum spot price (APSP) is a simple average of Brent, Dubai Fateh, and West Texas Intermediate (WTI) spot prices.
[2]CBOE = Chicago Board Options Exchange.

Figure 1.SF.3. Base Metal Spot Prices
(Indices; January 1, 2007 = 100)

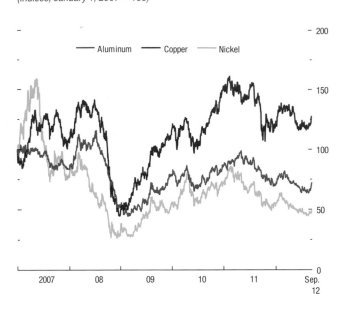

Sources: Bloomberg, L.P.; and IMF staff calculations.
Note: As of September 11, 2012.

Figure 1.SF.4. Food Prices and Volatility

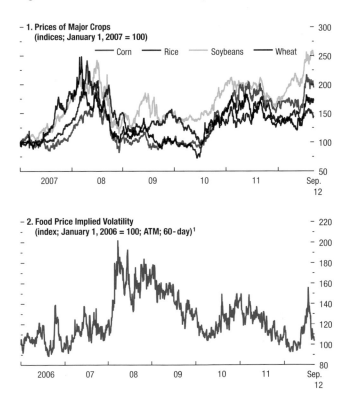

Sources: Bloomberg, L.P.; and IMF staff calculations.
Note: As of September 11, 2012.
[1] ATM = at the money.

First, on occasion, causality goes the other way: supply disruptions can sometimes lead to price spikes and declines in economic activity (Hamilton, 2008). Second, developments on the supply side or concerns about supply depletion can be important enough to break the tight connection between economic activity and commodity prices even if they are not significant enough to derail economic activity (see Benes and others, 2012, for the case of oil prices). Third, concerns that speculative commodity trading has decoupled price movements from economic activity have been a constant refrain during the past few years despite the lack of conclusive supporting evidence.[1]

These caveats notwithstanding, a tight link between economic activity and commodity price fluctuations is evident in the data, and this appears to be the leading factor behind the broad commodity price declines during the second quarter. Commodity markets rallied somewhat in early 2012 on the back of recovering market confidence in response to the European Central Bank's longer-term refinancing operations as well as better-than-expected global growth in the first quarter. However, with renewed setbacks to the global recovery in the beginning of the second quarter, leading indicators pointed to a synchronized slowing in the momentum of global activity. In particular, growth in a number of major emerging market economies, notably China, has slowed significantly. These common macroeconomic factors affect commodity prices through changes in current and prospective demand and the cost of carrying inventories.

Principal components analysis

The influence of common macroeconomic factors on commodity markets can be examined using principal component analysis, which extracts key factors that account for most of the variance in the observed variables. Individual commodity prices are affected by both commodity-wide and commodity-specific factors. The first principal component of commodity prices captures price movements driven by commodity-wide factors. The strong correla-

[1] See Box 1.4 of the September 2011 *World Economic Outlook* for a detailed discussion.

SPECIAL FEATURE

tion between this first principal component and actual commodity prices across the board—more than 0.85 for all major commodity groups, including crude oil, food, and base metals—implies that individual commodity prices have been significantly affected by commodity-wide factors (Figure 1.SF.5, panel 1). Similarly, the first principal component from industrial production indices (IPs), purchasing managers' indices (PMIs), and equity returns (using MSCI)—which are good proxies for global economic activity, economic sentiment, and broad asset market performance, respectively—capture the underlying common macroeconomic factors (Figure 1.SF.5, panel 2).

The strong correlations between the first principal components for commodity prices and aggregate economic activity suggest that commodity-wide factors have mainly reflected common macroeconomic developments. Especially during the second quarter, the first principal component of commodity prices has shown a declining trend in line with the first principal component of IPs, PMIs, and equity returns, implying that the recent declines in commodity prices over this period were largely driven by global economic conditions (Figure 1.SF.6).

Metal prices and Chinese activity

The link between prices and activity is also apparent for base metal prices. The slow recovery of advanced economies continued to exert a drag on base metal consumption, but it was the significant slowdown in major emerging market economies, notably China, that led to a sharp decline in global base metal consumption. In China, growth has been steadily moderating as the authorities have pursued policies aimed at slowing the economy to a more sustainable pace. Reflecting these policies, growth in industrial production fell to single digits after April for the first time since mid-2009, and real estate investment also slowed in recent months. China's base metal consumption, which has been steadily increasing and now accounts for more than 40 percent of global consumption (Figure 1.SF.7, panel 1), slowed sharply in the second quarter. As a result, growth in global consumption of base metals slowed significantly in the second quarter (Figure 1.SF.7, panel 2). In line with this trend, base metal

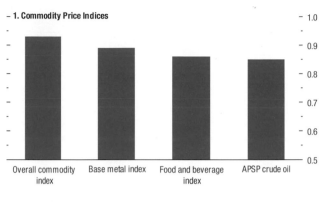

Figure 1.SF.5. Influence of Common Factors: Pairwise Correlations with First Principal Components

1. Commodity Price Indices

(bars, left to right: Overall commodity index, Base metal index, Food and beverage index, APSP crude oil)

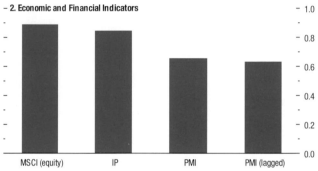

2. Economic and Financial Indicators

(bars, left to right: MSCI (equity), IP, PMI, PMI (lagged))

Source: IMF staff calculations.
Note: APSP = average petroleum spot price; IP = industrial production index; PMI = purchasing managers' index.

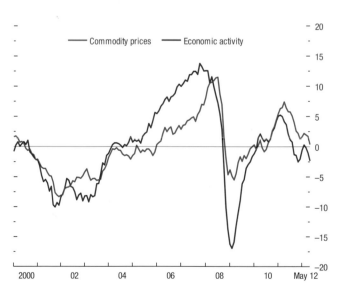

Figure 1.SF.6. Commodity Prices and Economic Activity: First Principal Components

Commodity prices — Economic activity

Source: IMF staff calculations.

prices declined the most among major commodities, despite some supply response to lower prices.

Demand factors play a critical role by driving commodity-wide movements in prices, but the role of commodity-specific factors—which generally reflect specific developments on the supply side—is important as well. In petroleum markets, production decisions by producers, supply disruptions, and geopolitical concerns are often decisive in determining the course of prices, particularly when inventories are low. For food prices, weather is the predominant commodity-specific factor. The next two sections discuss the supply-demand balance in oil and food markets, respectively.

Supply-Demand Balance in Oil Markets

Supply surge

Oil supply expanded at an annual rate of 3.2 percent during the first half of 2012—on average by 2.4 million barrels a day (mbd)—more than double the growth rate during 2011 (Table 1.SF.2). Since then, supply has moderated.

- *Organization of Petroleum Exporting Countries (OPEC):* As of the end of June, increased supply reflected an eight-month ramp-up in OPEC production (an increase of 2.1 mbd), well above the cartel's production quota ceiling of 30 mbd for crude oil. The OPEC crude oil production quota is only a guideline, however, and actual production was considerably higher (by 1.9 mbd) during the first half of 2012 (Figure 1.SF.8, panel 1), largely attributed to the recovery in Libyan production and increased Saudi output. While still above quota, OPEC production moderated (by 0.5 mbd) during the third quarter.[2]

---

[2]Before the full effects of the sanctions and oil embargo kicked in, Iranian crude oil during the second quarter was at half of peak production (in 1974, at more than 6 mbd), hovering at an average of 3.2 to 3.3 mbd between April and June 2012, only to fall to below 2.9 mbd in August (according to the International Energy Agency, IEA). Given the use of flagging out and floating storage, the IEA suggests caution when interpreting the data, especially pre-July data. The EU oil embargo also barred European insurance companies from insuring Iranian oil-related transactions. As the insurance market for Iranian oil disappeared, Japan decided to provide its own insurance and Iran offered to provide insurance coverage to tankers carrying Iranian oil.

Figure 1.SF.7. Demand for Base Metals

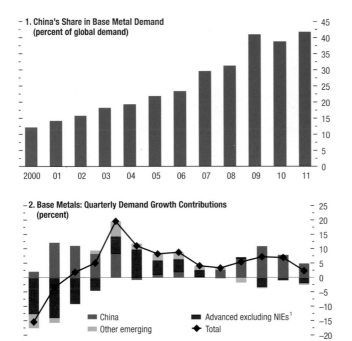

1. China's Share in Base Metal Demand (percent of global demand)

2. Base Metals: Quarterly Demand Growth Contributions (percent)

China
Other emerging
Advanced excluding NIEs[1]
Total

Sources: World Bureau of Metal Statistics; and IMF staff calculations.
Note: Weighted sum of aluminum, copper, lead, nickel, tin, and zinc.
[1]NIEs = newly industrialized Asian economies.

SPECIAL FEATURE

Table 1.SF.2. Global Oil Supply and Demand by Region
(Million barrels a day)

	2010	2011	2012 Proj.	2011 H2	2012 H1	2005–07 Avg.	2008	2009	2010	2011	2012 Proj.	2011 H2	2012 H1
						Year-over-Year Percent Change							
World Production	**87.3**	**88.4**	**89.8**	**88.9**	**90.8**	**0.9**	**1.2**	**−1.5**	**2.1**	**1.3**	**1.5**	**1.2**	**3.2**
OPEC (current composition)[1,2]	34.6	35.7	36.6	35.9	37.6	1.7	3.3	−5.9	1.8	3.0	2.6	2.8	6.3
Of Which:													
Saudi Arabia	9.7	10.8	. . .	11.1	11.4	−0.2	4.9	−9.5	2.2	11.6	. . .	13.2	8.7
Iran	4.2	4.2	. . .	4.1	3.8	1.7	−1.5	−1.9	−0.0	−1.7	. . .	−2.5	−10.2
Nigeria	2.5	2.6	. . .	2.6	2.6	−1.9	−7.6	−0.4	15.7	3.9	. . .	−0.3	−1.7
Venezuela	2.7	2.7	. . .	2.6	2.7	1.8	0.8	−3.6	−4.6	−1.2	. . .	−4.0	−2.7
Iraq	2.4	2.7	. . .	2.7	2.9	2.0	14.3	2.7	−2.0	12.9	. . .	12.3	5.4
Libya	1.7	0.5	. . .	0.3	1.4	4.3	0.8	−9.7	0.0	−70.8	. . .	−81.1	116.2
Kuwait	2.2	2.4	. . .	2.6	2.7	1.9	8.0	−11.3	1.6	9.8	. . .	15.3	14.8
Non-OPEC[2]	52.6	52.8	53.2	53.0	53.2	0.4	−0.2	1.5	2.4	0.3	0.8	0.1	1.1
Of Which:													
North America	14.1	14.6	15.7	14.9	15.6	−1.2	−3.4	1.8	3.6	3.5	7.8	4.5	8.8
United States	7.8	8.1	8.9	8.3	8.9	−1.8	−1.2	6.5	4.7	4.6	10.0	5.6	11.5
Canada	3.4	3.5	3.9	3.6	3.8	2.6	−2.2	−0.8	4.8	4.5	10.5	6.5	11.4
North Sea	3.8	3.4	3.1	3.3	3.3	−7.0	−4.7	−5.3	−8.6	−9.8	−8.0	−8.8	−5.8
Russia	10.5	10.6	10.7	10.6	10.7	2.5	−0.7	2.0	2.4	1.4	1.0	1.4	1.4
Other Former Soviet Union[3]	3.1	3.0	2.9	2.9	3.0	9.8	3.1	8.7	0.6	−3.0	−1.5	−5.6	−2.4
Other Non-OPEC	21.3	21.2	20.7	21.3	20.6	1.4	3.0	1.6	4.0	−0.2	−2.3	−1.1	−2.6
Of Which:													
Brazil	2.1	2.2	2.2	2.2	2.2	6.2	3.4	6.8	5.6	2.6	0.7	2.6	0.6
World Demand	**88.1**	**88.9**	**89.8**	**89.7**	**89.1**	**1.5**	**−0.7**	**−1.2**	**3.1**	**1.0**	**0.9**	**0.5**	**1.0**
Advanced Economies	45.9	45.4	45.0	45.6	44.7	−0.1	−3.6	−3.9	1.8	−1.2	−0.8	−1.7	−0.9
Of Which:													
United States	19.5	19.3	19.1	19.3	18.9	−0.1	−5.9	−3.7	2.2	−0.9	−0.9	−1.7	−2.1
Euro Area	10.5	10.2	9.9	10.3	9.8	−0.4	−0.4	−5.6	−0.3	−3.3	−3.1	−4.3	−3.8
Japan	4.4	4.5	4.6	4.6	4.8	−1.8	−4.8	−8.1	0.7	0.6	4.0	2.8	9.6
Newly Industrialized Asian Economies	5.0	4.9	4.9	4.9	4.8	2.4	−2.6	3.5	5.5	−2.4	−0.0	−1.8	−0.2
Emerging Market and Developing Economies	42.1	43.6	44.7	44.0	44.4	3.8	3.0	2.1	4.5	3.4	2.7	2.9	3.0
Of Which:													
Commonwealth of Independent States	4.2	4.4	4.6	4.6	4.5	2.2	6.1	−4.7	3.2	6.7	3.6	7.4	4.1
Developing Asia	25.1	26.0	26.9	25.9	27.0	3.7	1.6	3.8	7.2	3.9	3.2	2.8	3.0
China	8.8	9.2	9.5	9.2	9.4	5.5	1.9	3.3	10.7	5.0	2.6	2.2	1.8
India	3.4	3.5	3.6	3.4	3.7	4.9	4.0	1.1	7.1	4.1	3.8	4.7	3.7
Middle East and North Africa	9.1	9.0	9.2	9.2	9.1	4.5	5.2	5.7	2.5	−1.3	2.8	−0.9	3.0
Western Hemisphere	5.9	6.2	6.4	6.3	6.3	3.6	6.4	0.5	4.9	4.4	2.4	4.3	3.1
Net Demand[4]	**0.8**	**0.5**	**. . .**	**0.8**	**−1.7**	**0.4**	**−0.4**	**0.0**	**0.9**	**0.6**	**. . .**	**0.9**	**−1.9**

Sources: International Energy Agency, *Oil Market Report*, September 2012; and IMF staff calculations.

[1]OPEC = Organization of Petroleum Exporting Countries. Includes Angola (subject to quotas since January 2007) and Ecuador, which rejoined OPEC in November 2007 after suspending its membership from December 1992 to October 2007.

[2]Totals refer to a total of crude oil, condensates, natural gas liquids, and oil from unconventional sources. Individual OPEC country production is for crude oil only.

[3]Other Former Soviet Union includes Azerbaijan, Belarus, Georgia, Kazakhstan, Kyrgyz Republic, Tajikistan, Turkmenistan, Ukraine, and Uzbekistan.

[4]Difference between demand and production. In the percent change columns, the figures are in percent of world demand.

- *Non-OPEC:* Non-OPEC production growth was centered in the Americas—namely, Canada and the United States, which added on average 1 mbd. This increase was largely attributable to the development of unconventional oil production in the United States with hydraulic fracturing technology (Box 1.4).The increase in the Americas offsets non-OPEC declines elsewhere—for example, in Sudan, Syria, and Yemen—and trend declines in other Organization for Economic Cooperation and Development (OECD) country supplies (United Kingdom), resulting in a net non-OPEC supply increase of 0.4

SPECIAL FEATURE

mbd during the first half of the year (Table 1.SF.2). Unplanned outages in Norway and those related to Hurricane Isaac in the United States, among others, led to some moderation (by about 1 mbd) in non-OPEC production during the third quarter.

Anemic demand

Demand growth was flat during the first half of 2012 relative to the 2011 average, at 89.1 mbd, thus contributing to the easing in crude oil prices, particularly toward the end of the second quarter. Year-over-year demand was up during the second quarter of 2012 (by about 1.2 mbd), but largely from Asia and the Pacific—namely, China, India, and Japan—and the Middle East; there was a slowdown relative to the last quarter of 2011 in other advanced economies (Figure 1.SF.8, panel 2; Table 1.SF.2). This slowdown is a continuation of the trend decline in OECD demand (except in Japan) owing to lower oil intensity. Much of China's demand increase was reportedly to add to the country's strategic petroleum reserve and, to a lesser extent, to support the still-expanding vehicle usage and growth in petrochemical demand. India's strong demand intensified initially from irrigation needs given a weak monsoon and then from electricity blackouts and power shortages during the third quarter. Increased Japanese demand reflects the use of oil for power generation after nuclear production was halted in the wake of the Fukushima disaster. Japanese demand is expected to remain high despite the restart of two nuclear plants during July 2012, given the country's recent decision to phase out nuclear power by 2040.

Reflecting these supply and demand developments, there was a replenishment of inventories among OECD countries. Inventory levels were close to their five-year averages in July 2012, while spare capacity in OPEC countries hovered at 2.5 mbd (Figure 1.SF.9).[3]

Figure 1.SF.8. Oil Supply and Demand

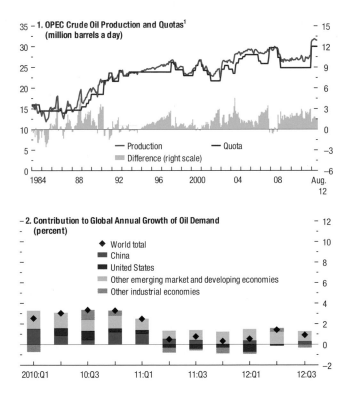

Sources: Bloomberg, L.P.; International Energy Agency; and IMF staff calculations.
[1]Excludes Iraq through December 2011.

[3]Reliable data on inventory accumulation from non-OECD economies are scarce. However, industry analysts report some buildup in forward demand (particularly in Asia), but this remains well below the OECD average (55 days) for many large emerging market economies (for example, India and Indonesia).

Supply Concerns in Food Markets

Supply setbacks

The prices of major crops—corn, soybeans, and wheat—have risen strongly amid concern about weather-related supply disruptions worldwide. Earlier in the year, the La Niña weather pattern contributed to drought in South America, which significantly hurt corn and soybean crops in Argentina, Brazil, and Paraguay. Since mid-June, other supply concerns have emerged as hot and dry weather in the U.S. Midwest lowered corn and soybean yields. At the same time, wheat crop estimates have been downgraded in the Black Sea region (Kazakhstan, Russia, Ukraine) and in China because of adverse weather conditions.

Robust demand

Food demand remained robust in 2012 despite the slowdown in global economic activity. Most of the demand growth for major crops—corn, wheat, soybeans, and rice—is expected to come from emerging market and developing economies this year, with China being the single largest contributor. Among individual food commodities, wheat accounts for more than half the global consumption growth for major crops.

Declining stocks

Global food markets are vulnerable to supply setbacks because of low buffers. Stock-to-use ratios remain below their long-term historical average levels for corn and rice and have been declining for wheat and soybeans. Compared with the 2007–08 food crisis, global stock-to-use ratios have improved significantly for rice and wheat but deteriorated most notably for soybeans and to a lesser extent for corn and other grains and oilseeds. (Figure 1.SF.10, panel 1). In the absence of adequate food reserves, threats of production shortages caused an immediate price response in grains, which has significant spillovers to other food commodities. Rising corn prices in particular have important spillover effects in meat and ethanol markets. The share of the U.S. corn crop going to fuel use declined noticeably with the expiration of government support for the ethanol industry through tariffs and tax credits to gasoline refiners. This year, all the growth in U.S. corn consumption is expected to come

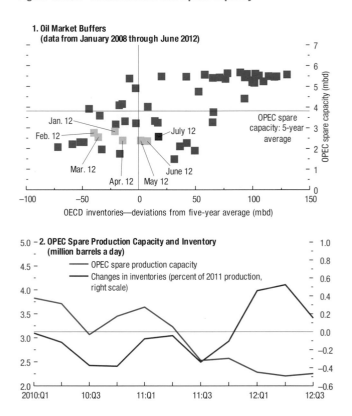

Figure 1.SF.9. Oil Inventories and Spare Capacity

1. Oil Market Buffers
(data from January 2008 through June 2012)

OECD inventories—deviations from five-year average (mbd)

OPEC spare capacity (mbd)

OPEC spare capacity: 5-year average

Jan. 12
Feb. 12
Mar. 12
Apr. 12
May 12
June 12
July 12

2. OPEC Spare Production Capacity and Inventory
(million barrels a day)

— OPEC spare production capacity
— Changes in inventories (percent of 2011 production, right scale)

Sources: International Energy Agency; U.S. Energy Information Administration; and IMF staff calculations.
Note: mbd = million barrels a day; OECD = Organization for Economic Cooperation and Development; OPEC = Organization of Petroleum Exporting Countries.

Figure 1.SF.10. Inventory Buffers for Food

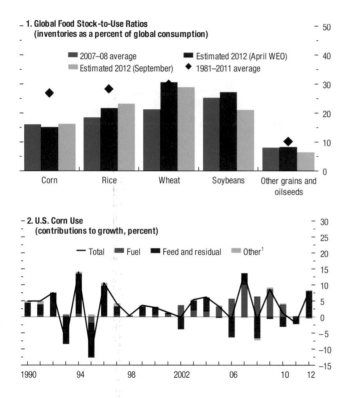

1. Global Food Stock-to-Use Ratios
   (inventories as a percent of global consumption)

2007–08 average   Estimated 2012 (April WEO)
Estimated 2012 (September)   1981–2011 average

Corn   Rice   Wheat   Soybeans   Other grains and oilseeds

2. U.S. Corn Use
   (contributions to growth, percent)

Total   Fuel   Feed and residual   Other¹

1990   94   98   2002   06   10   12

Sources: U.S. Department of Agriculture; and IMF staff estimates.
¹Includes use for cereal and other food products, seed, starch, high-fructose corn syrup, glucose and dextrose, and alcohol for beverages and manufacturing.

from its use as animal feed (Figure 1.SF.10, panel 2). Although other grains can be substituted for corn in animal feedstock, corn remains the primary feed grain in the United States. Another key grain, rice, posted only a marginal price change since mid-June because markets are well supplied, despite some concern about the Indian harvest from a weaker monsoon season, but global rice output is projected to reach record levels next year. Substitution on the supply and demand sides between rice and other grains is also less prevalent, and the rice market is more segmented.

Macroeconomic impact

The current food price shock is less severe than the shock in 2007–08 because it has not affected all key crops uniformly and has not been aggravated by trade restrictions and high energy input costs (Box 1.5). However rising food prices could have a number of macroeconomic implications. First, rising prices translate into higher headline inflation, which erodes consumers' buying power. This erosion is felt particularly sharply in low- and middle-income countries, where the share of food in the consumption basket is higher and the pass-through from international to domestic prices is larger than in advanced economies. Second, they erode the fiscal balance through higher government subsidies and safety net measures for affected households. And finally, rising food prices have a negative effect on the trade balances of food-importing countries. Rising food prices also have political economy dimensions: they contribute to widespread discontent, thus destabilizing fragile post-conflict political systems. Therefore, countries should avoid protective trade policies such as export bans and export taxes and quotas, which further drive up food prices and volatility, and instead should adopt appropriate policies to maintain macroeconomic stability while protecting the poor.[4]

In the near term, countries should expect rising inflation and balance of payments pressures. During the 2007–08 food price surge, low- and middle-income countries bore the brunt of the inflationary impact, because volatile items such as food and fuel

[4]So far this year, there is no evidence of widespread export restrictions on food commodities or panic buying by importers, as seen during 2007–08.

SPECIAL FEATURE

account for a large share in the consumption basket. Recent IMF research suggests that, despite a variety of appropriate monetary policy tools to combat rising inflation across countries, commodity importers are better off targeting underlying inflation rather than headline inflation, which includes volatile food and fuel, thus improving central bank credibility by stabilizing both output and inflation volatility.[5] In this context, near-term macroeconomic policies should also include scaling up well-targeted social safety nets and other fiscal transfers where space is available, allowing the real exchange rate to move flexibly for net importers, and accessing multilateral finance to support balance of payments needs.

Outlook for Commodity Markets

For all their faults, futures prices remain the most favored way to gauge the outlook for spot prices (Chinn and Coibion, 2009). The predictions by futures markets for the main commodities are shown in Figure 1.SF.11, and market assessments of the balance of risks from the prices of futures options are shown in Figure 1.SF.12.[6]

- *Oil:* With the decline in inventory buffers and their return in May to five-year averages, futures curves for the Brent crude oil variety—the predominant price benchmark outside the North American market—continue to exhibit backwardation, implying a gradual decline in oil prices to less than $100 in the medium term. However, reflecting physical market (for example, North Sea) disruptions, ongoing geopolitical risks and concern about associated potential supply disruptions, and expectations of stimulus in China, the United States, and Europe, the risk to oil prices is tilted to the upside. In contrast, futures curves for WTI are still sloping upward at the front end, reflecting localized pockets of excess supply in the landlocked

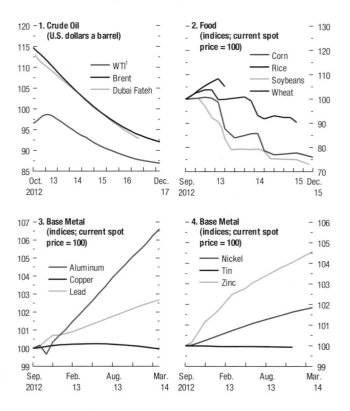

Figure 1.SF.11. Futures Prices

Sources: Bloomberg, L.P.; IMF, Primary Commodity Price System; and IMF staff calculations.
Note: As of September 11, 2012.
[1]WTI = West Texas Intermediate.

---

[5]See Chapter 3 of the September 2011 *World Economic Outlook* for a detailed discussion.

[6]The time duration of the fan chart depends on the depth of available futures options. Options for many commodities are either unavailable or, as for aluminum, are not liquid enough to construct a fan chart.

SPECIAL FEATURE

areas of the North American oil supply system.[7] However, because still-limited transportation capacity constrains the scope for arbitrage to reduce price differentials, and given that these constraints are expected to persist, current futures prices imply that markets expect WTI to be priced at a discount to Brent through 2015. Overall, risks around the APSP baseline are more balanced than at the time of the April 2012 *World Economic Outlook,* although upside risks are wide and thus cannot be easily dismissed (see Figure 1.SF.12).

- *Food:* Although short-term supply constraints are likely to keep food prices elevated, in the medium term the current food price spike should subside in the absence of major additional disruptions to supply and resulting trade restrictions. Futures price curves indicate that markets expect the prices of key food crops to moderate by the end of 2013.

- *Metals:* Markets are expecting some rebound after the sharp price declines in recent quarters. This could reflect anticipation of a pickup in economic activity beginning in the fourth quarter of 2012 and the impact of possible stimulus measures in China.

[7]With above-average temperatures in the United States during June and July coinciding with the summer driving season, oil spot prices rose in response to strong refinery runs, reduced imports, and falling stocks. The upward-sloping WTI futures curve at the front end, however, reflects still-large stocks in the mid-continent—from increased light tight oil in the United States and heavy crude oil from Canada—and a lack of pipeline capacity to ship crude oil to Gulf Coast refineries. The buildup in landlocked crude oil has driven the price of WTI below that of Brent, in part as a reflection of the higher cost of moving surplus crude oil to market by rail, barge, and truck. The ahead-of-schedule reversal of the direction of the Seaway pipeline, which now delivers heavy crude oil from Cushing, Oklahoma, to Gulf Coast refineries, helped alleviate at the margin some congestion this spring at Cushing—where stockpiles had been at an all-time high—but not enough to remove the surplus. The WTI-Brent spread is likely to persist until new pipelines to the Gulf Coast are built, existing pipelines expanded, and new refining capacity comes online to handle the increase in heavy crude: the first large-scale refining facility is scheduled to open in Indiana in mid-2013. The expected narrowing of the WTI-Brent spread is reflected in the middle and back end of both futures curves: both slope downward, reflecting expectations of future lower prices.

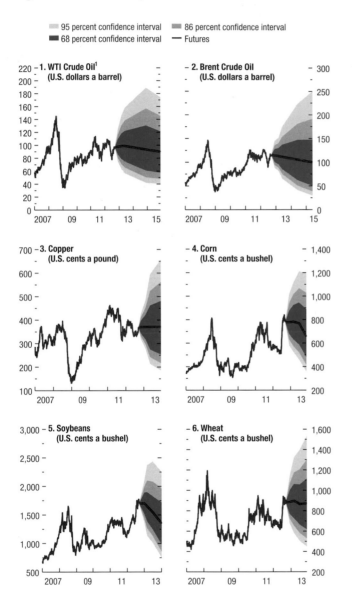

Figure 1.SF.12. Price Prospects for Selected Commodities

Sources: Bloomberg, L.P.; and IMF staff estimates.
Note: Derived from prices of futures options on September 11, 2012.
[1]WTI = West Texas Intermediate.

SPECIAL FEATURE

Box 1.1. Are We Underestimating Short-Term Fiscal Multipliers?

With many economies in fiscal consolidation mode, a debate has been raging about the size of fiscal multipliers. The smaller the multipliers, the less costly the fiscal consolidation. At the same time, activity has disappointed in a number of economies undertaking fiscal consolidation. So a natural question is whether the negative short-term effects of fiscal cutbacks have been larger than expected because fiscal multipliers were underestimated.

This box sheds light on these issues using international evidence. The main finding, based on data for 28 economies, is that the multipliers used in generating growth forecasts have been systematically too low since the start of the Great Recession, by 0.4 to 1.2, depending on the forecast source and the specifics of the estimation approach. Informal evidence suggests that the multipliers implicitly used to generate these forecasts are about 0.5. So actual multipliers may be higher, in the range of 0.9 to 1.7.

Forecast Errors and Fiscal Multipliers

Our basic approach is the following: focusing on the recent episode of widespread fiscal consolidation, we regress the forecast error for real GDP growth during 2010–11 on forecasts of fiscal consolidation for 2010–11 that were made in early 2010. Under rational expectations, and assuming that the correct forecast model has been used, the coefficient on planned fiscal consolidation should be zero. The equation estimated is

$$\textit{forecast error of growth} = \alpha + \beta \textit{ forecast of fiscal consolidation} + \varepsilon. \qquad (1.1.1)$$

The forecast error of growth is equal to actual cumulative real GDP growth during 2010–11 minus the forecast of growth in the April 2010 *World Economic Outlook*. The forecast of fiscal consolidation is the forecast of the change in the structural fiscal balance as a percentage of potential GDP during 2010–11 as of the April 2010 WEO. We also investigate forecasts other than the WEO. If the fiscal multipliers used for forecasting are accurate, the slope coefficient, β, should be zero. Our baseline sample consists of 28 economies: the major advanced economies included in the G20 and the member countries of the EU for which forecasts are available.

The authors of this box are Olivier Blanchard and Daniel Leigh.

What Do the Data Show?

We find the coefficient on planned fiscal consolidation to be large, negative, and significant. The baseline estimate suggests that a planned fiscal consolidation of 1 percent of GDP is associated with a growth forecast error of about 1 percentage point (Table 1.1.1 and Figure 1.1.1, panel 1). This result indicates that the multipliers underlying growth projections have been too low by about 1. The systematic relationship between fiscal consolidation and growth holds up to a battery of robustness tests. Overall, depending on the forecast source and the specification, our estimation results for the unexpected output loss associated with a 1 percent of GDP fiscal consolidation are in the range of 0.4 to 1.2 percentage points. First, we establish that the baseline result is not driven by crisis economies—those that had IMF programs—or other outliers (Table 1.1.1).[1]

Next, we check whether the results are robust to controlling for additional variables that could plausibly have triggered both planned fiscal consolidation and lower-than-expected growth. The omission of such variables could bias the analysis toward finding that fiscal multipliers were larger than assumed. We consider two groups of variables: those that were known when the growth forecasts were made and those that were not (Table 1.1.1).

- *Variables known at the time the forecasts were made:* We start by considering the role of sovereign debt problems. Are the baseline results picking up greater-than-expected effects of sovereign debt problems rather than the effects of fiscal consolidation? Reassuringly, the results are robust to controlling for the initial (end-2009) government-debt-to-GDP ratio and for initial sovereign credit default swap (CDS) spreads. Controlling for the possible role of banking crises—based on the data set of systemic banking crises of Laeven and Valencia (2012)—yields similar results. The baseline finding also holds up to controlling for the fiscal consolidation of trading partners. To the extent that fiscal consolidations were synchronized, fiscal consolidation by

[1]Similarly, the results are unchanged when other (non-EU) advanced economies are included (Iceland, Israel, Norway, Switzerland, Taiwan Province of China).

Box 1.1. *(continued)*

Table 1.1.1. Growth Forecast Errors and Fiscal Consolidation

(Forecast error of growth = $\alpha + \beta$ forecast of fiscal consolidation + $\gamma X + \varepsilon$)

Additional Control	β		γ		Obs	R^2
Baseline	−1.164***	(0.244)			28	0.506
Excluding Possible Outliers						
Exluding IMF Programs	−0.918***	(0.279)			24	0.256
Excluding CEE	−1.054***	(0.267)			22	0.480
Excluding Largest Adjustment	−0.974***	(0.314)			27	0.325
Excluding Cook's D Outliers	−1.058***	(0.240)			23	0.506
Additional Controls in Forecasters' Information Set						
Initial Government Debt	−1.165***	(0.249)	0.000	(0.007)	28	0.506
Initial Sovereign CDS	−0.971***	(0.250)	−0.669	(0.509)	27	0.533
Systemic Banking Crisis	−1.172***	(0.247)	0.192	(0.705)	28	0.508
Initial Growth Forecast	−1.194***	(0.264)	−0.068	(0.113)	28	0.511
Partner Fiscal Consolidation	−1.183***	(0.264)	−0.794	(1.289)	28	0.513
Additional Controls not in Forecasters' Information Set						
Change in Sovereign CDS	−0.938***	(0.315)	−0.092	(0.055)	27	0.540
Revision to Initial Debt	−1.171***	(0.284)	0.820	(10.7)	28	0.507
Unexpected Fiscal Consolidation	−1.146***	(0.230)	−0.142	(0.190)	28	0.513

Sources: Bloomberg, L.P.; Laeven and Valencia (2012); and IMF staff calculations.

Note: *, **, and *** denote significance at the 10 percent, 5 percent, and 1 percent levels, respectively. Obs denotes the number of observations. A constant term (α) is included in the specification but is not reported in the table. Unexpected fiscal consolidation is actual fiscal consolidation minus forecast. Estimation results for the constant term are not reported. IMF Programs denotes Greece, Ireland, Portugal, and Romania. CEE denotes Bulgaria, Czech Republic, Hungary, Poland, Romania, and Slovak Republic. Initial CDS denotes credit default swap spread at end-2009. Change in CDS is from end-2009 to end-2011.

others may be driving the results. However, when we control for trade-weighted fiscal consolidation of other countries (scaled by the share of exports in GDP), the results are virtually unchanged. Finally, to investigate the role of precrisis external imbalances that may have triggered both fiscal consolidation and larger-than-expected headwinds to growth, we try controlling for the precrisis (2007) current-account-deficit-to-GDP ratio and find similar results.[2]

- *Variables not known at the time the forecasts were made:*[3] We consider the role of the sharp increase in sovereign and financial market stress during 2010–11, measured by the change in the sovereign CDS spreads. Controlling for these developments again yields similar results. We also address the possibility that, even if the assumed multipliers were correct, countries with more ambitious consolidation programs may have implemented more fiscal consolidation than originally planned.

As Table 1.1.1 reports, including unexpected fiscal consolidation does not significantly affect the results, suggesting that the baseline specification is appropriate.[4] In line with this result, we find that there was no systematic tendency for economies with larger initial fiscal consolidation plans to implement larger additional consolidation.

GDP Components, Unemployment, and Different Forecasters

When we decompose GDP, we find the largest coefficient for forecasts of investment and the most statistically significant coefficient for forecasts of consumption (Figure 1.1.1, panel 2). The coefficient associated with forecasts of the unemployment rate is also large and significant.

We also consider four different sets of forecasts: those of the WEO, the European Commission (EC), the Organization for Economic Cooperation and Development (OECD), and the Econo-

---

[2]The baseline results also hold up to additional robustness checks, including controlling for the initial forecast for 2010–11 growth and for initial trade openness and its interaction with planned fiscal consolidation.

[3]It is possible that developments that occurred after the forecasts were made could be partly the *result* of lower-than-expected growth rather than the *cause* of lower growth.

[4]Unexpected consolidation is defined as the actual (ex post) change in the structural fiscal balance minus the forecast—that is, the forecast error of fiscal consolidation. The results also hold up to additional robustness checks, including controlling for the revision to the initial (end-2009) debt-to-GDP ratio, defined as the actual debt ratio in 2009 minus the estimate of the debt ratio published in the April 2010 WEO.

Box 1.1. *(continued)*

Figure 1.1.1. Growth Forecast Errors and Fiscal Consolidation Plans

Activity over the past few years has disappointed more in economies with more aggressive fiscal consolidation plans, suggesting that fiscal multipliers used in making growth forecasts have been systematically too low. This relationship holds for different components of GDP, the unemployment rate, and forecasts made by different institutions.

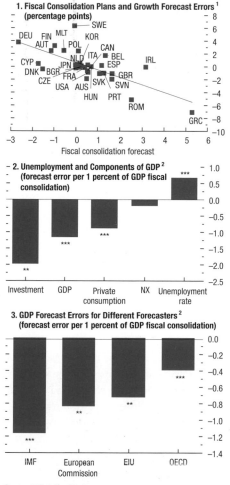

Source: IMF staff estimates.
Note: Figure identifies economies based on World Bank ISO three-letter codes (http://data.worldbank.org/node/18). NX = net exports contribution to growth. EIU = Economist Intelligence Unit.
[1]Vertical axis displays WEO forecast error for real GDP growth in 2010 and 2011 (actual forecast made in April 2010); horizontal axis displays WEO forecast of change in structural-fiscal-balance-to-GDP ratio in 2010 and 2011 (forecast made in April 2010).
[2]*, **, and *** denote significance at the 10 percent, 5 percent, and 1 percent levels, respectively.

mist Intelligence Unit (EIU—Figure 1.1.1, panel 3).[5] The largest estimated coefficient is associated with the WEO forecasts and the smallest with the OECD forecasts. The coefficient is statistically significant in all cases.

What Does This Say about Actual Fiscal Multipliers?

These results suggest that actual fiscal multipliers were larger than forecasters assumed. But what did forecasters assume about fiscal multipliers? Answering this question is complicated by the fact that not all forecasters make these assumptions explicit. Nevertheless, a number of policy documents, including IMF staff reports, suggest that fiscal multipliers used in the forecasting process are about 0.5. In line with these assumptions, earlier analysis by the IMF staff suggests that, on average, fiscal multipliers were near 0.5 in advanced economies during the three decades leading up to 2009.[6]

If the multipliers underlying the growth forecasts were about 0.5, as this informal evidence suggests, our results indicate that multipliers have actually been in the 0.9 to 1.7 range since the Great Recession. This finding is consistent with research suggesting that in today's environment of substantial economic slack, monetary policy constrained by the zero lower bound, and synchronized fiscal adjustment across numerous economies, multipliers may be well above 1 (Auerbach and Gorodnichenko, 2012; Batini, Callegari, and Melina, 2012; IMF, 2012b; Woodford, 2011; and others). More work on how fiscal multipliers depend on time and economic conditions is warranted.

[5]Data for EC forecasts are from the May 2010 *European Economic Forecast*. Data for OECD forecasts are from the June 2010 *Economic Outlook*. Data for EIU forecasts of real GDP are from the April 2010 *Country Forecast,* and the forecasts of fiscal consolidation are from the April 2010 WEO. (The EIU does not publish forecasts of the structural fiscal balance.)
[6]See Chapter 3 of the October 2010 *World Economic Outlook*.

Box 1.2. The Implications of High Public Debt in Advanced Economies

The analysis presented in this box examines the potential long-term macroeconomic implications of advanced economies' accumulation of large quantities of public debt, as currently forecast in the *World Economic Outlook* baseline scenario. Two models are used to illustrate the implications. The first is the Global Integrated Monetary and Fiscal Model (GIMF),[1] and the second is a small stochastic macroeconomic model that emphasizes uncertainty in fiscal dynamics (FiscalMod). The GIMF is used to illustrate the implications for the baseline of an accumulation of large stocks of debt by advanced economies, while the FiscalMod is used to illustrate the distribution of outcomes around possible baselines in an uncertain world with macroeconomic surprises.

Some Stylized GIMF Simulations

A stylized simulation that incorporates some aspects of recent economic experience in the G3 (euro area, Japan, United States) is used to illustrate the long-term implications for the baseline of higher public debt. In recent years G3 countries' fiscal positions have deteriorated, resulting in a sharp increase in public debt levels. This was driven largely by the financial crisis: public spending was increased to address financial institution problems and help maintain output in the face of diminished private demand. In addition, weak private demand has also led to lower public revenue. The GIMF simulation, represented by the blue line in Figure 1.2.1, replicates this development and shows a rise in G3 debt-to-GDP ratios over roughly a 10-year period by the amounts forecast in the WEO baseline between 2007 and 2017. In the simulation, the weakness in private demand also initially results in low real interest rates. However, once private demand normalizes and public debt converges to a new higher level, the increased demand for savings from G3 economies raises the global real interest rate, which over

the long term rises almost 40 basis points above the baseline. Although the following discussions focus largely on the macroeconomic implications of these higher real interest rates, this simulation analysis necessarily abstracts from the potential long-term benefits of the stimulus. The stimulus was likely instrumental in averting a potential deflationary spiral and protracted period of exceedingly high unemployment, macroeconomic conditions that general equilibrium models such as the GIMF are not well suited to capture.

Higher real interest rates have two important implications for the subsequent level of economic activity. First, higher real interest rates raise the servicing cost of outstanding public debt. To finance those increased debt-service costs, fiscal policy adjustments must occur.

It is assumed that higher labor income taxes and consumption taxes each account for 30 percent of the required funding, with an additional 10 percent coming from higher taxes on capital income and the final 30 percent coming from a reduction in transfers to households. Higher labor and capital income taxes reduce the amount of labor and capital used in production, and hence output, and lower transfers; and higher consumption taxes reduce household demand. The effects jointly lead to a lower level of sustainable output.[2] Second, higher real interest rates raise the cost of capital, further reducing the level of capital stock, firms' labor demand, and ultimately sustainable output. Together these two effects lead to GDP converging to a new long-term level roughly 1 percent below the previous baseline (as shown by the blue line in Figure 1.2.1). (This analysis does not consider the possibility of a simultaneous rise in the sovereign risk premium in these economies with higher public debt. Should that occur, the new long-term level of output would be even lower than simulated here.)

Although the run-up in public debt in G3 economies represents a significant decrease in

The main authors of this box are Ali Alichi, Derek Anderson, Ben Hunt, and Douglas Laxton.

[1] See Kumhof and others (2010) and Anderson and others (forthcoming).

[2] Relying on a different mix of fiscal instruments to generate the improvement in the primary fiscal balance necessary to cover increased debt-service costs would lead to slightly different outcomes for long-term sustainable GDP.

Box 1.2. *(continued)*

Figure 1.2.1. Implications of Higher Debt Levels in Advanced Economies
(Percent or percentage point deviation from control)

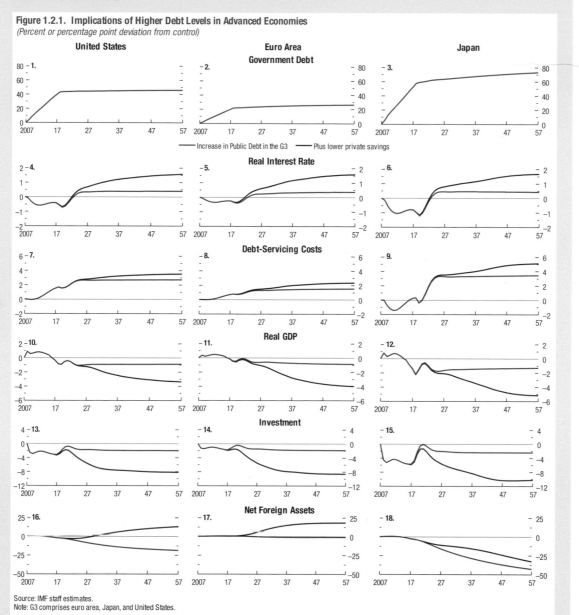

Source: IMF staff estimates.
Note: G3 comprises euro area, Japan, and United States.

public saving, another worry is that private saving rates could also decline. In emerging markets, notably emerging Asia, private saving rates have been very high and are likely to moderate in the future. In G3 economies, aging is likely to have a negative impact on private saving rates. The red line in Figure 1.2.1 represents the macro

implications if, in addition to the reduction in public saving, private saving rates also decline. A reduction in the private saving rate as a share of GDP in emerging market economies of roughly 2 percentage points is considered in this analysis. For the G3 economies, the decline in the saving rate is estimated using the United Nations' low-

Box 1.2. *(continued)*

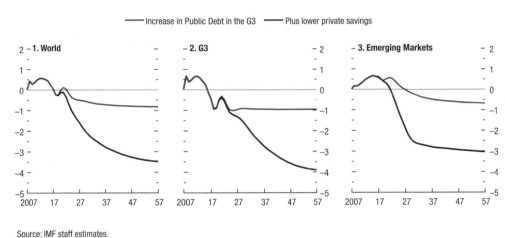

Figure 1.2.2. **Implications of Higher Debt Levels for the Global Economy**
(Percent or percentage point deviation from control)

Source: IMF staff estimates.
Note: G3 comprises euro area, Japan, and United States.

working-age population projections. For every 1 percent decline in the working-age population, it is assumed that saving declines by 0.7 percent.[3] The first point to note is that this implies that the real interest rate must rise by an additional 120 basis points. Higher real interest rates then lead to more of the behavior noted above. Tighter fiscal policy to finance increased debt-service costs further reduces the incentive to work, invest, and consume. Higher real interest rates further increase the cost of capital, adding to a decline in the incentive to invest. The net result is that GDP falls even further below the baseline if private saving rates decline along with the projected decline in public saving rates in the G3.

Focusing on relative impacts, Japan becomes worse off compared with the United States and the euro area because it had the highest debt level in the initial control and the largest increase in

[3]We abstract from the direct impact on output from the decline in the labor force itself and focus purely on the implications for saving. Implicitly, this assumes that the impact of the decline in the labor force on output and all the fiscal implications, such as pension and health care expenditures, are built into the baseline.

the initial scenario. The rising real interest rate adds to debt-service costs in Japan, so the fiscal adjustment to pay those costs is larger, as is the resulting impact on the incentive to work, invest, and consume.

Moreover, higher public debt in advanced economies does not reduce only their potential baseline GDP outcomes: all countries suffer because higher global real interest rates affect everyone. Figure 1.2.2 shows the outcomes for global GDP, GDP in the aggregate of the G3, and GDP in the aggregate of all other countries. Even though the G3 suffer the worst outcomes, all countries are worse off.

The simulated impact on real interest rates and thus on real GDP of higher debt and lower private saving in advanced economies is highly dependent on the rate at which households are willing to substitute consumption at some point in the future for consumption today—the intertemporal elasticity of substitution. The simulations presented in Table 1.2.1 assume an intertemporal elasticity of substitution of 0.5, roughly in the middle of the range of the empirical estimates. However, given the uncertainty

Box 1.2. *(continued)*

Table 1.2.1. Importance of the Intertemporal Elasticity of Substitution

| | Intertemporal Elasticity of Substitution | | | | | |
| | 0.25 | | 0.5 | | 1.0 | |
	Higher Debt	Plus Lower Savings	Higher Debt	Plus Lower Savings	Higher Debt	Plus Lower Savings
Global Real GDP	−1.75	−7.25	−1.0	−3.50	−0.07	−1.75
Global Real Interest Rate	0.80	3.30	0.40	1.20	0.20	0.80

Source: IMF staff calculations.

about this key parameter, Table 1.2.1 compares the long-term impact on global GDP and real interest rates under three values for the intertemporal elasticity of substitution.

Stochastic Analysis

GIMF simulations are a useful way to trace potential long-term trend outcomes for GDP when G3 countries have high public debt, but in an uncertain world, the distributions around those trend outcomes must be considered, given the potential range of future macroeconomic surprises. To compute the distributions for the outcomes for GDP, public debt, and real interest rates, a small empirical model, FiscalMod, is used. This model is semistructural, with a maturity structure of government debt and a yield curve. The model includes stochastic shocks to output, potential output, deficits, inflation, and interest rate term premiums and is simulated around an extended WEO baseline for a typical advanced economy. Illustrative base-case distributions (showing 90 percent confidence intervals) for the outcomes for GDP, the output gap, public debt, inflation, and real interest rates are presented in Figure 1.2.3.

To illustrate the risks associated with allowing debt to drift upward, Figure 1.2.3 presents a scenario that makes the following two assumptions. First, reduced world private saving rates (for example, due to aging) drive up the world real interest rate. Second, after the WEO horizon (2017) the baseline (median) value of net debt is allowed to increase to more than 100 percent of GDP. The distributions around this baseline are based on a fiscal policy rule allowing it to be easier to increase government deficits during bad economic times than it is to cut deficits during

good economic times—that is, it is assumed that there is a bias toward higher debt ratios even if the macroeconomic shocks are symmetric. Because of this assumption, outcomes around the baseline are asymmetrical: the upward drift in debt, combined with the assumption that high debt leads to higher risk and term premiums, results in positive skewness in real interest rates. Given the negative relationship between real interest rates and GDP, the result is negative skewness in GDP.[4]

Scenarios that involve very high levels of debt and real interest rates not only result in lower growth, but they imply a higher risk of default when fiscal dynamics are perceived to be unstable. In the model these scenarios would result in explosive dynamics and simulation failures. To illustrate the importance of these disaster scenarios, Figure 1.2.3, panel 6, shows the probability of net debt rising to more than 100 percent of GDP and the proportion of scenarios that fail because of unstable debt dynamics. As the distribution of debt drifts up, the proportion of scenarios with unstable debt dynamics rises because of a larger gap between an economy's real interest rate and real growth rate.

This analysis shows the importance of prudent fiscal policy frameworks that gradually reduce debt over time and prevent debt from drifting up too high. Still, it is important to consider the speed at which debt is reduced, given advanced economies' weakness and constraints on mon-

[4]The asymmetry in the distributions also reflects nonlinearity in which incremental increases in real interest rates caused by increases in debt become larger when the baseline value of debt is higher. For empirical evidence on the link between government debt and real interest rates, see Engen and Hubbard (2004); Gale and Orszag (2004); and Laubach (2009).

Box 1.2. *(continued)*

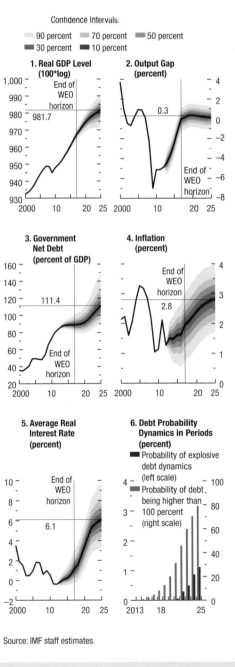

Figure 1.2.3. Illustrative Effects of Allowing Government Debt to Drift Higher

Confidence Intervals:
90 percent   70 percent   50 percent
30 percent   10 percent

1. Real GDP Level (100*log)

2. Output Gap (percent)

3. Government Net Debt (percent of GDP)

4. Inflation (percent)

5. Average Real Interest Rate (percent)

6. Debt Probability Dynamics in Periods (percent)
Probability of explosive debt dynamics (left scale)
Probability of debt being higher than 100 percent (right scale)

Source: IMF staff estimates.

etary policy to offset the contractionary effects of fiscal consolidation. As shown in Figure 1.2.3, the WEO baseline assumes a gradual closing of the output gap and little risk of a deflationary spiral (negative inflation and larger output gaps). Although it is not illustrated with an alternative scenario, the same model suggests that an excessively rapid reduction in debt would risk reducing growth and pushing the advanced economies into a deflationary spiral.

Box 1.3. How Does Uncertainty Affect Economic Performance?

Bouts of elevated uncertainty have been one of the defining features of the sluggish recovery from the global financial crisis. In recent quarters, high uncertainty has once again coincided with weakness in the global recovery. Many commentators argue that uncertainty is a major cause of escalating financial stress and recession in the euro area, stalling labor markets in the United States, and slowing growth in emerging market and developing economies.

This box explores the role of uncertainty in driving macroeconomic outcomes. Specifically, it addresses three major questions: How is uncertainty measured? How does it evolve over the business cycle? And what is the impact of uncertainty on growth and business cycles? To address these questions, the box briefly analyzes the main features of various measures of uncertainty and their association with growth and business cycles in advanced economies, and it interprets the evidence in light of findings from recent research.

Uncertainty is shown to have a harmful impact on economic activity. First, the adverse effects are transmitted through multiple channels, with financial market imperfections and institutional constraints often magnifying them, so the effects of uncertainty are likely to vary across sectors and countries. Second, as experienced acutely since the global financial crisis, uncertainty is highly countercyclical. Third, cross-country evidence indicates that high uncertainty is often associated with deeper recessions and weaker recoveries.

How Is Uncertainty Measured?

Economic uncertainty frequently refers to an environment in which little or nothing is known about the future state of the economy. Shocks that lead to economic uncertainty can stem from a variety of sources, including changes in economic and financial policies, dispersion in future growth prospects, productivity movements, wars, acts of terrorism, and natural disasters (Bloom, 2009). Although uncertainty is difficult to quantify because of its latent nature, it can be measured

The authors of this box are M. Ayhan Kose and Marco E. Terrones, with research support from Ezgi O. Ozturk.

indirectly in a number of ways. These measures emphasize distinct aspects of uncertainty facing an economy over time. Some of the measures focus on macroeconomic uncertainty, including the volatility of stock returns, variation in aggregate productivity, dispersion in unemployment forecasts, and the prevalence of terms such as "economic uncertainty" in the media. Others consider uncertainty at the microeconomic level, which is often measured by various indicators of dispersion across sectoral output, firm sales, and stock returns.

Because we are concerned primarily with macroeconomic uncertainty, we concentrate on four measures based on the volatility of stock returns and economic policy. The first is the monthly standard deviation of daily stock returns in each advanced economy in our sample.

The second is the Chicago Board Options Exchange Volatility Index (VXO), which is an indicator of the implied volatility of equity prices calculated from S&P 100 options. The third refers to uncertainty surrounding economic policies.[1] The fourth, which represents uncertainty at the global level, is the estimated dynamic common factor of the first measure using the series of the six major advanced economies with the longest available data.

How Does Uncertainty Evolve?

Both macroeconomic and policy measures of uncertainty tend to rise during global recessions (Figure 1.3.1). Policy uncertainty in the United States and the euro area has remained high since the global financial crisis and the recent sovereign debt problems in the euro area. Moreover, during the lethargic global recovery, uncertainty has been unusually high and volatile. This contrasts with the recoveries following the other three global reces-

[1]The economic policy uncertainty measure employed here is from Baker, Bloom, and Davis (2012), who use a weighted average of the following three indicators: the frequency with which terms like "economic policy" and "uncertainty" appear together in the media, the number of tax provisions that will expire in coming years, and the dispersion of forecasts of future government outlays and inflation. Because most of this information refers to outcomes it does not distinguish between uncertainty about policy goals and uncertainty about policy instruments.

Box 1.3. *(continued)*

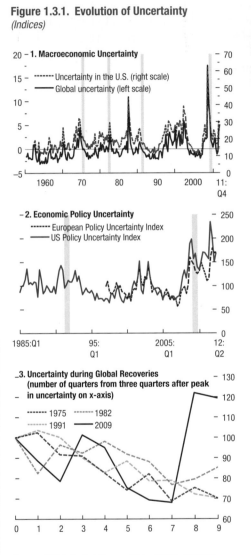

Figure 1.3.1. Evolution of Uncertainty
(Indices)

1. Macroeconomic Uncertainty
- - - - - Uncertainty in the U.S. (right scale)
——— Global uncertainty (left scale)

2. Economic Policy Uncertainty
- - - - - European Policy Uncertainty Index
——— US Policy Uncertainty Index

3. Uncertainty during Global Recoveries
(number of quarters from three quarters after peak in uncertainty on x-axis)
- - - - - 1975   · · · · · 1982
- - - - - 1991   ——— 2009

Sources: IMF staff calculations; and Baker, Bloom, and Davis (2012).
Note: In panels 1 and 2, shaded areas denote the periods of global recession. These global recessions (1975, 1982, 1991, 2009) are identified following Kose, Loungani, and Terrones (2009). In panel 2, economic policy uncertainty in the United States and the euro area is from Baker, Bloom, and Davis (2012). Since these indicators are based on different measures, their levels are not strictly comparable. In panel 3, each line presents the evolution of uncertainty in the United States starting three quarters after uncertainty reached its peak during the respective global recession.

sions shown in Figure 1.3.1, which were accompanied by steady declines in uncertainty.

Uncertainty is highly countercyclical. Macroeconomic uncertainty varies over different phases of the business cycle: during expansions in advanced economies uncertainty is, on average, much lower than during recessions, regardless of the measure (Table 1.3.1). Microeconomic uncertainty, measured by the volatility of movements in plant-level productivity in the United States, also behaves countercyclically and reached a post-1970 high during the Great Recession (Bloom and others, 2012).

Causality between uncertainty and the business cycle is difficult to establish—does uncertainty drive recessions or do recessions lead to uncertainty? Empirical findings on this question are mixed.[2] However, economic theory, as discussed next, points to clear channels through which uncertainty can have a negative impact on growth. Some uncertainty is likely to be an intrinsic feature of the business cycle: firms and households will learn only over time which sectors of the economy will do better and which will do worse—and for how long—in response to the shocks that cause recessions.

What Is the Impact of Uncertainty on Growth and Business Cycles?

Economic theory suggests that macroeconomic uncertainty can have an adverse impact on output through a variety of channels. On the demand side, for example, when faced with high uncertainty, firms reduce investment demand and delay their projects as they gather new information, because investment is often costly to reverse (Bernanke, 1983; Dixit and Pindyck, 1994). Households' response to high uncertainty is similar to that of

---

[2]Bachmann and Moscarini (2011) find that the direction of causality runs from recessions to uncertainty. In contrast, Baker and Bloom (2011) offer evidence, using disaster data as instruments, that the causality runs from uncertainty to recessions, and Bloom and others (2012) report that growth does not cause uncertainty. Predictions of theory and findings from empirical studies collectively indicate that uncertainty can play a dual role over the business cycle: it can be an impulse as well as a propagation mechanism.

Box 1.3. *(continued)*

Table 1.3.1. Uncertainty over the Business Cycle

	Country-Specific Uncertainty	Uncertainty in the United States	Economic Policy Uncertainty	Global Uncertainty
Recession	1.29***	24.12***	134.59***	1.61***
	(0.08)	(0.50)	(2.78)	(0.18)
Expansion	0.93***	19.03***	100.56***	−0.24**
	(0.03)	(0.06)	(0.51)	(0.02)
Number of Observations	3,138	4,158	2,268	4,347
Number of Economies	21	21	21	21
R^2 Adjusted	0.77	0.89	0.92	0.07
Test (*p* Values)				
h0: Recession Coefficient = Expansion Coefficient	0.00	0.00	0.00	0.00

Source: IMF staff calculations.

Note: The dependent variable is the level of uncertainty. Recessions and expansions in regressions refer to dummy variables taking the values of 1 and zero when the economy is in recession and expansion, respectively. The periods of recession and expansion are defined following Claessens, Kose, and Terrones (2012). Country-specific uncertainty refers to the monthly standard deviation of daily stock returns in each country. Daily returns are calculated using each country's stock price index. Data series cover the period 1960–2011, but coverage varies across economies. Uncertainty in the United States refers to the Chicago Board Options Exchange VXO index, which is calculated from S&P 100 options. Prior to 1986, this series has been extended following Bloom (2009). The policy uncertainty measure is an index of economic policy uncertainty for the United States from Baker, Bloom, and Davis (2012). It refers to the weighted average of three indicators, including the frequency of the appearance of terms like "economic policy" and "uncertainty" in the media, the number of tax provisions that will expire in coming years, and the dispersion of forecasts of future government outlays and inflation. Global uncertainty is the estimated dynamic common factor of the first measure using the series of France, Italy, Germany, Japan, the United Kingdom, and the United States. (These countries have the longest series of stock market indices.) *** denotes that the coefficients are statistically significant at the 1 percent level. Standard errors are in parentheses.

firms: they reduce their consumption of durable goods as they wait for less uncertain times. On the supply side, firms' hiring plans are also negatively affected by higher uncertainty, reflecting costly adjustment of personnel (Bentolila and Bertola, 1990).

Financial market imperfections can amplify the negative impact of uncertainty on growth. In theory, uncertainty leads to a decline in expected returns on projects financed with debt and makes it harder to assess the value of collateral. Thus, creditors charge higher interest rates and limit lending during uncertain times, which reduces firms' ability to borrow. The decline in borrowing causes investment to contract, especially for credit-constrained firms, and results in slower productivity growth because of reduced spending on research and development. These factors together can translate into a significant reduction in output growth (Gilchrist, Sim, and Zakrajsek, 2010).

The impact of uncertainty differs across sectors and countries. The sectors that produce durable goods—including machinery and equipment, automobiles, houses, and furniture—are often the most affected by increases in uncertainty. The impact of an uncertainty shock on consumption and investment is larger in emerging market economies than in advanced economies, probably because the

former group tends to have less developed financial markets and institutions (Carrière-Swallow and Céspedes, 2011).

Empirical evidence suggests that uncertainty tends to be detrimental to economic growth. The growth rate of output is negatively correlated with macroeconomic uncertainty (Table 1.3.2). A 1 standard deviation increase in uncertainty is associated with a decline in output growth of between 0.4 and 1.25 percentage points depending on the measure of macroeconomic uncertainty. There were indeed multiple episodes during which uncertainty rose by 1 standard deviation or more, including at the onset of the Great Recession and during the recent debt crisis in the euro area. High uncertainty tends to be associated with a larger drop in investment than in output and consumption growth. These findings lend support to the validity of different theoretical channels through which uncertainty adversely affects economic activity. They are also consistent with recent studies documenting a negative relationship between growth and uncertainty.[3]

[3]Empirical evidence based on vector autoregression (VAR) models points to a significant negative impact of uncertainty shocks on output and employment (Bloom, 2009; Hirata and others, 2012). These results also echo the findings in a broader area of research on the negative impact of macroeconomic and policy volatility on economic growth (Ramey and

Box 1.3. *(continued)*

Table 1.3.2. Uncertainty and Growth

	Output				Consumption				Investment			
	(1)	(2)	(3)	(4)	(1)	(2)	(3)	(4)	(1)	(2)	(3)	(4)
Country-Specific Uncertainty	−0.65*				−0.23				−1.18			
	(0.37)				(0.38)				(0.99)			
Uncertainty in the U.S.		−0.18***				−0.12***				−0.41***		
		(0.01)				(0.01)				(0.06)		
Economic Policy Uncertainty			−0.01***				−0.01				−0.02**	
			(0.00)				(0.00)				(0.01)	
Global Uncertainty				−0.46***				−0.31***				−0.87***
				(0.03)				(0.04)				(0.164)
Number of Observations	3,117	4,157	2,267	4,283	3,115	4,155	2,265	4,281	3,111	4,041	2,265	4,123
Number of Countries	21	21	21	21	21	21	21	21	21	21	21	21
R^2 Adjusted	0.42	0.38	0.44	0.38	0.09	0.13	0.06	0.13	0.31	0.25	0.35	0.25

Source: IMF staff calculations.

Note: Dependent variable is the year-over-year growth of the respective macroeconomic aggregate. All specifications include country fixed and time effects. See notes to Table 1.3.1 for explanations of uncertainty measures. *, **, and *** denote significance at the 10 percent, 5 percent, and 1 percent levels, respectively. Standard errors are in parentheses.

Table 1.3.3. Uncertainty and Business Cycles

	Recessions		Recoveries	
	With High Uncertainty	Others	With High Uncertainty	Others
Output				
Duration	4.00	3.89	4.81	4.54
Amplitude	−3.66**	−1.85	2.31*	3.06
Slope	−0.78*	−0.49	0.66*	0.77
Cumulative Loss	−5.81*	−2.99	. . .	. . .
Consumption	−0.46	−0.37	1.53	2.21
Investment	−9.44	−5.22	−0.48**	3.28
Number of Episodes	28	83	28	82

Source: IMF staff calculations.

Note: A recession is associated with high uncertainty if the level of uncertainty at its trough falls in the top quartile of uncertainty measured at the troughs of all recessions. A recovery is associated with high uncertainty if the average uncertainty during the recovery is in the top quartile of average uncertainty of all recovery episodes. The periods of recession and recovery are defined following Claessens, Kose, and Terrones (2012). All statistics except "Duration" correspond to sample median. For duration, means are shown. For recessions, duration is the number of quarters between peak and trough. Duration for recoveries is the time it takes to attain the level at the previous peak after the trough. The amplitude for recessions is calculated based on the decline in output during the recession and expressed in percent. The amplitude for the recoveries is calculated based on the one-year change in output after the trough and expressed in percent. The slope of the recessions is the amplitude from peak to trough divided by the duration. The slope of recoveries is the amplitude from the trough to the period where output has reached the level at its last peak divided by the duration. Cumulative loss combines information about duration and amplitude to measure the overall cost of a recession and is expressed in percent.** and * denote that features of recessions (recoveries) with high uncertainty differ significantly from those of other recessions (recoveries) at the 5 percent and 10 percent levels, respectively.

Policy-induced uncertainty is also negatively associated with growth. The adverse impact of policy uncertainty on economic growth works mainly through two channels. First, it directly affects the behavior of households and firms as they postpone investment and consumption decisions when uncertainty about future policies is elevated. Second, it breeds macroeconomic uncertainty, which in turn reduces growth. As noted, policy uncertainty has increased to record levels since the Great Recession. Specifically, the increase in policy uncertainty between 2006 and 2011 was about 5 standard deviations. This sharp increase in policy uncertainty may have stymied growth in advanced economies by 2½ percentage points during this period.[4]

Ramey, 1995; Kose, Prasad, and Terrones, 2006; Fatas and Mihov, forthcoming).

[4]This finding is consistent with results from a recent study by Baker, Bloom, and Davis (2012). They employ a VAR model and report that a jump in policy uncertainty, such as the one observed between 2006 and 2011 in the United

Box 1.3. *(continued)*

The degree of economic uncertainty also appears to be related to the depth of recessions and strength of recoveries. In particular, recessions accompanied by high uncertainty are often deeper, longer, and more severe than other recessions. Moreover, recessions in highly uncertain environments are associated with cumulative output losses roughly two times larger than those during other recessions (Table 1.3.3). Similarly, recoveries coinciding with periods of elevated uncertainty are weaker and slower than other recoveries.[5] Both consumption

and investment tend to grow at a slower pace during recoveries associated with high uncertainty.

Global Recovery in Times of Manifold Uncertainty

Elevated uncertainty historically coincides with periods of lower growth, and the recent pickup in uncertainty raises the specter of another global recession. Policymakers can do little to alleviate the intrinsic uncertainty economies typically face over the business cycle. However, policy uncertainty is unusually high, and it contributes significantly to macroeconomic uncertainty. By implementing bold and timely measures, policymakers can reduce policy-induced uncertainty and help kick-start economic growth. What precisely policymakers need to do is discussed in the main text of Chapter 1.

States, is associated with about a 3 percent decline in real GDP and a 16 percent contraction in private investment.

[5]The unusually high levels of uncertainty the global economy experienced since the 2007–09 financial crisis and the associated episodes of deep recessions and weak recoveries play an important role in explaining these findings. Uncertainty shocks account for about one-third of business cycle variation in advanced economies and up to half of cyclical volatility in emerging market and developing economies, implying that these shocks play a sizable role in driving the dynamics of recessions and expansions (Bloom and others,

2012; Baker and Bloom, 2011). Other relevant research concludes that shocks associated with uncertainty and financial disruptions were the primary factors that led to the Great Recession (Stock and Watson, forthcoming).

Box 1.4. Unconventional Energy in the United States

U.S. natural gas and oil production has increased in recent years, driven largely by the commercialization of horizontal drilling and hydraulic fracturing ("fracking") technology from shale rock.[1,2] The "unconventional energy revolution" began in the natural gas sector during the past decade, and gas production rose 28 percent between 2005 and 2011, and continued to climb in 2012 albeit at diminishing rates.[3] The rise in unconventional gas contributed to the plunge in natural gas prices, and producers have since focused on liquids-rich gas plays or have migrated to pure oil (or tight oil) plays.

Since 2005, application of this technology has put an end to the trend decline in U.S. oil output by increasing oil production from unconventional formations—first by maintaining total U.S. oil production at about 7 million barrels a day (mbd) until 2008 (8 percent of daily global production). More recently, from 2009 to the first half of 2012, oil output rose by about 2 mbd to about 9 mbd (10 percent of daily global oil production). This more recent rise stems largely from tapping unconventional shale deposits in North Dakota and Texas for "tight" oil and other liquid by-products (that is, natural gas liquids) through the use of techniques similar to those pioneered to tap unconventional shale gas (see Table 1.SF.2).

The boom in unconventional energy affects other energy markets as well. The downturn in natural gas prices has led to displacement of coal in the U.S. electric power sector and decoupling of U.S. natural gas from crude oil prices. The displacement of coal is largely attributed to the shift from coal to natural gas by U.S. electric power companies in response to lower natural gas prices. On the one hand, coal displacement in the United States has been beneficial to Europe, where demand has increased because of substitution away from higher-priced fuels—notably (non-U.S.) natural gas, whose price is still linked to that of oil—and from a phaseout of nuclear power. On the other hand, rising unconventional natural gas production has also led to a decoupling of U.S. natural gas prices from crude oil prices; gas prices have fallen to their lowest level in a decade.[4] Rising unconventional oil production has also contributed to the stock buildup in the mid-continent, which led to a large discount in the price of U.S. West Texas Intermediate crude oil compared with internationally traded crude oil varieties—for example, Brent and Dubai Fateh.

The future of unconventional extraction is uncertain given its relative cost: crude oil prices would have to range between $50 and $90 a barrel to guarantee commercial viability (break-even). Hence a drop in crude oil prices to levels seen during the 2008 slump could set back U.S. unconventional oil production. Despite uncertainty, industry analysts suggest that U.S. production could increase by 1 mbd annually until 2015, and possibly beyond. Moreover, because there are large tight oil reserves in other regions of the world, if commercially viable, extraction could offset declining production in maturing conventional fields, thus alleviating concern about oil scarcity. Finally, abundant unconventional energy might not keep oil prices from rising in the short term, but it could have that effect in the

---

The authors of this box are Samya Beidas-Strom and Akito Matsumoto.

[1] Hydraulic fracturing involves pumping a mix of water, sand, and chemicals into wells at high pressure, thereby cracking the rock containing the liquids. Horizontal drilling enables greater access to pockets of liquids, allowing more to be pumped to the surface. Application of this technique to hydrocarbon liquids (oil) was previously considered too challenging or uneconomic and has raised environmental concerns—notably about possible contamination of aquifers.

[2] "Oil" in this box refers to crude (conventional) oil, condensates, natural gas liquids, and unconventional oil.

[3] Unconventional natural gas is found in locations requiring special extraction technologies such as horizontal drilling and fracking. It includes shale gas, tight gas, and coal-bed methane; this gas is similar to conventional natural gas, with the only difference being that their extraction requires unconventional methods. Unconventional oil, such as shale oil (or tight oil), is recovered from shale using the same unconventional technologies as for shale gas but is conventional oil, similar in quality to light crude oil.

[4] Until the early 1990s, natural gas prices were heavily regulated, with regulators using oil prices as a reference for gas prices. Deregulation and restructuring of the pipeline sector led to a competitive market with direct gas-on-gas competition.

Box 1.4. *(continued)*

long term—because higher energy prices would stimulate unconventional oil development if oil prices remain above $80 a barrel. At the same time, energy substitutability depends on a number of factors: electric power companies switched from coal to natural gas as did the petrochemical sector, but a shift from oil to natural gas in transportation has proved to be much slower.[5]

[5]See Chapter 3 of the April 2011 *World Economic Outlook* for a detailed discussion.

Box 1.5. Food Supply Crunch—Who Is Most Vulnerable?

Food prices are increasing worldwide, raising fears of another food crisis like that in 2007–08. How is 2012 different? Which regions are most vulnerable to the current food price surge?[1] The current food price shock is less severe than that of 2007–08 because it has not affected all key crops uniformly and has not been aggravated by trade restrictions and high energy input costs. However, when focusing on vulnerability, there are significant variations across regions: the African, Central American, Caribbean, and Middle Eastern regions appear to be the most exposed to rising food prices amid low inventory buffers and high dependence on the global market for their food supplies.

The 2007–08 food crisis was exacerbated by various forms of export restrictions by major food exporters;[2] in contrast, no such policies have been implemented by major food exporters during 2012. Since the last food crisis, supply has responded to robust demand and relatively high prices through higher acreage and yields as well as productivity gains. As a result, global inventory buffers, measured by stock-to-use ratios, have improved significantly, especially for rice and wheat.

The author of this box is Marina Rousset.

[1]Regional composition is as defined by the U.S. Department of Agriculture. Note that North America includes Mexico, and Oceania includes Australia and New Zealand. Pacific island nations, which are vulnerable to food price shocks, could not be disaggregated from Oceania due to data limitations.

[2]A survey by the U.N. Food and Agriculture Organization prepared in 2008 showed that of the 77 surveyed countries, roughly one-quarter imposed some form of export restrictions during the food crisis.

Spillovers from energy markets are much more limited in 2012. Energy prices feed into global food prices through two main channels: cost push and demand pull. First, energy-intensive inputs such as ammonia-based nitrogen fertilizers and power provide a transmission mechanism from energy prices into food prices. Second, the diversion of crops from food to fuel production has become an important factor in recent years—corn and sugar have been increasingly used for ethanol production and soybeans and other oilseeds for biodiesel production. Energy prices surged alongside food prices during the 2007–08 food crisis, intensifying the spillover through both channels, but energy prices have recently declined, limiting the spillover to food prices. The expiration of government subsidies to the U.S. ethanol industry in 2011 also helped reduce the use of food crops for energy production. Therefore, the pass-through from energy prices to food prices plays a less important role than in 2007–08.

Nevertheless, countries in Africa, Central America, the Caribbean, and the Middle East are vulnerable to rising food prices. Despite significant heterogeneity, regions with low inventory buffers, high dependence on the global market for their food supply, and a high share of food in final consumption seem to be the most vulnerable to recent food price hikes (Table 1.5.1, Figure 1.5.1).[3]

[3]Compared with 2007–08, the extent of regional exposure to global food price fluctuations has not changed significantly.

Table 1.5.1. Regional Food Vulnerability

	Low Food Inventories (that is, low stock-to-use ratios)	High Dependence on Global Food Imports	High Share of Food in Final Consumption
Caribbean	*	*	*
Central America	*		
East Asia			
European Union			
Former Soviet Union		*	*
Middle East	*	*	*
North Africa		*	*
North America	*		
Oceania			
Other Europe			
South America	*		*
South Asia			*
Southeast Asia			*
Sub-Saharan Africa	*	*	*

Sources: U.S. Department of Agriculture; World Trade Organization; IMF, World Economic Outlook database; and IMF staff calculations.

Box 1.5. *(continued)*

Figure 1.5.1. Regional Food Vulnerabilities

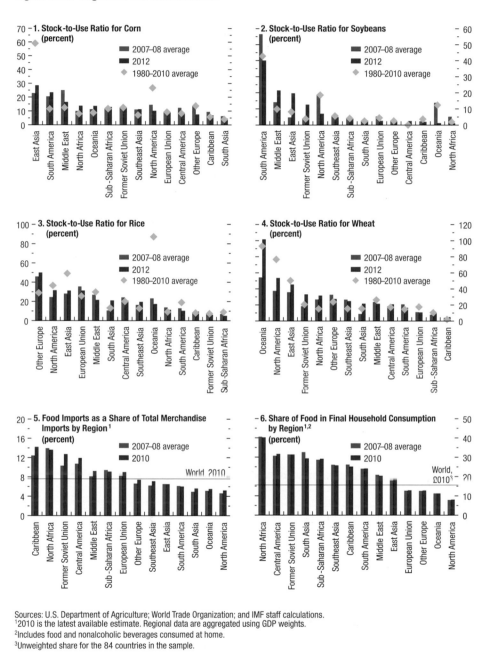

Sources: U.S. Department of Agriculture; World Trade Organization; and IMF staff calculations.
[1]2010 is the latest available estimate. Regional data are aggregated using GDP weights.
[2]Includes food and nonalcoholic beverages consumed at home.
[3]Unweighted share for the 84 countries in the sample.

Box 1.5. *(continued)*

- Naturally, regions that are not self-sustaining in agricultural production, and therefore dependent on the global food market, are the most exposed to the effects of global price instability. These regions include Caribbean and Central American nations, which import three-quarters and one-half of their corn demand, respectively, and have lower inventory buffers than in 2007–08.
- Countries in the Middle East and sub-Saharan Africa, which import more than half of their wheat consumption and whose stock-to-use ratios for wheat and rice are below historical averages, could also be heavily affected if global wheat prices rise further because of lower inventory buffers.
- North Africa, where about 40 percent of final consumption is food, is also vulnerable to high food prices given significant reliance on food imports.

Exposure to global food price volatility for other regions is crop specific. The former Soviet Union region has a high share of imports and household consumption dedicated to food, but, because of interregional trade, its exposure to global markets for wheat—its main consumption and trade crop—is fairly limited. East Asia, in particular

China, depends on the global market to satisfy a large portion of its domestic soybean demand but has accumulated substantial inventory buffers. Although inventory buffers in North America, which is a net exporter of major crops, have deteriorated significantly, especially for corn, food expenditures in North America account for a lower share of imports and household income than in other regions, making North America less vulnerable to food price increases.

On the global level, the current stock-to-use ratios for corn and soybeans are lower than they were during 2007–08, but are higher for rice and wheat. Many regions have undertaken self-sufficiency initiatives to reduce their dependence on global food markets, and some regions increased their precautionary demand for key grains to mitigate food price increases while others initiated food and fertilizer subsidies and farm lending programs. However, alleviating the burden of global food price volatility calls for broader policy reforms, including to address agricultural infrastructure improvement, effective safety nets for the poor, and climate change, as well as to encourage additional agricultural food production (and eliminate policies that discourage it).

References

Anderson, D., B. Hunt, M. Kortelainen, D. Muir, and S. Snudden (forthcoming), "Getting to Know the GIMF: The Simulation Properties of the Global Integrated Monetary and Fiscal Model," IMF Working Paper (Washington: International Monetary Fund).

Auerbach, Alan, and Yuriy Gorodnichenko, 2012, "Fiscal Multipliers in Recession and Expansion," in *Fiscal Policy after the Financial Crisis*, ed. by Alberto Alesina and Francesco Giavazzi (Cambridge, Massachusetts: National Bureau of Economic Research).

Bachmann, Rudiger, and Giuseppe Moscarini, 2011, "Business Cycles and Endogenous Uncertainty," University of Michigan Working Paper (Ann Arbor, Michigan).

Baker, Scott, and Nicholas Bloom, 2011, "Does Uncertainty Drive Business Cycles? Using Disasters as a Natural Experiment," Stanford University Working Paper (Stanford, California).

——, and Steven J. Davis, 2012, "Measuring Economic Policy Uncertainty," Stanford University Working Paper (Stanford, California).

Barkbu, Bergljot, Jesmin Rahman, Rodrigo Valdés, and a staff team, 2012, "Fostering Growth in Europe Now," IMF Staff Discussion Note No. 12/07 (Washington: International Monetary Fund). www.imf.org/external/pubs/ft/sdn/2012/sdn1207.pdf.

Batini, Nicoletta, Giovanni Callegari, and Giovanni Melina, 2012, "Successful Austerity in the United States, Europe, and Japan," IMF Working Paper No. 12/190 (Washington: International Monetary Fund).

Benes, Jaromir, Marcelle Chauvet, Ondra Kamenik, Michael Kumhof, Douglas Laxton, Susanna Mursula, and Jack Selody, 2012, "The Future of Oil: Geology versus Technology," IMF Working Paper No. 12/109 (Washington: International Monetary Fund).

Bentolila, Samuel, and Giuseppe Bertola, 1990, "Firing Costs and Labour Demand: How Bad Is Eurosclerosis?" *Review of Economic Studies*, Vol. 57, No. 3, pp. 381–402.

Bernanke, Ben, 1983, "Irreversibility, Uncertainty, and Cyclical Investment," *The Quarterly Journal of Economics*, Vol. 98, No. 1, pp. 85–106.

Bloom, Nicholas, 2009, "The Impact of Uncertainty Shocks," *Econometrica*, Vol. 77, No. 3, pp. 623–85.

——, Max Floetotto, Nir Jaimovich, Itay Saporta-Eksten, and Stephen Terry, 2012, "Really Uncertain Business Cycles," NBER Working Paper No. 18245 (Cambridge, Massachusetts: National Bureau of Economic Research).

Carrière-Swallow, Yan, and Luis Felipe Céspedes, 2011, "The Impact of Uncertainty Shocks in Emerging Economies," Central Bank of Chile Working Paper No. 646 (Santiago).

Chinn, Menzie David, and Olivier Coibion, 2009, "The Predictive Content of Commodity Futures," La Follette School of Public Affairs Working Paper No. 2009–016 (Madison, Wisconsin: University of Wisconsin). http://ssrn.com/abstract=1490043 or http://dx.doi.org/10.2139/ssrn.1490043.

Christiano, Lawrence, Martin Eichenbaum, and Sergio Rebelo, 2011, "When Is the Government Spending Multiplier Large?" *Journal of Political Economy*, Vol. 119, No. 1, pp. 78–121.

Claessens, Stijn, M. Ayhan Kose, and Marco E. Terrones, 2012, "How Do Business and Financial Cycles Interact?" *Journal of International Economics*, Vol. 87, No. 1, pp. 178–90.

Decressin, Jörg, and Douglas Laxton, 2009, "Gauging Risks for Deflation," IMF Staff Position Note No. 09/01 (Washington: International Monetary Fund).

Dixit, Avinash K., and Robert S. Pindyck, 1994, *Investment Under Uncertainty* (Princeton, New Jersey: Princeton University Press).

Elekdag, Selim, and Prakash Kannan, 2009, "Incorporating Market Information into the Construction of the Fan Chart," IMF Working Paper No. 09/178 (Washington: International Monetary Fund).

Elmendorf, Douglas W., and N. Gregory Mankiw, 1999, "Government Debt," in *Handbook of Macroeconomics*, Vol. 1C, ed. by J.B. Taylor and M. Woodford (Amsterdam: North-Holland).

Engen, Eric M., and R. Glenn Hubbard, 2004, "Federal Government Debt and Interest Rates," *NBER Macroeconomics Annual*, Vol. 19 (Cambridge, Massachusetts: National Bureau of Economic Research), pp. 83–138.

European Council (EC), 2012, "Towards a Genuine Economic and Monetary Union," June 26 report by European Council President Herman Van Rompuy (Brussels). http://consilium.europa.eu/uedocs/cms_data/docs/pressdata/en/ec/131201.pdf.

Fatas, Antonio, and Ilian Mihov, forthcoming, "Policy Volatility, Institutions and Economic Growth," *Review of Economics and Statistics*.

Gale, William, and Peter Orszag, 2004, "Budget Deficits, National Saving, and Interest Rates," *Brookings Papers on Economic Activity*, Vol. 2, pp. 101–87.

Gilchrist, Simon, Jae Sim, and Egon Zakrajsek, 2010, "Uncertainty, Financial Frictions, and Investment Dynamics," Boston University Working Paper (Boston, Massachusetts).

Hamilton, James D., 2008, "Oil and the Macroeconomy," in *New Palgrave Dictionary of Economics*, ed. by Steven Durlauf and Lawrence Blume (Houndmills, United Kingdom: Palgrave McMillan, 2nd ed.).

Hirata, Hideaki, M. Ayhan Kose, Christopher Otrok, and Marco E. Terrones, 2012, "Global House Price Fluctuations: Synchronization and Determinants," NBER Working Paper No. 18362 (Cambridge, Massachusetts: National Bureau of Economic Research).

International Monetary Fund (IMF), 2012a, *Euro Area Policies,* IMF Country Report No. 12/181 (Washington). www.imf.org/external/pubs/ft/scr/2012/cr12181.pdf.

———, 2012b, *Fiscal Monitor* (Washington, April).

———, 2012c, *Greece: Staff Report for the 2012 Article IV Consultation*, Country Report No. 12/57 (Washington).

———, 2012d, *Pilot External Sector Report* (Washington). www.imf.org/external/np/pp/eng/2012/070912.pdf.

———, 2012e, *2012 Spillover Report* (Washington). www.imf.org/external/np/pp/eng/2012/070912.pdf.

———, 2012f, *Toward Lasting Stability and Growth: Umbrella Report for the G-20 Mutual Assessment Process* (Washington). www.imf.org/external/np/g20/pdf/062012.pdf.

———, 2012g, *The United Kingdom: Staff Report for the 2012 Article IV Consultation*, IMF Country Report No. 12/190 (Washington).

Kose, M. Ayhan, Eswar Prasad, and Marco E. Terrones, 2006, "How Do Trade and Financial Integration Affect the Relationship between Growth and Volatility," *Journal of International Economics*, Vol. 69 (June), pp. 176–202.

Kose, M. Ayhan, Prakash Loungani, and Marco E. Terrones, 2009, "Out of the Ballpark," *Finance & Development*, Vol. 46 (June), pp. 25–28.

Kumar, Manmohan S., 2003, "Deflation: Determinants, Risks, and Policy Options," IMF Occasional Paper No. 221 (Washington: International Monetary Fund).

———, and Jaejoon Woo, 2010, "Public Debt and Growth," IMF Working Paper No. 10/174 (Washington: International Monetary Fund).

Kumhof, Michael, Douglas Laxton, Dirk Muir, and Susanna Mursula, 2010, "The Global Integrated Monetary and Fiscal Model (GIMF)—Theoretical Structure," IMF Working Paper No. 10/34 (Washington: International Monetary Fund).

Laeven, Luc, and Fabián Valencia, 2012, "Systemic Banking Crises Database: An Update," IMF Working Paper No. 12/163 (Washington: International Monetary Fund).

Laubach, Thomas, 2009, "New Evidence on the Interest Rate Effects of Budget Deficits and Debt," *Journal of the European Economic Association*, Vol. 7, No. 4, pp. 858–85.

Matheson, Troy D., 2011, "New Indicators for Tracking Growth in Real Time," IMF Working Paper No. 11/43 (Washington: International Monetary Fund).

Ramey, Garey, and Valerie Ramey, 1995, "Cross-Country Evidence on the Link between Volatility and Growth," *American Economic Review*, Vol. 85, No. 5, pp. 1138–51.

Stock, James H., and Mark W. Watson, forthcoming, "Disentangling the Channels of the 2007–09 Recession," *Brookings Papers on Economic Activity* (Washington: Brookings Institution).

Woodford, Michael, 2011, "Simple Analytics of the Government Expenditure Multiplier," *American Economic Journal: Macroeconomics,* Vol. 3, No. 1, pp. 1–35.

CHAPTER 2

COUNTRY AND REGIONAL PERSPECTIVES

Global growth slowed again during the second quarter of 2012 after rebounding during the first. The slowing has been observed in all regions. This synchronicity suggests an important role for common factors, many of which reflected wide-ranging spillovers from large country-specific or regional shocks. A first shock was the ratcheting up of financial stress in the euro area periphery in the second quarter. Second, domestic demand in many economies in Asia and Latin America (notably Brazil, China, and India, but also others) slowed, owing not just to weaker external demand from Europe but also to domestic factors. Growth also decelerated in the United States.

The theme of spillovers runs throughout this chapter, because spillovers are important to both the baseline projections and the risks to the outlook. With respect to the former, near-term growth projections across most regions have been revised down relative to the April 2012 *World Economic Outlook* (Figure 2.1). Activity is projected to gradually gather speed beginning in late 2012, later than had been expected in April, led by a pickup in emerging market economies owing to recent policy easing. The relatively small revisions to global growth under the baseline are predicated on the assumption that there will be sufficient policy action for financial conditions in the euro area periphery to gradually ease and that the fiscal cliff will be avoided in the United States.

Downside risks have increased relative to the April 2012 WEO and also have important global spillover potential.[1] The most immediate downside risk—that delayed or insufficient policy action will further escalate the euro area crisis—remains in place. Other short-term risks are the looming U.S. "fiscal cliff" and delays in raising the U.S. debt ceiling.

[1] The *2012 Spillover Report* (IMF, 2012b) discusses policy-related spillover risks emanating from the five largest systemically important economies (China, euro area, Japan, United Kingdom, United States).

Figure 2.1. Revisions to WEO Growth Projections for 2012 and 2013

(Percentage point difference from April 2012 WEO projections)

Revisions to the outlook have generally been downward but to varying degrees. The largest revisions apply to Europe, Asia, and Latin America.

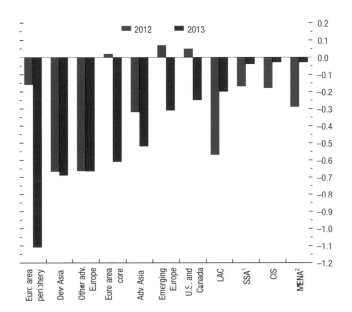

Source: IMF staff estimates.
Note: Adv. Asia = advanced Asia; CIS = Commonwealth of Independent States; Dev. Asia = developing Asia; LAC = Latin America and the Caribbean; MENA = Middle East and North Africa; SSA = sub-Saharan Africa. Emerging Europe (listed as central and eastern Europe in the Statistical Appendix): Albania, Bosnia and Herzegovina, Bulgaria, Croatia, Hungary, Kosovo, Latvia, Lithuania, FYR Macedonia, Montenegro, Poland, Romania, Serbia, Turkey; Euro area core: Austria, Belgium, Estonia, Finland, France, Germany, Luxembourg, Malta, Netherlands, Slovak Republic, Slovenia; Euro area periphery: Cyprus, Greece, Ireland, Italy, Portugal, Spain; other advanced Europe (Other adv. Europe): Czech Republic, Denmark, Iceland, Norway, Sweden, Switzerland, United Kingdom.
[1] Excludes South Sudan.
[2] Excludes Libya and Syria.

Figure 2.2. The Effects of Lower Potential Growth
(Peak deviation of real GDP growth from WEO baseline; percentage points)

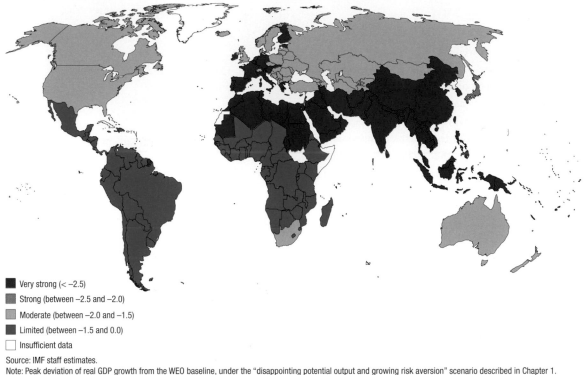

■ Very strong (< –2.5)
■ Strong (between –2.5 and –2.0)
■ Moderate (between –2.0 and –1.5)
■ Limited (between –1.5 and 0.0)
□ Insufficient data

Source: IMF staff estimates.
Note: Peak deviation of real GDP growth from the WEO baseline, under the "disappointing potential output and growing risk aversion" scenario described in Chapter 1. Simulations were conducted using the IMF's Global Economic Model, a six-region model (supplemented with satellite models) that does not explicitly model individual countries (except the United States and Japan).

A medium-term risk is the possibility of lower-than-expected growth in many major economies and regions, including China, because of lower medium-term growth potential and temporarily higher global risk aversion. As illustrated by the corresponding scenario analysis in Chapter 1, if this risk materializes, sharply lower growth will be experienced in all regions—including regions with no or only minor declines in potential growth, which underscores the large spillovers (Figure 2.2).

The Spillover Feature in this chapter assesses the potential transmission of financial stress in advanced economies via capital flows, sovereign yields, and equity prices. The analysis highlights the strong response of global capital flows and asset prices to increased financial stress in advanced economies during several recent episodes, pointing to important differences across episodes depending on the source of stress (Figure 2.3). It also shows that stress related to downswings in China's real activity has become a source of financial market contagion, particularly for

commodity-exporting emerging market and developing economies. Because capital flows and asset prices affect domestic financial conditions and business and household confidence, the real effects can be important.

Europe: In the Orbit of the Euro Area Crisis

Financial stress in the euro area periphery has ratcheted up. The recession in most of the periphery is increasingly spilling into other economies in the region. The measures agreed to at the June 29, 2012, European Union (EU) summit and the European Central Bank's (ECB's) establishment of the Outright Monetary Transactions (OMT) program were steps in the right direction and have improved financial conditions, which nevertheless remain fragile. The baseline outlook for the region, weaker now than expected in the April 2012 WEO (Figure 2.4), is for further anemic growth or contraction in 2012 and a moderate pickup in growth in 2013. The possibility that the euro area crisis will escalate remains a major downside risk to growth and financial sector stability until the underlying issues are resolved.

Activity in Europe contracted by about ¼ percent during the first half of 2012. The main new development was a further escalation of financial stress during the second quarter in the euro area periphery, which, despite some easing, did not fully reverse in the third quarter through mid-September. The impact is most direct in these economies themselves, and all except Ireland are in recession now. But spillovers are increasingly reaching other economies in the region, given strong trade and financial linkages (Figure 2.5). Rising uncertainty about the viability of the Economic and Monetary Union (EMU) has been another drag on the region. Tellingly, there has been no contribution to growth from investment, in sharp contrast to other advanced economies and major emerging market economies. Finally, precrisis legacy issues, including high household debt following housing booms, have constrained private consumption, notably in Spain, but also in Denmark and the United Kingdom.

Another factor has been the diminishing offset from trade with faster-growing emerging market and advanced economies. Economies in the region with higher growth, including in the euro area core,[2] have benefited from stronger trade linkages with faster-growing economies outside the region. Still, robust growth in Russia has provided some offset to the weaker euro area external demand in emerging Europe. On the financial side, capital outflows from the periphery to perceived safe haven economies in the region (Germany, Switzerland, Scandinavian countries) have continued. These flows contributed to declining yields on government bonds and have fostered expanded domestic lending in recipient economies, including for housing.

Monetary policy remains accommodative across the region. But with increasing financial market segmentation due to country risk premiums in the euro area, the transmission of conventional monetary policy impulses to the periphery is impaired. The fiscal policy stance has been contractionary overall, especially in the euro area periphery, where the structural fiscal

[2]Austria, Belgium, Estonia, Finland, France, Germany, Luxembourg, Malta, Netherlands, Slovak Republic, and Slovenia.

Figure 2.3. Weekly Equity and Bond Fund Flows during Financial Stress in Advanced Economies
(Percent of 2011 weekly GDP, two weeks before and after stress)

Financial stress in advanced economies tends to be associated with swings in global capital flows. Flows are lower during the weeks following stress than during the weeks before.

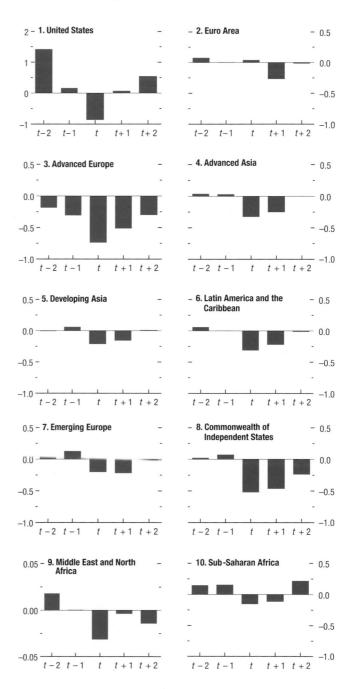

Sources: Emerging Portfolio Fund Research; and IMF staff calculations.
Note: Stress events are during January 2010–June 2012. See the Spillover Feature for details. See Table 2.SF.2 for the country composition of each group.

Figure 2.4. Europe: Revisions to 2013 GDP Growth Forecasts
(Change in percentage points from April 2012 WEO projections)

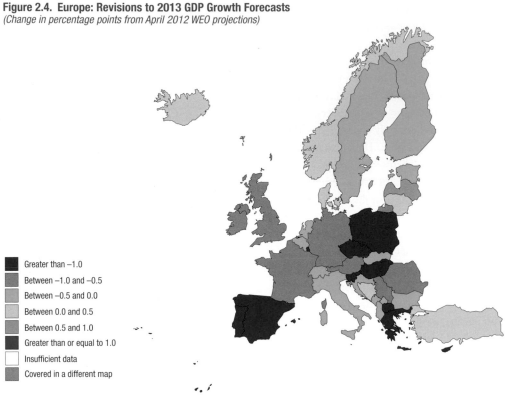

- Greater than −1.0
- Between −1.0 and −0.5
- Between −0.5 and 0.0
- Between 0.0 and 0.5
- Between 0.5 and 1.0
- Greater than or equal to 1.0
- Insufficient data
- Covered in a different map

Source: IMF staff estimates.

deficit as a share of GDP is expected to decline by about 2½ percentage points in 2012, compared with a decline of about ½ percentage point in 2011.

Near-term prospects for Europe are weaker now than they were at the time of the April 2012 WEO. The forecast assumes that policymakers in the euro area succeed in containing the crisis through a combination of continued crisis management (including implementation of reforms agreed to at the June summit), supportive demand management, and further advancement of measures to deepen fiscal integration and create a full-fledged banking union. Still, uncertainty will constrain confidence and activity for some time, and downside risks loom large.

The baseline projects that economic activity will pick up gradually, primarily in 2013 (Table 2.1). This increasing activity reflects a number of factors, including improving external demand due to the pickup in growth in some major emerging market economies, a moderating pace of fiscal consolidation throughout much of the region—Spain is an exception given that consolidation must accelerate to meet deficit targets in 2012–13—and a gradual further easing of financial

stress in the euro area periphery as fiscal adjustment advances, policy support increases, and policy credibility and confidence improve. There are broad differences among European economies.

- In the euro area, real GDP is projected to contract at a rate of ½ percent in 2012 and to increase by ¼ percent in 2013. In the core economies, growth will broadly stall in 2012, except in the Netherlands, where intensified fiscal consolidation is expected to contribute to contraction. Except for Ireland, which is in a bumpy recovery, the recessions in the economies of the euro area periphery have been deeper, and recovery is generally expected to begin only in 2013, once adjustment moderates.

- Growth in other advanced economies in Europe is projected to moderate to ¼ percent in 2012 before picking up in 2013. Domestic demand has generally remained stronger in many economies, reflecting lower precrisis imbalances and balance sheet pressure, which, together with declining yields from safe haven inflows, have helped cushion the spillovers from the euro area crisis. One exception is the United Kingdom, where the financial sector was hit hard by the global financial crisis and where ongoing repair of overstretched private and public balance sheets weighs on domestic demand.

- Emerging Europe was significantly affected by the euro area crisis during the past year, including through the deleveraging of western European banks and declining capital inflows (see Chapter 2 of the October 2012 *Global Financial Stability Report*). Credit growth, in turn, decreased significantly. Trade with the euro area also decelerated rapidly, and growth slowed sharply from late 2011. Nevertheless, unlike in 2008, risk contagion from the euro area crisis has remained limited, and credit default swap spreads for most countries in the region remain well below those for the economies of the euro area periphery. Growth is projected to strengthen from 2 percent in 2012 to about 2½ percent in 2013, largely owing to improving conditions elsewhere in Europe.

Headline inflation generally moderated in 2012 and is projected to decline further in the remainder of 2012–13. In fact, where inflation either increased or remained above target recently, the causes were primarily one-time factors such as increases in energy prices and indirect taxes. Although core inflation has remained relatively stable over the past year, it is expected to decrease as well, given the slowdown in activity and large output gaps. With large downside risks to the near-term growth outlook, there is a risk of core inflation undershooting targets, especially in other advanced Europe.

Downside risks predominate in Europe's near-term growth prospects. The most immediate risk remains that delayed or insufficient policy action will lead to further escalation of the euro area crisis. Until the crisis is resolved, the situation remains precarious, and the broad interconnections among most economies in the region point to larger spillovers in Europe than in other regions.

The growth implications and spillovers from any further escalation of the crisis will depend on the scale and reach of the deterioration in confidence and the response of capital flows.[3] If the deterio-

[3]Chapter 2 of the April 2012 *World Economic Outlook* provides an in-depth analysis of these linkages. It highlights the important role of adverse feedback loops between rising funding pressure in the banking system, increasing fiscal vulnerability, and slowing aggregate demand and growth.

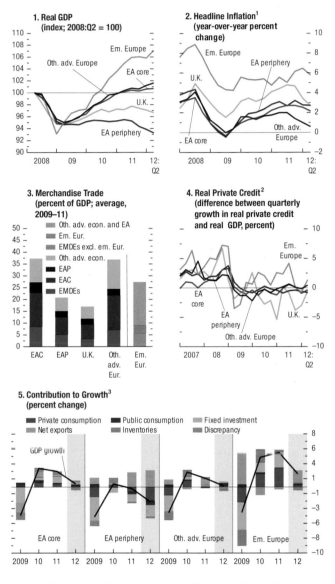

Figure 2.5. Europe: In the Midst of Economic and Financial Stress

Activity has slowed throughout Europe, with recession in the euro area periphery and the United Kingdom. Increased uncertainty about policy and prospects has weighed on confidence and investment throughout the region. Growth in real private credit has fallen below that of GDP in some economies, highlighting pressure from bank balance sheet deleveraging and funding problems.

Sources: IMF, Direction of Trade Statistics database; IMF, International Financial Statistics database; and IMF staff estimates.
Note: EA = euro area; EAC = euro area core; EAP = euro area periphery; EMDEs = emerging market and developing economies; Em. Eur. = emerging Europe; U.K. = United Kingdom. See Figure 2.1 for regional country compositions, except other advanced Europe (Oth. adv. Eur.): Czech Republic, Denmark, Iceland, Norway, Sweden, Switzerland; and other advanced economies (Oth. adv. econ.): advanced economies excluding euro area, other advanced Europe, and United Kingdom.
[1]Emerging Europe excludes Albania, Kosovo, FYR Macedonia, and Montenegro.
[2]Real GDP and private credit data are seasonally adjusted.
[3]Due to data limitations, Kosovo and FYR Macedonia are excluded from emerging Europe. Other advanced Europe includes the United Kingdom.

Table 2.1. Selected European Economies: Real GDP, Consumer Prices, Current Account Balance, and Unemployment

(Annual percent change unless noted otherwise)

	Real GDP			Consumer Prices[1]			Current Account Balance[2]			Unemployment[3]		
		Projections			Projections			Projections			Projections	
	2011	2012	2013	2011	2012	2013	2011	2012	2013	2011	2012	2013
Europe	**2.0**	**0.1**	**0.8**	**3.3**	**2.8**	**2.1**	**0.4**	**0.8**	**1.0**	**. . .**	**. . .**	**. . .**
Advanced Europe	**1.4**	**−0.3**	**0.4**	**2.9**	**2.3**	**1.7**	**1.1**	**1.5**	**1.7**	**9.4**	**10.2**	**10.4**
Euro Area[4],[5]	1.4	−0.4	0.2	2.7	2.3	1.6	0.0	1.1	1.3	10.2	11.2	11.5
Germany	3.1	0.9	0.9	2.5	2.2	1.9	5.7	5.4	4.7	6.0	5.2	5.3
France	1.7	0.1	0.4	2.1	1.9	1.0	−1.9	−1.7	−1.7	9.6	10.1	10.5
Italy	0.4	−2.3	−0.7	2.9	3.0	1.8	−3.3	−1.5	−1.4	8.4	10.6	11.1
Spain	0.4	−1.5	−1.3	3.1	2.4	2.4	−3.5	−2.0	−0.1	21.7	24.9	25.1
Netherlands	1.1	−0.5	0.4	2.5	2.2	1.8	8.5	8.2	8.2	4.4	5.2	5.7
Belgium	1.8	0.0	0.3	3.5	2.8	1.9	−1.0	−0.1	0.3	7.2	7.4	7.9
Austria	2.7	0.9	1.1	3.6	2.3	1.9	1.9	1.9	1.6	4.2	4.3	4.5
Greece	−6.9	−6.0	−4.0	3.3	0.9	−1.1	−9.8	−5.8	−2.9	17.3	23.8	25.4
Portugal	−1.7	−3.0	−1.0	3.6	2.8	0.7	−6.4	−2.9	−1.7	12.7	15.5	16.0
Finland	2.7	0.2	1.3	3.3	2.9	2.3	−1.2	−1.6	−1.7	7.8	7.6	7.8
Ireland	1.4	0.4	1.4	1.2	1.4	1.0	1.1	1.8	2.7	14.4	14.8	14.4
Slovak Republic	3.3	2.6	2.8	4.1	3.6	2.3	0.1	0.8	0.3	13.5	13.7	13.5
Slovenia	0.6	−2.2	−0.4	1.8	2.2	1.5	0.0	1.1	1.0	8.2	8.8	9.0
Luxembourg	1.6	0.2	0.7	3.7	2.5	2.3	7.1	7.3	7.1	5.7	6.2	6.1
Estonia	7.6	2.4	3.5	5.1	4.4	3.2	2.1	0.7	−0.1	12.5	10.1	9.1
Cyprus	0.5	−2.3	−1.0	3.5	3.1	2.2	−10.4	−3.5	−2.0	7.8	11.7	12.5
Malta	2.1	1.2	2.0	2.5	3.5	2.2	−1.3	−1.5	−1.6	6.5	6.0	5.8
United Kingdom[5]	0.8	−0.4	1.1	4.5	2.7	1.9	−1.9	−3.3	−2.7	8.0	8.1	8.1
Sweden	4.0	1.2	2.2	3.0	1.4	2.0	6.9	7.2	7.8	7.5	7.5	7.7
Switzerland	1.9	0.8	1.4	0.2	−0.5	0.5	10.5	10.1	10.0	2.8	3.4	3.6
Czech Republic	1.7	−1.0	0.8	1.9	3.4	2.1	−3.0	−2.4	−2.2	6.7	7.0	8.0
Norway	1.5	3.1	2.3	1.3	1.0	2.2	14.5	15.2	15.6	3.3	3.1	3.1
Denmark	0.8	0.5	1.2	2.8	2.6	2.0	6.7	5.0	4.6	6.1	5.6	5.3
Iceland	3.1	2.9	2.6	4.0	5.6	4.4	−6.2	−2.7	−2.1	7.4	6.1	5.7
San Marino	−2.6	−2.6	0.5	2.0	3.0	2.1	. . .	. . .	. . .	5.5	6.6	6.1
Emerging Europe[6]	**5.3**	**2.0**	**2.6**	**5.3**	**5.6**	**4.4**	**−6.1**	**−5.0**	**−4.9**	**. . .**	**. . .**	**. . .**
Turkey	8.5	3.0	3.5	6.5	8.7	6.5	−10.0	−7.5	−7.1	9.8	9.4	9.9
Poland	4.3	2.4	2.1	4.3	3.9	2.7	−4.3	−3.7	−3.8	9.6	10.0	10.2
Romania	2.5	0.9	2.5	5.8	2.9	3.2	−4.4	−3.7	−3.8	7.4	7.2	7.0
Hungary	1.7	−1.0	0.8	3.9	5.6	3.5	1.4	2.6	2.7	11.0	10.9	10.5
Bulgaria	1.7	1.0	1.5	3.4	1.9	2.3	0.9	−0.3	−1.5	11.3	11.5	11.0
Serbia	1.6	−0.5	2.0	11.1	5.9	7.5	−9.5	−11.5	−12.6	24.4	25.6	25.6
Croatia	0.0	−1.1	1.0	2.3	3.0	3.0	−1.0	−1.2	−1.3	13.7	14.2	13.3
Lithuania	5.9	2.7	3.0	4.1	3.2	2.4	−1.5	−1.1	−1.4	15.4	13.5	12.5
Latvia	5.5	4.5	3.5	4.2	2.4	2.2	−1.2	−1.6	−2.8	16.2	15.3	13.9

[1]Movements in consumer prices are shown as annual averages. December–December changes can be found in Tables A6 and A7 in the Statistical Appendix.

[2]Percent of GDP.

[3]Percent. National definitions of unemployment may differ.

[4]Current account position corrected for reporting discrepancies in intra-area transactions.

[5]Based on Eurostat's harmonized index of consumer prices.

[6]Also includes Albania, Bosnia and Herzegovina, Kosovo, FYR Macedonia, and Montenegro.

ration is confined to the periphery economies—broadly mirroring developments during the past two years—private capital outflows from crisis to core economies will increase. The direct negative impact on the periphery through external current accounts and domestic demand would remain limited, however, because the euro system provides for automatic, offsetting inflows. Still, financial conditions would tighten as prospective bank losses increase; banks in the periphery and, to a lesser extent, in the core economies (largely because of cross-border asset holdings in the periphery) would increase provisions and precautionary cash holdings; and lending rates would rise.

In contrast, if the euro area core economies were hit by contagion—for example, resulting from rapidly intensifying concerns about the integrity of the EMU and its ability to manage the crisis—the loss of investor confidence would also hit the core. Sovereign risk premiums and yields would increase in the periphery and the core, requiring additional fiscal adjustment everywhere. Increased capital outflows from the euro area as a whole would cause depreciation of the euro by more than in the case of limited contagion. Current accounts throughout the euro area would adjust. Obviously, the output losses in Europe and also outside the region would be larger under this scenario.

The highest policy priority in Europe is to resolve the crisis in the euro area. All other economies in the region need a policy mix that supports their recoveries in a weak global growth environment, and many also need to address fiscal sustainability challenges and financial sector vulnerabilities.

Resolving the euro area crisis requires progress toward banking and fiscal union in combination with short-term demand support and crisis management at the euro area level.[4]

- The agreements reached at the June 29, 2012, EU summit, if fully implemented, will create a banking union and help break the adverse feedback loops between sovereigns and banks—once an effective single supervisory mechanism for euro area banks is established, the ESM, which will be operational beginning in October 2012, could be

able to recapitalize banks directly. But implementation hurdles are a concern, and additional steps are needed. Banking union also requires a pan-European deposit insurance guarantee program and a bank resolution mechanism with common backstops.

- Regarding demand support, the ECB should keep its policy rate low for the foreseeable future or reduce it even further. OMTs, which the ECB will consider for countries under a macroeconomic adjustment or precautionary program with the European Financial Stability Facility and its successor, the European Stability Mechanism (ESM), should help ensure that low policy rates transmit to borrowing costs in countries in the periphery with a program. The ECB should also continue to provide ample liquidity to banks.

- The viability of the EMU must be supported by wide-ranging structural reforms throughout the euro area to raise growth and competitiveness, thereby helping the resolution of intra-euro-area current account imbalances.

- Fiscal consolidation plans in the euro area must be implemented. In general, attention should be paid to meeting structural fiscal targets, rather than nominal targets that will likely be affected by economic conditions. Automatic stabilizers should thus be allowed to operate fully in economies not subject to market pressure. Considering the large downside risks, economies with limited fiscal vulnerability should stand ready to implement fiscal contingency measures if such risks materialize.

In other advanced economies in the region, monetary policy needs to respond effectively to a much weaker near-term environment that will dampen price pressures, including through the use of further unconventional measures. In the United Kingdom, further monetary easing through unconventional measures may be necessary, depending on the effects of the easing measures implemented recently. With the prospect of somewhat weaker global growth, automatic stabilizers should be allowed to operate fully, and economies with limited fiscal vulnerability (see the October 2012 *Fiscal Monitor*) should stand ready to implement fiscal contingency measures if large downside risks materialize.

---

[4]See also the discussion in Chapter 1 and in IMF (2012c).

In emerging Europe, the need for fiscal consolidation varies widely; economies with a high public debt burden and exposed to market volatility must continue with steady consolidation (Hungary). Inflation pressure is set to decline rapidly in many countries, giving central banks new room for easing.

The United States and Canada: Growth Continues, but Slack Remains

In the United States, a modest recovery with weak job creation continues amid a weak global environment, although the housing market is stabilizing. In Canada, the recovery has been more robust, reflecting partly the effects of favorable financing conditions with less pressure for balance sheet adjustment and the commodity boom. The expansion is expected to remain modest throughout 2012–13 (Figure 2.6). Both external and domestic downside risks to the outlook remain elevated. In the United States, it is imperative to avoid excessive fiscal consolidation (the fiscal cliff) in 2013, to raise the debt ceiling promptly, and to agree on a credible medium-term fiscal consolidation plan. In Canada, a priority is to limit risks related to elevated house prices and household debt levels.

Output in the United States rose above the precrisis peak in the second half of 2011, sooner than in many other advanced economies (Figure 2.7, panels 1 and 2). Still, compared with earlier recoveries, growth remains sluggish, consistent with the broad evidence of significant legacy effects of financial crises and housing busts. Job creation, which accelerated in the second half of 2011, slowed again in 2012. Weaker external conditions and the confluence of global spillovers discussed above explain much of the slowing, with a payback from the unusually warm winter weather also temporarily weighing on growth in the second quarter. On the demand side, growth in business investment lost some momentum, in part due to the partial expiration of bonus depreciation allowances, although uncertainty related to the fiscal and economic outlook may have also played a role. Private consumption has also moderated since early 2012. The

Figure 2.6. United States and Canada: Revisions to 2013 GDP Growth Forecasts
(Change in percentage points from April 2012 WEO projections)

- Greater than −1.0
- Between −1.0 and −0.5
- Between −0.5 and 0.0
- Between 0.0 and 0.5
- Between 0.5 and 1.0
- Greater than or equal to 1.0
- Insufficient data
- Covered in a different map

Source: IMF staff estimates.

housing market is showing signs of stabilizing after a sharp correction (Figure 2.7, panels 3 and 4).

In Canada, growth has been constrained by the sluggish expansion in the United States—a result of the two economies' deep economic and financial linkages—and the ongoing fiscal consolidation. Still, activity has recovered at a faster pace than in the United States. Domestic demand—both business investment and private consumption—has been supported by exceptionally favorable financing conditions, including low interest rates and credit availability. These factors, along with the commodity boom, have also boosted the housing sector, especially in provinces with strong mining activity. However, housing-related credit and household leverage have risen markedly since the Great Recession, despite measures to limit mortgage growth (Figure 2.7, panels 4 and 5).

The U.S. and Canadian economies are both projected to grow at about 2 percent during 2012–13 under the baseline, with uncertainty and weaker external demand weighing on aggregate demand (Table 2.2). U.S. inflation will stay subdued, given lower commodity prices and persistent economic slack, averaging 2 percent this year and declining to 1¾ percent in 2013.

The near-term growth outlook is subject to large downside risks from both external and domestic factors. The main external risk pertains to a further escalation of the euro area crisis. Although safe haven capital flows into the United States could help to lower bond yields, supporting interest-sensitive components of aggregate demand, they also have been associated with real appreciation pressures, which dampen exports. As noted above, U.S. growth will also fall sharply if potential output in the United States and its major trading partners disappoints and risk aversion increases (Figure 2.2).

A major U.S. domestic risk is the potential for much sharper fiscal contraction (Figure 2.7, panel 6) if policymakers fail to reach agreement to prevent large automatic tax increases and spending cuts scheduled to take effect at the beginning of 2013. At the extreme, the fiscal cliff could result in a fiscal withdrawal of more than 4 percent of GDP in 2013—about 3 percentage points of GDP larger than the fiscal adjustment assumed under the

Figure 2.7. United States and Canada: A Weak Recovery

Growth in the United States has been sluggish, and job creation has weakened. The recovery is expected to remain tepid, given a weaker global environment and significant domestic policy uncertainty, including about the fiscal cliff. In Canada, easy financing conditions, strong credit growth, and robust commodity market conditions have supported domestic demand, and activity has expanded at a faster pace than in other major advanced economies.

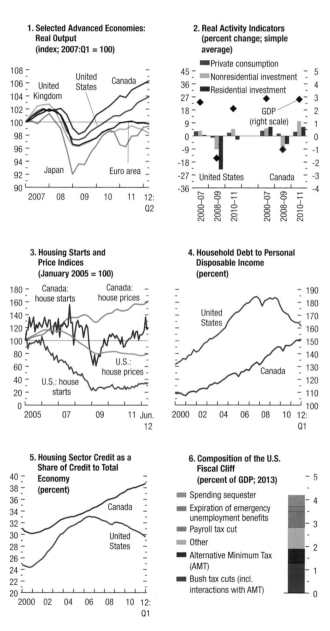

Sources: Congressional Budget Office; Haver Analytics; and IMF staff estimates.

Table 2.2. Selected Advanced Economies: Real GDP, Consumer Prices, Current Account Balance, and Unemployment
(Annual percent change unless noted otherwise)

	Real GDP			Consumer Prices[1]			Current Account Balance[2]			Unemployment[3]		
		Projections			Projections			Projections			Projections	
	2011	2012	2013	2011	2012	2013	2011	2012	2013	2011	2012	2013
Advanced Economies	**1.6**	**1.3**	**1.5**	**2.7**	**1.9**	**1.6**	**−0.2**	**−0.4**	**−0.3**	**7.9**	**8.0**	**8.1**
United States	1.8	2.2	2.1	3.1	2.0	1.8	−3.1	−3.1	−3.1	9.0	8.2	8.1
Euro Area[4,5]	1.4	−0.4	0.2	2.7	2.3	1.6	0.0	1.1	1.3	10.2	11.2	11.5
Japan	−0.8	2.2	1.2	−0.3	0.0	−0.2	2.0	1.6	2.3	4.6	4.5	4.4
United Kingdom[4]	0.8	−0.4	1.1	4.5	2.7	1.9	−1.9	−3.3	−2.7	8.0	8.1	8.1
Canada	2.4	1.9	2.0	2.9	1.8	2.0	−2.8	−3.4	−3.7	7.5	7.3	7.3
Other Advanced Economies[6]	3.2	2.1	3.0	3.1	2.2	2.4	4.7	3.7	3.3	4.5	4.5	4.6
Memorandum												
Newly Industrialized Asian Economies	4.0	2.1	3.6	3.6	2.7	2.7	6.6	5.6	5.5	3.6	3.5	3.5

[1]Movements in consumer prices are shown as annual averages. December–December changes can be found in Table A6 in the Statistical Appendix.
[2]Percent of GDP.
[3]Percent. National definitions of unemployment may differ.
[4]Based on Eurostat's harmonized index of consumer prices.
[5]Current account position corrected for reporting discrepancies in intra-area transactions.
[6]Excludes the G7 economies (Canada, France, Germany, Italy, Japan, United Kingdom, United States) and euro area countries.

baseline. Growth would stall in 2013 with the full materialization of the cliff and, as detailed in the *2012 Spillover Report* (IMF, 2012b), would inflict large spillovers on major U.S. trading partners and also on commodity exporters (because of declines in commodity prices).

Another fiscal risk, although relatively more medium term, relates to a potential jump in the risk premium on U.S. Treasury bonds, reflecting investor concerns about the sustainability of U.S. debt levels in the absence of a credible plan for medium-term consolidation. The rise in long-term interest rates would lead to lower aggregate demand and growth, particularly in the United States but also elsewhere through asset price and trade spillovers (see IMF, 2012b). More generally, a deterioration in economic conditions in the U.S. economy that hurts investor confidence and raises risk aversion at the global level could induce sharp swings in global capital flows and asset prices (see the Spillover Feature).

Given its strong economic and financial ties with the U.S. economy, Canada is equally exposed to the risks facing its trading partner. In addition, an important domestic vulnerability in Canada relates to the housing market. A sharp or sustained decline in house prices could seriously set back the leveraged household sector and domestic demand.

The urgent policy priorities in the United States are to avoid excessive fiscal contraction in the short term, promptly raise the debt ceiling, and agree on a credible fiscal consolidation plan—centered around entitlement and tax reforms—that places government debt on a sustainable path in the medium term. The latter would also contribute to global demand rebalancing, given that the U.S. current account position is estimated to be weaker and the real effective exchange rate stronger than they would be if a more desirable path for fiscal deficits over the medium term were in place (IMF, 2012a). Notwithstanding recent steps and nascent signs of stabilization in the housing market, more must be done to reduce the rate of foreclosures and remove impediments to the transmission of low long-term policy rates to mortgage rates.[5] In this regard, the recent measures by the Federal Reserve on additional quantitative easing and the extension of its low-interest-rate guidance until mid-2015 were timely in limiting downside risks. Monetary policy needs to remain accommodative while the government and household sectors continue to consolidate

[5]Key measures include increasing the participation of government-sponsored enterprises in the principal reduction program, supporting refinancing on a larger scale, and converting foreclosed property into rental property to limit the downward price pressure. See IMF (2012c) and Chapter 3 of the April 2012 *World Economic Outlook*.

their balance sheet positions. These and other priorities—including financial regulatory, labor market, and structural reforms—are discussed in detail in Chapter 1 and in previous WEO reports.

In Canada, the key priority is to ensure that risks from the housing sector and increases in household debt remain well contained and do not create financial sector vulnerabilities. Thus far, mortgage credit growth has slightly decelerated in response to the measures taken by the authorities, including tighter mortgage insurance standards. If household leverage continues to rise, additional measures may need to be considered.

Asia: Calibrating a Soft Landing

Growth in Asia has moderated further with weaker external demand and the soft landing of domestic demand in China. The outlook is for a modest pickup in growth on the back of recent policy easing. Limited direct financial spillovers and some room for policy easing should be helpful in minimizing external downside risks. Balancing external and internal risks will be important, however, given that output gaps are still positive in some economies in the region while credit growth remains strong and that lower-than-expected potential output growth and domestic imbalances are still risks.

Growth continued to moderate in much of Asia during the first half of 2012. Slower growth in import demand in most advanced economies corresponded with weaker export growth in Asia. Growth in China slowed further in the second quarter of 2012, as the economy continued to adjust to the policy tightening undertaken in 2010–11. The tightening of monetary and credit policies has been partly reversed in 2012, as price pressures have eased and the residential real estate market has cooled. This easing, however, has not yet gained the traction expected earlier in the year. Slowing growth in China has affected activity in the rest of Asia, a consequence of the deepening of linkages throughout the region in the past decade.

In other parts of Asia, activity was boosted by recovery from natural disasters and reconstruction, notably in Japan and Thailand, but also in Australia and New Zealand. In Australia, continued strong mining activity and related investment have

also supported growth. In India, growth weakened more than expected in the first half of 2012, an outcome of stalled investment caused by governance issues and red tape, and a deterioration in business sentiment against the backdrop of a rising current account deficit and the recent rupee depreciation.

Compared with the region's growth performance in recent years, the near- and medium-term outlooks are less buoyant. This view reflects weaker anticipated external demand resulting from the tepid growth prospects in major advanced economies and a downshift in China's and India's growth prospects, with a return to double-digit growth in China unlikely given the policy objectives laid out in the 12th Five-Year Plan. The main impetus for a moderate pickup in growth from late 2012 will come from recent policy easing in China and elsewhere. Specifically, growth in the region is projected to average 5½ percent this year and rise to 5¾ percent in 2013 (Table 2.3), downward revisions of more than ½ percentage point for both years relative to the April 2012 WEO (Figure 2.8).

- Growth in China is projected to be about 7¾ percent this year and then to strengthen to 8¼ percent in 2013 as domestic demand growth, especially investment growth, picks up with the policy easing now under way.
- Growth in India is projected to average 5 to 6 percent in 2012–13, more than 1 percentage point lower than in the April 2012 WEO. The downgrade reflects both an expectation that current drags on business sentiment and investment will persist and a weaker external environment.
- In Japan, growth is expected to reach almost 2¼ percent in 2012. Much of the recent strength is attributable to reconstruction activity and some rebound in manufacturing activity in the first half of the year following the supply shocks associated with the March 2011 earthquake and tsunami and the Thai floods in October 2011. The effects of these factors will fade, however, and growth is projected to moderate to 1¼ percent in 2013.
- Weaker external demand is the main factor underpinning generally modestly weaker growth in the ASEAN-5[6] economies in 2012 (Figure 2.9, panels

[6]The Association of Southeast Asian Nations (ASEAN) has 10 members; the ASEAN-5 are Indonesia, Malaysia, the Philippines, Thailand, and Vietnam.

Table 2.3. Selected Asian Economies: Real GDP, Consumer Prices, Current Account Balance, and Unemployment
(Annual percent change unless noted otherwise)

	Real GDP			Consumer Prices[1]			Current Account Balance[2]			Unemployment[3]		
		Projections			Projections			Projections			Projections	
	2011	2012	2013	2011	2012	2013	2011	2012	2013	2011	2012	2013
Asia	**5.8**	**5.4**	**5.8**	**5.0**	**3.9**	**3.8**	**1.9**	**1.2**	**1.3**	...	...	...
Advanced Asia	**1.3**	**2.3**	**2.3**	**1.6**	**1.2**	**1.2**	**2.3**	**1.5**	**1.6**	**4.3**	**4.3**	**4.2**
Japan	−0.8	2.2	1.2	−0.3	0.0	−0.2	2.0	1.6	2.3	4.6	4.5	4.4
Australia	2.1	3.3	3.0	3.4	2.0	2.6	−2.3	−4.1	−5.5	5.1	5.2	5.3
New Zealand	1.3	2.2	3.1	4.0	1.9	2.4	−4.2	−5.4	−5.9	6.5	6.6	5.7
Newly Industrialized Asian Economies	**4.0**	**2.1**	**3.6**	**3.6**	**2.7**	**2.7**	**6.6**	**5.6**	**5.5**	**3.6**	**3.5**	**3.5**
Korea	3.6	2.7	3.6	4.0	2.2	2.7	2.4	1.9	1.7	3.4	3.3	3.3
Taiwan Province of China	4.0	1.3	3.9	1.4	2.5	2.0	8.9	6.9	7.3	4.4	4.5	4.3
Hong Kong SAR	5.0	1.8	3.5	5.3	3.8	3.0	5.3	4.1	3.8	3.4	3.4	3.3
Singapore	4.9	2.1	2.9	5.2	4.5	4.3	21.9	21.0	20.7	2.0	2.1	2.1
Developing Asia	**7.8**	**6.7**	**7.2**	**6.5**	**5.0**	**4.9**	**1.6**	**0.9**	**1.1**	...	...	...
China	9.2	7.8	8.2	5.4	3.0	3.0	2.8	2.3	2.5	4.1	4.1	4.1
India	6.8	4.9	6.0	8.9	10.2	9.6	−3.4	−3.8	−3.3	...	...	...
ASEAN-5	**4.5**	**5.4**	**5.8**	**5.9**	**4.0**	**4.3**	**2.9**	**0.6**	**0.2**	...	...	...
Indonesia	6.5	6.0	6.3	5.4	4.4	5.1	0.2	−2.1	−2.4	6.6	6.2	6.1
Thailand	0.1	5.6	6.0	3.8	3.2	3.3	3.4	−0.2	0.1	0.7	0.7	0.7
Malaysia	5.1	4.4	4.7	3.2	2.0	2.4	11.0	7.5	6.9	3.1	3.1	3.0
Philippines	3.9	4.8	4.8	4.7	3.5	4.5	3.1	3.0	2.6	7.0	7.0	7.0
Vietnam	5.9	5.1	5.9	18.7	8.1	6.2	0.2	0.3	−0.9	4.5	4.5	4.5
Other Developing Asia[4]	**5.0**	**5.1**	**4.9**	**10.6**	**8.9**	**8.2**	**−0.6**	**−1.5**	**−1.5**	...	...	...
Memorandum												
Emerging Asia[5]	7.3	6.1	6.7	6.1	4.7	4.6	2.4	1.6	1.7	...	...	...

[1]Movements in consumer prices are shown as annual averages. December–December changes can be found in Tables A6 and A7 in the Statistical Appendix.
[2]Percent of GDP.
[3]Percent. National definitions of unemployment may differ.
[4]Other Developing Asia comprises Afghanistan, Bangladesh, Bhutan, Brunei Darussalam, Cambodia, Fiji, Kiribati, Lao P.D.R., Maldives, Myanmar, Nepal, Pakistan, Papua New Guinea, Samoa, Solomon Islands, Sri Lanka, Timor-Leste, Tonga, Tuvalu, and Vanuatu.
[5]Emerging Asia comprises all economies in Developing Asia and Newly Industrialized Asian Economies.

1 and 2). The main exception is Thailand, where growth has bounced back sharply, led by reconstruction and investment after the devastating floods in October 2011. Overall, growth in the ASEAN-5 is projected to accelerate slightly to 5¾ percent in 2013, up from about 5½ percent in 2012.

- In Korea, growth is projected to moderate to 2¾ percent this year but to pick up to about 3½ percent in 2013 because of a rebound in exports and private investment, which is geared toward the tradables sector.

Inflation in the region is projected to decline from 5 percent in 2011 to about 4 percent during 2012–13. This is due, in part, to the recent decline in commodity prices but also to the lagged effect of the policy tightening during 2010–11 put in place to relieve overheating pressure.

The balance of risks to the near-term growth outlook is tilted to the downside, reflecting external and, to a lesser extent in the near term, internal risks to the region. In the short term, a further escalation of the euro area crisis and failure to address the U.S. fiscal cliff are the main external risks for the region. If these risks were to materialize, Asia's open, trade-oriented economies would be faced with lower external demand and other spillovers (for example, on confidence), and growth could be substantially lower.

Much of the discussion of spillovers from advanced economies to economies in emerging Asia has focused on spillovers through trade and confidence channels. However, as discussed in the Spillover Feature, emerging Asia, like other emerging markets, has become more integrated with global

Figure 2.8. Asia: Revisions to 2013 GDP Growth Forecasts
(Change in percentage points from April 2012 WEO projections)

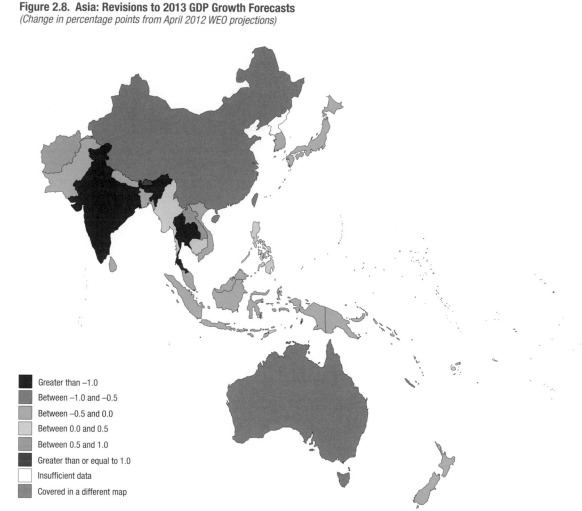

Greater than −1.0
Between −1.0 and −0.5
Between −0.5 and 0.0
Between 0.0 and 0.5
Between 0.5 and 1.0
Greater than or equal to 1.0
Insufficient data
Covered in a different map

Source: IMF staff estimates.

financial markets (Figure 2.9, panels 3 and 4). With the resulting higher exposure to financial shocks, increases in financial stress in advanced economies during the past few years have indeed been associated with lower capital flows and asset price declines in the region. Overall, though, private capital flows to the region have remained sizable and credit growth strong (Figure 2.9, panel 5). With increased exposure, volatility in global capital markets also can have larger effects, including through effects on exchange rates (as illustrated by safe haven effects and the recent yen appreciation).

Among internal risks to the region, lower-than-expected potential growth in emerging Asia in the medium term is a key risk. As noted in Chapter 1,

the housing boom and similar temporary factors in the major advanced economies may have contributed to the recent strong growth performance in the region. China experienced residential real estate and investment booms of its own, which accelerated during 2009–10 subsequent to macroeconomic policy stimulus actions taken in response to the global financial crisis. Strong credit growth has supported demand across emerging market economies more broadly, including in Asia, but cannot continue at its recent pace without creating large financial stability risks. In the event of simultaneous lower potential growth in emerging Asia and in other regions, the impact on growth would be sizable in Asia, as would be the outward spillovers on commodity exporters

Figure 2.9. Asia: Activity Decelerates

Growth in Asia has moderated further, given weaker external demand and the soft landing in China. The downgrading of medium-term growth prospects in China will affect regional growth performance because of China's expanding trade linkages with other economies in the region. The region has been exposed to financial spillovers from advanced economies, but capital flows to its emerging market economies and credit growth both remain strong.

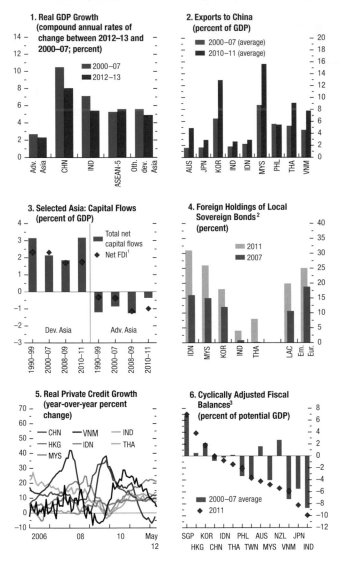

Sources: CEIC; Haver Analytics; IMF, Balance of Payments Statistics database; IMF, Direction of Trade Statistics database; IMF, International Financial Statistics database; IMF, *Regional Economic Outlook: Asia and Pacific* (October 2011); national sources; and IMF staff estimates.
Note: Advanced Asia (Adv. Asia): Australia (AUS), Hong Kong SAR (HKG), Japan (JPN), Korea (KOR), New Zealand (NZL), Singapore (SGP), Taiwan Province of China (TWN); ASEAN-5: Indonesia (IDN), Malaysia (MYS), Philippines (PHL), Thailand (THA), Vietnam (VNM); other developing Asia (Oth. dev. Asia): Afghanistan, Bangladesh, Bhutan, Brunei Darussalam, Cambodia, Kiribati, Lao P.D.R., Maldives, Myanmar, Nepal, Pakistan, Papua New Guinea, Samoa, Solomon Islands, Sri Lanka, Timor-Leste, Tonga, Vanuatu; developing Asia (Dev. Asia): ASEAN-5 and other developing Asia; CHN = China; IND = India.
[1] FDI = foreign direct investment.
[2] Em. Eur. = emerging Europe (see Figure 2.1 for regional country compositions); LAC = Latin America and the Caribbean; India: total bond market.
[3] Indonesia: average of 2004–07; New Zealand: average of 2005–07; Vietnam: in percent of fiscal year nominal GDP.

(see Figure 2.2). A related risk is that the recent surge in investment in China could be reversed and result in a sharper-than-expected investment slowdown in the future. Such a shock would strongly affect economies in the highly interlinked Asian supply chain—for example, Korea, Malaysia, Taiwan Province of China, and Thailand—including indirectly through the large effects on other major manufacturing exporters, especially Germany and Japan.[7]

Policies must strike the right balance between managing external and internal risks and orchestrating a soft landing. External risks have been more pressing, and the recent shift toward monetary easing across much of the region seems appropriate for most economies, given decelerating inflation in both advanced and emerging Asia. Even so, recent rate cuts have used some of the available space in emerging Asia—output gaps are still positive and real policy rates remain well below their precrisis averages. In India, where inflation is still high, monetary policy should stay on hold until a sustained decrease in inflation materializes. In Japan, the easing of monetary policy announced in September should help support economic growth and exit from deflation. Further easing of monetary policy may, however, be needed for inflation accelerating toward the Bank of Japan's goal of 1 percent.

Should downside risks materialize, some economies (ASEAN-5, China, Korea) still have the fiscal space to allow automatic stabilizers to operate fully, if appropriate, or to use discretionary fiscal stimulus (Figure 2.9, panel 6). In a number of economies, however, addressing debt sustainability through credible fiscal consolidation remains a priority (India, Japan, Vietnam). In Japan, the recent approval of a gradual doubling of the consumption tax rate to 10 percent by 2015 is an important step toward putting public debt on a sustainable trajectory, although further consolidation measures are needed to achieve this goal. Structural fiscal policy reform is needed in a number of economies in the region, including China, to address social spending and protection as well as infrastructure needs. By reducing distortions that hold back private consumption, such reforms would lower

[7] IMF (2012b) presents a more detailed analysis of spillovers from investment shocks in China.

risks of a buildup in domestic imbalances and are part of the set of desirable policies that would help rebalance global demand. Indeed, in a number of Asian economies—including China, Korea, Malaysia, Singapore, and Thailand—current account positions are stronger and currencies are weaker than they would be with a more desirable set of policies.[8]

Against the risks of deteriorating credit quality while growth is slowing, policymakers in many Asian economies also need to guard against financial stability risks arising from recent rapid credit growth, including by closely monitoring balance sheet health and funding conditions in the banking and shadow banking systems. In the event of global or local liquidity shortages, central banks should stand ready to backstop liquidity.

Latin America and the Caribbean: Losing Some Buoyancy

With slowing growth, overheating pressures and inflation in Latin America and the Caribbean (LAC) have declined. Private capital flows remain strong and financing conditions favorable. The outlook has deteriorated compared with the April 2012 WEO (Figure 2.10). Growth is expected to pick up later this year, as recent policy easing gains traction. Risks to the near-term growth outlook are to the downside, as elsewhere. With continued rapid credit growth and inflation above the midpoint of the target band in many economies in the region, however, the priority is to rebuild macroeconomic policy space unless downside risks materialize.

Growth in the LAC region decelerated further in the first half of 2012. Activity outside the region moderated more than expected, including in emerging Asia, which weakened external demand for LAC goods and services. Together with weaker near-term global prospects, this slump in activity also led to lower prices for most commodities and terms-of-trade losses for commodity exporters, which account for three-quarters of the region's output. Domestic demand growth, especially investment, cooled on the back of past policy tightening. The pickup in growth was lower than expected in Brazil—an important cause of the weaker regional growth performance—an acknowledgment of

[8]See also IMF (2012a).

both poorer external conditions and slower transmission of the monetary policy easing since August 2011 as a result of an increase in nonperforming loans after several years of rapid credit growth.

The LAC region has been exposed to financial spillovers from the euro area crisis and concerns about global growth prospects, but their effects have been contained. These spillovers contributed to increased risk aversion and temporarily reduced capital flows to the region but have not caused a reversal of flows (Figure 2.11). Foreign currency debt spreads have increased, as in other emerging markets, but they remain well below recent highs. At the same time, most of the region's currencies have appreciated, with the notable exception of the Brazilian *real* (Figure 2.11, panels 1 and 2).

Spillovers from the region's exposure to the operations of European banks, predominantly Spanish banks, have also been contained, primarily because the LAC operations of these banks are largely conducted by subsidiaries and funded by local deposits. Credit growth throughout the region has thus remained robust, notwithstanding slowing activity.

Growth in the region is projected to moderate to 3¼ percent in 2012, before strengthening to about 4 percent in 2013 (Table 2.4). Among the commodity exporters, recent monetary policy easing is expected to spur stronger growth in Brazil from late 2012, led by domestic demand. Employment growth is also expected to remain robust, primarily in the domestic services sectors. In most other commodity exporters, growth is expected to remain close to potential for the remainder of 2012 and in 2013, after moderating gradually during the past year or so. In Mexico, growth has remained strong in 2012 but is expected to moderate with the weaker near-term U.S. growth prospects. Overall, growth is forecast to average 3¾ percent in 2012–13, somewhat above potential. In Central America, where the outlook is closely tied to developments in the United States, growth is expected to moderate by ½ percentage point from 2011 to 4¼ percent in 2012–13. In the Caribbean, high public debt and weak tourism and remittance flows continue to constrain the outlook, and growth is expected to remain lackluster at about 2¾ to 3½ percent.

Risks to the growth outlook are to the downside, and the main risks are broadly aligned with those

Figure 2.10. Latin America and the Caribbean: Revisions to 2013 GDP Growth Forecasts
(Change in percentage points from April 2012 WEO projections)

Greater than −1.0
Between −1.0 and −0.5
Between −0.5 and 0.0
Between 0.0 and 0.5
Between 0.5 and 1.0
Greater than or equal to 1.0
Insufficient data
Covered in a different map

Source: IMF staff estimates.

affecting the global economy. The main near-term risks relate to an escalation of the euro area crisis and the U.S. fiscal cliff. The euro area risk scenario analysis in Chapter 1 suggests that the peak decline in regional output could amount to about ½ percent relative to the baseline. This is modest compared with other regions and reflects the LAC region's relatively low level of trade with Europe (only about 10 percent of goods exports) and limited financial linkages. If global growth slowed sharply because the United States failed to avoid the fiscal cliff, the impact on the LAC region would be relatively larger because of stronger linkages with the U.S. economy. In both cases, countercyclical policy responses in the region could help dampen the spillover effects on domestic output.

In view of the region's dependence on commodity market developments, particularly in the Southern Cone, the medium-term risks that have the greatest impact on commodity prices are of particular concern. The Chapter 1 risk scenario of lower potential growth in systemically important economies and temporarily higher global risk aversion illustrates this concern. Even if potential growth in the LAC region were only ½ percentage point lower, the short-term growth impact would be considerably larger because a commodity price bust would follow the large output declines in emerging Asia and the advanced economies. A sharper-than-expected investment slowdown in China is another important medium-term risk that could affect the LAC region. China's economic boom of the past decade has been commodity intensive, boosting its market share in global commodity markets, especially in industrial base metals and raw materials, and leading to much greater trade linkages with the LAC region. Among the commodity exporters, the largest spillover effects of an investment shock in China would be on undiversified exporters specializing in metal extraction and trade; diversified exporters such as Brazil would be relatively less affected (see IMF, 2012b).

Lower potential growth also is a risk from an intraregional perspective because growth in the region has been above historical trends during the past decade or so, supported in part by financial deepening and rapid credit growth. This success may well have generated overly optimistic expectations about potential growth in the medium term. There are related risks of domestic financial instability after years of rapid credit growth.

Against this backdrop, policymakers in the region must be alert to spillovers from weaker prospects in advanced economies and major emerging markets outside the region, volatile capital flows, and emerging domestic financial risks. Nevertheless, policymakers must carefully balance these downside risks with the remnants of recent overheating and reduced policy space. Despite recent declines, inflation is still above the midpoint of target bands, and output gaps are close to zero or still positive. Concerns about upside risks to inflation are particularly acute in Venezuela and Argentina, where policies have not been tightened noticeably and inflation continues at high levels. Still, monetary policy should be the first line of defense if global growth slows more than expected, especially in economies with established and tested inflation-targeting frameworks. As for risks related to capital flows and financial stability, policies must build on a strong foundation of prudential measures and further enhance risk-based prudential regulation and supervision. At the same time, liquidity provision may also be needed if a change in global risk sentiment leads to acute funding pressure in the region's banking systems.

Fiscal policy should continue to rebuild room for maneuvering unless large downside risks materialize. New fiscal space is particularly important for commodity exporters to buffer the downside risks to global growth and commodity prices.

Figure 2.11. Latin America: A Moderate Slowdown

Private capital flows to Latin America remain strong despite increased global risk aversion and concerns about domestic strains. Inflation and overheating risks have declined, but with continued rapid credit growth and inflation above the midpoint of the target band in many economies in the region, the priority remains to rebuild macroeconomic policy space and build on progress in macroprudential regulation and supervision unless downside risks materialize.

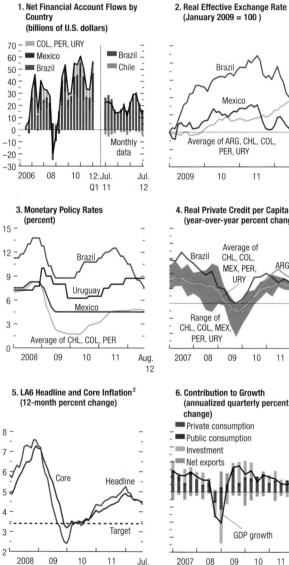

Sources: Haver Analytics; and IMF staff calculations.
Note: ARG = Argentina; CHL = Chile; COL = Colombia; MEX = Mexico; PER = Peru; URY = Uruguay.
[1]Nominal variables for Argentina are deflated using IMF staff estimates of average provincial inflation.
[2]LA6: Brazil, Chile, Colombia, Mexico, Peru, and Uruguay.

Table 2.4. Selected Western Hemisphere Economies: Real GDP, Consumer Prices, Current Account Balance, and Unemployment

(Annual percent change unless noted otherwise)

	Real GDP			Consumer Prices[1]			Current Account Balance[2]			Unemployment[3]		
		Projections			Projections			Projections			Projections	
	2011	2012	2013	2011	2012	2013	2011	2012	2013	2011	2012	2013
North America	**2.0**	**2.3**	**2.2**	**3.1**	**2.1**	**1.9**	**−2.9**	**−3.0**	**−3.0**	...	...	...
United States	1.8	2.2	2.1	3.1	2.0	1.8	−3.1	−3.1	−3.1	9.0	8.2	8.1
Canada	2.4	1.9	2.0	2.9	1.8	2.0	−2.8	−3.4	−3.7	7.5	7.3	7.3
Mexico	3.9	3.8	3.5	3.4	4.0	3.5	−1.0	−0.9	−1.1	5.2	4.8	4.8
South America[4]	**4.8**	**2.9**	**4.0**	**7.8**	**6.8**	**6.9**	**−1.0**	**−1.5**	**−1.7**	...	...	...
Brazil	2.7	1.5	4.0	6.6	5.2	4.9	−2.1	−2.6	−2.8	6.0	6.0	6.5
Argentina[5]	8.9	2.6	3.1	9.8	9.9	9.7	−0.1	0.3	−0.1	7.2	7.2	7.2
Colombia	5.9	4.3	4.4	3.4	3.2	2.8	−3.0	−2.9	−2.9	10.8	11.0	10.5
Venezuela	4.2	5.7	3.3	26.1	23.2	28.8	8.6	6.7	5.6	8.1	8.0	8.1
Peru	6.9	6.0	5.8	3.4	3.7	2.5	−1.9	−3.0	−3.0	7.7	7.5	7.5
Chile	5.9	5.0	4.4	3.3	3.1	3.0	−1.3	−3.2	−3.0	7.1	6.6	6.9
Ecuador	7.8	4.0	4.1	4.5	5.1	4.3	−0.3	−0.3	3.0	6.0	5.8	6.2
Uruguay	5.7	3.5	4.0	8.1	7.9	7.6	−3.1	−3.0	−1.9	6.0	6.7	7.0
Bolivia	5.2	5.0	5.0	9.9	4.8	4.7	2.2	1.8	1.1	...	...	...
Paraguay	4.3	−1.5	11.0	6.6	5.0	5.0	−1.0	−1.1	−0.4	5.6	5.8	5.4
Central America[6]	**4.7**	**4.3**	**4.1**	**5.6**	**5.0**	**4.9**	**−6.9**	**−7.2**	**−6.9**	...	...	...
Caribbean[7]	**2.7**	**2.8**	**3.5**	**7.2**	**5.5**	**5.3**	**−6.3**	**−5.9**	**−5.8**	...	...	...
Memorandum												
Latin America and the Caribbean[8]	4.5	3.2	3.9	6.6	6.0	5.9	−1.3	−1.7	−1.9	...	...	...
Eastern Caribbean Currency Union[9]	−1.1	0.7	1.3	3.5	3.3	2.6	−20.3	−20.5	−19.8	...	...	...

[1]Movements in consumer prices are shown as annual averages. December–December changes can be found in Tables A6 and A7 in the Statistical Appendix.

[2]Percent of GDP.

[3]Percent. National definitions of unemployment may differ.

[4]Also includes Guyana and Suriname.

[5]Figures are based on Argentina's official GDP and consumer price index (CPI-GBA) data. The IMF has called on Argentina to adopt remedial measures to address the quality of the official GDP and CPI-GBA data. The IMF staff is also using alternative measures of GDP growth and inflation for macroeconomic surveillance, including data produced by private analysts, which have shown significantly lower real GDP growth than the official data since 2008, and data produced by provincial statistical offices and private analysts, which have shown considerably higher inflation figures than the official data since 2007.

[6]Central America comprises Belize, Costa Rica, El Salvador, Guatemala, Honduras, Nicaragua, and Panama.

[7]The Caribbean comprises Antigua and Barbuda, The Bahamas, Barbados, Dominica, Dominican Republic, Grenada, Haiti, Jamaica, St. Kitts and Nevis, St. Lucia, St. Vincent and the Grenadines, and Trinidad and Tobago.

[8]Latin America and the Caribbean comprises Mexico and economies from the Caribbean, Central America, and South America.

[9]Eastern Caribbean Currency Union comprises Antigua and Barbuda, Dominica, Grenada, St. Kitts and Nevis, St. Lucia, and St. Vincent and the Grenadines as well as Anguilla and Montserrat, which are not IMF members.

More generally, the move to countercyclical macroeconomic policies has been an important factor underpinning greater resilience in emerging market economies (see Chapter 4). With output gaps close to zero or still positive in many economies in the region, a countercyclical policy stance would indicate that fiscal policy needs to remain tight. Many economies in the region should also include structural reforms aimed at boosting medium-term growth. In Brazil, for example, infrastructure bottlenecks are a constraint on growth. Recent steps to grant private concessions to develop critical road and railway

infrastructure are a welcome step forward, but increased public investment is also needed. Greater resolve is required to reduce debt overhang in the Caribbean while addressing weak competitiveness.

Commonwealth of Independent States: Growth Is Still Robust

Growth in the Commonwealth of Independent States (CIS) is expected to moderate slightly in line with the projected small decline in commodity prices and a weaker external environment. The region remains vulnerable to stress from advanced economies, given the CIS's deeper economic and financial linkages with the euro area. The region should take advantage of the still-favorable current economic conditions to rebuild policy space.

Growth remained robust in the CIS through the beginning of 2012, supported by high prices for key commodities, good harvests in 2011, and strong remittance flows. However, financial conditions in the three largest CIS economies (Kazakhstan, Russia, Ukraine) have been significantly affected by increased financial stress in the euro area periphery and higher global risk aversion: sovereign spreads have widened; stock prices have fallen; and capital outflows have risen. Investment growth has weakened, but expansionary fiscal policies and strong credit growth in Russia and other energy exporters have dampened the overall growth impact.

Regional growth is expected to average 4 percent during 2012–13 compared with close to 5 percent in 2011, in response to a weaker external environment

and terms-of-trade losses from the slight decline in commodity prices (Table 2.5; Figures 2.12 and 2.13).

- Russia's growth is projected at about 3¾ percent during 2012–13, led by domestic demand, which is supported by an expansionary fiscal stance and a rebound in credit growth. Growth is projected to moderate in the region's other energy-exporting economies, mainly owing to weaker growth in the energy sector, although strong public spending should help sustain activity in other sectors.

- The global growth slowdown is projected to have a larger impact on some of the region's energy-importing economies. Growth in Ukraine will slow to 3 percent in 2012 compared with more than 5 percent in 2011, driven by weaker export and domestic demand growth. In Belarus, lower domestic demand after the 2011 currency crisis will weigh on growth. In the Kyrgyz Republic and Tajikistan, activity is supported by strong remittances and import demand from Russia

Table 2.5. Commonwealth of Independent States: Real GDP, Consumer Prices, Current Account Balance, and Unemployment

(Annual percent change unless noted otherwise)

	Real GDP			Consumer Prices[1]			Current Account Balance[2]			Unemployment[3]		
		Projections			Projections			Projections			Projections	
	2011	2012	2013	2011	2012	2013	2011	2012	2013	2011	2012	2013
Commonwealth of Independent States (CIS)[4]	**4.9**	**4.0**	**4.1**	**10.1**	**6.8**	**7.7**	**4.6**	**4.2**	**2.9**	...	...	...
Net Energy Exporters	**4.7**	**4.0**	**4.1**	**8.5**	**5.3**	**6.7**	**6.1**	**5.6**	**4.2**	...	...	...
Russia	4.3	3.7	3.8	8.4	5.1	6.6	5.3	5.2	3.8	6.5	6.0	6.0
Kazakhstan	7.5	5.5	5.7	8.3	5.0	6.6	7.6	6.2	4.5	5.4	5.4	5.3
Uzbekistan	8.3	7.4	6.5	12.8	12.9	10.7	5.8	4.7	3.3	0.2	0.2	0.2
Azerbaijan	0.1	3.9	2.7	7.9	3.0	6.0	26.5	20.4	16.1	6.0	6.0	6.0
Turkmenistan	14.7	8.0	7.7	5.3	4.3	6.0	2.0	−1.5	−1.6	...	...	...
Net Energy Importers	**5.7**	**3.8**	**4.2**	**18.2**	**14.7**	**12.7**	**−7.9**	**−6.8**	**−6.9**	...	...	...
Ukraine	5.2	3.0	3.5	8.0	2.0	7.4	−5.5	−5.6	−6.6	7.9	7.8	7.7
Belarus	5.3	4.3	3.4	53.2	60.2	30.6	−10.5	−3.6	−5.8	0.6	0.6	0.6
Georgia	7.0	6.5	5.5	8.5	0.2	5.5	−11.8	−12.6	−11.2	15.1	14.2	13.8
Armenia	4.6	3.9	4.0	7.7	2.8	4.2	−10.9	−9.8	−9.3	19.0	19.0	18.5
Tajikistan	7.4	6.8	6.0	12.4	6.0	8.1	0.6	−0.4	−1.5	...	...	...
Mongolia	17.5	12.7	15.7	7.7	14.1	11.7	−31.8	−31.4	−10.1	7.7	6.8	6.1
Kyrgyz Republic	5.7	1.0	8.5	16.6	2.9	9.4	−6.3	−12.8	−6.2	7.9	7.7	7.6
Moldova	6.4	3.0	5.0	7.6	5.1	5.0	−11.5	−11.4	−10.7	6.7	5.8	6.4
Memorandum												
Low-Income CIS Countries[5]	7.3	6.1	6.1	11.6	8.2	8.6	−1.5	−2.3	−2.3	...	...	...
Net Energy Exporters Excluding Russia	6.8	5.8	5.5	8.9	6.3	7.3	10.6	8.1	6.0	...	...	...

[1]Movements in consumer prices are shown as annual averages. December–December changes can be found in Table A7 in the Statistical Appendix.

[2]Percent of GDP.

[3]Percent. National definitions of unemployment may differ.

[4]Georgia and Mongolia, which are not members of the Commonwealth of Independent States, are included in this group for reasons of geography and similarities in economic structure.

[5]Low-income CIS economies comprise Armenia, Georgia, Kyrgyz Republic, Moldova, Tajikistan, and Uzbekistan.

Figure 2.12. Commonwealth of Independent States: Revisions to 2013 GDP Growth Forecasts
(Change in percentage points from April 2012 WEO projections)

Greater than −1.0
Between −1.0 and −0.5
Between −0.5 and 0.0
Between 0.0 and 0.5
Between 0.5 and 1.0
Greater than or equal to 1.0
Insufficient data
Covered in a different map

Source: IMF staff estimates.
Note: Includes Georgia and Mongolia.

(deferred gold production increases planned for 2012 will temporarily lower growth in the Kyrgyz Republic).

Inflation is projected to moderate during 2012–13 compared with 2011, reflecting favorable harvests in many economies of the region, monetary policy tightening in some, and a slight retreat in commodity prices. The recent surge in global food prices, however, could push prices up temporarily, and demand pressures remain strong in energy exporters.

As in other regions, the balance of risks to the near-term outlook is tilted to the downside. In view of the region's strong dependence on commodity exports, most major risks to global growth discussed in Chapter 1 would be of concern to the CIS region because they would involve large commodity price

declines. For the energy importers in the region, direct trade spillovers from a further escalation of the euro area crisis would also be sizable given that Europe is the most important trading partner outside the region.

If downside risks materialize, external balances would deteriorate, which would tend to exacerbate capital outflows and put pressure on currencies, especially in energy importers with large external financing needs (Ukraine). More flexible exchange rates and a reduction in balance sheet mismatches (Kazakhstan, Russia) would help cushion the growth impact compared with the 2009 downturn. The impact on Russia, should any of the downside risks materialize, would be critical for the region as a whole, given the tight linkages between Russia and other CIS economies via trade, foreign direct investment (FDI), and remittances.

Against this backdrop, the major CIS economies should take advantage of the current, still-robust economic conditions to rebuild fiscal policy buffers. In Russia, the non-oil fiscal deficit is more than three times larger than it was before the Great Recession. In energy importers, the fiscal adjustment should aim to put public debt on a downward trajectory (Kyrgyz Republic, Tajikistan), which would also lower external vulnerabilities by reducing large current account deficits (Armenia, Georgia).

Consolidation efforts should be accompanied by structural reforms, a strengthening of fiscal frameworks, and improvements in the quality and efficiency of public spending.

In some economies, further monetary policy tightening is needed to rein in inflation expectations (Belarus, Mongolia, Uzbekistan). If downside risks materialize, however, monetary and fiscal policies may need to be eased, maintaining a balance between immediate stabilization needs and medium-term objectives.

Global risks also call for speeding up financial system repair and improving the region's resilience to negative external spillovers of financial stress (see the Spillover Feature). Although progress has been made to strengthen the banking system, bank balance sheets are still impaired in a number of economies faced with a significant share of nonperforming loans (Ukraine) and poor capital adequacy (Kazakhstan, Kyrgyz Republic, Tajikistan).

Middle East and North Africa: A Two-Speed Region

Differences in the economic performance of oil exporters and oil importers have widened. Higher government spending in most oil exporters has supported robust growth. Elsewhere, uncertainties from political and economic change after the Arab Spring, slowing growth in major trading partners, and, in some cases, internal conflict have led to a marked weakening in activity. For oil importers, the policy priority will be preserving or rebuilding macroeconomic stability while defining and implementing a reform agenda to accelerate growth. For

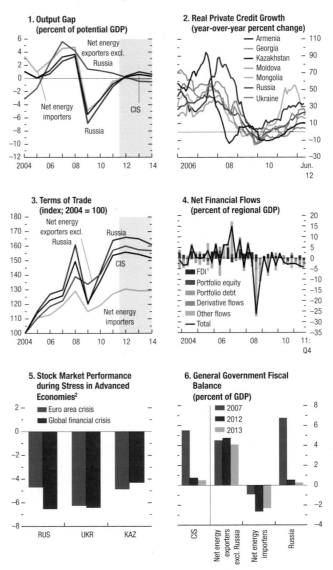

Figure 2.13. Commonwealth of Independent States: Vulnerable to Negative Spillovers

Growth in the CIS has remained robust, supported by high prices for key commodities and good harvests in 2011, although indicators suggest some moderation of activity in recent months. Financial conditions in the three largest CIS economies (Kazakhstan, Russia, Ukraine) have deteriorated with increased financial stress in the euro area periphery and higher global risk aversion. Given downside risks, the priority is to strengthen policies by improving fiscal balances, accelerating financial system reform, and tightening the monetary stance where inflation risks are high.

Sources: Haver Analytics; IMF, Balance of Payments Statistics database; IMF, International Financial Statistics database; Thomson Reuters Datastream; and IMF staff estimates.
Note: Net energy exporters: Azerbaijan, Kazakhstan (KAZ), Russia (RUS), Turkmenistan, Uzbekistan. Net energy importers: Armenia, Belarus, Georgia, Kyrgyz Republic, Moldova, Mongolia, Tajikistan, Ukraine (UKR).
[1]FDI = foreign direct investment.
[2]Percent change in average level of index five days after and five days before stress in advanced economies. The periods for euro area crisis and global financial crisis are respectively: January 2010–June 2012 and January 2007–December 2009. See the Spillover Feature for details.

Table 2.6. Selected Middle East and North African Economies: Real GDP, Consumer Prices, Current Account Balance, and Unemployment
(Annual percent change unless noted otherwise)

	Real GDP			Consumer Prices[1]			Current Account Balance[2]			Unemployment[3]		
		Projections			Projections			Projections			Projections	
	2011	2012	2013	2011	2012	2013	2011	2012	2013	2011	2012	2013
Middle East and North Africa	**3.3**	**5.3**	**3.6**	**9.7**	**10.4**	**9.1**	**14.2**	**12.2**	**10.6**	...	...	...
Oil Exporters[4]	**3.9**	**6.6**	**3.8**	**10.1**	**11.1**	**9.4**	**18.7**	**16.4**	**14.2**	...	...	...
Iran	2.0	−0.9	0.8	21.5	25.2	21.8	12.5	3.4	1.3	12.3	14.1	15.6
Saudi Arabia	7.1	6.0	4.2	5.0	4.9	4.6	26.5	26.1	22.7	...	...	...
Algeria	2.4	2.6	3.4	4.5	8.4	5.0	10.0	6.2	6.1	10.0	9.7	9.3
United Arab Emirates	5.2	4.0	2.6	0.9	0.7	1.6	9.7	9.3	10.1	...	...	...
Qatar	14.1	6.3	4.9	1.9	2.0	3.0	30.2	29.6	26.8	...	...	...
Kuwait	8.2	6.3	1.9	4.7	4.3	4.1	44.0	44.1	39.2	2.1	2.1	2.1
Iraq	8.9	10.2	14.7	5.6	6.0	5.5	8.3	0.3	6.1	...	...	...
Oil Importers[5]	**1.4**	**1.2**	**3.3**	**8.5**	**8.3**	**8.3**	**−5.2**	**−6.9**	**−5.8**	...	...	...
Egypt	1.8	2.0	3.0	11.1	8.6	10.7	−2.6	−3.4	−3.3	12.1	12.7	13.5
Morocco	4.9	2.9	5.5	0.9	2.2	2.5	−8.0	−7.9	−5.4	8.9	8.8	8.7
Tunisia	−1.8	2.7	3.3	3.5	5.0	4.0	−7.3	−7.9	−7.7	18.9	17.0	16.0
Sudan[6]	−4.5	−11.2	0.0	18.3	28.6	17.0	−0.5	−7.8	−6.6	12.0	10.8	9.6
Lebanon	1.5	2.0	2.5	5.0	6.5	5.7	−14.0	−16.2	−15.6	...	...	...
Jordan	2.6	3.0	3.5	4.4	4.5	3.9	−12.0	−14.1	−9.9	12.9	12.9	12.9
Memorandum												
Israel	4.6	2.9	3.2	3.4	1.7	2.1	0.8	−2.1	−1.3	7.1	7.0	7.0
Maghreb[7]	−1.9	19.0	6.0	4.0	6.4	3.6	2.2	4.4	2.9	...	...	...
Mashreq[8]	1.8	2.0	3.0	10.0	8.2	9.8	−4.9	−6.0	−5.4	...	...	...

[1]Movements in consumer prices are shown as annual averages. December–December changes can be found in Tables A6 and A7 in the Statistical Appendix.
[2]Percent of GDP.
[3]Percent. National definitions of unemployment may differ.
[4]Also includes Bahrain, Libya, Oman, and Yemen.
[5]Also includes Djibouti, Mauritania, and Syria. Excludes Syria for 2011 onward.
[6]Data for 2011 exclude South Sudan after July 9. Data for 2012 and onward pertain to the current Sudan.
[7]The Maghreb comprises Algeria, Libya, Mauritania, Morocco, and Tunisia.
[8]The Mashreq comprises Egypt, Jordan, Lebanon, and Syria. Excludes Syria for 2011 onward.

oil exporters, the priority is to take advantage of current high oil prices to diversify their economies.

Growth in the Middle East and North Africa (MENA) region was relatively subdued at 3¼ percent in 2011, but is projected to strengthen to 5¼ percent in 2012 on account of oil exporters (Table 2.6).[9] Growth in oil exporters is expected to accelerate from about 4 percent in 2011 to 6½ percent in 2012, largely as a result of a strong rebound of activity in Libya since late 2011. In most other oil exporters, non-oil GDP growth is expected to remain robust in 2012, supported by ratcheted-up

[9]Syria has been excluded from regional aggregates, including projections, because of the ongoing civil war. Regional aggregates do include Libya, where activity has been strongly affected by its civil war, with a collapse in output in 2011 and a sharp rebound in 2012.

government spending as oil prices remain at historically high levels, while oil sector growth is forecast to moderate somewhat after a strong increase in 2011 (Figure 2.14). The boost from Libya will moderate in 2013, when growth in the oil exporters of the region is projected to be 3¾ percent.

In contrast, growth in oil importers has been about 1¼ percent during 2011–12, reflecting the effects of social unrest and political uncertainty, weak external demand, and high oil prices. Uncertainty and unrest have led to a pullback from the region, evidenced most dramatically in steep declines in tourism and FDI (Figure 2.15). At the same time, the contraction of activity in advanced Europe—a major trading partner for most economies in the group—has been a drag on growth. Looking forward, uncertainty is expected to decrease as political transitions stabilize, while external demand

Figure 2.14. Middle East and North Africa: Revisions to 2013 GDP Growth Forecasts
(Change in percentage points from April 2012 WEO projections)

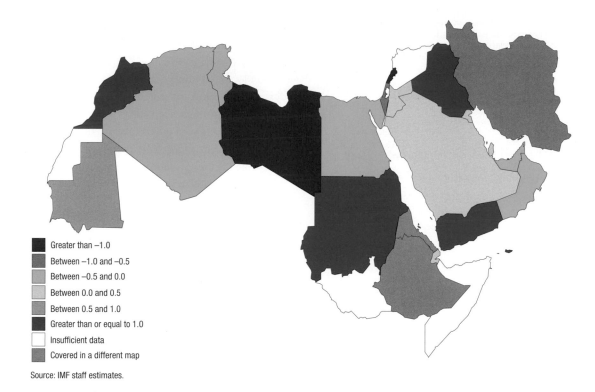

Greater than −1.0
Between −1.0 and −0.5
Between −0.5 and 0.0
Between 0.0 and 0.5
Between 0.5 and 1.0
Greater than or equal to 1.0
Insufficient data
Covered in a different map

Source: IMF staff estimates.

picks up, and growth in oil importers is projected to recover to 3¼ percent in 2013.

Risks to the near-term outlook for oil exporters revolve primarily around oil prices and global growth, given that all major risks to global growth discussed in Chapter 1 involve lower oil prices. For oil exporters, government expenditures have risen to such a degree that substantial declines in the price of oil could undermine fiscal positions. Despite significant accrued financial buffers, such declines could put at risk ongoing infrastructure investment and growth. On the upside, Iran-related and other geopolitical risks could lead to higher oil prices.

Oil importers face both external and internal risks. On the external side, they are vulnerable to trade spillovers if downside risks to growth in major economies materialize.[10] Another concern is risks to internal and external balances from upside risks

to food and fuel prices (see the Special Feature in Chapter 1). Because of extensive food and fuel subsidies in most economies, the immediate concern with spikes in commodity prices is not the effect on inflation and disposable income, but rather the strain on budgets and foreign exchange reserves. More broadly, meeting social demands when growth has slowed and political uncertainty has increased has resulted in higher budget deficits and declines in foreign exchange reserves in non-oil importers.

A general policy priority in the MENA region is to secure economic and social stability through more inclusive medium-term growth. Achieving this goal will require institutional and regulatory reform to stimulate private sector activity and ensure greater and more equal access to economic opportunities and measures to address chronically high unemployment, particularly among the young.

Maintaining macroeconomic stability while supporting strong, inclusive medium-term growth will be an important policy challenge. Increased spending on food and fuel subsidies, along with pressure to raise civil ser-

[10] The November 2012 *Regional Economic Outlook: Middle East and Central Asia* provides a detailed analysis of spillovers from the economies of the Gulf Cooperation Council to other MENA economies.

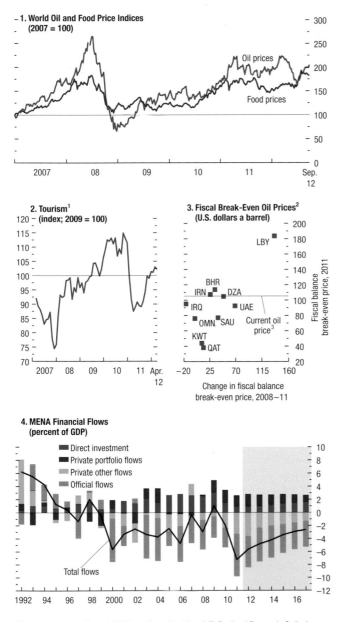

Figure 2.15. Middle East and North Africa: An Uneven Recovery

Continued high oil prices, increased oil production, and increased government spending have supported robust activity in oil exporters. Internal conflicts and their aftermath remain a source of uncertainty, and tourism has not yet recovered. The increases in government expenditure in oil exporters in the region have raised the break-even oil price (the price at which oil revenue covers the non-oil budget deficit), implying that significant oil price declines could undermine fiscal positions.

Sources: Bloomberg Financial Markets; Haver Analytics; IMF, *Regional Economic Outlook: Middle East and Central Asia*, November 2012; and IMF staff estimates.
[1]Index of tourism is calculated based on the simple average of tourism receipts of Egypt, Jordan, Lebanon, Morocco, and Tunisia. Morocco's figures are based on nonresident entries instead of tourist arrivals because of a lack of data.
[2]DZA = Algeria; BHR = Bahrain; IRN = Iran; IRQ = Iraq; KWT = Kuwait, LBY = Libya; OMN = Oman; QAT = Qatar; SAU = Saudi Arabia; UAE = United Arab Emirates.
[3]Current oil price as of August 2012.

vice wages and pensions, risks straining public finances. In oil exporters, it will be critical to contain increases in spending on entitlements that are hard to reverse. Instead, the focus should be on productivity-enhancing spending on human capital and infrastructure investment, which could also support diversification of their economies. In oil importers, policy buffers have been diminished, creating pressures for fiscal consolidation. Structural fiscal reforms aimed at reorienting government spending toward poverty reduction and the promotion of productive investment will be crucial to improving the budget outlook. Improved targeting of subsidies, especially through fuel subsidy reforms, will be an important step in this respect.

Sub-Saharan Africa: A Continued Favorable Outlook

Sub-Saharan Africa is expected to continue growing strongly in the near term, with regional differences in prospects reflecting in part economies' varying exposure to external shocks (Figure 2.16). As elsewhere, external risks remain elevated. Policymakers in the region should use the window provided by strong growth to rebuild budgetary space and normalize monetary conditions to be better prepared for downside risks.

Economic activity in sub-Saharan Africa (SSA) has expanded by more than 5 percent in each of the past three years—continuing a decade-long run of strong performance that was only briefly interrupted by the global downturn in 2009 (Figure 2.17, panels 1 and 2). Most SSA economies are participating in this solid expansion, with the notable exception of South Africa, which has been hampered by its strong linkages with Europe, as well as some countries in western Africa affected by drought and civil conflict. More recently, some food importers in the region have also been hit by the sharp increase in global food prices for a few major crops—leading to higher headline inflation and widening trade imbalances—although so far with less severe effects than during the 2007–08 food price shocks (see Chapter 1, Box 1.5).

The region's recent growth has occurred against a backdrop of difficult external conditions, including the escalation of the euro area crisis. But apart from South Africa, financial spillovers from Europe to the region have been modest (Figure 2.17, panel 3).

Figure 2.16. Sub-Saharan Africa: Revisions to 2013 GDP Growth Forecasts
(Change in percentage points from April 2012 WEO projections)

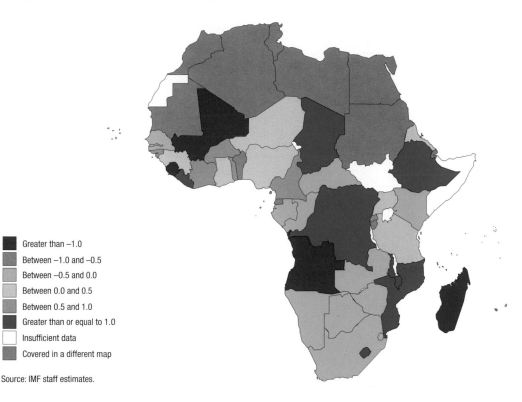

Greater than –1.0
Between –1.0 and –0.5
Between –0.5 and 0.0
Between 0.0 and 0.5
Between 0.5 and 1.0
Greater than or equal to 1.0
Insufficient data
Covered in a different map

Source: IMF staff estimates.

Export diversification has reduced exposure to weak demand from advanced economies, and high commodity prices have supported the region's commodity exporters and boosted investment in resource extraction. However, as documented in Chapter 4, improved policy frameworks and judicious use of policy space in response to adverse shocks have been important elements in these economies' improved performance during the past decade.

In the baseline scenario, under which strains in the euro area remain contained and the global economy expands by 3¼ to 3½ percent this year and next, growth in SSA will continue above 5 percent during 2012–13 (Table 2.7).

- Growth in the oil-exporting economies is projected to remain high, near 6 percent in 2012; increased oil production in Angola will expand its GDP by close to 6¾ percent this year. In Nigeria, non-oil GDP growth will moderate with the softer external environment and tighter macroeconomic policies, but a slight rebound in oil output will keep overall GDP growth at 7 percent.

- Among the middle-income countries, growth in South Africa is projected to be 2½ percent in 2012—below most estimates of potential growth—largely because of strong linkages with Europe. Growth is expected to rebound to 3 percent next year under the relatively favorable external conditions of the WEO baseline. Output growth in Cameroon is expected to strengthen this year and next, with the non-oil sector being supported by major public investment projects and measures to boost agricultural productivity.

- The region's low-income economies face varying outlooks. In Ethiopia, growth is projected to decelerate moderately this year and next, reflecting weaker external demand and an increasingly constrained environment for private sector activity. In Kenya, tight monetary conditions have slowed consumption, but construction activity and corporate investment remain buoyant and will support an acceleration of growth to 5 percent this year and 5½ percent in 2013.

Figure 2.17. Sub-Saharan Africa: A Strong Expansion

Economic activity in sub-Saharan Africa has been expanding by 5 percent or more a year throughout the past decade, except during the global downturn in 2008–09. High commodity prices have supported the region's commodity exporters and boosted investment in resource extraction. Better policy frameworks and judicious use of policy space in responding to adverse shocks have also contributed to this improved performance. But with macroeconomic policies still accommodative in much of the region, rebuilding policy buffers is a priority.

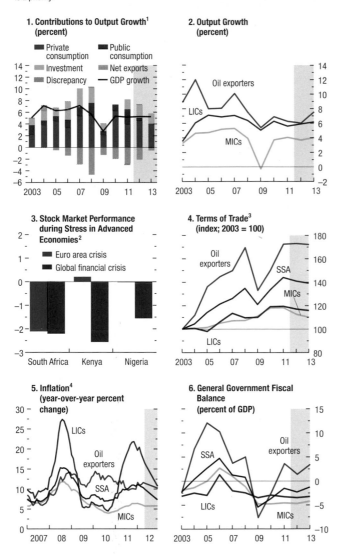

Sources: Bloomberg Financial Markets; Haver Analytics; and IMF staff estimates.
Note: LIC = low-income country (SSA); MIC = middle-income country (SSA); SSA = sub-Saharan Africa.
[1]Liberia, South Sudan, and Zimbabwe are excluded due to data limitations.
[2]Percent change in average level of index five days after and five days before stress in advanced economies. The periods for euro area crisis and global financial crisis are respectively: January 2010–June 2012 and January 2007–December 2009. See the Spillover Feature for details.
[3]Excludes South Sudan due to data limitations.
[4]Due to data limitations, the following are excluded: Chad and Equatorial Guinea from oil exporters; Cameroon and Swaziland from MICs; Burkina Faso, Central African Republic, Comoros, Democratic Republic of the Congo, Eritrea, The Gambia, Guinea, Guinea-Bissau, Liberia, Mozambique, São Tomé and Príncipe, and Zimbabwe from LICs.

Risks to the outlook remain high, primarily because of global uncertainties. If the euro area crisis escalates further and global growth slows further, SSA's prospects will be less favorable. The primary channel for spillovers is trade. South Africa, strongly linked to Europe, would be particularly affected, with possible repercussions for some economies in southern Africa, and softer commodity prices would adversely affect the region's natural resource export-ers.[11] Another key risk relates to the possible further elevation of global food prices, which would under-mine the external and fiscal balances of the food importers in the region. For the medium term, a potential sharp slowdown in China would also affect the region adversely, not only because of the region's deepening trade linkages with China in the past sev-eral years (see Figure 2.SF.7) or through the effect on global commodity prices (see IMF, 2012b), but also because of China's increasingly important contribu-tion to the region's FDI and official financing.[12]

The priority in much of the region is to continue to strengthen policy buffers and prepare contingency plans if downside risks materialize. Macroeconomic policies have remained generally accommodative, although a surge in inflation during 2011 prompted a sharp tightening of monetary policy in several east African economies. In several countries, some fiscal consolida-tion is also under way. If downside risks to the global economy materialize, economies without significant financing constraints should stand ready to ease policies in response. But countries that are in the process of reducing elevated inflation will need to maintain tight monetary policies. The situation is different in South Africa, where four years of macroeconomic stimulus have significantly diminished the policy space avail-able to deal with an adverse shock. This constraint is particularly acute on the fiscal side, where fiscal space will shrink further in a global slowdown; under such a scenario the authorities may need to rely more heavily on countercyclical monetary policy to cushion the economy against adverse spillovers.

[11]See Chapter 2 of the October 2012 *Regional Economic Outlook: Sub-Saharan Africa* for a detailed analysis of spillover channels from the region's two largest economies, South Africa and Nigeria, to the rest of the region.
[12]See Chapter 3 of the October 2011 *Regional Economic Outlook: Sub-Saharan Africa.*

Table 2.7. Selected Sub-Saharan African Economies: Real GDP, Consumer Prices, Current Account Balance, and Unemployment
(Annual percent change unless noted otherwise)

	Real GDP			Consumer Prices[1]			Current Account Balance[2]			Unemployment[3]		
		Projections			Projections			Projections			Projections	
	2011	2012	2013	2011	2012	2013	2011	2012	2013	2011	2012	2013
Sub-Saharan Africa	**5.1**	**5.0**	**5.7**	**9.7**	**9.1**	**7.1**	**−1.7**	**−3.2**	**−3.3**	...	...	...
Oil Exporters[4]	**6.2**	**6.0**	**7.5**	**11.2**	**10.8**	**8.9**	**5.5**	**3.8**	**3.4**	...	...	...
Nigeria	7.4	7.1	6.7	10.8	11.4	9.5	3.6	3.5	3.1	23.9	...	...
Angola	3.9	6.8	5.5	13.5	10.8	8.6	9.6	8.5	6.6	...	...	...
Equatorial Guinea	7.8	5.7	6.1	6.3	5.4	7.0	−6.0	−7.7	−7.7	...	...	...
Gabon	6.6	6.1	2.0	1.3	2.3	2.6	10.6	9.1	4.1	...	...	...
Republic of Congo	3.4	4.9	5.3	1.8	5.1	4.5	0.8	−0.6	−0.4	...	...	...
Middle-Income[5]	**4.1**	**3.7**	**4.0**	**5.4**	**5.7**	**5.5**	**−3.4**	**−5.3**	**−5.3**	...	...	...
South Africa	3.1	2.6	3.0	5.0	5.6	5.2	−3.3	−5.5	−5.8	23.9	24.4	24.7
Ghana	14.4	8.2	7.8	8.7	9.8	10.9	−9.2	−9.1	−7.0	...	...	...
Cameroon	4.2	4.7	5.0	2.9	3.0	3.0	−4.1	−4.1	−3.8	...	...	...
Côte d'Ivoire	−4.7	8.1	7.0	4.9	2.0	2.5	6.7	−3.1	−1.6	...	...	...
Botswana	5.1	3.8	4.1	8.5	7.5	6.2	1.6	3.9	3.4	...	...	...
Senegal	2.6	3.7	4.3	3.4	2.3	2.1	−6.4	−8.5	−6.9	...	...	...
Low-Income[6]	**5.6**	**5.9**	**6.1**	**15.1**	**12.5**	**7.6**	**−10.9**	**−11.1**	**−11.2**	...	...	...
Ethiopia	7.5	7.0	6.5	33.1	22.9	10.2	0.6	−6.1	−7.7	...	...	...
Kenya	4.4	5.1	5.6	14.0	10.0	5.8	−10.6	−8.5	−8.6	...	...	...
Tanzania	6.4	6.5	6.8	12.7	15.6	9.8	−13.7	−15.4	−13.4	...	...	...
Uganda	5.1	4.2	5.7	18.7	14.6	6.1	−11.4	−11.0	−11.7	...	...	...
Democratic Republic of the Congo	6.9	7.1	8.2	15.5	10.4	9.5	−11.5	−12.5	−14.3	...	...	...
Mozambique	7.3	7.5	8.4	10.4	3.0	8.6	−12.8	−11.6	−12.4	...	...	...
Memorandum												
Sub-Saharan Africa Excluding												
South Sudan	5.2	5.3	5.3	9.3	8.9	7.0	−2.0	−3.1	−3.5	...	...	...

[1]Movements in consumer prices are shown as annual averages. December–December changes can be found in Table A7 in the Statistical Appendix.

[2]Percent of GDP.

[3]Percent. National definitions of unemployment may differ.

[4]Also includes Chad and South Sudan.

[5]Also includes Cape Verde, Lesotho, Mauritius, Namibia, Seychelles, Swaziland, and Zambia.

[6]Also includes Benin, Burkina Faso, Burundi, Central African Republic, Comoros, Eritrea, The Gambia, Guinea, Guinea-Bissau, Liberia, Madagascar, Malawi, Mali, Niger, Rwanda, São Tomé and Príncipe, Sierra Leone, Togo, and Zimbabwe.

Spillover Feature: The Financial Transmission of Stress in the Global Economy

Four years after the global financial crisis, the world economy is still struggling to achieve sustained expansion amid major downside risks. This Spillover Feature sheds light on a number of concerns relating to the weak recovery: Could a major intensification of the euro area crisis or renewed U.S. financial stress induce contagion effects? Have such spillovers increased over time? Can a sharp economic slowdown in China affect financial conditions elsewhere?

Financial markets react differently to stress depending on the strength of offsetting factors. Capital may flow out of economies under stress to regions in which perceived economic prospects and financial returns are higher. However, if banks in the economies under stress are forced to reduce leverage by unwinding their cross-border exposures, this would cause capital outflows from across the world.[1] Stress could also dampen risk appetite more generally and precipitate a flight to safety out of all risky assets, depressing asset prices and financing conditions more broadly.

We assess the nature of global contagion during episodes of financial stress in the United States and the euro area as well as the contagion of shocks to real activity specific to China. We gauge this contagion by tracking developments in weekly bond and equity flows to advanced and emerging market economy funds and daily equity prices and sovereign yields in the immediate aftermath of these stress episodes. However, the spillovers evident in the analysis should be interpreted as associations rather than drivers of stress because we do not identify the factors underlying the stress nor control for common factors that may be affecting global financial markets concurrently.[2]

The findings confirm that global financial conditions are vulnerable to stress in major economies. Global capital flows and asset prices tend to be weaker in the period after stress compared with the period before. However, the magnitudes of the spillovers are generally smaller now than they were during the global financial crisis. Stress related to sharp economic downswings in China has also become a source of financial contagion, although more so for emerging market and developing economies than for advanced economies. For many emerging market and developing economy regions, stress during the euro area crisis has been transmitted more quickly to equity than to bond flows, whereas in the aftermath of the global financial crisis, both bond and equity flows were similarly affected by stress. The greater persistence of bond flows may be indicative of increased investor confidence about these economies, but could also be the result of a search for yield in a time of low global interest rates.

The consequences of stress vary by region, likely reflecting differences in underlying vulnerabilities and in exposures to the various types of stress. The Commonwealth of Independent States (CIS) and emerging Europe—which have deeper economic and financial ties with the euro area—have experienced somewhat larger swings in financial conditions than others during the euro area crisis. Spillovers for other regions are relatively smaller. Stress emanating from China coincides with sharper declines in financial conditions in Latin America and the Caribbean (LAC), sub-Saharan Africa (SSA) and the Middle East and North Africa (MENA) than elsewhere—possibly because of these regions' ties with China for oil and other commodity exports. These findings resonate with recent studies highlighting the role of spillovers.[3]

The main author of this feature is Rupa Duttagupta with support from Gavin Asdorian, Sinem Kilic Celik, Nadia Lepeshko, and Bennet Voorhees.

[1]The potential global consequences of bank deleveraging in the euro area, as observed in late 2011, were analyzed in the Spillover Feature in Chapter 2 of the April 2012 *World Economic Outlook.*
[2]For instance, IMF (2012b) finds that the spillover consequences of increased volatility in euro area sovereign bond markets depend on the level of global risk repricing.

[3]Fratzscher, Lo Duca, and Straub (2012) analyze the spillover consequences of unconventional monetary policy announcements by the Federal Reserve. Bayoumi and Bui (2011) document the consequences of U.S. fiscal, financial, and monetary policies on asset prices for a number of systemically important economies. IMF (2011a, 2012b) consider other scenarios to analyze the potential global effects of a further intensification of the crisis

Defining Stress

To compare the consequence of stress in recent years with that during the global financial crisis, we distinguish between two sample periods: (1) January 2007 through 2009, which included the U.S. subprime mortgage meltdown and culminated in the global financial crisis; and (2) January 2010 to mid-2012, the period of the euro area crisis.

Financing conditions for sovereigns in the euro area periphery have sharply deteriorated only with the escalation of their debt crises.[4] The volatility in their financing conditions, as measured by the range of daily 10-year sovereign spread changes relative to German bunds, has also increased (Figure 2.SF.1, panels 1 and 3). Conversely, U.S. financial market uncertainty, as measured by the Chicago Board Options Exchange Market Volatility Index (VIX), is relatively lower now (Figure 2.SF.1, panels 2 and 4). However, the VIX has experienced occasional volatility in recent years: in May 2010, possibly related to contagion from the outbreak of the Greek crisis, and in late 2011 during the acrimonious U.S. debt-ceiling debate and the escalation of sovereign funding pressure in Italy.

How were episodes of financial stress in the advanced economies chosen? Drawing on Romer (2012), episodes of high stress in a euro area periphery economy are defined as days in which the change in the daily 10-year sovereign spread was in the 95th percentile of its distribution for the given sample period (see Figure 2.SF.1). The euro area periphery as a whole is considered to have been under stress when all periphery economies were under stress as defined by the above metric. For the United States, stress is defined as days in which the VIX level is higher than 30 and the daily VIX increase is in the 95th percentile of the distribution.[5] We filter out

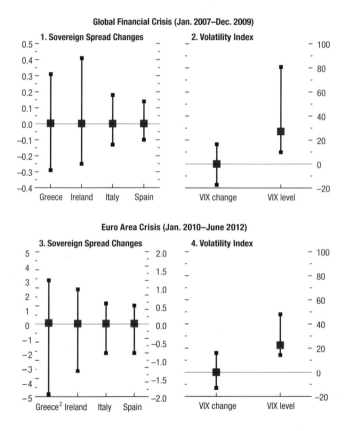

Figure 2.SF.1. Financing Conditions for Euro Area Periphery Economies and the United States, 2007–12
(Percentage points for daily spread changes and points for VIX)[1]

Financing conditions faced by the euro area periphery economies sharply deteriorated during the euro area crisis. In contrast, U.S. financial market stress is somewhat lower now than during the global financial crisis.

Global Financial Crisis (Jan. 2007–Dec. 2009)

1. Sovereign Spread Changes

2. Volatility Index

Euro Area Crisis (Jan. 2010–June 2012)

3. Sovereign Spread Changes

4. Volatility Index

Sources: Bloomberg Financial Markets; and IMF staff calculations.
[1]VIX: Chicago Board Options Exchange Market Volatility Index.
[2]Greek sovereign spread changes are on the left scale.

---

in the euro area. See also Chapter 4 of the October 2009 *World Economic Outlook.*

[4]The euro area periphery economies considered here comprise Greece, Ireland, Italy, and Spain.

[5]Although the U.S. 10-year sovereign yield could serve as an alternative proxy for tracking U.S. stress, this yield has declined in periods of stress in part because of the dollar's status as a safe haven currency and in part because of the Federal Reserve's unconventional measures to lower rates (see IMF, 2012b, for the effects of unconventional Federal Reserve measures on U.S. sovereign yields). Therefore, the VIX is a better gauge of U.S. financial stress.

Figure 2.SF.2. Changes in Stress Indicators, 2007–12
(percentage points for daily sovereign spread and points for VIX)[1]

Financial stress is proxied by sharp increases in sovereign spreads for the euro area periphery economies and in the VIX for the United States.

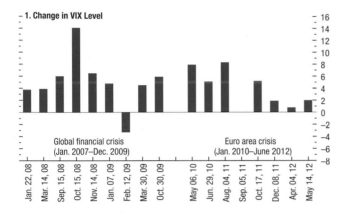

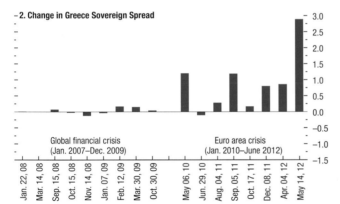

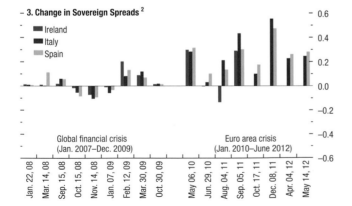

Sources: Bloomberg Financial Markets; and IMF staff calculations.
[1]VIX: Chicago Board Options Exchange Market Volatility Index.
[2]Data on Irish 10-year bond yields were discontinued after October 11, 2011. Beyond this date, stress in the euro area reflects data on Greece, Italy, and Spain.

consecutive days of stress in a region by restricting each stress episode to those that occur at least one month after the previous episode. The final number of stress episodes is determined by the days during which the euro area periphery, the United States, or both were under stress.

Focusing on the euro area crisis period, we identify episodes of real activity-related stress from China as periods during which China's manufacturing activity is weaker than can be explained by its external trade links. Specifically, we first single out residuals from a 12-month rolling regression of the Chinese manufacturing purchasing managers' index (PMI) on U.S. and euro area PMIs only when they are in the bottom quartile of the distribution. Among these, episodes since 2011 that do not coincide with the episodes of advanced economy stress are considered China-induced stress events.[6]

The above criteria identify 15 stress episodes for the advanced economies and 2 for China (Figure 2.SF.2, Table 2.SF.1). As expected, during the global financial crisis, stress was experienced mainly in the United States, whereas during 2010 through mid-2012, stress was experienced by both the United States and the euro area periphery, although increasingly by only the latter since late 2011.

Transmission of Stress

Spillovers through Cross-Border Capital Flows

We use data on portfolio capital flows compiled by Emerging Portfolio Fund Research (EPFR) to track capital flow movements at a weekly frequency. These data suggest a drying up of capital flows from most regions at the outbreak of the global financial crisis (Figure 2.SF.3, panels 1 and 2).[7] However,

[6]Manufacturing PMIs are released on the first working day of the month, so the specific China-induced stress date is the first working day of the month identified as a stress episode. Even so, given the lower frequency for the PMI data, the case for a correctly identified shock emanating from China is weaker than for the advanced economies, whose stress dates were identified using daily data. Thus, the results relating to China-specific stress should be treated with caution.

[7]These data are not available at daily frequency for most regions. Although EPFR funds do not cover all portfolio flows, recent studies find a close match between EPFR and balance of payments gross portfolio flows (Fratzscher, 2011; Miao and Pant, 2012).

SPILLOVER FEATURE

Table 2.SF.1. Behavior of Stress Indicators, 2007–12

| | Chicago Board Options Exchange Market Volatility Index (VIX) | | Daily Changes in 10-year Sovereign Spreads | | | | | | | | | |
| | | | Greece | | Ireland | | Italy | | Spain | | |
Stress Dates	VIX Level	Change in VIX Level	Spread Level[1]	Change in Spread[2]	Spread Level[1]	Change in Spread[2]	Spread Level[1]	Change in Spread[2]	Spread Level[1]	Change in Spread[2]	Stress Experienced by
Stress during the Global Financial Crisis (January 2007—December 2009)											
Jan. 22, 2008	31.01	3.83	0.37	0.01	0.22	0.01	0.38	0.01	0.19	0.01	United States
Mar. 14, 2008	31.16	3.87	0.68	−0.00	0.41	0.01	0.63	0.01	0.41	0.11	United States
Sep. 15, 2008	31.70	6.04	0.80	0.07	0.42	0.02	0.72	0.06	0.47	0.06	United States
Oct. 15, 2008	69.25	14.12	0.84	−0.03	0.60	−0.02	0.69	−0.05	0.47	−0.09	United States
Nov. 14, 2008	66.31	6.48	1.39	−0.13	0.78	−0.07	0.95	−0.10	0.46	−0.10	United States
Jan. 07, 2009	43.39	4.83	2.11	−0.04	1.38	−0.01	1.25	−0.06	0.80	−0.04	United States
Feb. 12, 2009	41.25	−3.28	2.64	0.17	2.23	0.20	1.41	0.08	1.17	0.13	Euro area periphery
Mar. 30, 2009	45.54	4.50	2.72	0.15	2.38	0.09	1.40	0.12	1.03	0.07	Both
Oct. 30, 2009	30.69	5.93	1.42	0.04	1.47	0.02	0.84	0.02	0.56	0.01	United States
Stress during the Euro Area Crisis (January 2010—June 2012)[3]											
May 06, 2010	32.80	7.89	8.52	1.21	3.00	0.30	1.49	0.28	1.63	0.31	Both
Jun. 29, 2010	34.13	5.13	7.89	−0.11	2.95	−0.00	1.57	0.03	2.05	0.10	United States
Aug. 4, 2011	31.66	8.28	12.87	0.28	8.10	−0.13	3.90	0.21	3.98	0.13	United States
Sep. 5, 2011	33.92	0.00	17.47	1.19	6.91	0.29	3.71	0.43	3.41	0.30	Both
Oct. 17, 2011	33.39	5.15	21.90	0.17	. . .	. . .	3.70	0.10	3.22	0.17	United States
Dec. 8, 2011	30.59	1.92	32.70	0.80	. . .	. . .	4.44	0.55	3.80	0.47	Euro area periphery
Apr. 4, 2012	16.44	0.78	20.34	0.86	. . .	. . .	3.58	0.23	3.90	0.26	Euro area periphery
May 14, 2012	21.87	1.98	26.13	2.89	. . .	. . .	4.24	0.25	4.77	0.28	Euro area periphery

China, Real Activity Stress	PMI[4]	Change from Previous Month	Unexplained PMI[5]
Feb. 1, 2011	51.7	−2.8	−2.0
Jun. 1, 2011	52.5	−1.5	−2.4

Source: IMF staff calculations. See Table 2.SF.2 for data sources.

[1]Daily spread with 10-year bunds.

[2]Daily spread change.

[3]Data on Irish 10-year bond yields were discontinued after October 11, 2011. (Stress in the euro area reflects data on Greece, Italy, and Spain only).

[4]Purchasing Managers' Index.

[5]The bottom quartile residuals from a 12-month rolling regression of China's manufacturing purchasing managers' index (PMI) on the U.S. and euro area manufacturing PMIs. (The residuals for months that coincided with months of advanced economy stress are filtered out.)

capital flow volatility increased even before the crisis—as early as January 2007 for developing Asia and late 2007 for LAC economies. Flows picked up for most regions from the second half of 2009, although volatility has increased again since early 2011. Since late 2009, there has also been a change in the composition of portfolio flows toward bond flows for both advanced and emerging market and developing economies (Figure 2.SF.3, panel 3). The rise in bond flows for the latter marks a shift from the steady decline in the share of debt-creating inflows in the run-up to the global financial crisis.[8]

[8]See Chapter 4 of the April 2011 *World Economic Outlook*.

Event studies based on the identified stress episodes confirm that stress in major economies tends to be associated with lower global capital flows. The exercise compares the level of capital flows to alternative regions in the week of and the weeks before and after stress, and then averages across all stress episodes within each sample period. Lower flows in the weeks of and after stress relative to the week before suggest that foreign investors' appetite for cross-border investment is lower during stress (Figure 2.SF.4). The poststress decline in flows during the euro area crisis is generally not as sharp as that observed during the global financial crisis, although there is considerable regional heterogeneity:

Figure 2.SF.3. Global Weekly Capital Flows
(Billions of U.S. dollars)[1]

Following a sharp decline during the global financial crisis, capital flows have steadily risen in most regions. Emerging market and developing economies have seen a buildup in both bond and equity flows, whereas equity flows have largely been negative in advanced economies.

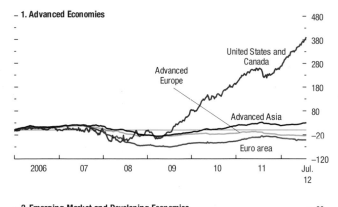

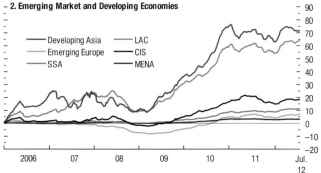

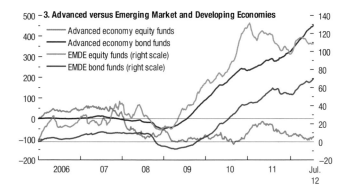

Sources: Emerging Portfolio Fund Research; and IMF staff calculations.
Note: LAC = Latin America and the Caribbean; CIS = Commonwealth of Independent States; SSA = sub-Saharan Africa; MENA = Middle East and North Africa; EMDE = emerging market and developing economy. See Table 2.SF.2 for the country composition of each group.
[1] Equity and bond fund flows, cumulated from January 2006.

- Advanced economies tend to experience greater declines in capital flows when their own economies are under stress compared with periods of China-specific stress (Figure 2.SF.4, panels 1–4). With the exception of advanced Asia, flows to advanced economies do not fall immediately after China-related stress and, in fact, increase for some.

- Although capital flows to emerging market and developing economies also dry up after stress, the scale varies by region (Figure 2.SF.4, panels 5–10). For the CIS, poststress capital outflows during the euro area crisis are larger than in other emerging market and developing economies and almost as sharp as outflows during the global financial crisis, whereas for emerging Europe flows continue to be lower even in the week after stress. This may reflect in part these regions' ties with the euro area and the effects of increased deleveraging by euro area banks, many of which have a strong presence in the CIS and emerging Europe.

- The evidence of contagion from China is stronger for emerging market and developing economies, particularly in the LAC, MENA, and SSA regions, likely reflecting commodity trade linkages, but also for emerging Europe.[9]

Stress has affected bond and equity flows differently over time, suggesting that investors are increasingly distinguishing between asset classes rather than between economies (Figure 2.SF.5).[10] During the euro area crisis, bond flows—including to emerging market and developing economies—have held up more than equity flows after stress, declining in level but not reversing immediately. The decline in equity flows is generally sharper. In contrast, during the global financial crisis, bond flows were generally negative and fell further after stress (equity flows behaved in a similar fashion). It is possible that investors increasingly consider that

[9] IMF (2012b) analyzes the consequences of potentially lower Chinese investment growth on growth in commodity exporters through direct trade linkages and global commodity prices.
[10] The EPFR database does not have data on bond and equity fund flow breakdowns for every country. Therefore, total flows for a country are included in the regional aggregates only if both bond and equity fund flows are available. See Table 2.SF.2 for details on the country coverage of the data.

SPILLOVER FEATURE

Figure 2.SF.4. Global Fund Flows during Stress
(Percent of 2011 weekly GDP)

Global capital flows are generally weaker during the week of and the week after advanced economy stress than during the week before stress. For most regions, the swings in flows around stress episodes are still somewhat smaller compared with those experienced during the global financial crisis. Stress from China also tends to coincide with lower flows but more dominantly for emerging market and developing economies that have strong trade-related ties with China.

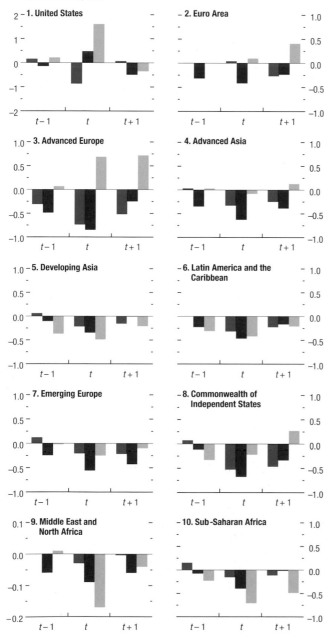

Sources: Emerging Portfolio Fund Research; and IMF staff calculations.
Note: *t* denotes the week of stress, and *t* − 1 and *t* + 1 refer to the weeks before and after stress, respectively. See Table 2.SF.2 for country composition in each group.

Figure 2.SF.5. The Composition of Capital Flows during Stress
(Percent of 2011 weekly GDP)

Bond flows have tended to be relatively more resilient to stress than equity flows during the euro area crisis.

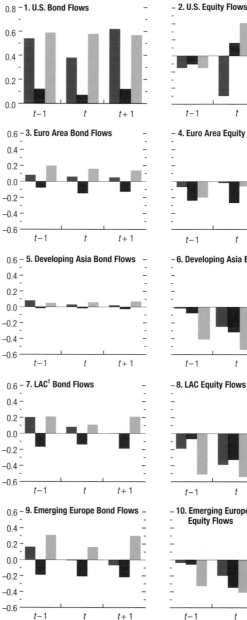

Sources: Emerging Portfolio Fund Research; and IMF staff calculations.
Note: *t* denotes the week of stress, and *t* −1 and *t* +1 refer to the weeks before and after stress, respectively. See Table 2.SF.2 for the country composition of each group.
[1]LAC: Latin America and the Caribbean.

Table 2.SF.2. Data for Spillover Feature

Variable	Definition/Description/Source
Sovereign Spreads Greece Ireland Italy Spain	Ten-year general government bond index. The spread is calculated as a country's indexed yield over German 10-year bonds. Source: Bloomberg Financial Markets.
VIX	Chicago Board Options Exchange Market Volatility Index. Source: Bloomberg Financial Markets.
Total, Bond, and Equity Fund Flows	Weekly total, bond, and equity fund flows to 10 regions. Source. Emerging Portfolio Fund Research.

Country Compositions for Each Region:

Total Flows

Euro Area	Austria, Belgium, Cyprus, Estonia, Finland, France, Germany, Greece, Ireland, Italy, Netherlands, Portugal, Slovak Republic, Slovenia, Spain
Advanced Europe	Czech Republic, Denmark, Iceland, Israel, Norway, Sweden, Switzerland, United Kingdom
Advanced Asia	Australia, Hong Kong SAR, Japan, Korea, New Zealand, Singapore, Taiwan Province of China
Developing Asia	China, India, Indonesia, Malaysia, Pakistan, Philippines, Sri Lanka, Thailand, Vietnam
Latin America and the Caribbean	Argentina, Bolivia, Brazil, Chile, Colombia, Dominican Republic, Ecuador, El Salvador, Guatemala, Mexico, Panama, Peru, Venezuela
Emerging Europe	Bulgaria, Croatia, Hungary, Latvia, Lithuania, Poland, Romania, Serbia, Turkey
Commonwealth of Independent States	Georgia, Kazakhstan, Mongolia, Russia, Ukraine
Sub-Saharan Africa	Botswana, Côte d'Ivoire, Ghana, Kenya, Mauritius, Namibia, Nigeria, South Africa, Zambia
Middle East and North Africa	Bahrain, Egypt, Jordan, Kuwait, Lebanon, Morocco, Oman, Qatar, Saudi Arabia, Tunisia, United Arab Emirates
United States and Canada	Canada, United States
United States	United States

Bond Flows: *Each region includes the same composition as Total Flows, with additional countries listed below.*

Developing Asia	Cambodia
Latin America and the Caribbean	Costa Rica, Jamaica, Nicaragua, Trinidad and Tobago, Uruguay
Emerging Europe	Albania, Bosnia and Herzegovina, FYR Macedonia
Commonwealth of Independent States	Azerbaijan, Belarus, Moldova
Sub-Saharan Africa	Angola, Democratic Republic of the Congo, Gabon, Liberia, Uganda
Middle East and North Africa	Algeria, Iran, Iraq, Libya
Advanced Economies	All countries listed under Euro Area, Advanced Europe, Advanced Asia, and United States and Canada
Emerging Market and Developing Economies	All countries listed under Developing Asia, Latin America and the Caribbean, Emerging Europe, Commonwealth of Independent States, Sub-Saharan Africa, and Middle East and North Africa

Equity Flows: *Each region includes the same composition as Total Flows, with additional countries listed below.*

Developing Asia	Bangladesh, Cambodia, Papua New Guinea
Commonwealth of Independent States	Turkmenistan

SPILLOVER FEATURE

Table 2.SF.2. *(continued)*

Variable	Definition/Description/Source
Sub-Saharan Africa	Malawi, Rwanda, Swaziland, Tanzania, Uganda, Zimbabwe
Middle East and North Africa	Iran, Yemen
Advanced Economies	All countries listed under Euro Area, advanced Europe, Advanced Asia, and United States and Canada
Emerging Market and Developing Economies	All countries listed under Developing Asia, Latin America and the Caribbean, Emerging Europe, Commonwealth of Independent States, Sub-Saharan Africa, and Middle East and North Africa
2011 Weekly GDP	2011 annual GDP in U.S. dollars divided by 52. Source: World Economic Outlook database (series NGDPD).
Sovereign Yields[1]	Ten-year government bond yields for most advanced economies; JPMorgan EMBIG Sovereign Yields for emerging market economies. Source: Bloomberg Financial Markets.
Country Compositions for Each Region	
Euro Area (core)	Belgium, Finland, France, Germany, Netherlands, Slovak Republic
Advanced Europe	Czech Republic, Denmark, Norway, Sweden, Switzerland, United Kingdom
Advanced Asia	Australia, Hong Kong SAR, Japan, Korea, New Zealand, Singapore, Taiwan Province of China
Developing Asia	China, India, Indonesia, Malaysia, Pakistan, Philippines, Sri Lanka, Thailand, Vietnam
Latin America and the Caribbean	Argentina, Belize, Brazil, Chile, Colombia, Dominican Republic, Ecuador, El Salvador, Jamaica, Mexico, Panama, Peru, Trinidad and Tobago, Uruguay, Venezuela
Emerging Europe	Bulgaria, Croatia, Hungary, Lithuania, Poland, Serbia, Turkey
Commonwealth of Independent States	Belarus, Georgia, Kazakhstan, Russia, Ukraine
Sub-Saharan Africa	Côte d'Ivoire, Gabon, Ghana, Nigeria, Senegal, South Africa
Middle East and North Africa	Egypt, Iraq, Jordan, Lebanon, Morocco, Tunisia
Equity Prices[1]	MSCI Equity Indices. Source: Bloomberg Financial Markets.
Country Compositions for Each Region	
Euro Area	Austria, Belgium, Finland, France, Germany, Greece, Ireland, Italy, Netherlands, Portugal, Spain
Advanced Europe	Czech Republic, Denmark, Norway, Sweden, Switzerland, United Kingdom
Advanced Asia	Australia, Hong Kong SAR, Japan, Korea, New Zealand, Singapore, Taiwan Province of China
Developing Asia	China, India, Indonesia, Malaysia, Pakistan, Philippines, Sri Lanka, Thailand
Latin America and the Caribbean	Argentina, Brazil, Chile, Mexico, Peru, Venezuela
Emerging Europe	Hungary, Poland, Turkey
Commonwealth of Independent States	Kazakhstan, Russia, Ukraine
Sub-Saharan Africa	Kenya, Nigeria, South Africa
Middle East and North Africa	Egypt, Israel, Jordan, Morocco
Financial Equity Prices[1]	MSCI Financial Equity Indices. Source: Bloomberg Financial Markets.
Country Compositions for Each Region	
Euro Area	Austria, Belgium, Finland, France, Germany, Greece, Ireland, Italy, Netherlands, Portugal, Spain
Advanced Europe	Czech Republic, Denmark, Norway, Sweden, Switzerland, United Kingdom

SPILLOVER FEATURE

Table 2.SF.2. *(continued)*

Variable	Definition/Description/Source
Advanced Asia	Australia, Hong Kong SAR, Japan, Korea, New Zealand, Singapore, Taiwan Province of China
Developing Asia	China, India, Indonesia, Malaysia, Pakistan, Philippines, Sri Lanka, Thailand
Latin America and the Caribbean	Argentina, Brazil, Chile, Colombia, Mexico, Peru
Emerging Europe	Hungary, Poland, Turkey
Commonwealth of Independent States	Russia
Sub-Saharan Africa	South Africa
Middle East and North Africa	Egypt, Israel, Jordan, Morocco
Purchasing Managers' Index (manufacturing) China Euro Area United States	Markit Economics Purchasing Managers' Index for the manufacturing sector (monthly data). Source: Haver Analytics.

[1]Regional aggregates are computed as a weighted average of the countries within the region, with weights based on 2012 U.S. dollar GDP weights from the April 2012 *World Economic Outlook.*

these economies issue higher-quality assets given the resilience of their expansions. However, it could also reflect a greater thirst for yield in an environment of ultra-low interest rates.

Contagion through Asset Prices

The above results using weekly capital flows are complemented by studying the poststress behavior of global sovereign yields and equity prices, the data for which are available at a daily frequency. Global asset prices tend to tighten in periods of stress—sovereign yields rise and equity prices fall (Figure 2.SF.6)—although the size of spillovers has typically varied across regions:

- During the euro area crisis, for emerging Europe, the CIS, and LAC, the average sovereign yields in the two days after stress were 8 to10 basis points higher compared with average yields in the two days before stress. During the global financial crisis, the rise in yields after stress was generally larger, particularly for the CIS. For developing Asia, stress has been associated with a decline in sovereign yields in both

crisis periods, but more so during the euro area crisis. This observation is consistent with the greater persistence of bond flows observed for emerging market and developing economies over time. Yields in most advanced economies also tend to be lower after stress, more so during the euro area crisis period, reflecting in part a flight to quality.

- Both equity and financial equity prices are lower after stress, with the poststress declines in financial equity prices slightly larger than those in overall equity prices for most regions. During the euro area crisis, for most regions, equity prices were lower by 1 to 3 percentage points for the two days after stress (compared with the average two-day prices before stress), while the decline was about 4 percentage points for the CIS and euro area economies. These declines were larger during stress in the global financial crisis.
- Sovereign yields do not exhibit any specific pattern during China-specific stress episodes. Equity and financial equity prices are generally weaker after such stress, particularly for commodity-exporting regions (LAC, MENA).

SPILLOVER FEATURE

Conclusions

The analysis confirms that financial or real stress in major economies can affect global financial conditions either because stress occurs concurrently everywhere or because of spillover effects. Global capital flows decline, equity prices fall, and sovereign yields generally rise following such stress. Although spillovers have been smaller in recent years than during the global financial crisis, economies with greater linkages to advanced economies—emerging Europe and the CIS region—remain vulnerable. Swings in financial conditions are also experienced around stress from downswings in Chinese real economic activity, particularly for commodity exporters. The recent shift in financial markets away from equity to bond flows in emerging market and developing economies could suggest that bonds issued by the latter are now considered safer for investors than before. However, it could also reflect a search for yield in the face of low global interest rates, which raises concerns about a potential increase in the exposure of these economies to such debt-creating flows.

The real implications of stress can be severe in the context of strong macrofinancial linkages in systemically important economies.[11] Growth spillovers from these economies can be large given the sizable trade linkages of most regions with these economies (Figure 2.SF.7). More generally, a sharp rise in global risk aversion—the proxy used here for U.S. financial strain—is also associated with a higher likelihood of the end of economic expansions in emerging market and developing economies (see Chapter 4).

Policymakers should focus on limiting the potential for such stress in the first place, which involves a range of policies, as discussed in Chapter 1. For economies at the receiving end, it is crucial to maintain strong macroeconomic and prudential policies that sustain market confidence and increase resilience to potential contagion.

[11]See Claessens, Kose, and Terrones (2011); Igan and others (2009); Reinhart and Rogoff (2009); and IMF (2012b).

Figure 2.SF.6. Global Asset Price Performance around Stress Episodes

Global sovereign yields tend to rise and equity prices to fall during periods of stress emanating from major economies.

■ Euro area crisis (Jan. 2010–June 2012) ■ Global financial crisis (Jan. 2007–Dec. 2009)
■ China real activity stress

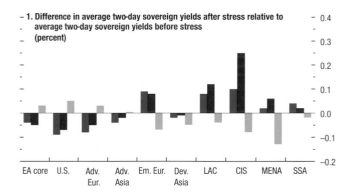

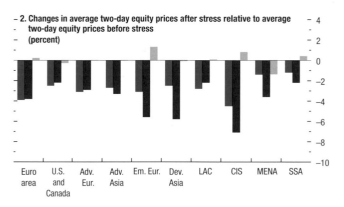

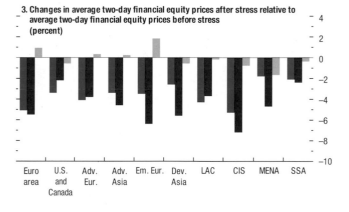

Sources: See Table 2.SF.2.
Note: EA core = euro area core; Adv. Eur. = advanced Europe; Adv. Asia = advanced Asia; Em. Eur. = emerging Europe; Dev. Asia = developing Asia; LAC = Latin America and the Caribbean; CIS = Commonwealth of Independent States; MENA = Middle East and North Africa; SSA = sub-Saharan Africa. See Table 2.SF.2 for the country composition of each group.

Figure 2.SF.7. Global Trade Linkages with Advanced Economies and China

Global trade linkages with advanced economies remain sizable, and those with China have been increasing in recent years.

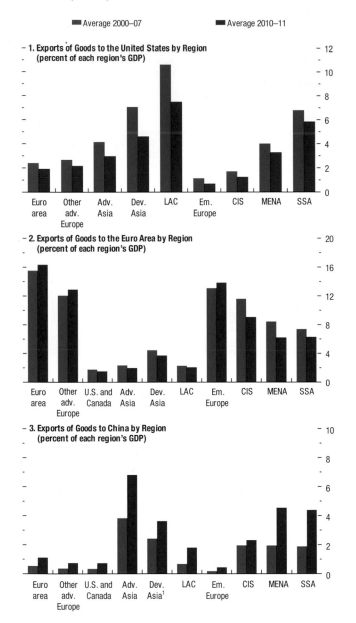

Sources: IMF, Direction of Trade Statistics database; and IMF staff calculations.
Note: Adv. Asia = advanced Asia; Dev. Asia = developing Asia; LAC = Latin America and the Caribbean; Em. Europe = emerging Europe; CIS = Commonwealth of Independent States; MENA = Middle East and North Africa; SSA = sub-Saharan Africa.
See the Statistical Appendix for regional country compositions, except other advanced Europe (Other adv. Europe): Czech Republic, Denmark, Iceland, Norway, Sweden, Switzerland, United Kingdom.
[1]Excluding China.

References

Anderson, Derek, Benjamin Hunt, Mika Kortelainen, Dirk Muir, and Stephen Snudden, forthcoming, "Getting to Know the GIMF: The Simulation Properties of the Global Integrated Monetary and Fiscal Model," IMF Working Paper (Washington: International Monetary Fund).

Bayoumi, Tamim, and Trung Bui, 2011, "Unforeseen Events Wait Lurking: Estimating Policy Spillovers from U.S. to Foreign Asset Prices," IMF Working Paper No. 11/183 (Washington: International Monetary Fund).

Claessens, Stijn, Ayhan M. Kose, and Marco Terrones, 2011, "How Do Business and Financial Cycles Interact?" IMF Working Paper No. 11/88 (Washington: International Monetary Fund).

Fratzscher, Marcel, 2011, "Capital Flows, Push versus Pull Factors and the Global Financial Crisis," ECB Working Paper No. 1364 (Frankfurt: European Central Bank).

_____, Marco Lo Duca, and Roland Straub, 2012, "Quantitative Easing, Portfolio Choice and International Capital Flows" (unpublished; Frankfurt: European Central Bank).

Hyndman, Rob, Anne B. Koeher, J. Keith Ord, and Ralph D. Snyder, 2008, *Forecasting with Exponential Smoothing: The State Space Approach* (Berlin: Springer-Verlag).

Igan, Deniz, Alain N. Kabundi, Franciso Nadal-De Simone, Marcelo Pinheiro, and Natalia T. Tamirisa, 2009, "Three Cycles: Housing, Credit, and Real Activity," IMF Working Paper No. 09/231 (Washington: International Monetary Fund).

International Monetary Fund (IMF), 2011a, *Euro Area Policies: Spillover Report for the 2011 Article IV Consulta-tion and Selected Issues,* IMF Country Report No. 11/185 (Washington). www.imf.org/external/pubs/ft/scr/2011/cr11185.pdf.

_____, 2011b, "Recent Experiences in Managing Capital Flows: Cross-Cutting Themes and Possible Policy Framework" (Washington). www.imf.org/external/np/pp/eng/2011/021411a.pdf.

———, 2012a, *Pilot External Sector Report* (Washington). http://www.imf.org/external/np/pp/eng/2012/070212.pdf.

_____, 2012b, *2012 Spillover Report* (Washington). www.imf.org/external/np/pp/eng/2012/070912.pdf.

_____, 2012c, *The United Kingdom: Staff Report for the 2012 Article IV Consultation,* IMF Country Report No. 12/190 (Washington).

Kamenik, Ondrej, 2011, OG research paper (unpublished; Prague: OGResearch). http://www.ogresearch.com/products.

Kumhof, Michael, Douglas Laxton, Dirk Muir, and Susanna Mursula, 2010, "The Global Integrated Monetary and Fiscal Model (GIMF)—Theoretical Structure," IMF Working Paper No. 10/34 (Washington: International Monetary Fund).

Miao, Yanliang, and Malika Pant, 2012, "Coincident Indicators of Capital Flows," IMF Working Paper No. 12/55 (Washington: International Monetary Fund).

Reinhart, Carmen M., and Kenneth S. Rogoff, 2009, *This Time Is Different: Eight Centuries of Financial Folly* (Princeton, New Jersey: Princeton University Press).

Romer, Christina, D., 2012, "Fiscal Policy in the Crisis: Lessons and Policy Implications" (unpublished; Berkeley: University of California).

THE GOOD, THE BAD, AND THE UGLY: 100 YEARS OF DEALING WITH PUBLIC DEBT OVERHANGS

Throughout the past century, numerous advanced economies have faced public debt burdens as high, or higher, than those prevailing today. They responded with a wide variety of policy approaches. We analyze these experiences to draw lessons for today and reach three main conclusions. First, successful debt reduction requires fiscal consolidation and a policy mix that supports growth. Key elements of this policy mix are measures that address structural weaknesses in the economy and supportive monetary policy. Second, fiscal consolidation must emphasize persistent, structural reforms to public finances over temporary or short-lived fiscal measures. In this respect, fiscal institutions can help lock in any gains. Third, reducing public debt takes time, especially in the context of a weak external environment.

Public debt in advanced economies has climbed to its highest level since World War II. In Japan, the United States, and several European countries, it now exceeds 100 percent of GDP (Figure 3.1). Low growth, persistent budget deficits, and high future and contingent liabilities stemming from population-aging-related spending pressure and weak financial sectors have markedly heightened concerns about the sustainability of public finances. These concerns have been reflected in ratings downgrades and higher sovereign borrowing costs, especially for some European countries. Correcting fiscal imbalances and reducing public debt have therefore become high priorities.

There is, however, a widespread and ongoing debate over the most appropriate policy mix for achieving a successful adjustment. According to some, fiscal austerity is essential to resolve the current crisis. Others argue that fiscal austerity is self-defeating, given its contractionary effect on output, and that reinvigorating growth through fiscal

The authors of this chapter are John Simon (team leader), Andrea Pescatori, and Damiano Sandri with support from Gavin Asdorian and Murad Omoev. Paolo Mauro, Cemile Sancak, and Ali Abbas provided helpful comments.

Figure 3.1. Public Debt in Advanced Economies

Gross public debt as a percent of GDP among advanced economies has reached historical highs: Japan, the United States, and many European countries currently have debt-to-GDP ratios close to or above 100 percent.

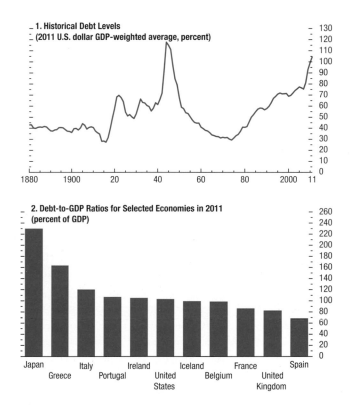

Sources: Abbas and others (2010); and IMF staff calculations.

stimulus is more important.[1] Still others point to the experience of financial repression after World War II and suggest this as a model for resolving the current debt overhang.[2]

This chapter informs the current policy debate by reviewing the historical experiences of advanced economies that have reached debt-to-GDP ratios as high as today's. The policy responses differed greatly, as did the outcomes. The richness of this historical experience provides insight into the full spectrum of policy options currently under consideration. In particular, the chapter addresses the following questions:

- How successful were countries in reducing high public debt ratios in the past?
- Which policy mix proved most effective? What were the contributions of fiscal, monetary, and financial sector policies?
- What were the macroeconomic consequences of the policies pursued?
- What does historical experience suggest for countries dealing with high debt today?

To address these points, we do not focus only on large debt reductions, as done in previous studies, but we review more broadly "what happens next?" after debt rises above 100 percent of GDP. This allows us to take in the full range of possible outcomes rather than just the successes, which might paint a distorted picture of debt dynamics. Indeed, some of the most instructive episodes are those in which public debt increased.[3]

We focus on six case studies spanning almost 100 years, from the United Kingdom in the immediate aftermath of World War I, through the United States after World War II, to Belgium, Canada, Italy, and Japan in the 1980s and 1990s. These episodes cover

a full range of policy approaches and economic outcomes. In-depth analysis allows us to more clearly identify the policy mix pursued by each country and assess its *relative* effectiveness. Importantly, we not only focus on fiscal policies, but also consider the broader macroeconomic environment encompassing the countries' monetary stance, financial sector policies, and external environment. That said, past country experiences are not necessarily prescriptions for the future, given changes in economic structures and in policy and regulatory frameworks. Moreover, we review actual policy strategies and do not consider whether other policies would have produced better outcomes. These caveats must be taken into account when drawing implications for today. Finally, given the high starting point, even relatively successful debt reductions can still leave countries with high debt and, thus, a vulnerability to renewed setbacks. For example, in Belgium, where debt was reduced substantially between 1993 and 2007, debt levels are again approaching 100 percent because of the setbacks from the Great Recession.

The next section looks at the full historical record, focusing on episodes that begin when public debt rose above 100 percent of GDP and reviewing the macroeconomic environment and outcomes. The chapter then discusses how the six cases were selected before turning to the in-depth case studies. It then synthesizes the findings from the case studies and, finally, draws lessons for today.

Historical Overview

The IMF Fiscal Affairs Department recently compiled a comprehensive database on gross government debt-to-GDP ratios covering nearly the entire IMF membership back to 1875.[4] We use these data to

---

[1]See, for example, Krugman (2012).

[2]Financial repression occurs "when governments implement policies to channel to themselves funds that in a deregulated market environment would go elsewhere" (Reinhart, Kirkegaard, and Sbrancia, 2011). It commonly involves explicit or indirect caps on government debt interest rates, combined with other regulations to ensure a market for this debt. See also Reinhart and Sbrancia (2011).

[3]By selecting the sample of episodes on the basis of ex ante criteria rather than ex post success, this chapter is similar in spirit to, though distinct from and complementary to, the approach of Mauro (2011), which looks at large planned fiscal consolidations and compares plans against outcomes for the G7 countries and EU member countries during the past few decades.

---

[4]See Abbas and others (2010) for a detailed description of the database, which is available at www.imf.org/external/datamapper/index.php?db=DEBT. The use of gross debt data reflects the difficulty of collecting net debt data on a consistent basis across countries and over time. Nonetheless, even gross debt data may not be immune to measurement problems (see Dippelsman, Dziobek, and Gutiérrez Mangas, 2012). We also use supplementary data on interest payments and primary deficits for 19 advanced economies from Abbas and others (2011) as well as real GDP data from Maddison (2003) and other data from Reinhart and Rogoff (2010).

identify all advanced economy episodes that begin when gross public debt rises above 100 percent of GDP.[5] High-debt episodes of emerging market and developing economies are not included in our analysis. This is not because they may not offer interesting insights. Rather, it is because their experiences typically differed in two important respects. First, their debt was mostly external and denominated in foreign currency, which presents different challenges from those faced by advanced economies today.[6] Second, their economic structures and institutions can differ substantially from the structures and institutions of advanced economies, especially going back in time.[7] Finally, narrowing our analysis to advanced economies is a simple and transparent criterion for selecting the sample.

The 100 percent threshold is used for a number of reasons. First, it is most relevant today given the number of countries currently close to or above that threshold. Second, 100 percent is high relative to historical experience: only 15 percent of the observations in our advanced economy database are above 100 percent. Third, our analysis suggests that political and economic forces do not tend to exert

[5]The starting date of an episode is the first year in which the debt-to-GDP ratio exceeds 100 percent, conditional on the ratio being below 100 percent in the previous year. In a few instances, missing data prevent us from identifying the exact year in which the debt-to-GDP ratio crossed the 100 percent threshold. In these cases, we interpolate the data linearly and date the episode from the time the interpolated data show the 100 percent threshold was crossed. Furthermore, given our focus on the 15 years after the 100 percent threshold is crossed, we consider only episodes that begin by 1997 and, thus, end by 2012. We have experimented with different windows (for example, 10 years and 20 years) and the results are essentially unchanged.

[6]The inability of emerging markets to borrow abroad in their own currency has been referred to in the literature as "original sin" (Eichengreen, Hausmann, and Panizza, 2005). In particular, a debt denominated in foreign currency, especially if issued at short-term maturities, introduces an exchange rate channel through which sharp depreciations of the currency, by increasing the debt burden, can fuel additional exchange rate depreciation and trigger a vicious cycle. The presence of this channel, then, has various ex ante implications—for example, posing a stricter limit on the amount of debt that can be issued and constraining the set of monetary policy options.

[7]Some of the earliest episodes in our sample involve economies that share features similar to those of emerging market economies (for example, Greece in 1888 or Greece in 1931). For the sake of completeness, we retain these episodes in the historical overview but do not include them in the case studies or draw important conclusions from them.

downward pressure on debt on average until public debt reaches this level.

The 26 identified episodes are shown in Figure 3.2, which also traces the evolution of the debt-to-GDP ratio for 15 years after the 100 percent threshold was crossed. The chart conveys three key insights.

• Public debt levels above 100 percent of GDP are not uncommon. Of the 22 advanced economies for which there is good data coverage, more than half experienced at least one high-debt episode between 1875 and 1997. Furthermore, several countries had multiple episodes: three for Belgium and Italy and two for Canada, France, Greece, the Netherlands, and New Zealand.

• The dynamics of the debt-to-GDP ratios are quite diverse, with some countries experiencing additional large increases and others witnessing sharp reductions.

• The episodes are clustered around four major eras: the last quarter of the 19th century, the periods following the two world wars, and the last quarter of the 20th century. The 19th century debt buildup was related mainly to nation building and the railroad boom. The post–World War II episodes are connected with the enormous and widespread military effort and subsequent rebuilding, although some start earlier, during the Great Depression. The episodes in the last cluster during the 1980s and 1990s have their genesis in the breakdown of the Bretton Woods system, when government policy struggled with social issues and the transition to current economic systems.

Figure 3.3, panel 1, combines the full set of episodes to trace the distribution of the debt-to-GDP ratio for 15 years after debt crosses the 100 percent threshold. The range of experiences is broad: the 10th and 90th percentiles are associated with a reduction of 60 percentage points and an increase of 90 percentage points in debt, respectively. Focusing on the median, the debt ratio does tend to fall, but only at a moderate pace. After 15 years, the median debt-to-GDP ratio is only about 10 percentage points lower than in the first year after debt rises above 100 percent.

This pattern of falling median debt ratios emerges only at high original debt ratios. Panel 2 of Figure

Figure 3.2. Debt-to-GDP Dynamics after Public Debt Reaches 100 Percent of GDP
(Percent of GDP, advanced economies)

Increases in public debt to above 100 percent are reasonably frequent, with very diverse dynamics of the debt-to-GDP ratios. These episodes are clustered around four major eras: the last quarter of the 19th century, the periods following the two world wars, and the last quarter of the 20th century.

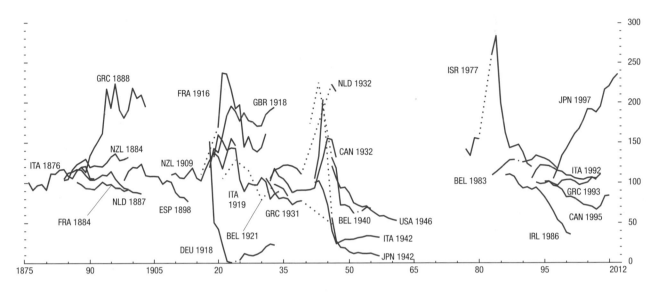

Sources: Abbas and others (2010); and IMF staff calculations.
Note: BEL = Belgium; CAN = Canada; DEU = Germany; ESP = Spain; FRA = France; GBR = United Kingdom; GRC = Greece; IRL = Ireland; ISR = Israel; ITA = Italy; JPN = Japan; NLD = Netherlands; NZL = New Zealand; USA = United States. We consider all historical episodes when gross public debt rose above 100 percent of GDP and trace the evolution of the debt-to-GDP ratios for the subsequent 15 years. Where data are missing, dotted lines represent linear interpolations between available observations.

3.3 repeats the same exercise shown in panel 1, but uses a 60 percent threshold. The interesting difference is that 15 years after debt rises above 60 percent, the median debt level shows no tendency to decrease, and the average debt level is actually higher (which can be inferred from the positively skewed distribution).

To provide a framework for thinking about the evolution of debt-to-GDP ratios during these episodes, one can think about four key variables that affect the stock of debt, b_t: the interest rate paid on the stock of debt, i_t; the inflation rate of the GDP deflator, π_t; the real GDP growth rate, g_t; and the primary deficit–to-GDP ratio, d_t. The relationships among these variables are described by the following formula:

$$b_t = \frac{1 + i_t}{(1 + \pi_t)(1 + g_t)} b_{t-1} + d_t + e_t, \qquad (3.1)$$

in which e_t is a residual that takes into account valuation effects and other accounting adjustments not fully captured by changes in the primary deficit.[8] As a result of compounding over long periods, the difference between the real interest rate and real GDP growth plays a crucial role in determining the stability of public debt. While a high difference can set debt on an unstable path, the difference is normally close to zero. In particular, for the 22 advanced economies in our database, the average difference is –0.7 percent.[9] Furthermore, primary deficits respond slowly to changes in debt—Ostry and others (2010)

[8]The residual can be significant and can vary across countries depending on, among other things, the accounting rules followed by governments (for further details see Appendix 4 of the September 2011 *Fiscal Monitor*). This residual is particularly pronounced in the periods preceding World War II, when accounting standards were not reliable or uniform.

[9]A differential of –0.7 percent implies that the term in front of b_{t-1} in the equation for debt dynamics is approximately equal to 0.99. Or, put another way, the half-life of public debt, abstracting from changes in the primary balance or other adjustments related to the stock of debt, would be almost 100 years. For additional details on the negative interest rate growth differential, see Escolano, Shabunina, and Woo (2011).

estimate that the elasticity of the primary balance to debt is quite low at about 0.05. Thus, the evolution of the stock of debt tends to be quite persistent and to undergo large, long swings, as evident in Figures 3.2 and 3.3.

This framework helps us explore other aspects of these countries' experiences. Panel 1 of Figure 3.4 shows the average growth rate of real GDP per capita and the change in the debt-to-GDP ratio for each high-debt episode. With the exception of Greece (1931),[10] the United Kingdom (1918) had the worst growth performance, with negative growth and a considerable increase in its debt burden. At the opposite extreme is Ireland (1986), with the fastest average growth rate, more than 6 percent, and substantial debt reduction. The largest debt reductions followed the world wars, usually as a result of hyperinflation. The United States (1946) stands out as an exception, as we discuss below; however, inflation was still an important contributor to debt reduction during this episode. Finally, there is no clear correlation between growth and debt reduction in this group of high-debt episodes.

Another way to look at these high-debt episodes is by tracking the average primary fiscal balance and the average inflation rate over the 15 years after public debt reaches 100 percent of GDP. Because these are the main targets of fiscal and monetary policy, they lay a foundation for examining the various policy approaches of the case studies. Figure 3.4, panel 2, shows that when these countries reached high levels of debt, their fiscal balances and inflation rates differed considerably. We see some obvious outliers in the United Kingdom (1918) and Japan (1997) along with a number of war-related high- or hyperinflation episodes, including in France, Germany, Greece, Italy, and Japan. By and large, however, the more modern episodes are much more tightly clustered, with modest inflation and modest primary surpluses. As is evident in the case studies below, the modern episodes differed in ways not readily apparent in the aggregate analysis.

Table 3.1 presents a third perspective on these episodes, which are separated into two broad

[10]The poor economic performance of Greece is explained mainly by the deep internal political instability after the 1919–22 war with Turkey and the foreign occupation during World War II.

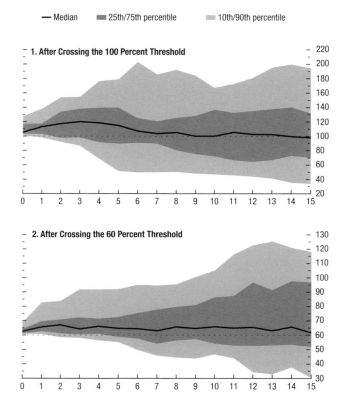

Figure 3.3. Debt-to-GDP Dynamics
(Percent of GDP, advanced economies)

After reaching 100 percent of GDP, the debt-to-GDP ratio tends to decline, even though at a very moderate pace. This tendency to reverse is not present at lower levels of debt, for example when debt rises above 60 percent of GDP.

Source: IMF staff calculations.
Note: The horizontal axis shows the number of years after the debt-to-GDP ratio crosses the threshold.

Figure 3.4. High Debt, Growth, and Inflation

After exceeding the 100 percent debt-to-GDP ratio, there is considerable variation in economies' growth, the change in their debt ratio, their primary fiscal balance, and their inflation rate.

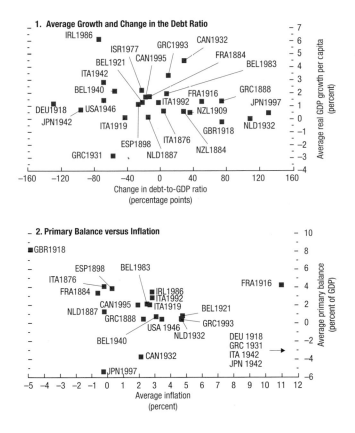

Sources: Abbas and others (2010); Maddison (2003); Reinhart and Rogoff (2010); and IMF staff calculations.
Note: The change in debt ratio, average growth rates, inflation, and primary balance are computed over the 15 years after debt reaches 100 percent of GDP. BEL: Belgium; CAN: Canada; DEU: Germany; ESP: Spain; FRA: France; GBR: United Kingdom; GRC: Greece; IRL: Ireland; ISR: Israel; ITA: Italy; JPN: Japan; NLD: Netherlands; NZL: New Zealand; USA: United States.

groups: those in which debt levels increased and those in which debt levels decreased. The primary fiscal surplus is, on average, about 2.4 percent of GDP during episodes where the debt-to-GDP ratio decreases, but it is only 1.2 percent where the debt ratio increases. This foreshadows a finding from our case studies—debt reduction ultimately requires primary surpluses. The relationship between inflation and debt reduction is more ambiguous. Although hyperinflation is clearly associated with sharp debt reduction, when hyperinflation episodes are excluded, there is no clear association between the average inflation rate and the change in debt. Finally, a relatively stronger growth performance is associated with debt reduction when hyperinflation episodes are excluded.

Among our 26 episodes, only 3 feature default: Germany (1918), which suspended war reparations in 1932, and Greece (1888, 1931), which defaulted in 1894 and 1932, respectively. These episodes have little relevance for the challenges faced by advanced economies today for at least two reasons. First, they involve very peculiar features that set them apart from others: the post–World War I political instability in Germany, the nation-building effort of Greece at the turn of the 19th century and the subsequent Greco-Turkish war of 1897, and a period of deep internal political instability in Greece after the 1919–22 war with Turkey. Second, in these defaults a large proportion of public debt was denominated in foreign currency (or gold), which made debt repayment subject to exchange rate fluctuations. For example, the Greek episodes are more similar to the sovereign debt crises commonly experienced by emerging markets, during which a sharp drop in the exchange rate leads to a dramatic increase in the value of foreign-currency-denominated liabilities.

Public Debt and Economic Growth

One particular concern with high public debt ratios is that they may lower economic growth. Several empirical papers document a negative correlation between public debt and GDP growth, with some suggesting that a debt-to-GDP ratio of 90 percent or more may constrain growth (Kumar and Woo, 2010; Reinhart and Rogoff, 2010; Cecchetti,

Table 3.1. Differentiating Episodes by the Change in the Debt-to-GDP Ratio

1. Episodes with an Overall Reduction in Debt to GDP over 15 Years

Episodes		Change in Debt to GDP (percent)	GDP Growth (percent)	Inflation (percent)	Primary Balance (percent of GDP)
Country	Start Year				
Germany	1918	−129	1.2	1.4×10^{10}	3.8
Japan	1942	−96	0.7	91.4	3.5
Ireland	1986	−74	6.1	2.8	1.7
Italy	1942	−68	2.8	41.5	3.5
United States	1946	−68	1.4	3.0	0.7
Greece	1931	−57	−2.8	90.0	2.0
Belgium	1940	−55	2.2	3.1	3.9
Italy	1919	−43	0.1	2.7	0.8
Spain	1898	−27	1.1	0.3	2.0
Israel	1977	−22	2.2	4.8	1.3
Belgium	1921	−22	1.3	1.9	3.3
Canada	1995	−18	1.7	−0.2	2.8
Netherlands	1887	−15	0.1	−0.6	. . .
France	1884	−13	1.7	2.8	. . .
Italy	1992	−2	1.3	. . .	. . .
Average		−47	1.4	1.0×10^{9}	2.4
Average Excluding Hyperinflation (>40 percent)		−33	1.8	2.1	2.2

2. Episodes with an Overall Increase in Debt to GDP over 15 Years

Episodes		Change in Debt to GDP (percent)	GDP Growth (percent)	Inflation (percent)	Primary Balance (percent of GDP)
Country	Start Year				
Italy	1876	4	0.6	−0.2	4.1
Belgium	1983	8	2.0	2.5	2.1
Greece	1993	10	3.3	4.7	0.4
New Zealand	1884	28	0.6	−1.6	−3.7
Canada	1932	29	4.5	2.1	4.2
New Zealand	1909	36	0.5	3.8	0.5
France	1916	50	1.4	11.0	8.2
Greece	1888	75	1.4	2.3	0.5
United Kingdom	1918	75	−0.2	−4.8	−5.4
Netherlands	1932	109	0.0	4.7	. . .
Japan	1997	131	0.5	−0.3	. . .
Average		51	1.3	2.2	1.2

Source: IMF staff calculations.

Mohanty, and Zampolli, 2011).[11] However, high debt may itself be the result of sluggish growth, or it could reflect a third factor that at the same time increases debt and reduces growth (for example, a war or a financial crisis). Indeed, Panizza and

Presbitero (2012), who use an instrumental variable approach to control for reverse causality, reject the hypothesis that high debt causes lower growth. We do not address the challenging causality issue here. Rather, by focusing on performance after a certain debt-to-GDP ratio has been crossed, we highlight a few additional and important stylized facts about debt and growth.

Figure 3.5, panel 1, explores whether entering a high-debt phase is followed by relatively low growth over the subsequent 15 years. Growth rates during each of the episodes are compared with those of a control

[11]Reinhart, Reinhart, and Rogoff (2012) find that debt above 90 percent reduces growth by 1 percent. Kumar and Woo (2010) find that when debt is at 90 percent, an additional 10 percent increase in the debt ratio reduces future growth by about 1 percent for advanced economies and that this is not the case for some selected lower levels of debt. Cecchetti, Mohanty, and Zampolli (2011) obtain a similar result when debt is in a range of 85 percent of GDP.

group of all other advanced economies during the same periods. If growth rates are unrelated to debt levels, the growth of countries with high debt should be, on average, about the same as those of other countries—that is, the points plotted in Figure 3.5, panel 1, should be randomly scattered around zero. The scatter plot, however, shows that countries that crossed the 100 percent threshold typically experienced lower GDP growth than the advanced economy average. In this respect at least, these results are consistent with the findings of Reinhart and Rogoff (2010).

Figure 3.5, panel 2, explores debt levels and growth performance in more breadth. This figure is also based on the difference between the average growth rate during a set of high-debt episodes and the average growth rate for all advanced economies during matching periods. But the threshold for selecting episodes varies between 10 percent of GDP and 140 percent of GDP, with the threshold increasing in 5 percentage point increments. For each threshold, the average growth rate during the selected episodes is plotted against the advanced economy average. Furthermore, in addition to episodes where debt is increasing when the threshold is crossed, the figure also shows relative growth for episodes where debt is decreasing when the threshold is crossed. This yields two interesting observations. First, it matters whether a country's debt level is increasing or decreasing. Among countries with the same debt levels, the growth performance over the subsequent 15 years in countries for which debt is decreasing when the threshold is crossed is better than in countries for which it is increasing. This difference is statistically significant across the whole sample. It is particularly striking for debt levels between 90 and 115 percent of GDP (where average growth is 0.5 percentage point higher).[12] Second, there is no particular threshold that consistently precedes subpar growth performance. In fact, Figure 3.5, panel 2, shows that countries with a debt level between 90 and 110 percent outperform the control group when debt is on a declining trajectory.

Figure 3.5. Debt and Growth Performance

Countries whose debt-to-GDP ratio rises above 100 percent tend to experience lower GDP growth than other advanced economies. However, countries with a debt level between 90 and 110 percent can actually grow faster than other advanced economies if debt is on a declining trajectory. In fact, the growth performance in countries whose debt is decreasing when crossing a given threshold is better than that in countries where it is increasing.

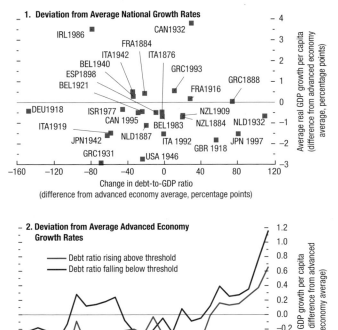

Sources: Abbas and others (2010); Maddison (2003); and IMF staff calculations.
Note: The change in debt ratio and average growth rates are computed over the 15 years after the debt ratio crosses the specified threshold. The blue line in panel 2 shows the difference in average growth for economies whose debt ratio rises above the threshold specified on the horizontal axis with respect to the average growth among all advanced economies over the same periods. The red line denotes the growth rate differential when the debt ratio falls below each given threshold. BEL: Belgium; CAN: Canada; DEU: Germany; ESP: Spain; FRA: France; GBR: United Kingdom; GRC: Greece; IRL: Ireland; ISR: Israel; ITA: Italy; JPN: Japan; NLD: Netherlands; NZL: New Zealand; USA: United States.

[12]Countries with very low debt levels (for example, below 25 percent of GDP) tend to have higher public debt levels after 15 years. In such cases, whether debt is increasing or decreasing at the time they cross the threshold has much less of an effect on the level of debt at the end of the episode.

Our analysis is not meant to dispute the notion that, all else equal, higher levels of debt may lead to higher real interest rates. Rather it highlights that there is no simple relationship between debt and growth. In fact, our subsequent analysis emphasizes that there are many factors that matter for a country's growth and debt performance. Moreover, there is no single threshold for debt ratios that can delineate the "bad" from the "good." For this reason, we explore public debt dynamics, the macroeconomic environment, and policies in a number of case studies.

Case Studies

We turn now from the aggregate analysis of the 26 high-debt episodes to more detailed analyses of 6 individual cases: the United Kingdom (1918), the United States (1946), Belgium (1983), Italy (1992), Canada (1995), and Japan (1997) (Figure 3.6). The selected cases meet three criteria: the episodes cover each of the main eras of high debt; they reflect the full range of outcomes; and they cover the full range of macroeconomic policy approaches.

The case studies cover the two postwar eras and the most recent era of debt buildup in peacetime. High-debt episodes that occurred before World War I are excluded because of the lack of detailed data and because the structure of economies was substantially different during that era, making comparisons with today less meaningful. For the interwar period, we consider the United Kingdom (1918) because it provides important lessons about fiscal austerity and the difficulties created by deflation.[13] Among post–World War II episodes, we analyze the United States (1946) because it is representative of the financial repression policies adopted after the war and that have recently been suggested as a possible solution to current debt problems (Reinhart and Sbrancia, 2011). The more recent cases of Belgium (1983), Canada (1995), Italy (1992), and Japan (1997)

[13]We did not select Germany because its experience was very extreme and that experience is already relatively well known: the limited ability to raise taxes combined with large expenditures and war-reparation requirements caused serious fiscal imbalances that led the Weimar Republic to monetize the fiscal deficits, producing bouts of hyperinflation.

Figure 3.6. Debt-to-GDP Dynamics after Crossing the 100 Percent Threshold
(Percent of GDP, advanced economies)

The selected case studies cover the broad range of debt-to-GDP dynamics historically experienced by advanced economies.

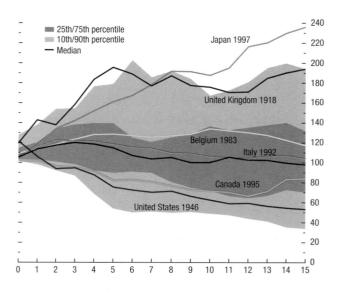

Sources: Abbas and others (2010); and IMF staff calculations.
Note: The horizontal axis shows the number of years after the debt-to-GDP ratio exceeds 100 percent.

capture a wide range of debt-to-GDP dynamics and policy approaches.[14] Together, the case studies capture the full range of debt outcomes for countries whose public debt rises above 100 percent of GDP. The cases are also representative of the range of policies pursued to address high public debt (see Figure 3.4, panel 2). The United Kingdom (1918) is an extreme case of large fiscal surpluses and strong deflation. Japan (1997) also endured deflation but pursued the opposite fiscal stance, with large and persistent fiscal deficits. Finally, the United States (1946), Belgium (1983), Italy (1992), and Canada (1995) are representative of the fiscal primary surplus and positive inflation policy mix followed by the majority of countries since World War II.[15]

We start with the United Kingdom after World War I, whose experience set a clear foundation for all subsequent thinking about public debt and economic policy. We follow with the United States after World War II, where initial circumstances were very similar but outcomes were very different. We then turn to more modern examples and emphasize not the extremes but the more typical experiences of Belgium, Canada, and Italy. Nonetheless, to reinforce the message that the United Kingdom's experience with deflation after World War I has not been consigned to the dustbin of history, we discuss Japan since the 1990s.

The United Kingdom in 1918: Deflation

In the aftermath of World War I, the United Kingdom's stock of debt had ballooned to about 140 percent of GDP and prices were more than double

their prewar level. Policymakers' priorities were twofold. First, return to the gold standard at the prewar parity to restore British trade, prosperity, and prestige (Pollard, 1992, p. 106). Second, pay off the debt to preserve Britain's proverbial creditworthiness. Indeed, by returning to prewar parity, the United Kingdom intended to prove its commitment to repay its debt in real terms, rather than in devalued currency.[16]

To achieve its objectives the U.K. government implemented a policy mix of severe fiscal austerity and tight monetary policy. The primary surplus was kept near 7 percent of GDP throughout the 1920s.[17] This was accomplished through large expenditure decreases, courtesy of the "Geddes axe," and a continuation of the higher tax levels introduced during the war.[18] On the monetary front, the Bank of England raised interest rates to 7 percent in 1920 to support the return to the prewar parity, which—coupled with the ensuing deflation—delivered extraordinarily high real rates.

The United Kingdom's resulting economic performance was very poor. Economic growth was weak and considerably below the advanced economy average, unemployment was high, and deflation was the order of the day (Figure 3.7). Real output in 1938 was barely above the level in 1918, and growth averaged about ½ percent a year. This was not merely because of the Great Depression—real output in 1928 was also below that in 1918. The export sector was particularly weak as a result of the revaluation of the currency—the real exchange rate drifted up initially as price and wage reductions failed to keep up with the nominal appreciation. Unemployment reached 11 percent in 1921. Indeed, the weakness

[14]Among the recent episodes of substantial debt reduction, Ireland (1986) stands out. Starting from a relatively low level of GDP per capita, however, this remarkable decline was driven mainly by the very high growth rate resulting from the process of catching up with the other European economies. Ireland experienced a structural transformation in the late 1980s from an agriculture-based economy, which had already occurred earlier in many other advanced economies (see Honohan and Walsh, 2002; and Perotti, 2012). We therefore have not included this episode in our case studies because it does not seem repeatable by countries currently dealing with high public debt.

[15]A number of countries experienced primary deficits and positive (usually hyper-) inflation, but these were all war related, with Germany (1918) the most extreme example. We do not investigate these cases further here because of their limited relevance for today.

[16]David Lloyd George, prime minister from 1916 to 1922, said this about the desire to pay off the debt and return to the gold standard: "It was not policy that determined the action of the government in Britain. It is just because a Briton has an ineradicable habit of paying what he owes and it never occurred to him to abandon that habit because he had fought a victorious war. Great Britain thought it her duty to uphold her credit, even at the highest cost." Lloyd George (1928)

[17]The headline balance remained slightly negative given the size of the debt and the interest rate on it.

[18]Sir Eric Geddes was appointed to chair a committee on ways to reduce expenditures in August 1921. It was, on its terms, very successful. But, as Pollard (1992) puts it, "The Geddes axe became a by-word for callous meanness" (p. 106).

of the labor market was part and parcel of the policy to induce large reductions in prices and, perforce, wages. A comparison with the other continental powers, particularly France and even Germany, suggests that the costs of this mix of tight fiscal and monetary policies were high. These outcomes led to the cynical observation from Keynes (1928, p. 218) that "assuredly it does not pay to be good."

If the policies pursued had successfully reduced debt and restored British growth and prosperity, the short-term costs perhaps would have been acceptable. Unfortunately, they did not. In fact, the policies had the opposite effect: British prosperity was hampered by the dual pursuit of prewar parity and fiscal austerity. Most European countries were enhancing their competitiveness through exchange rate devaluation, and British export industries suffered accordingly. Furthermore, managing the exchange rate forced the Bank of England to maintain high interest rates, which increased the burden of the national debt and generally constrained economic activity—further undermining tax receipts.

The policy of fiscal austerity, pursued to pay down the debt, further limited growth. Debt continued to rise and was about 170 percent of GDP in 1930 and more than 190 percent of GDP in 1933. It was not until 1990 that debt approached its pre–World War I level. Lloyd George (1928) observed about Britain that "her present activity and profit-earning power have been sacrificed in large measure to the maintenance of integrity and good faith to all her creditors at home and abroad."

The effects of deflation, economic growth, interest rates, and fiscal austerity on the public debt can be seen in Figure 3.7, panel 3. This figure calculates the average annual contribution to the change in the debt-to-GDP ratio over five-year periods from 1919 to 1933 and for the period as a whole. The calculation is based on the formula for debt dynamics given in equation (3.1). Primary surpluses contributed on average about 7 percentage points a year, but they were easily overwhelmed by deflation and high interest rates, which added 12 percentage points a year to the stock of debt. Furthermore, there was little to no positive contribution from economic growth. Only during 1924–28, when the United Kingdom experienced modest growth, did the debt level actually decline.

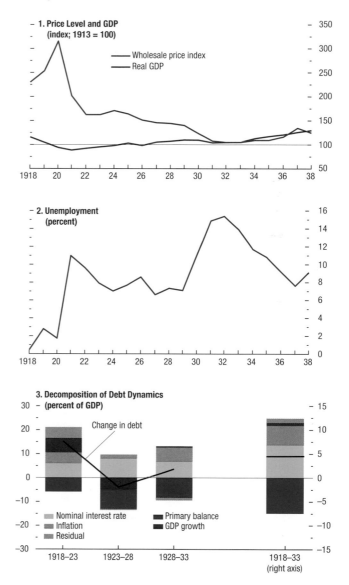

Figure 3.7. United Kingdom: Deflation in the Aftermath of World War I

After World War I, the United Kingdom experienced strong deflation, anemic growth, and high unemployment. Despite large primary surpluses, the debt ratio continued to increase due to high nominal interest rates and deflation.

1. Price Level and GDP
(index; 1913 = 100)

— Wholesale price index
— Real GDP

2. Unemployment
(percent)

3. Decomposition of Debt Dynamics
(percent of GDP)

Change in debt

■ Nominal interest rate   ■ Primary balance
■ Inflation   ■ GDP growth
■ Residual

1918–23   1923–28   1928–33   1918–33
(right axis)

Sources: Abbas and others (2010); Feinstein (1972); Mitchell (1998); and IMF staff calculations.
Note: The decomposition of debt dynamics is based on a linearized version of equation (3.1).

The U.K. interwar episode is an important reminder of the challenges of pursuing a tight fiscal and monetary policy mix, especially when the external sector is constrained by a high exchange rate.

The United States in 1946: Financial Repression and Surprise Inflation

By the end of World War II the U.S. stock of debt had swelled to 10 times higher than it was before the war, about 120 percent of GDP. The U.S. economy was also confronting a rapid rise in inflation associated with the removal of wartime price controls and the release of pent-up demand. In this respect, at least, the U.S. situation was similar to that of the United Kingdom after World War I. Many feared a similar outcome.[19] The success of the Keynesian revolution in economic thinking and the fear of repeating the mistakes of the interwar period, however, led to a very different policy approach and to better economic results.

Between 1946 and 1948, U.S. public finances swung quickly from deficit to surplus, as is common in postwar periods. The primary balance went from a deficit of 5 percent of GDP in 1946 to a surplus of 6½ percent of GDP in 1948 before stabilizing near 2 percent through most of the 1950s. In this respect, U.S. performance was qualitatively, if not quantitatively, similar to that of both the United States and the United Kingdom after World War I.

The monetary policy situation was, however, very different. In fact, unlike after World War I, various extraordinary measures used to support wartime deficits were removed only partially or slowly. In particular, the bond-support program, which placed a floor under the price of government bonds during the war, was continued, and this prevented the Federal Reserve from raising interest rates to

control inflation.[20] Despite proposals to remove this restriction on the operation of monetary policy, fear of repeating the mistakes of the past and causing a repeat of the boom-bust cycle after World War I persuaded policymakers to stay the course.[21]

The removal of price controls in mid-1946 led to a burst of inflation in late 1946 and 1947, which was ended by the 1949 recession and the concomitant mild deflation. Notwithstanding the burst of inflation, between 1946 and 1948 there was a widespread belief that prices were destined to fall quickly, which—coupled with a high government surplus and the fear of a major recession—meant that the Federal Reserve did not actually have to intervene to support government bond prices.[22] Serious inflation pressure was building nonetheless, and it emerged at the outset of the Korean War in 1950. To mitigate the rise in inflation without disrupting the bond market, consumer credit limits were reintroduced and there was a call for voluntary restraints on bank credit.[23] Nonetheless, between 1950 and 1951 inflation increased substantially again. This second burst of inflation coupled with that during 1946–47 contributed substantially to lower U.S. public debt, which by 1951 was down to 75 percent of GDP.

The Korean War finally demonstrated that the policies being pursued by the government made inflation rather than deflation the real danger. This

[19]"As the year 1947 opens America has never been so strong or so prosperous. Nor have our prospects ever been brighter. Yet in the minds of a great many of us there is a fear of another depression, the loss of our jobs, our farms, our businesses…The job at hand today is to see to it that America is not ravaged by recurring depressions and long periods of unemployment, but that instead we build an economy so fruitful, so dynamic, so progressive that each citizen can count upon opportunity and security for himself and his family." (Truman, 1947)

[20]Under the program, the Federal Reserve was responsible for intervening in the market to buy bonds if the price fell below par. The practical effect was to cap nominal interest rates at various maturities, with the Treasury bill rate at 0.375 percent and the long-term bond rate at 2½ percent.
[21]"The financial world should rest easy that the investment market will not be subject to the demoralization which swept over it in 1920 when the unsupported market for Government bonds fell about 20 percent below par" (Truman, 1947, p. 202).
[22]Friedman and Schwartz (1963) and Meltzer (2003) provide various arguments in support of the thesis that there was a "willingness on the part of the public to hold relatively large amounts of money and government securities at fairly low rates of interest" as reflected by the relatively small rise in the money stock over that period. In their view the "expectation of subsequent contraction and price decline […] induced [the public] to hold larger real money balances than it otherwise would have been willing to. In this way it made the postwar rise more moderate." (Friedman and Schwartz, 1963)
[23]The Defense Production Act, enacted September 8, 1950, in response to the start of the Korean War, sought, among other things, to restrain inflation through control of consumer and real estate credit.

realization enabled the Federal Reserve to regain some independence in setting interest rates.[24] The Federal Reserve was formally freed from the obligation to support the government bond market in 1951, although this was only the first step in dismantling the bond-support program.[25] Still, the idea of capping nominal interest rates while limiting the quantity of credit (credit controls) permeated U.S. economic policy at the time and persisted at least until the 1980s.

Figure 3.8 shows the contributions of the various forces to changes in the U.S. public debt level and the two distinct phases of the debt reduction. In the early years, high rates of surprise inflation combined with low nominal interest rates to reduce the debt by almost 35 percentage points. The rest of the debt reduction is attributable to solid growth, which contributed 2 percentage points each year; primary surpluses contributed an additional 2 percentage points.[26]

In summary, financial repression evolved logically and gradually from the reality of high public debt and the fear of what would happen if interest rates were raised to fend off postwar inflation. But, because direct control of quantities replaced the price mechanism, controls had to be in place across a wide range of activities. Credit controls and higher reserve requirements were imposed on banks. Bank competition was limited by various rules such as

[24]As noted by Friedman and Schwartz, "World War II was widely expected to be followed by severe unemployment. The Reserve System girded itself for the possibility and welcomed the bond-support program, because the System thought it would be consistent with the easy-money policies which would be required after the war. In the event, inflation rather than deflation loomed as a greater danger and, under the added impetus to inflation given by the Korean War, the Federal Reserve was finally led to divest itself of the self-imposed chains of the bond-supporting program." (Friedman and Schwartz, 1963, p. 700)

[25]In March 1951 an agreement was reached by President Truman, the Treasury, and the Federal Reserve (the 1951 Accord) that relieved the Federal Reserve of the responsibility of supporting the government securities market. Support for government securities, however, continued under the principle of "bills only" or "bills preferably," which facilitated large-scale Treasury refunding operations during times of stringent money market conditions. See Young and Yager (1960).

[26]Although strong, the U.S. growth rate after World War II was below the advanced economy average (see Figure 3.8). This was largely because of the high growth rates in Europe, which resulted from the reconstruction efforts.

Figure 3.8. United States: Debt Dynamics after World War II
(Percent of GDP)

The United States sharply reduced its debt-to-GDP ratio in the five years following World War II thanks to a combination of high negative real interest rates, fiscal surpluses, and strong growth.

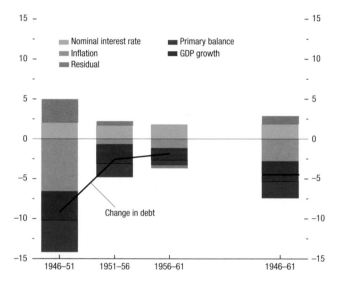

Sources: Abbas and others (2010); Haver Analytics; Reinhart and Rogoff (2010); and IMF staff calculations.
Note: The decomposition of debt dynamics is based on a linearized version of equation (3.1).

Regulation Q and limits on branching.[27] Some of these restrictions (for example, interest ceilings on deposits) were eventually circumvented by financial innovation (for example, money market funds) and thus led to additional intervention in later years (for example, the extension of credit controls by the Consumer Credit Protection Act of 1969). More generally, these restrictions only partially succeeded in stabilizing inflation. In fact, even though the U.S. exchange rate policy fixing the gold value at $35 an ounce did not destabilize prices,[28] inflation remained very volatile throughout the episode and beyond.[29]

Japan 1997: Deflation Redux

Gross Japanese public debt rose above 100 percent of GDP in 1997, during the middle of Japan's "lost decade"—an extended period of mild deflation and output growth near zero, a growth level considerably below that of other advanced economies and Japan's own historical levels (see Figure 3.5, panel 1).[30] The primary cause of the rising debt was a bursting of the stock market and real estate bubbles in 1989–90 and the subsequent weakness in the financial and real sectors of the economy. The initial policy response involved fiscal stimulus, with a sharp deterioration of the fiscal

balance, and interest rate cuts (Figure 3.9). The sharp reduction of inflation expectations, however, was larger than the reduction in interest rates, leading to a real exchange rate appreciation.[31] Moreover, this policy response did not directly address the structural weaknesses in Japan's financial sector. There was a moderate recovery that ended in 1997 when a confluence of events weakened the economy. Though there was a tightening of fiscal policy through a rise in consumption and payroll taxes that had been induced by the growing public debt and rising social security expenditures, the main causes of the economic downturn were as follows. First, the Asian financial crisis occurred and the exchange rate appreciated substantially. Moreover, structural weakness in the banking sector was exacerbated by the poor economic performance, resulting in the onset of a serious banking crisis. The end result was a severe recession that forced the government to abandon its fiscal consolidation plan and led to continued increases in public debt levels.

Monetary policy in this period had limited effect in stimulating economic activity. Although interest rates were close to zero, no credit or quantitative easing policies were implemented. Furthermore, and more seriously, structural problems in the banking sector remained, and this compromised the transmission of monetary policy to lending conditions. Finally, a premature increase in interest rates in 2000 and repercussions from the bursting of the dot-com bubble in the United States exacerbated the situation. The economy again fell into recession in 2001.

There was a second and more effective phase of policy action beginning in 2001. The government turned its attention to fixing the underlying structural problems in the economy. The authorities took significantly more resolute steps to resolve problems in the financial sector, forcing the write-down of bad loans and the recapitalization of banks with private and public funds. The Bank of Japan also began a program of quantitative easing and in

[27]From 1933 to 1986 Regulation Q imposed maximum interest rates on various types of bank deposits, such as demand deposits, savings accounts, and time deposits, which limited competition among banks for funding. Interstate branching was not allowed until 1994.

[28]Given widespread concern about competitive devaluations, the overriding objective of postwar U.S. exchange rate policy was the maintenance of a fixed par value of the dollar as established by the Bretton Woods agreement. Moreover, given that there were relatively few revaluations or devaluations of foreign currencies against gold, the overall system ensured fairly stable exchange rates during this high-debt episode.

[29]Inflation volatility during the episode was more than four times higher than U.S. inflation volatility from 1997 to 2012.

[30]In the case of Japan, the difference between gross and net debt is significant. Due to large gross lending and borrowing positions within the public sector, the net debt-to-GDP ratio in 1997 was only 34 percent. However, both gross debt and net debt have followed a similar trend, with net debt currently exceeding 130 percent of GDP.

[31]The yen's real trade-weighted exchange rate appreciated by about 60 percent in early 1990s, peaking in 1995; after that, it depreciated temporarily during the economic recovery, only to rise again during the Asian crisis.

2002 publicly committed to keeping interest rates low until stable positive inflation returned. The structural reforms to the financial sector and the more accommodative monetary policy environment reversed the downward trend in inflation and led to a relatively strong recovery phase that finally allowed for a mild correction of the fiscal imbalance. A weakening exchange rate and very favorable external environment also contributed to the positive outcomes.[32] During this period, the debt-to-GDP ratio stabilized at about 185 percent. Since then, the Great Recession pushed Japan back into recession, leading to yet another large deterioration in the fiscal balance.

The various phases of this episode are summarized in Figure 3.9, panel 3, which shows the decomposition of Japan's debt dynamics. Growth and inflation made virtually no direct contribution to debt dynamics during this period as a whole—although the increase in debt slowed between 2002 and 2007, when the policy response emphasized monetary measures and growth was stronger. The largest contribution to debt dynamics, however, comes from the primary deficit.

This episode highlights the need to deal with banking sector weakness and ensure a supportive monetary environment before fiscal consolidation can succeed. It also highlights the difficulties that can be created by adverse external developments when domestic conditions are already stretched. When structural weakness in the financial system prevents the normal transmission of monetary stimulus and when policy rates are constrained by the zero lower bound, the risk of anemic and fragile growth is high regardless of the fiscal setting. Such a macroeconomic environment clearly precluded successful fiscal consolidation: whenever such measures were taken the economy dipped into recession.

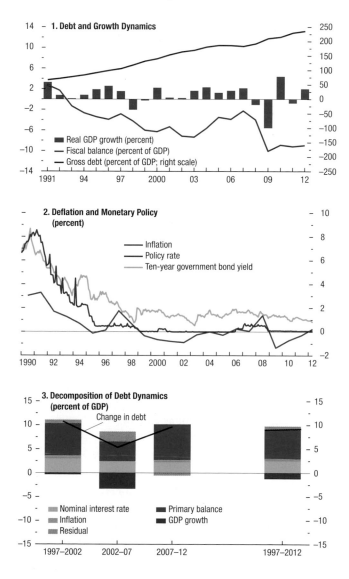

Figure 3.9. Japan: Lost Decade

After stock market and real estate bubbles burst, Japan's weak growth and large fiscal deficits caused a strong increase in the debt-to-GDP ratio. The gradual reduction in policy rates to the zero bound was not sufficient to prevent deflation.

Sources: Abbas and others (2010); Thomson Reuters Datastream; Haver Analytics; and IMF staff calculations.
Note: The decomposition of debt dynamics is based on a linearized version of equation (3.1).

---

[32]The real exchange rate devalued by about 20 percent between 2004 and 2007, thanks, in part, to the more accommodative monetary policy stance.

Italy in 1992: European Monetary Union

Italy's ratio of public debt to GDP rose 70 percentage points in the quarter-century after World War II, a period marked by relatively high inflation and the subordination of monetary policy to the government's desire for low financing costs. In 1992, the debt-to-GDP ratio rose swiftly past 100 percent, peaking at about 120 percent between 1994 and 1996. It subsequently declined moderately, reaching a trough of 104 percent in 2004, as a result of Italy's strong political desire to be a founding member of the euro area.

The criteria of the 1992 Maastricht Treaty, which set out the conditions for membership in the euro area, however, were a serious challenge to Italian ambitions because they required a very strong monetary and fiscal effort from Italian policymakers. Unfortunately, the European exchange rate mechanism (ERM) crisis in September 1992 and the disintegration of long-standing Italian political parties following widespread corruption scandals appeared to further complicate Italian hopes of participating in the euro area. In practice, however, the political instability reinforced a pro-Europe sentiment at various levels of society and opened the door to three technocratic governments that were able to implement a substantial fiscal adjustment and initiate unpopular structural reforms.[33]

On the fiscal front, the consolidation effort included structural reforms that affected pension payments, health services, local authority finance, wage setting, and public employment. An important step was breaking the wage-price spiral, which was accomplished with the suspension and subsequent removal of wage indexation (*scala mobile*) in December 1991 and July 1993.[34] This smoothed the way for the transition to a low-inflation monetary policy regime in line with the Maastricht criteria. In 1993 the government was granted special power to cut primary spending, thus breaking with the past practice of using one-time measures as the main vehicle for deficit reduction, and action was taken to curb the Parliament's power to implement new spending initiatives. Pension reform was particularly important given the rapidly aging population and a generous pension provision that gave Italy one of highest ratios of pension spending to GDP in the world—14 percent in 1994. The reform was a step in the right direction, but there were two drawbacks: first, it was not enough given the demographic trends, and second, the transition phase was particularly long.[35] Thus, although necessary, the benefits of the reform took a long time to directly affect public finances. Despite these promising developments, and reflecting the delay in bottom-line results from some of them, almost half the consolidation was achieved through tax increases.[36]

On the monetary front, 1992 was a year of market turbulence, with Italy's exit from the ERM and the subsequent devaluation of the lira. The currency crisis had two distinct implications for public finances. On one hand, it delivered gains in competitiveness much needed by Italian export industries, thus supporting economic growth. On the other hand, the sharp devaluation stoked inflation and, especially, inflation expectations, which led the Bank of Italy to raise interest rates significantly. The burden of interest payments rose to more than 11 percent of GDP between 1993 and 1995, and this prevented a significant reduction in the overall deficit, which remained stuck above 7 percent.

[33]The technocratic governments were led by Giuliano Amato (June 1992–April 1993), Carlo Azeglio Ciampi (April 1993–May 1994), and Lamberto Dini (January 1995–May 1996) after a brief interlude under Silvio Berlusconi.

[34]The new labor agreement in July 1993 sought greater employer and trade union support for policy targets by explicitly mentioning the policy goals of reducing inflation, cutting the budget deficit, and stabilizing the exchange rate (OECD, 1994).

[35]The 1995 Dini reform of the public pension system was intended to ensure the long-term viability of pension funds by instituting sustainable contribution rates (the system shifted from linking old-age pensions to earnings, *sistema retributivo*, to linking benefits to lifetime contributions, *sistema contributivo*); linking benefits to residual life expectancy at the time of retirement; reviewing pensions for the disabled and survivors; and reviewing guaranteed minimum pensions. The 1995 Dini reform would have eliminated the possibility of retiring after 35 years of service regardless of age (*pensioni di anzianità*), which constituted one of the more generous provisions of the old system, by 2013; starting in 2008, seniority pensions would have required 40 years of service. A few years later, the Prodi Agreement tried to shorten the very long transition phase.

[36]The fiscal consolidation amounted to 13.6 percent of GDP from 1992 to 1995, of which just over 40 percent was from tax increases—the primary balance went from –4 percent in 1987 to 2.9 percent in 1995 (see Devries and others, 2011).

In 1996, immediately after taking office, the government led by Romano Prodi declared as its primary objective Italy's admission to the euro area as a founding member. Prodi's goal was to break the vicious cycle of high expected inflation, high interest rates, high deficits, and again to high expected inflation that would have prevented admission. He gained support from unions and the public to embark on further substantial fiscal consolidation, and this led to implementation of additional measures that eventually reduced the overall deficit to 2.7 percent in 1997, reaching a record primary surplus of 6.1 percent of GDP in 1997.[37] This consolidation topped a 10-year period during which Italy improved its primary balance by slightly more than 10 percentage points—an exceptional performance by historical standards.

Furthermore, the credibility of Italy's commitment to European integration and the feasibility of meeting the Maastricht criteria as perceived by the markets led to a dramatic drop in interest rates in early 1996. This effectively broke the previous vicious cycle and replaced it with a virtuous one. Given the tight timetable, however, some of the deficit reduction inevitably consisted of one-time measures. This is exemplified by the 0.6 percent of GDP "tax for Europe" and by the fact that part of the debt reduction was achieved with substantial proceeds from privatization.[38]

Joining the euro area lowered borrowing costs for the Italian Treasury and made it possible to extend the average maturity of its debt (Figure 3.10), which helped reduce the public debt over the following seven years. After 1998, however, the zeal gradually faded and no substantial additional discretionary consolida-

[37]The convergence was assessed in 1998 on figures for 1997.

[38]From 1990 to 2000, Italy's privatization proceeds were estimated at about $108 billion—the highest relative to GDP among Organization for Economic Cooperation and Development (OECD) countries in both absolute and relative terms (OECD, 2003b). Over the entire episode, privatization receipts accounted for about 10 percentage points of GDP. This means that more than half of the peak-to-trough debt reduction can be attributed to privatization receipts. It is also worth noting that, according to the Maastricht Treaty, privatization proceeds are treated as financing, and therefore they matter for debt reduction but not for the deficit target. In our analysis, however, privatization receipts are included in the primary deficit.

Figure 3.10. Italy: Fading Zeal

In order to meet the Maastricht criteria, Italy achieved large primary surpluses at the end of the 1990s. The debt ratio also started to decline thanks to the reduction in real interest rates. Fiscal consolidation efforts, however, waned during the 2000s.

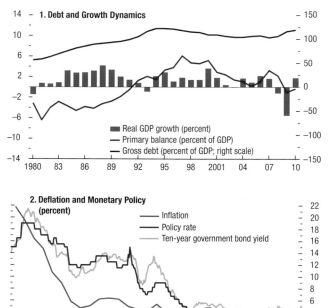

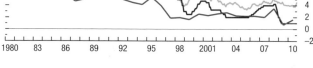

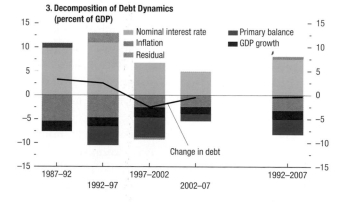

Sources: Abbas and others (2010); Bank of Italy; Thomson Reuters Datastream; Haver Analytics; and IMF staff calculations.
Note: The decomposition of debt dynamics is based on a linearized version of equation (3.1).

tion efforts were undertaken.[39] Moreover, because some of the fiscal measures were temporary, the primary surplus started to decline after peaking in 1997. As a result the speed of debt reduction was modest and reflected momentum more than ongoing effort.

These developments can be seen in the debt decomposition summary in Figure 3.10, panel 3. A move into primary surplus during 1993–97 was offset by tight monetary policy, but with the easing of monetary conditions during 1998–02, debt dropped more significantly—at least until the primary surpluses faded away during 2003–07. Also notable is that GDP growth made a very modest contribution to debt reduction throughout this period. Indeed, the economy's growth rate remained weak, considerably below the advanced economy average (see Figure 3.5, panel 1).

Belgium in 1983: Ten Years of Consolidation before Currency Union

A comparison of the Italian experience with that of Belgium is quite instructive, because Belgium experienced, eventually, a more successful outcome under very similar circumstances. The Belgian story starts approximately 10 years earlier with the debt-to-GDP ratio crossing the 100 percent threshold in 1983. As in Italy, Belgium's large primary deficits, slow growth, and the central bank's relatively tight anti-inflation stance combined to put the debt-to-GDP ratio on an unsustainable path.

From 1982 to 1987 Belgium embarked on a serious fiscal consolidation effort that culminated with the 1987 "Sint-Anna" or "Val Duchesse" deficit reduction plan. This plan consisted mainly of structural reforms that delivered permanent spending cuts of 2.8 percent of GDP. The plan, coupled with previous fiscal consolidation efforts (again, mainly structural and spending based), led to substantial primary surpluses and even a temporary reduction in the debt-to-GDP ratio. Over the 10-year period from 1981 to 1991, Belgium improved its primary

balance by 11 percentage points—the largest consolidation over any 10-year period among advanced economies since World War II.[40]

The policies pursued focused on trimming the share of public employment, reducing an excessively generous system of welfare payments, cutting family allowances and unemployment insurance benefits, and increasing the retirement age. In the business sector, there was little scope for privatization compared with other countries such as Italy, but corporate tax expenditures and subsidies—among the highest in the OECD—were reduced substantially.[41] These priorities were a reaction to policies pursued between the mid-1970s and early 1980s that markedly increased subsidies to business, public sector employment, and transfer payments to households. Finally, in the early 1990s, under the "global plan," pension expenditures and health care costs were curbed further. [42] However, during the past 30 years there was no relevant structural reform to improve the flexibility and efficiency of the labor market, which has left Belgium plagued with low labor participation and high short- and long-term unemployment for most of the high-debt episode and beyond. The main achievement with respect to the labor market was the wage moderation process, which since the mid-1980s has linked wage increases to those in Belgium's major trading partners (Germany, France, Netherlands).[43]

---

[39]During the period 2003–05 the European Union Stability and Growth Pact was watered down, in part because of core European countries' poor growth performance. In any case, Italy undertook some additional consolidation from 2004 to 2007, after the 2003 recession.

[40]For a list of the largest primary balance improvements in advanced economies and emerging markets, see Abbas and others (2010).

[41]It was estimated that "total aid to business—subsidies, capital transfers, loans and government equity investment has averaged 5.5 percent of GNP (gross national product) a year since the early 1970s, attaining 8.9 per cent in 1982" (OECD, 1986, p. 25). For comparison, in Italy business subsidies were equal to only about 3 percent of business sector value added during 1980–87 (OECD, 1994, p. 54).

[42]On November 17, 1993, a comprehensive plan for employment, competitiveness, and the social security system was approved by the Belgian government. OECD (2003a) reports that "a new method of calculating pensions will be introduced (the base period for calculating pensions will be longer, and pensions for men and women will be harmonized)"; other constraints and cost-cutting measures are mentioned for health care costs. The age limit for early retirement was raised from 55 to 58.

[43]Also, like Italy, Belgium was listed among OECD countries as having the most market-unfriendly product market regulation, mainly because of barriers to entrepreneurship (see OECD, 2003a).

Belgium's fiscal effort was hampered by monetary conditions at the time and by a slowdown in global activity in the early 1990s.[44] Although the wage moderation process helped break the wage-price spiral, which contributed to endemic inflation, it still took some time and a period of high interest rates (aimed at maintaining the peg to the European Currency Unit) for monetary policy to succeed in delivering low and stable inflation. Hence, the debt-to-GDP ratio started to rise again in 1990 and peaked at 134 percent in 1993, a recession year. Even during the recession, however, the Belgian government was able to run a primary surplus—highlighting how beneficial the structural measures taken in the 1980s were for public finances.

A second multiyear convergence plan was enacted in the early 1990s to meet the Maastricht criteria by reducing the budget deficit to less than 3 percent by 1997.[45] This plan included a mix of additional spending cuts and tax increases—but it was fundamentally built on the foundation established by the successful 1980s consolidation. Moreover, the fiscal framework was strengthened: first, in 1989 the High Council of Finance was vested with a renewed advisory role for budgetary policy; second, in 1994, the National Accounting Institute was established to provide macroeconomic forecasts for use in budget preparation. Both actions were fundamental to increasing government accountability for budgetary policy.[46]

On the monetary front, the successful fiscal consolidation of the 1980s gave markets confidence that the convergence plan would likewise be successful. As a result, in 1993 short-term bond rates were on a steep downward path, and long-term bond rates soon followed.[47] Inflation, which had been reduced in the

[44]The real growth rate deteriorated from more than 3 percent in 1990 to –0.7 percent in 1993, in line with other advanced economies.

[45]The fiscal consolidation of the 1990s included privatization and sales of assets (such as the central bank gold reserve). The impact of these temporary measures, however, was minor in Belgium compared with Italy.

[46]See European Commission (2012).

[47]The decomposition in Figure 3.11, panel 3, shows that the more benign monetary conditions, evidenced by falling interest rates during the episode, contributed significantly to the reduction in debt levels.

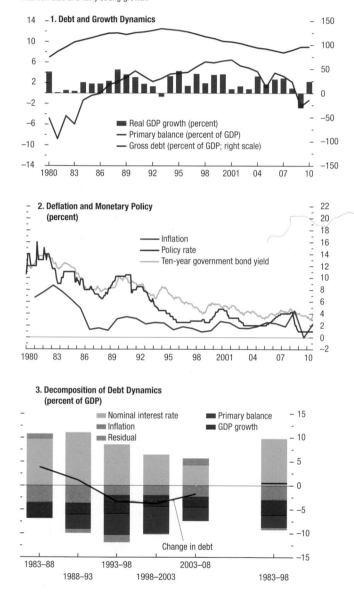

Figure 3.11. Belgium: A Marathon Not a Sprint

Belgium achieved large primary surpluses in the late 1980s and maintained them for about 15 years. The debt ratio also fell considerably in the 1990s thanks to a reduction in real interest rates and fairly strong growth.

1. Debt and Growth Dynamics

- Real GDP growth (percent)
- Primary balance (percent of GDP)
- Gross debt (percent of GDP; right scale)

2. Deflation and Monetary Policy
(percent)

- Inflation
- Policy rate
- Ten-year government bond yield

3. Decomposition of Debt Dynamics
(percent of GDP)

- Nominal interest rate
- Inflation
- Residual
- Primary balance
- GDP growth

Change in debt

1983–88   1993–98   2003–08
1988–93   1998–2003   1983–98

Sources: Abbas and others (2010); Thomson Reuters Datastream; Haver Analytics; and IMF staff calculations.
Note: The decomposition of debt dynamics is based on a linearized version of equation (3.1).

late 1980s, oscillated around 2 percent.[48] One consequence was that, in contrast to the first effort, this convergence plan led to a sustained drop in debt.

In sum, Belgium's public finances were already on a sounder footing than Italy's by the end of the 1980s. The permanent structural measures taken in the 1980s projected beneficial effects into the future. As a result Belgium required a milder fiscal adjustment to meet the Maastricht criteria than Italy, and the changes in the fiscal framework adopted in the 1990s helped prevent slippages and the onset of fiscal consolidation fatigue. At the same time, given the credibility attached to the 1992 convergence plan, Belgium benefited from a much needed reduction in real interest payments earlier than Italy. It is hard to say whether this is what contributed to its relatively better growth performance, but between 1993 and 2007 Belgium reduced its debt-to-GDP ratio by 50 percentage points—substantially more than Italy.

Canada in 1995: Success from Failure

As in Belgium, there were two phases to Canada's fiscal consolidation: an initial unsuccessful phase in the second half of the 1980s and a later successful consolidation starting in 1995. We discuss them both here because the earlier consolidation effort provides a valuable comparison with the ultimately successful consolidation in the mid-1990s.

In the early 1980s, a combination of high primary deficits and tight monetary policy put the Canadian general government debt on an unstable path—from 1981 to 1986 the debt increased by about 25 percentage points (Figure 3.12, panel 1). This prospect induced the newly elected government of Brian Mulroney to embark on a multiyear fiscal consolidation plan that, beginning in 1985, aimed at stabilizing the debt-to-GDP ratio at 65 percent by 1990–91.

The actual implementation of the 1985 plan implied a fiscal consolidation that was split roughly evenly between tax hikes and spending cuts (see Guajardo, Leigh, and Pescatori, 2011) and was able to achieve a temporary balanced primary budget in

1989. The overall debt performance was less successful. In fact, given the high real and nominal interest payments followed by the sharp 1990–91 recession, the debt-to-GDP ratio kept rising and peaked at 102 percent in 1995. The recession left a large scar on fiscal revenue,[49] while government spending kept increasing in real terms until 1993, mainly as a result of automatic stabilizers.

Various reasons have been advanced for the failure of the 1985 consolidation.[50] One explanation is that the adjustment in expenditures relied mainly on poorly specified across-the-board cuts and efficiency gains that did not impose fundamental changes in the way government expenses were determined and so did not persist. Moreover, some of the measures were also temporary. For example, the plan imposed a temporary surtax on higher-income individuals and large corporations and garnered some savings from privatization. Thus, while the primary balance did improve during the 10 years from 1985 to 1995, the improvement amounted to just under 6 percentage points of GDP because it was interrupted by the recession of the early 1990s. The consolidation effort did, however, introduce a number of permanent measures that helped future Canadian governments, including a change from full to partial indexation of tax brackets. Another factor, which becomes clearer on examination of the 1995 consolidation, is that both the monetary and external environments were hostile to debt reduction. Monetary policy was particularly tight because the Bank of Canada was attempting to reduce inflation with high real interest rates during this time (Figure 3.12, panel 2), and the recession, which coincided with a global slowdown, undermined growth and government finances (more below).

In 1995, after having crossed the 100 percent debt-to-GDP threshold and with substantial public support, the Canadian government launched another ambitious fiscal consolidation plan.[51] Given the

---

[48]As for various other European countries, 1994, the year after the ERM collapse, was an exception.

[49]Revenue recovered slowly, possibly due to the performance of the housing market: housing prices dropped by 7 percent from their peak in 1990 and did not recover quickly, while stock prices started to increase only in 1995.

[50]See, for example, Sancak, Liu, and Nakata (2011) for a more detailed discussion of the Canadian experience.

[51]Convincing the public of the importance of reducing public debt was an important element in the government's approach to

already high level of taxation and disappointment with the earlier consolidation, this plan was mainly spending based and tackled some fundamental structural issues behind the fiscal imbalances. In particular, the plan implemented structural reforms to the unemployment insurance system, the system of transfers to provinces, and the pension system.[52] The reduction in transfers to the provinces imposed additional fiscal discipline at the subnational level, with the effect of improving provincial finances as well. Moreover, the consolidation was supported by the fact that in the mid-1990s, most Canadian provinces legislated some form of fiscal regulation that explicitly imposed specific limits on fiscal indicators such as budgetary balances, spending, and taxation.[53] This helped boost the persistence of the fiscal effort. As a result, the primary balance moved to a consistent strong surplus, and debt fell by 35 percentage points over the subsequent 10 years.

The success of the fiscal consolidation effort of the 1990s was clearly amplified by the benign external and domestic environment. Domestically, after the Bank of Canada adopted an inflation-targeting framework in 1991, the country was enjoying the benefits of relatively low interest rates in an environment of low and stable inflation, while the exchange rate depreciated slowly but steadily over the period.[54] As a consequence, real rates dropped substantially along with the premium associated with the risk of resurgent inflation. The debt-service burden fell from almost 10 percent of GDP in 1995 to about 7 percent in 2000. Moreover, the United States, Canada's foremost trading partner, experienced an extraordinary boom in the late 1990s. This, coupled with a strong decrease in the real effective exchange rate, helped spur the Canadian export sector: the contribution of exports to GDP growth averaged more than 3 percentage points between 1993 and 2000. Despite the propitious monetary and exter-

the issue. Furthermore, unfavorable comparisons of Canada with Mexico by the *Wall Street Journal* in the wake of the peso crisis and Moody's credit watch on Canada prior to the 1995 budget underscored the importance for the public of dealing with debt.

[52]See Sancak, Liu, and Nakata (2011) for further details.
[53]See Millar (1997).
[54]The depreciation of the Canadian dollar was supported by the relatively stronger performance of the U.S. economy at the time and by declines in commodity prices during the 1990s.

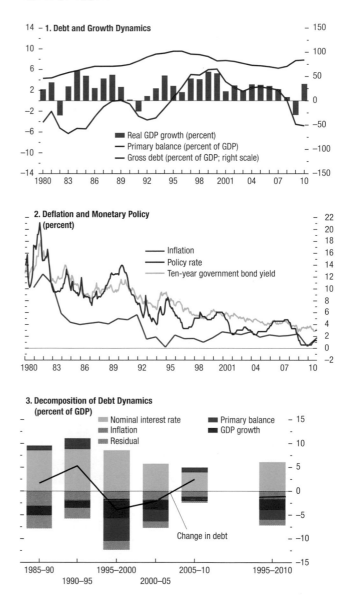

Figure 3.12. Canada: Fiscal Consolidation after 1985

Canada went through two distinct consolidation phases in the 1980s and 1990s, the latter leading to larger primary surpluses and declining debt. The 1990s debt reduction was also supported by strong growth.

1. Debt and Growth Dynamics

- Real GDP growth (percent)
— Primary balance (percent of GDP)
— Gross debt (percent of GDP; right scale)

2. Deflation and Monetary Policy
(percent)

— Inflation
— Policy rate
— Ten-year government bond yield

3. Decomposition of Debt Dynamics
(percent of GDP)

Nominal interest rate   Primary balance
Inflation   GDP growth
Residual

Change in debt

Sources: Abbas and others (2010); Thomson Reuters Datastream; Haver Analytics; and IMF staff calculations.
Note: The decomposition of debt dynamics is based on a linearized version of equation (3.1).

Figure 3.13. Decomposition of Debt Dynamics in Case Study Countries
(Percent of GDP)

Despite large fiscal surpluses, the United Kingdom experienced sharply higher debt due to very high real interest rates caused by deflation. The United States successfully reduced debt through a combination of negative real interest rates and growth. Japan's increase in debt resulted mostly from its large fiscal deficits. The second phase of debt reduction for Belgium, Canada, and Italy was supported by larger fiscal surpluses and lower real interest rates.

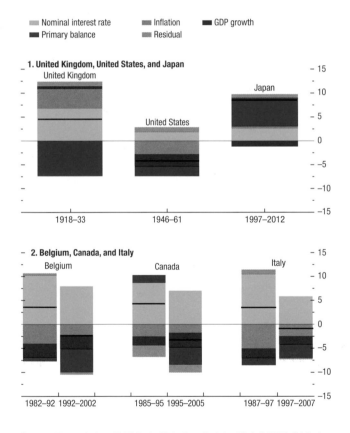

Sources: Abbas and others (2010); Bank of Italy; Haver Analytics; Mitchell (1998); Reinhart and Rogoff (2010); and IMF staff calculations.
Note: The decomposition of debt dynamics is based on a linearized version of equation (3.1).

nal environment, GDP growth remained below the advanced economy average (see Figure 3.5, panel 1).

Figure 3.12, panel 3, shows the decomposition of the debt dynamics over these years. Given the relevance of the 1985 consolidation, two bars are added to cover this period, although the average is still for the 15 years following 1995. Strong growth, a large primary surplus, and falling real interest rates contribute strongly to debt reduction after 1995. Finally, the effect of the Great Recession is visible in the last bar—weak growth and countercyclical fiscal stimulus added to the debt during this period.

Overall, this episode highlights how fiscal, monetary, and external factors all contribute to the outcome. The shift in the composition of fiscal efforts toward structural reforms and a rule-based fiscal framework at the subnational level contributed to the success of consolidation in 1995. But the influence of both monetary and external conditions is also evident. In the 1985 plan, both monetary and external conditions hampered contraction, whereas in 1995 these influences were supportive. Furthermore, even in a sound monetary and fiscal setting, the effects of the Great Recession show that external events can still compromise domestic debt reduction.

Analysis

This section draws together the experiences of the countries covered in the case studies by comparing the policy objectives pursued, the instruments used (such as policy rates, exchange rates, primary surpluses, and institutional frameworks), and the outcomes achieved. To facilitate this comparison, Figure 3.13 shows debt decompositions for the six cases. This comparison yields a number of lessons on how to best deal with high levels of public debt.

The first key lesson is that a supportive monetary environment is a necessary condition for successful fiscal consolidation. This is evident from the cases of the United Kingdom, the United States, and Japan (Figure 3.13, panel 1). In the United Kingdom, despite substantial fiscal efforts that achieved and sustained large primary surpluses, public debt ratios were not reduced. The reason is the simultaneous pursuit of a return to the gold standard at the prewar parity, which required a tight monetary policy stance and exceptionally high real interest rates, which offset the contribution of fiscal surpluses to debt reduction. At the same time, domestic prices did not fall enough to produce a real exchange rate depreciation due to the concomitant appreciation of the pound to prewar parity. Furthermore, this combination of tight fiscal and monetary policies delivered negative growth, exacerbating the debt problem.

Given that both fiscal and monetary policies were tight in the United Kingdom, it is conceivable that either or both were to blame for the poor outcomes. However, the cases of Japan, which had tight monetary conditions and loose fiscal conditions, and the United States, which had loose monetary and tight fiscal conditions, allow us to attribute the outcomes more clearly to the monetary stance, as explained below.

In Japan, monetary policy was constrained by the zero lower bound after the bursting of the stock market and real estate bubbles in the early 1990s. In addition, the monetary transmission mechanism was impaired by financial sector problems. With low growth and deflation, the Japanese authorities were in a difficult position with respect to fiscal consolidation. Attempts to tighten fiscal policies were either quickly abandoned after economic conditions deteriorated or not seriously pursued. If Japan had persisted with tight fiscal policy, it seems likely that it would have experienced even stronger deflation and lower growth, just as in the United Kingdom. Still, despite an expansionary fiscal policy stance, growth remained anemic and public debt ratios kept increasing.

In the United States after World War II, vivid memories of the Great Depression led people to fear deflation more than inflation. The high level of war debt and the associated potentially high interest burden were also a source of concern. The authorities adopted a policy mix that resulted in an exceptionally supportive monetary environment combined with tight fiscal policy. Specifically, they adopted various policy measures (often referred to as "financial repression") that aimed at keeping the nominal rates on government bonds low, while controlling inflation with a tight fiscal stance and credit controls. This policy mix resulted in two substantial bursts of inflation, which led to large negative real rates and a sharp reduction in the debt-to-GDP

ratio. The supportive monetary stance was also instrumental in lowering private borrowing rates, thus providing stimulus to the economy. Based on growth and fiscal performance, this policy mix was undoubtedly successful—although inflation volatility remained relatively high. Thus, we conclude that a supportive monetary policy stance is a key ingredient in successful debt reduction.

What is less clear, however, is whether this approach could be applied in today's economic and financial environment. The set of controls and regulations needed for financial repression to be effective would lead to a much less internationally integrated financial system than we have today. Furthermore, an unexpected burst of inflation—which accounted for much of the debt reduction in the United States episode—could jeopardize the institutional framework built by central banks over the past 30 years for controlling inflation.[55]

Leaving aside the possibility of large inflation surprises and financial repression, the most realistic policy options for today appear to be those followed by Belgium, Canada, and Italy. All three countries implemented large fiscal adjustment in an environment where the goal of reaching or maintaining low inflation was considered necessary for economic stability. Their degrees of success in reducing public debt, however, varied.[56] This variation leads us to three additional conclusions and reinforces our first conclusion about the importance of monetary policy in successful debt reduction.

First, even in an environment where inflation is low, a supportive monetary environment with low real rates is important to facilitate a reduction in public debt. The monetary environment was tight in the 1980s (and in Italy until the mid-1990s) because of disinflationary efforts by central banks. As a result, debt continued to increase in all three countries. Figure 3.13, panel 2, shows that high real

---

[55]It is also worth noting that the period of financial repression ended with the collapse of the Bretton Woods international monetary system because of the loss of U.S. competitiveness vis-à-vis its trading partners, which opened the doors to the great inflation of the 1970s.

[56]This can be seen from Figure 3.13, panel 2, where we present the debt decompositions for each country across the two main phases (that is, a tight or supportive monetary policy stance) that we have identified in the previous case studies.

interest rates contributed to the rise in debt levels in the initial years of each episode, despite tight fiscal policies. It was only when real rates fell—after disinflation was achieved and credible monetary policy frameworks were established—that all countries were able to reduce their debt.

Second, debt reduction is larger when fiscal measures are permanent or structural and buttressed by a fiscal framework that supports the measures implemented. Italian fiscal adjustment efforts led to a considerable improvement in the fiscal balance. However, especially before 1992, they were biased toward temporary measures that failed to put public debt on a steadily decreasing path—in part because of the lack of a fiscal framework to lock in the fiscal gains achieved.[57] In fact, faced with very high levels of taxation, fiscal efforts waned after Italy entered the EMU. Similarly, Canada in the 1980s complemented tax hikes with spending cuts, but the reduction in spending was achieved with across-the-board cuts that proved to be short lived. In contrast, in the 1990s, Canada's fiscal plans were much more successful in persistently reducing public debt. This is because they were based on well-targeted and structural measures, including pension and entitlement reforms in a context of tight fiscal rules at the subnational level. Similarly, Belgium's ability to achieve large and persistent primary surpluses can largely be explained by structural spending cuts, which involved reductions in public employment and reforms to the excessively generous welfare system in the context of a fiscal framework that enhanced accountability.

Third, the relatively successful experiences of Belgium and Canada in the 1990s were facilitated by a boost from strong external demand (Figure 3.14).[58] While external demand is influenced by various factors, currency depreciation helped in both cases (Canada in the first half of the 1990s, Belgium in the second half of the 1990s). The Italian economy benefited from the sharp devaluation after the 1992 ERM crisis, but, in part because of its relatively more closed economy, the

Figure 3.14. Contribution to GDP from Exports
(Percent of GDP)

The debt reductions in the 1990s for Belgium and Canada were achieved in the context of strong export performance.

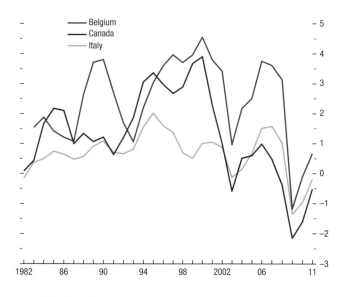

Source: IMF staff calculations.

---

[57]As a matter of fact, Italy passed important entitlement reforms in the mid-1990s, but their major benefits accumulated only very gradually over time.

[58]The average ratio of exports to GDP between 1992 and 2007 in Belgium, Canada, and Italy was 0.65, 0.34, and 0.23, respectively.

export contribution to output growth was smaller and relatively short lived. Hence, although precise attribution is difficult here, a supportive external environment clearly contributes to the relatively better growth performance and relatively better debt reduction in Canada and Belgium compared with Italy.

Fourth, it takes time to turn around primary deficits. Emblematic is the case of Belgium, which, despite achieving the largest peacetime improvement in the primary balance since World War II between 1981 and 1991, still took 10 years to move from a deficit of about 7 percent to a surplus of 4 percent. The effect of this transition on the level of debt is visible in Figure 3.13, panel 2: the average contribution of the primary balance to debt reduction between 1982 and 1992 was actually very small. The observation that it takes time to turn around primary balances is confirmed by looking at the full sample of countries. Among advanced economies since 1980, improvements of greater than 10 percentage points over a 10-year period are exceedingly rare. Canada's best improvement was 6.7 percentage points between 1990 and 2000, and Italy achieved a 10.2 percentage point improvement between 1987 and 1997—both among the best since 1980 among advanced economies. In short, sustained improvements of more than 1 percentage point a year are rare, and this means that, when starting from a primary deficit, debt reduction takes a particularly long time.

Summing up, historical experience suggests that countries dealing with high debt burdens are unlikely to experience strong improvements in their debt ratios while real rates are high and monetary conditions remain tight. Assuming that sufficiently supportive monetary conditions can be achieved, fiscal policy focused on permanent or structural reforms appears to provide larger and more enduring debt reductions than do policies based on more temporary measures.

Conclusion

For countries currently struggling with high public debt burdens, the historical record offers both instructive lessons and cautionary tales. The first lesson is that fiscal consolidation efforts need to be complemented by measures that support growth: structural

issues need to be addressed and monetary conditions need to be as supportive as possible. In Japan, for example, weaknesses in the banking system and corporate sector limited monetary policy efficacy and led to weak growth, which prevented fiscal consolidation. As a result, debt continued climbing until these issues were addressed. In Italy, Belgium, and Canada, debt did not fall until monetary conditions were supportive. Here, reforms to wage-setting mechanisms that broke the wage-price spiral were an important contributor to the establishment of the supportive monetary environment. Furthermore, monetary easing also fostered exchange rate depreciation, which supported external demand and growth.

The case of the United Kingdom reinforces this message but also offers a cautionary lesson for countries attempting internal devaluation. The combination of tight monetary and tight fiscal policy, aimed at significantly reducing the price level and returning to the prewar parity, had disastrous outcomes. Unemployment was high, growth was low, and—most relevant—debt continued to grow. Although the price level reduction the United Kingdom was attempting to achieve is larger than anything likely to happen as a result of internal devaluation today, similar dynamics are evident. A reduction in the price level, a necessary part of internal devaluation, comes at a high cost, and determining whether the cost outweighs the benefit to competitiveness from internal devaluation requires further work.

The case of the United States, although supporting the general finding about the contribution of monetary policy, points to more outside-the-box possibilities. U.S. monetary policy was very supportive in the immediate postwar years as a result of limits on nominal interest rates and bursts of inflation. This particular combination quickly reduced the debt ratio while growth remained robust. Whether financial repression could assist in reducing debt burdens in today's environment, however, is much harder to gauge. Given that the major problem for the United States in those years was controlling excess demand and inflation—which is not a problem faced by the countries struggling with public debt today—it seems likely that financial repression as practiced by the United States after World War II would not be effective today for countries already benefiting from historically low sovereign interest rates. Moreover, the inflationary consequences of financial repression could endanger the institutional frameworks established over the past 30 years to control inflation. Whether policies inspired by this experience could help remains an open question.

The implications vary for countries dealing with high debt levels today. For some, such as the United States, where financial sector weakness has largely been addressed and monetary policy is as supportive as possible, it would seem that conditions are in place for fiscal consolidation. In others, such as the European periphery, where financial sectors remain weak and fundamental issues relating to monetary union remain to be addressed, progress may be limited until these issues are resolved.

A second lesson is that consolidation plans should emphasize persistent, structural reforms over temporary or short-lived measures. Belgium and Canada were ultimately much more successful than Italy in reducing debt, and a key difference between these cases is the relative weight placed on structural improvements versus temporary efforts. Moreover, both Belgium and Canada put in place fiscal frameworks in the 1990s that preserved the improvement in the fiscal balance and mitigated consolidation fatigue.

A third lesson is that fiscal repair and debt reduction take time—with the exception of postwar episodes, primary deficits have not been quickly reversed. A corollary is that this increases the vulnerability to significant setbacks when shocks hit. The sharp increases in public debt since the Great Recession—including in the relatively successful cases of Belgium and Canada—exemplify such vulnerability. Furthermore, the external environment has been an important contributor to outcomes in the past. The implications for today are sobering—widespread fiscal consolidation efforts, deleveraging pressures from the private sector, adverse demographic trends, and the aftermath of the financial crisis are unlikely to provide the supportive external environment that played an important role in a number of previous episodes of debt reduction. Expectations about what can be achieved need to be set realistically.

Based on these lessons, we suggest a road map for successful resolution of the current public debt over-

hangs. First, support for growth is essential to cope with the contractionary effects of fiscal consolidation. Policies must emphasize the resolution of underlying structural problems within the economy, and monetary policy must be as supportive as possible. Such policy support is particularly important at this point because all major economies must address public debt overhangs, which means they cannot rely on favorable external conditions. Second, because debt reduction takes time, fiscal consolidation should focus on enduring structural change. In this respect, fiscal institutions can help. Third, while realism is needed when it comes to expectations about future debt trajectories and setting debt targets in a relatively weaker global growth environment, the case of Italy in the 1990s suggests that debt reduction is still possible even without strong growth.

References

Abbas, S.M. Ali, Olivier Basdevant, Stephanie Eble, Greetje Everaert, Jan Gottschalk, Fuad Hasanov, Junhyung Park, Cemile Sancak, Ricardo Velloso, and Mauricio Villafuerte, 2010, "Strategies for Fiscal Consolidation in the Post-Crisis World," Fiscal Affairs Department Paper No. 10/04 (Washington: International Monetary Fund).

Abbas, S. Ali, Nazim Belhocine, Asmaa ElGanainy, and Mark Horton, 2010, "A Historical Public Debt Database," IMF Working Paper No. 10/245 (Washington: International Monetary Fund).

———, 2011, "Historical Patterns and Dynamics of Public Debt—Evidence From A New Database," *IMF Economic Review*, Vol. 59, No. 4, pp. 717–42.

Cecchetti, Stephen G., M.S. Mohanty, and Fabrizio Zampolli, 2011, "The Real Effects of Debt," BIS Working Paper No. 352 (Basel: Bank for International Settlements).

Devries, Pete, Jaime Guajardo, Daniel Leigh, and Andrea Pescatori, 2011, "An Action-Based Analysis of Fiscal Consolidation in OECD Countries," IMF Working Paper No. 11/128 (Washington: International Monetary Fund).

Dippelsman, Robert, Claudia Dziobek, and Carlos A. Gutiérrez Mangas, 2012, "What Lies Beneath: The Statistical Definition of Public Sector Debt," IMF Staff Discussion Note No. 12/09 (Washington: International Monetary Fund).

Eichengreen, Barry, Ricardo Hausmann, and Ugo Panizza, 2005, "The Pain of Original Sin," in *Other People's Money: Debt Denomination and Financial Instability in Emerging Market Economies,* ed. by Barry Eichengreen and Ricardo Hausmann (Chicago: University of Chicago Press), pp. 13–47.

Escolano, Julio, Anna Shabunina, and Jaejoon Woo, 2011, "The Puzzle of Persistently Negative Interest Rate–Growth Differentials: Financial Repression or Income Catch-Up?" IMF Working Paper No. 11/260 (Washington: International Monetary Fund).

European Commission, 2012, "Fiscal Frameworks across Member States: Commission Services Country Fiches from the 2011 EPC Peer Review," European Commission Occasional Paper No. 91 (Brussels).

Feinstein, Charles H., 1972, *National Income, Expenditure and Output of the United Kingdom, 1855–1965* (Cambridge, United Kingdom: Cambridge University Press).

Friedman, Milton, and Anna Jacobson Schwartz, 1963, *A Monetary History of the United States: 1867–1960* (Princeton, New Jersey: Princeton University Press).

Guajardo, Jaime, Daniel Leigh, and Andrea Pescatori, 2011, "Expansionary Austerity: New International Evidence," IMF Working Paper No. 11/158 (Washington: International Monetary Fund).

Honohan, Patrick, and Brendan Walsh, 2002, "Catching Up with the Leaders: The Irish Hare," *Brookings Papers on Economic Activity, No. 1* (Washington: Brookings Institution).

Keynes, Maynard, 1928, "The Stabilization of the Franc," *New Republic*, Vol. 55, No. 711, p. 218.

Krugman, Paul, 2012, *End this Depression Now!* (New York: W.W. Norton & Company).

Kumar, Manmohan S., and Jaejoon Woo, 2010, "Public Debt and Growth," IMF Working Paper No. 10/174 (Washington: International Monetary Fund).

Lloyd George, David, 1928, "Franc Stabilization Is Crowning Triumph," *Pittsburgh Post-Gazette*, July 8, p. 10.

Maddison, Angus, 2003, *The World Economy: Historical Statistics* (Paris: Organization for Economic Cooperation and Development).

Mauro, Paulo, ed., 2011, *Chipping Away at Public Debt: Sources of Failure and Keys to Success in Fiscal Adjustment* (Washington: International Monetary Fund).

Meltzer, Allan, 2003, *A History of the Federal Reserve: Volume 1: 1913-1951* (Chicago: University of Chicago Press).

Millar, Jonathan, 1997, "The Effects of Budget Rules on Fiscal Performance and Macroeconomic Stabilization," Bank of Canada Working Paper No. 97-15 (Ottawa: Bank of Canada).

Mitchell, B. R., 1998, *International Historical Statistics: Europe 1750–1993* (London: Macmillan Reference).

Organization for Economic Cooperation and Development (OECD), 1986, *Economic Survey of Italy* (Paris).

———, 1994, *Economic Survey of Italy* (Paris).

———, 2003a, *Economic Survey of Belgium* (Paris).

———, 2003b, *Economic Survey of Italy* (Paris).

Ostry, Jonathan, Atish Ghosh, Jun Kim, and Mahvash Qureshi, 2010, "Fiscal Space," IMF Staff Position Note No. 10/11 (Washington: International Monetary Fund).

Panizza, Ugo, and Andrea F. Presbitero, 2012, "Public Debt and Economic Growth: Is There a Causal Effect?" MoFiR Working Paper No. 65 (Ancona, Italy: Money and Finance Research Group).

Perotti, Roberto, 2012, "The 'Austerity Myth': Gain Without Pain?" in *Fiscal Policy after the Financial Crisis*, ed. by Alberto Alesina and Francesco Giavazzi (Chicago: University of Chicago Press).

Pollard, Sidney, 1992, *The Development of the British Economy 1914-1990* (London: Edward Arnold).

Reinhart, Carmen M., Jacob F. Kirkegaard, and M. Belén Sbrancia, 2011, "Financial Repression Redux," *Finance & Development*, Vol. 48, No. 2, pp. 22–26.

Reinhart, Carmen M., Vincent Reinhart, and Kenneth S. Rogoff, 2012, "Public Debt Overhangs: Advanced Economy Episodes Since 1800," *Journal of Economic Perspectives*, Vol. 26, No. 3, pp. 69–86.

Reinhart, Carmen M., and Kenneth S. Rogoff, 2010, "Growth in a Time of Debt," *American Economic Review: Papers and Proceedings*, Vol. 100, No. 2, pp. 573–78.

Reinhart, Carmen M., and M. Belén Sbrancia, 2011, "The Liquidation of Government Debt," NBER Working Paper No. 16893 (Cambridge, Massachusetts: National Bureau of Economic Research).

Sancak, Cemile, Lucy Qian Liu, and Taisuke Nakata 2001, "Canada: A Success Story," in *Chipping Away at Public Debt: Sources of Failure and Keys to Success in Fiscal Adjustment*, ed. by Paolo Mauro (Hoboken, New Jersey: John Wiley & Sons).

Truman, Harry S., 1947, *Economic Report of the President*, January 9.

Young, Ralph A., and Charles A. Yager, 1960, "The Economics of 'Bills Preferably,' " *The Quarterly Journal of Economics*, Vol. 74, No. 3, pp. 341–73.

CHAPTER 4

RESILIENCE IN EMERGING MARKET AND DEVELOPING ECONOMIES: WILL IT LAST?

Many emerging market and developing economies have done well over the past decade and through the global financial crisis. Will this last? This chapter documents the marked improvement in these economies' resilience over the past 20 years. These economies did so well during the past decade that for the first time, emerging market and developing economies spent more time in expansion and had smaller downturns than advanced economies. Their improved performance is explained by both good policies and a lower incidence of external and domestic shocks: better policies account for about three-fifths of their improved performance, and less-frequent shocks account for the rest. However, should the external environment worsen, these economies will likely end up "recoupling" with advanced economies. Homegrown shocks could also pull down growth. These economies will need to rebuild their buffers to ensure that they are able to respond to potential shocks on the horizon.

During 2003–07 growth in emerging market and developing economies accelerated (Figure 4.1, panel 1), even as growth in advanced economies remained weak. This stimulated a vigorous debate on whether emerging market and developing economies had decoupled from the advanced economies.[1] That debate was silenced temporarily by the global crisis that emanated from the United States and Europe—in fact, more than half of emerging market and developing economies experienced negative growth in 2009 (Figure 4.1, panel 2). But they quickly bounced back, and during 2010–11 many of them grew at or above precrisis rates. As a result, they now account for virtually all of global growth (Figure 4.1, panel 3).

The question on policymakers' minds now is whether this strong performance will last. Beyond

The authors of this chapter are Abdul Abiad (team leader), John Bluedorn, Jaime Guajardo, and Petia Topalova, with support from Angela Espiritu and Katherine Pan.

[1]For a summary of this debate, see Kose (2008) and, in the *World Economic Outlook,* Chapter 4 of the April 2007 report and Chapter 1 of the April 2008 report.

Figure 4.1. The Strong Performance of Emerging Market and Developing Economies
(Percent)

Growth in emerging market and developing economies accelerated in the mid-2000s, leading to talk of their decoupling from advanced economies. Emerging market and developing economies were not spared during the global downturn; most experienced negative growth in 2009. But many have recovered and are growing at or above precrisis rates, despite continued weakness in advanced economies. As a result, they now account for almost all global growth.

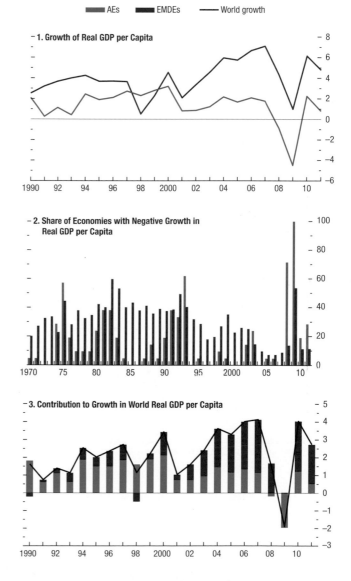

Sources: World Economic Outlook database; World Bank World Development Indicators database; Penn World Tables 7.0; and IMF staff calculations.
Note: Economy groups are defined in Table 4.3 of Appendix 4.1. AE = advanced economy; EMDE = emerging market and developing economy.

Figure 4.2. Diverse Paths of Output

Unlike the smooth hills that characterize advanced economies' output paths, output in emerging market and developing economies is marked by mountains, cliffs, plateaus, and plains. Expansions and downturns can last just a few years or stretch over many years.

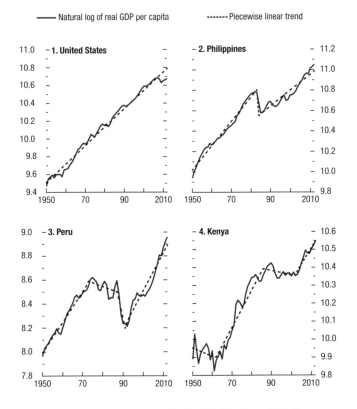

Sources: World Economic Outlook database; World Bank World Development Indicators database; Penn World Tables 7.0; and IMF staff estimates.

the de facto evidence of their resilience over the past decade and through the largest global shock in the past half-century, optimists can point to their improved policy frameworks and the ample policy space—room to maneuver without undermining sustainability—these improvements have created. These economies have also become more diversified along many dimensions—in their economic structure, trading patterns, and the composition of their capital flows. On the other hand, recent growth in some emerging market and developing economies has been supported by capital inflows, strong credit growth, and for those that export commodities, by the continued strength of commodity prices. These factors are prone to reversal, which suggests that these economies' prospects might not be that robust (Frankel, 2012). Some of the policy space they built over the past decade was used during the global crisis and has not yet been fully rebuilt. And there are now signs that growth in some of these economies is slowing.

This chapter studies the resilience of these economies, defined as their ability to sustain longer and stronger expansions and to experience shorter and shallower downturns and more rapid recoveries.[2] Previous studies have attempted to directly explain the growth of emerging market and developing economies and have had only modest success, in part because the behavior of output in these economies is much more complex and diverse than in advanced economies (see, for example, Easterly, 2001, and Figure 4.2). Easterly and others (1993) found very low persistence in their growth rates across decades, which is hard to reconcile with the high persistence of "fundamentals"—such as investment rates, education levels, trade, financial development, and institutional quality—that typically enter growth regressions. Pritchett (2000) characterized

---

[2]This is consistent with the general definition of resilience, which encompasses the same two aspects. The *Oxford English Dictionary*, for example, defines resilience as "the quality or fact of being able to recover quickly or easily from, or resist being affected by, a misfortune, shock, or illness." Increased resilience would result in longer and stronger expansions, but the latter could also result from fewer shocks—a possibility we explore in this chapter. Shorter and shallower downturns and more rapid recoveries are fully consistent with the aforementioned definition of resilience, since downturns are the result of negative shocks.

their output paths as being composed of "mountains, plateaus, cliffs, and plains" and documented large and abrupt changes in growth performance at the country level. Some emerging market and developing economies grow at reasonable rates for many years and then, without any obvious change in fundamentals, stagnate for decades, whereas others experience long periods of stagnation interrupted periodically by bursts of fast growth. Severe economic crises are not uncommon and tend to happen more often in these economies. These crises have large output costs because they often represent declines in the trend rather than fluctuations around a trend (Aguiar and Gopinath, 2007; Cerra and Saxena, 2008). As a result, expansions and recoveries in these economies have lasted anywhere from a few years to several decades.

Analyzing the length of expansions and the speed of recoveries could be an intermediate step in investigating the processes underlying growth—shifts in long-term growth or in the volatility of growth will show up in changing duration of expansions and speed of recoveries. Another reason for studying their duration is to help policymakers identify the factors that tend to halt or prolong expansions and hasten recoveries.[3]

This chapter helps shed light on the past, present, and prospective resilience of emerging market and developing economies by addressing the following questions:

- How has the resilience of these economies changed over time? Have expansions become longer and stronger, and have downturns and recoveries become shallower and shorter?

- What factors, both external and domestic, are associated with the duration of expansions and the speed of recoveries in these economies?

- If performance has improved over time, to what extent has it been due to less frequent or less

severe shocks, to improved policymaking, and to structural changes such as shifts in these economies' trade and financial linkages?

The chapter examines the evolution of output per capita in more than 100 emerging market and developing economies over the past 60 years.[4] It identifies periods of expansion, downturn, and recovery in their output paths. Using a variety of tools, including event studies, statistical associations, and duration analysis, it analyzes how these durations have changed over time and how they relate to various shocks, policies, and structural characteristics. These are the chapter's main findings:

- The resilience of emerging market and developing economies has increased markedly during the past two decades. They are spending more time in expansion, and downturns and recoveries have become shallower and shorter. The performance of the past decade was particularly good, with emerging Europe being a notable exception. In fact, the past decade was the first time that emerging market and developing economies spent more time in expansion, and had smaller downturns, than advanced economies.

- Various shocks, both external and domestic, are associated with the end of expansions in these economies. Among external shocks, sudden stops in capital flows, advanced economy recessions, spikes in global uncertainty, and terms-of-trade busts all increase the likelihood that an expansion will end. Among domestic shocks, credit booms double and banking crises triple the probability that an expansion will shift into a downturn by the following year.

- Good policies are associated with increased resilience. Specifically, greater policy space (characterized by low inflation and favorable fiscal and external positions) and improved policy frameworks (countercyclical policy, inflation targeting, and flexible exchange rate regimes) are associated with longer expansions and faster recoveries.

- It is more difficult to tease out the effects on resilience of these economies' structural characteristics—such as trade patterns, financial openness and the composition of capital flows, and income

---

[3]In analyzing the length of expansions and speed of recoveries, we contribute to a growing literature that tries to shed light on growth transitions. Examples include Hausmann, Pritchett, and Rodrik (2005), who investigate growth accelerations; Berg, Ostry, and Zettelmeyer (2012) and Virmani (2012), who study periods of sustained growth; and Rodrik (1999); Becker and Mauro (2006); and Hausmann, Rodriguez, and Wagner (2006), who focus on growth collapses.

[4]Appendix 4.1 outlines the data sources for the analysis.

distribution. Few of these characteristics are robustly associated with the duration of expansions and the speed of recoveries.

- Improvements in policymaking and the buildup of policy space in many of these economies account for the bulk of the increased resilience since 1990. Some shocks, such as spikes in global uncertainty, have become more frequent in the past decade, but other shocks have become less frequent, such as banking crises and credit booms. Overall, the fact that there have been fewer shocks accounts for about two-fifths of the improved performance in emerging market and developing economies. Greater policy space and better policy frameworks account for the remaining three-fifths of the improvement in their performance.

The rest of the chapter is structured as follows. The first section documents how resilience has evolved for various country groupings and regions over time and relates these changes to deeper shifts in steady-state growth rates and the variability of growth. The second section relates the duration of expansions and the speed of recoveries to external and domestic shocks, to policy space and policy frameworks, and to structural characteristics of these economies. It uses standard tools of duration analysis, including both bivariate and multivariate models, to examine these correlates in a comprehensive and integrated manner. It then evaluates whether the nature of these associations has changed over time. The final section synthesizes the chapter with an examination of how these economies' policies and structure, as well as the shocks that buffet them, have changed over time. It then quantifies their relative contributions to the rise in resilience, and concludes with a few words on the prospective resilience of these economies.

How Has Resilience Varied across Countries and over Time?

We begin by establishing some stylized facts about the depth and duration of downturns, recoveries, and expansions for various country groups and how these have changed over the past six decades. For the purposes of this chapter the economies of the world

are split into three groups.[5] Following Pritchett (2000), we define advanced economies primarily by membership in the Organization for Economic Cooperation and Development prior to 1990, with the exception of Turkey.[6] All other economies are classified as emerging market and developing economies, which we further subdivide into two groups: low-income countries, which are defined as the 51 economies currently eligible for concessional IMF loans, and the remaining 69 economies, which we classify as emerging markets. Appendix 4.1 lists the countries included in the analysis according to their classifications.

The primary variable of interest is the evolution of real output per capita. We focus on this variable for consistency with most of the literature on development, because it is the relevant measure of output for welfare analysis, and since it accounts for differences in population growth rates across countries. Most of the chapter's findings continue to hold if one uses real output instead (see Appendix 4.4).

To identify expansions, downturns, and recoveries in output per capita, we use the statistical algorithm of Harding and Pagan (2002), which detects turning points in the log level of a time series. The algorithm searches for local maximums (peaks) and minimums (troughs) that meet specified conditions for the length of cycles and phases. Because we are using annual data and some downturns and expansions can be as short as one year, the only condition imposed is on the minimum length of the cycle (a contiguous expansion and downturn), which is specified to be five years.[7] Expansions are defined as

[5]Throughout, we restrict our analysis to economies that have had an average population of at least 1 million inhabitants over the sample period.

[6]This implies that some economies currently classified as advanced by the *World Economic Outlook* are classified as emerging markets in this chapter. We do this because over the past 60 years they were more like emerging markets than advanced economies and because their experience—especially their ability to grow sufficiently to attain advanced economy status—provides valuable lessons.

[7]This is not too restrictive a constraint. In advanced economies, cycles have averaged 8½ years (see Chapter 3 of the April 2002 *World Economic Outlook*). As noted, expansions and downturns in emerging market and developing economies can often be much more protracted. The imposition of a five-year minimum cycle length serves mainly to filter out high-frequency fluctuations in

the period from the year after a trough to the year of the peak, inclusive, and downturns are defined as the period from the year after a peak to the year of the trough, inclusive. Recoveries are defined as the period from the year after a trough to the year when output per capita reaches or exceeds the previous peak's level. When output is well behaved, as is the case for most advanced economies, recoveries are a subset of expansions. For emerging market and developing economies, however, an expansion following a deep downturn may not reach the previous peak's output per capita until several cycles are completed, in which case a recovery can span several cycles. Application of the Harding-Pagan methodology identifies 117 expansions and 105 downturns in advanced economies and 576 expansions and 496 downturns in emerging market and developing economies.[8]

How has resilience changed over time? Figures 4.3 and 4.4 plot the dynamics of output per capita during the 10 years following a peak, with peaks grouped by the decades during which they occurred. We begin by looking at output dynamics following peaks in the 1950s and 1960s—the dark blue lines in the figures. These were golden decades for the advanced economies and good decades for emerging market and developing economies—the median downturn for the latter during these decades was shallow, less than 3 percent, and it took four years for median output per capita to regain or surpass its previous peak (Figure 4.3, panel 2).

Emerging market and developing economies took a sharp turn for the worse in the 1970s and 1980s (Figure 4.3, panels 2 to 4, red lines). The median downturn was much deeper and more protracted—even 10 years later median output per capita failed to recover its losses relative to the previous peak. There were substantial variations across regions, however (see Figure 4.4). Emerging and developing Asia was relatively resilient in these decades, with the median downturn and recovery lasting only four years. This was in sharp contrast to Latin America,

---

emerging market and developing economies' output, which is typically much more volatile than output in advanced economies.

[8]The number of expansions and downturns are not equal due to the presence of incomplete cycles at the start and end of the time series.

Figure 4.3. Dynamics of Output per Capita following Peaks
(Median output per capita; peak = 100; years on x-axis)

The 1950s and 1960s were good decades for emerging market economies—less so for low-income countries. But the 1970s and 1980s were cruel to both—median output per capita remained below predownturn levels 10 years after the peak. The 1990s saw shallower downturns and faster recoveries in emerging market economies, while the improvement in low-income countries was most evident during 2000–06. Both groups did comparatively well during the Great Recession.

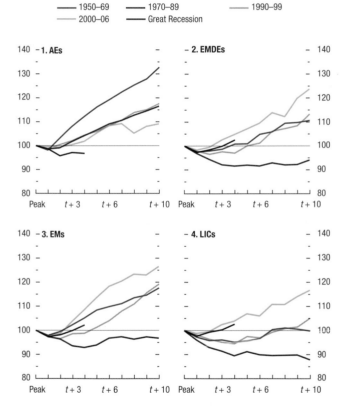

Source: IMF staff calculations.
Note: Economy groups are defined in Table 4.3 of Appendix 4.1. AE = advanced economy; EM = emerging market economy; EMDE = emerging market and developing economy; LIC = low-income country. Peaks in output per capita are identified using the Harding-Pagan algorithm (Harding and Pagan, 2002). Output per capita at the peak (*t*) is normalized to 100, and the median output per capita is plotted in years (*t* + 1) through (*t* + 10) for each group.

Figure 4.4. Emerging Market and Developing Economy Regions: Dynamics of Output per Capita following Peaks
(Median output per capita; peak = 100; years on x-axis)

There were differences in performance across emerging market and developing economy regions over the past decades. The 1970s and 1980s were difficult for most regions (especially sub-Saharan Africa), but emerging and developing Asia fared better. The 1990s were tough for emerging and developing Asia, but the performance of other regions improved. All regions did better in the 2000s, except emerging Europe during the Great Recession.

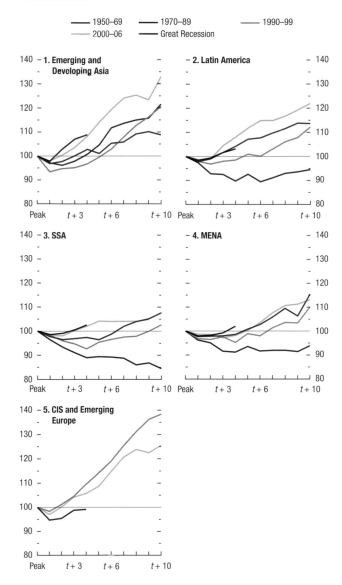

Source: IMF staff calculations.
Note: Economy groups are defined in Table 4.3 of Appendix 4.1. CIS = Commonwealth of Independent States; MENA = Middle East and North Africa; SSA = sub-Saharan Africa. Peaks in output per capita are identified using the Harding-Pagan algorithm (Harding and Pagan, 2002). Output per capita at the peak (t) is normalized to 100, and the median output per capita is plotted in years ($t + 1$) through ($t + 10$) for each region.

where many economies went through wrenching debt crises in the 1980s, and to sub-Saharan Africa and the Middle East and North Africa. In all three of the latter regions, median output per capita 10 years later remained below (in some cases well below) the previous peak.

Things began improving for emerging market and developing economies in the 1990s (Figure 4.3, light blue lines). Median output per capita followed a path closer to that observed in the 1950s and 1960s, although again with some variation across regions (see Figure 4.4). The 1990s were not a great decade for emerging and developing Asia: many economies experienced sharp downturns during the 1997–98 Asian financial crisis. By contrast, many countries in emerging Europe grew rapidly following their transition-related declines in output.

But the strong performance of emerging market and developing economies in the early 2000s and throughout the Great Recession was unprecedented (Figure 4.3, yellow and black lines).[9] The decline in median output per capita during downturns between 2000 and 2006 was smaller than in previous decades, and it only took two years to recover—this was true for both the emerging market and low-income country subgroups. Even through the Great Recession—arguably the largest external shock in the past half-century—both these subgroups performed well, with median output per capita recovering to its precrisis peak by the third year. The strong performance in the aftermath of the global crisis is evident in most regions, with the exception of emerging Europe, where median output per capita has yet to recover to its precrisis level (Figure 4.4, black lines). Employment in many emerging market and developing economies has also performed well: unemployment fell below precrisis levels by 2011 (see Box 4.1 for an analysis of the relationship between employment and growth in these economies).

[9] The improved performance of these economies is not driven by a subset of well-performing countries. If emerging market and developing economies are split into commodity exporters—which have benefited greatly in recent years from high commodity prices—and non–commodity exporters, the same pattern of improvement is evident in both groups. Similarly, isolating the largest emerging markets from the rest does not alter the picture materially. These splits are reported in Figure 4.15 in Appendix 4.4.

These economies did so well in the past decade that for the first time, they spent more time in expansion and had smaller downturns than advanced economies (Figure 4.5, panel 1). In the 1970s and 1980s, emerging market and developing economies spent more than a third of their time in downturns. In the 2000s, however, they spent more than 80 percent of their time in expansion. In contrast, the advanced economies have spent less time in expansion over the decades, and in the 2000s they were in downturns more than a fifth of the time. Although emerging market and developing economies have been spending more time in expansion, the median growth rate during expansions has not shown a clear trend over the past decades—median growth during recent expansions is not much different than during the expansions of the 1970s and 1980s (Figure 4.5, panel 2). But their downturns have become much less severe and are now shallower than downturns in the advanced economies (Figure 4.5, panel 3).

Why Has Resilience Changed? Taking a Look at Steady-State Growth and Variability

Longer expansions and shorter downturns are, in the end, simply manifestations of deeper changes. One possible underlying change is that steady-state or trend growth of emerging market and developing economies has been increasing—a higher rate of trend growth would mean that shocks that would have previously caused a downturn now cause only a slowdown. A second possibility is that the variability of growth has lessened, so that the longer expansions and faster recoveries are the result of fewer large, negative fluctuations.[10] Or both changes could be at work.

---

[10]A third possibility is that the propagation mechanism has changed—that is, the effect of shocks has become more (or less) persistent over time. But such a change would have ambiguous effects on resilience as defined in this chapter. Greater persistence would mean longer-lasting effects for positive shocks, which would prolong expansion, but it would also mean more protracted effects for negative shocks, which would result in slower recoveries. As it turns out, the estimated autoregressive coefficient (from an AR(1) growth model) for emerging market and developing economies has not changed significantly over the past 40 years. See Appendix 4.2.

Figure 4.5. Along Which Dimensions Has Emerging Market and Developing Economy Growth Improved?
(Percent)

Emerging market and low-income economies have spent more time in expansion during the past two decades relative to the 1970s and 1980s. The 2000s was the first decade during which both groups spent more time than advanced economies in expansion. Median growth in output per capita during expansions has not risen much, but downturns have become shallower.

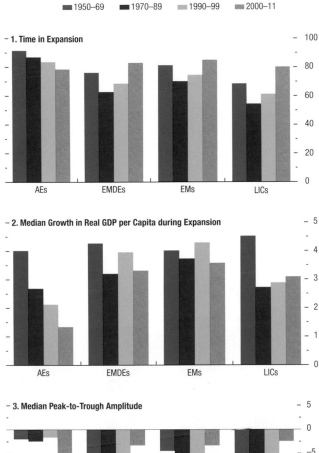

Source: IMF staff calculations.
Note: Economy groups are defined in Table 4.3 of Appendix 4.1. AE = advanced economy; EM = emerging market economy; EMDE = emerging market and developing economy; LIC = low-income country. Peaks and troughs in output per capita are identified using the Harding-Pagan algorithm (Harding and Pagan, 2002).

Figure 4.6. Why Have Emerging Market and Developing Economies Become More Resilient?
(Percent)

The longer expansions and shorter recoveries observed in these economies during the past two decades are a manifestation of two underlying changes: higher steady-state growth and less variability in growth.

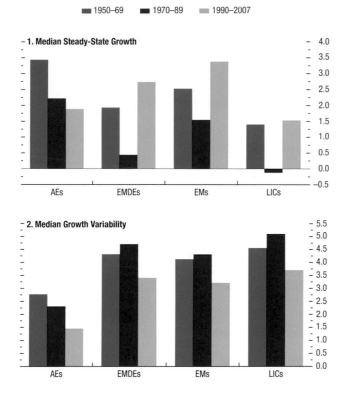

Source: IMF staff calculations.
Note: Economy groups are defined in Table 4.3 of Appendix 4.1. AE = advanced economy; EM = emerging market economy; EMDE = emerging market and developing economy; LIC = low-income country. Growth in output per capita is modeled as an AR(1) process, and the model is estimated for all countries over three subperiods—1950–69, 1970–89, and 1990–2007. See Appendix 4.2 for further details. The results are nearly identical for 1990–2011 and 1990–2007.

Although estimating potential growth is difficult, including for advanced economies, one way to shed light on which of these various possibilities is at work is to follow Blanchard and Simon (2001) by modeling output growth as a simple autoregressive process—that is, by letting the growth rate of output per capita be a function of its lagged value and a constant, plus an innovation term. With such a model, we can calculate measures of steady-state growth and the variability of growth. We estimate such a model for all countries over three subperiods—the 1950s and 1960s, 1970s and 1980s, and 1990s and 2000s—and extract the median estimates for steady-state growth and the variability of growth for each of these periods (see Appendix 4.2).

As Figure 4.6 shows, longer expansions, shallower downturns, and faster recoveries are the result of both higher steady-state growth and lower variability in growth. For emerging markets, median steady-state growth fell from 2½ percent in the 1950s and 1960s to 1½ percent in the 1970s and 1980s; but it more than doubled, to 3½ percent, in the 1990s and 2000s. At the same time, the standard deviation of growth fell to 3¼ percent, from 4¼ percent in the 1970s and 1980s.[11] The same pattern holds true for low-income countries, for which steady-state growth markedly improved since the stagnation of the 1970s and 1980s and growth variability fell. The improvements in emerging market and developing economies along both dimensions differ from what is observed in the advanced economies, where the variability of growth has been falling over time (a phenomenon often referred to as the Great Moderation). On its own, this would be expected to improve resilience, but it has been offset by lower trend growth—median steady-state growth is less than 2 percent, about half of what it was in the 1950s and 1960s.

[11]The changes in steady-state growth and growth variability are both statistically significant for the emerging market and developing economies.

What Factors Are Associated with Resilience?

Having established the stylized facts regarding the changing duration of expansions and speed of recoveries in emerging market and developing economies, we now ask which factors are associated with these durations.[12] Specifically, we explore the following, in turn:

- What kinds of shocks, both external and domestic, tend to derail expansions?
- Do good policies help lengthen expansions and/or hasten recoveries?
- What structural characteristics help strengthen resilience?

What Shocks Tend to End Expansions?

A large number of shocks could potentially derail expansions in emerging market and developing economies. We focus on a subset of economic and financial disturbances, both domestic and external, the risks of which are now heightened in a number of countries:[13]

- *External shocks:* We consider increases in global uncertainty and world interest rates, recessions in advanced economies, sharp declines in an economy's terms of trade, and sudden stops in capital inflows. Sharp increases in world interest rates, which we proxy with the U.S. real interest rate, have triggered crises in the past, as have spikes in global uncertainty and recessions in advanced economies. Similarly, adverse movements in a country's terms of trade or capital flows can be destabilizing.

- *Domestic shocks:* We consider credit booms and banking crises. Although strong credit growth tends to be associated with strong output growth, excessively high credit tends to generate domestic vulnerabilities such as asset price bubbles or consumption and investment booms, and there is often a downturn when they burst. Similarly, banking crises frequently have very negative macroeconomic consequences.[14]

The shocks under consideration differ in one important dimension. Many external shocks, such as a rise in global uncertainty or global interest rates or recession in advanced economies, are clearly exogenous to emerging market and developing economies. Therefore, we examine the contemporaneous effect of these external shocks on the probability that the expansion ends.[15] But domestic shocks, such as a banking crisis, might be triggered by developments in output—for example, financial sector distress may be the result of a downturn rather than its cause. To gauge whether banking crises tend to derail expansions—while minimizing potential reverse causality issues—we examine the likelihood of an expansion ending in the period immediately following a banking crisis. For credit booms, the deleterious effects of which may take time to materialize, we examine the likelihood of an expansion ending in the subsequent period if there has been a credit boom during the previous three years.

The domestic and external shocks under consideration are strongly associated with expansions coming to an end. Figure 4.7 compares the probability of an expansion ending when these shocks occur with the probability of an expansion ending in the absence of such a shock. Among external shocks, spikes in global uncertainty, recessions in advanced economies, sudden stops in capital flows,

---

[12]It is important to emphasize that it is very difficult to establish causality from factors such as policies and structural characteristics on the one hand to the duration of expansions and recoveries on the other. Many of the variables we explore, including measures of policy space such as low inflation or stronger fiscal balances, are endogenous to the growth process in general. In particular, they could be a function of how long the economy has been in expansion.

[13]For a related analysis of output drops and shocks, see Becker and Mauro (2006). Adler and Tovar (2012) look specifically at the resilience of emerging markets to global financial shocks. Other shocks, such as political turmoil and civil unrest, have also been important, particularly in low-income countries; see Hausmann, Rodriguez, and Wagner (2006) and Berg, Ostry, and Zettelmeyer (2012).

[14]See Chapter 4 of the October 2009 *World Economic Outlook*.

[15]The case of sudden stops in capital flows is less clear-cut, because a reversal in net capital flows could be driven by changes in domestic conditions. The findings reported here for sudden stops are not sensitive to whether the contemporaneous or lagged values of the sudden stop indicators are used. In addition, Appendix 4.4 reports a robustness test intended to minimize potential endogeneity, in which we focus on the subset of sudden stop episodes referred to in the literature as "systemic sudden stops," which are those that coincide with a sharp rise in global uncertainty. The results hold in this case as well.

Figure 4.7. Emerging Market and Developing Economies: Effects of Various Shocks on the Likelihood that an Expansion Will End
(Percent)

Various shocks, both external and domestic, are associated with expansions coming to an end. Among external shocks, sudden stops in capital flows, spikes in global uncertainty, recessions in advanced economies, and terms-of-trade busts all significantly increase the likelihood that an expansion will end. Among domestic shocks, credit booms double and banking crises triple the likelihood that an expansion will shift to a downturn by the following year.

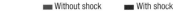

■ Without shock   ■ With shock

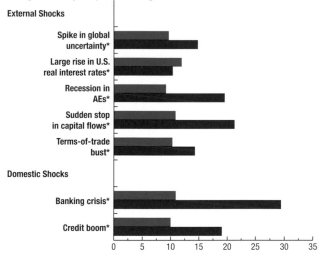

Source: IMF staff calculations.
Note: AE = advanced economy. The bars show the average probability of exiting an expansion in the absence or presence of various types of external and domestic shocks. For external shocks, which are more likely to be exogenous, the red bars present the contemporaneous effect, that is, the probability that the expansion will end and the downturn will begin in the same year as the shock. For domestic shocks, for which endogeneity is more of a concern, the red bars are the lagged effect, that is, the probability that the expansion will end and the downturn will begin in the year after the shock. The probability of exit conditional on a shock also depends on the length of the expansion at the time the shock occurs; the average probability is used as a summary measure of the distribution of conditional probabilities. Statistically significant differences at the 10 percent level between the underlying distributions are denoted by starred and bolded labels.

and terms-of-trade busts all significantly increase the likelihood that an expansion will end. Sudden stops and advanced economy recessions have the most pronounced effects; they raise the likelihood that an expansion will end by a factor of two. The effect of domestic shocks is just as strong if not stronger—credit booms double the likelihood that an expansion will shift into a downturn by the following year, and banking crises triple the likelihood.

How Are Policies Associated with Resilience?

We now turn to the role of monetary, fiscal, and exchange rate policies. One of the arguments put forward in the literature to explain higher resilience among emerging market and developing economies is these economies' improved policy frameworks and increased policy space (see, for example, Kose and Prasad, 2010). For example, many have adopted inflation targeting and have reduced inflation since the early 1990s (Schmidt-Hebbel, 2009). Similarly, some have graduated from procyclical fiscal policy and now have a greater ability to implement countercyclical fiscal policy than in the late 1990s (Frankel, Végh, and Vuletin, 2011) or have reduced their fiscal deficits and public debt.[16] Finally, many have moved away from hard exchange rate pegs, and their more flexible exchange rates act as a shock absorber and reduce the vulnerability of the public and financial sectors to the sudden and severe currency depreciations characteristic of currency crises (Chang and Velasco, 2004).

We analyze both improved policy frameworks and enhanced policy space for fiscal, monetary, and exchange rate policies as follows:

- *Monetary policy:* We consider whether the central bank has adopted inflation targeting. To measure policy space, we consider whether the economy had an inflation rate above or below 10 percent.[17]

---

[16]Végh and Vuletin (2012) also find that monetary policy in many emerging market and developing economies has graduated from being procyclical to being more countercyclical.

[17]Our results are robust to choosing a more stringent threshold for low inflation. See Appendix 4.4 for details.

- *Fiscal policy:* We consider whether fiscal policy was countercyclical or procyclical.[18] We also measure policy space—the scope for further increases in public debt without undermining sustainability (Ostry and others, 2010, p. 4). We use two measures: whether the government was running a fiscal surplus or deficit, and whether it had a low or high ratio of public debt to GDP, with the threshold for "high" public debt at 50 percent of GDP.[19]

- *Exchange rate policy:* We consider whether the economy had a pegged exchange rate or not. For policy space, we look at whether the economy had a current account surplus or deficit, a high or low ratio of external debt to GDP (above or below 40 percent), and a high or low ratio of international reserves to GDP (above or below the sample median).[20]

To assess the role of policies, we relate the duration of expansions and the speed of recoveries to the various policy measures using nonparametric duration analysis methods—that is, without imposing any structure or model on the data.[21] Specifically, we use the standard Kaplan-Meier survivor function estimator to gauge whether policy frameworks and the availability of policy space help lengthen

expansions and hasten recoveries. As with domestic shocks, we use lagged values of the policy variables to minimize reverse causality, so that policy characteristics in the current year are related to the likelihood that an expansion or recovery will end in the next year.

We find that good policy frameworks have helped emerging market and developing economies prolong their expansions and hasten their recoveries. Figure 4.8 illustrates how their average duration is associated with the various measures of policy frameworks and policy space.[22] With regard to policy frameworks, inflation targeting and a countercyclical fiscal policy significantly increase the length of expansions and hasten recoveries.[23] In addition, not having a pegged exchange rate tends to lengthen expansions, but has no significant effect on the speed of recoveries.

Adequate policy space also appears to provide a cushion. Figure 4.8 shows that having a low inflation rate significantly lengthens expansions and hastens recoveries. Having a fiscal surplus in the previous year leads to significantly longer expansions, but there is no significant impact of this variable on the speed of recoveries. Economies with low levels of public debt tend to recover much faster from downturns, but this variable has no significant effect on the length of expansions. Finally, a strong external position (characterized by current account surpluses, low external debt, and high international reserves) significantly lengthens expansions and hastens recoveries.[24]

---

[18]The cyclicality of fiscal policy is measured by the correlation between the cyclical component of real government expenditure and the cyclical component of real GDP (Kaminsky, Reinhart, and Végh, 2004) measured over the previous 10 years. A negative correlation reflects a countercyclical fiscal policy; a positive correlation reflects a procyclical fiscal policy.

[19]Mendoza and Ostry (2008) find that fiscal solvency in emerging markets diminishes beyond a public debt threshold of 50 percent of GDP, with fiscal solvency measured by the responsiveness of the primary balance to changes in the debt level. Due to the poor coverage of data on fiscal balances across economies and over time, we proxy the fiscal balance by the change in the ratio of public debt to GDP adjusted by nominal GDP growth. See Appendix 4.1 for details.

[20]Reinhart, Rogoff, and Savastano (2003, p. 10) find that "default in emerging markets can and does occur at ratios of external debt to GDP that would not be considered 'excessive' for the typical advanced economy." About one-fifth of defaults they study in these countries occurred when external debt was less than 40 percent of GDP, and one-third occurred when external debt was between 40 and 60 percent of GDP.

[21]Duration analysis goes by many names, including "survival" or "event history" analysis. Historically, such methods arose in medical research on the determinants of human mortality (the origin of the term "survival analysis"). See Appendix 4.3 for details.

[22]The average recovery duration shown in Figure 4.8 may be somewhat surprising to those used to the much shorter recoveries in advanced economies, but recall from Figure 4.3 that the *median* path of output per capita following peaks in the 1970s and 1980s did not recover to the previous peak's level even 10 years later.

[23]This result is in line with de Carvalho Filho (2011), who documents that inflation-targeting economies fared better during the Great Recession.

[24]Several studies find that the strength of the countries' external position (low levels of foreign-currency-denominated debt, low current account deficits) was an important factor in explaining the cross-country incidence of the Great Recession. See, for example, Blanchard, Faruqee, and Das (2010) and Lane and Milesi-Ferretti (2010). Didier, Hevia, and Schmukler (2012) document the importance of foreign reserves in explaining the speed of recovery in the aftermath of the global crisis.

Figure 4.8. Emerging Market and Developing Economies: Effects of Policies on Expansion Duration and Speed of Recovery
(Years)

Good policies have contributed to emerging market and developing economies' resilience. Specifically, greater policy space (as measured by low inflation and favorable fiscal and external positions) and improved policy frameworks (as measured by countercyclical policy, the adoption of inflation targeting, and more flexible exchange rate regimes) are associated with longer expansions and faster recoveries.

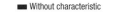

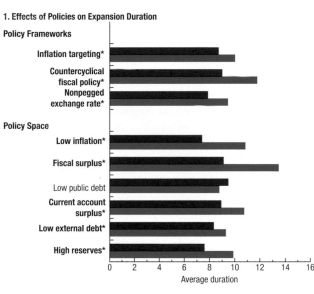

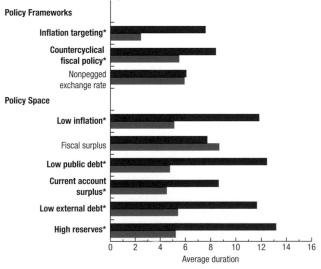

Source: IMF staff calculations.
Note: The bars show the average duration of expansions and recoveries in the absence or presence of the given characteristic. The average duration is used as a summary measure of the underlying duration distribution conditional on the characteristic. Statistically significant differences at the 10 percent level between the underlying distributions are denoted by starred and bolded labels.

How Are Structural Characteristics Associated with Resilience?

In addition to macroeconomic policies, an economy's structural characteristics shape its performance in general and its response to shocks in particular. Various hypotheses have been put forward in recent years that relate changes in the resilience of emerging market and developing economies to shifts in their economic structures. Although many potential characteristics could affect resilience, we focus on the following:

- *Increased trade openness and diversification:* There has been a significant shift in both the trade openness and trading patterns of emerging market and developing economies. Trade openness has increased substantially over time as trade regimes have been liberalized and the costs of transportation and communication have fallen. Greater trade openness helps reduce dependence on domestic demand and vulnerability to domestic shocks, but it may also make economies more vulnerable to slowdowns in external demand. Greater diversification across trading partners would help reduce these economies' vulnerability to slowdowns in specific trading partners. In this regard, the dramatic increase in trade among these economies is thought to have helped them weather the recent advanced economy crisis, although prospectively it may increase their vulnerability to a slowdown in large emerging markets like China (Box 4.2).
- *Increased financial openness and changes in the composition of capital flows:* As with trade, there has been a steady move toward greater financial openness in many regions. Increased capital account openness can facilitate risk sharing, but it can also leave countries more vulnerable to financial shocks or sudden stops in capital flows. For some emerging market and developing economies, susceptibility to the volatility of capital flows has been mitigated by a change in their composition—toward foreign direct investment (FDI), which is thought to be more stable.
- *Income equality:* Rodrik (1999) posits that when social divisions run deep, the effects of external shocks are magnified by the distributional conflicts they trigger. Adjustment to external shocks often has distributional consequences, and in

economies where "latent social conflict" is high—as measured by proxies such as income inequality, ethnic and linguistic fractionalization, and social mistrust—adjustment tends to be inadequate, prolonging the negative effects of the shock. More recent papers such as Berg and Ostry (2011) find that greater income equality enables countries to sustain periods of rapid growth.

Although the effects of shocks and policies on the duration of expansions are apparent and almost always significant, the effects of structural characteristics are less clear-cut (Figure 4.9, panel 1). We use the same techniques as in previous subsections to examine their effects on the duration of expansions and the speed of recoveries, again using lagged values to mitigate reverse causality, so that structural characteristics in the current year are related to the likelihood that an expansion or recovery will end in the following year. Greater trade openness and trade liberalization are not significantly associated with the duration of expansions. Nor are the extent of trade among emerging market and developing economies or greater financial integration. In contrast, greater FDI flows are associated with a small but statistically significant increase in the average duration of expansions. The strongest structural correlate of expansion duration, at least in this bivariate exercise, is income inequality—countries with below-median income inequality have expansions that last about five years longer than those with above-median income inequality.

The effects of structural factors on the speed of recovery are more distinct (Figure 4.9, panel 2). Greater trade openness and diversification, lower financial integration, higher capital account openness, and higher FDI are all significantly associated with faster recoveries. But greater income equality does not have a significant effect on the speed of recovery.

Putting It All Together: Multivariate Analysis

To this point, the chapter has examined individual variables and their association with the resilience of emerging market and developing economies. However, these determinants rarely change in isolation and often move together, and so a proper assessment of

Figure 4.9. Emerging Market and Developing Economies: Effects of Structural Characteristics on Expansion Duration and Speed of Recovery
(Years)

It is more difficult to tease out the effects of economies' structural characteristics—such as trade patterns, composition of capital flows, and the degree of financial integration—on resilience. Among these characteristics, only FDI flows and low income inequality were significantly associated with longer expansion. The effects of structural factors on the speed of recovery are more distinct: greater trade openness and diversification, lower financial integration, higher capital account openness, and higher FDI are all significantly associated with faster recoveries. Income inequality does not have a significant effect on the speed of recovery.

■ Without characteristic   ■ With characteristic

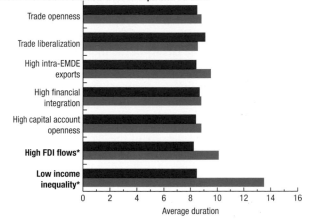

1. Effects of Structural Characteristics on Expansion Duration

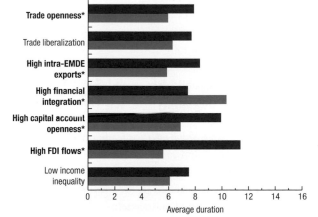

2. Effects of Structural Characteristics on Recovery Duration

Source: IMF staff calculations.
Note: EMDE = emerging market and developing economy; FDI = foreign direct investment. The bars show the average duration of expansions and recoveries in the absence or presence of the given characteristic. The average duration is used as a summary measure of the underlying duration distribution conditional on the characteristic. Statistically significant differences at the 10 percent level between the underlying distributions are denoted by starred and bolded labels.

each variable's influence requires controlling for movements in the other variables. To do this, we undertake a multivariate analysis of resilience. We do this using the tools of parametric duration analysis, which allow the duration of an expansion or the speed of recovery to be modeled as a function of several variables simultaneously. This analysis provides a sense of how each variable is related to the chances that the episode under study will last—that is, whether the variable tends to increase or decrease the expected length of an episode at a given time. Appendix 4.3 contains details on the duration model used here.

The large number of potential correlates and the poor data availability for some of these necessitate a parsimonious approach to the multivariate analysis. As noted, a wide array of factors have been identified as possible factors in the improved resilience of emerging market and developing economies, but there is only limited historical experience on which to draw to test the simultaneous impact of these various factors. For example, the data are extremely sparse for our measure of the cyclicality of fiscal policy prior to the 1990s. As a result, we focus on a selected subset of the variables explored in the previous section:

- *External shocks:* global uncertainty, the U.S. real interest rate, indicators of terms-of-trade busts, sudden stops in capital inflows, and advanced economy recessions;
- *Domestic shocks:* indicators of credit booms and systemic banking crises;
- *Domestic policies:* indicators of single-digit inflation and public debt levels below 50 percent of GDP, and a measure of international reserves to GDP; and
- *Structural characteristics:* trade openness, financial openness, and income equality.

Apart from the external shocks, the explanatory variables are lagged as in the previous section to mitigate potential endogeneity.

What Ends Expansions?

The first column of Table 4.1 shows how the expected duration of an expansion is associated with these variables. The estimates are based on an accelerated failure time model, which breaks the

determinants of duration into two components: a baseline expected duration, which captures how long an episode is likely to last at a particular time, independent of other variables, and a "shifter" that scales this baseline and is a function of a set of explanatory variables. The Weibull shape parameter for the model indicates that an expansion has a greater chance of ending the longer it lasts (the parameter is greater than 1). The effects of the explanatory variables on the baseline are given by the time ratios, which are the numbers shown in the table for each variable. The magnitude of these time ratios denotes the factor by which the expected duration of the expansion is increased relative to the baseline. If the time ratio is greater than 1, the variable tends to lengthen the expansion or slow the recovery relative to the baseline; if it is less than 1, it tends to shorten the expansion or hasten the recovery.

The multivariate duration analysis for expansions mostly confirms the bivariate relationships reported above. External and domestic shocks tend to reduce the length of expansions. For example, a 1 point rise in global uncertainty reduces the expected duration of an expansion by about 5 percent (because the baseline expected duration is multiplied by 0.951). A 1 percentage point rise in the U.S. real interest rate has a similar effect. Sudden stops, advanced economy recessions, credit booms, and banking crises reduce the expected duration of an expansion by about 40 percent. These shocks have statistically significant effects, with the exception of terms-of-trade busts and the U.S. real interest rate.

The policy-related variables tend to increase the length of expansions, although the statistical significance of these effects varies. Low inflation lengthens the expansion by about 47 percent, whereas a 10 percent of GDP increase in international reserves lengthens it by about 9 percent. In the multivariate model, a low public debt level does not have a statistically significant effect on expansion duration.

The structural characteristics tend to have little to no effect. Only higher income inequality and greater financial integration reduce the expected expansion duration in a statistically significant manner, but even then, the magnitudes are small.

Table 4.1. What Ends Expansions and Recoveries?

Explanatory Variable	Expansions			Recoveries		
	All Years	Pre-1990	Post-1989	All Years	Pre-1990	Post-1989
Implied S&P 100 Volatility (VXO)[1]	0.951***	0.981	0.943***	1.054***	1.060**	1.042**
	(−4.179)	(−0.985)	(−4.565)	(2.846)	(2.143)	(2.012)
U.S. Ex Ante Real Interest Rate	0.956	0.993	0.835***	1.085	0.960	1.068
	(−1.461)	(−0.158)	(−3.479)	(1.502)	(−0.397)	(0.748)
Terms-of-Trade Bust Indicator	0.968	0.802	1.134	1.751	1.819	1.726*
	(−0.214)	(−1.034)	(0.740)	(1.582)	(1.065)	(1.944)
Sudden Stop (capital inflows) Indicator	0.590***	0.497*	0.841	0.921	1.208	0.834
	(−2.927)	(−1.885)	(−1.254)	(−0.171)	(0.168)	(−0.452)
Advanced Economy Recession Indicator	0.642***	0.668**	0.680*	1.271	1.006	1.012
	(−4.074)	(−2.420)	(−1.911)	(0.922)	(0.0209)	(0.0372)
Credit Boom during Past Three Years	0.616***	0.591***	0.705***	1.449	1.200	1.546
	(−3.913)	(−2.621)	(−2.610)	(0.875)	(0.300)	(0.867)
Banking Crisis Indicator	0.550***	0.504***	0.538***			
	(−3.376)	(−3.302)	(−2.830)			
Single-Digit Inflation Indicator	1.473***	1.574**	1.276**	0.692	0.788	1.132
	(3.185)	(2.474)	(2.102)	(−1.465)	(−0.674)	(0.457)
Low Public Debt to GDP Indicator	1.009	0.998	1.019	0.550***	0.623	0.472***
	(0.0713)	(−0.0117)	(0.132)	(−2.648)	(−1.308)	(−2.969)
International Reserves to GDP	1.009***	1.006	1.004	0.993	1.001	0.998
	(2.866)	(1.289)	(0.903)	(−0.927)	(0.0636)	(−0.241)
Income Inequality (Gini coefficient)	0.986**	0.976***	0.997			
	(−2.144)	(−2.833)	(−0.459)			
Trade Openness (exports plus imports to GDP)	0.999	1.001	1.000	0.993**	0.987**	1.000
	(−0.451)	(0.373)	(−0.170)	(−2.327)	(−2.324)	(−0.0371)
Financial Openness (external assets plus liabilities to GDP)	0.999***	0.999***	1.000	1.001**	1.004	1.000
	(−3.121)	(−4.840)	(−0.549)	(2.154)	(1.183)	(−0.488)
Observations		1,264			832	
Number of Episodes		188			144	
Number of Exits		126			118	
Number of Economies		75			76	
Weibull Shape Parameter	1.516	1.408	2.277	0.829	0.857	1.024
Z Statistic of Shape Parameter	6.829	3.258	2.928	−3.792	−1.846	1.713
Log Likelihood	−103.0	−88.1		−201.1	−189.1	
Model Chi-Squared p Value	0.000	0.000		0.000	0.000	

Source: IMF staff calculations.

Note: Exponentiated coefficients shown are time ratios, which indicate whether the variable tends to shorten (less than 1) or lengthen (greater than 1) the expected time-in-episode. Z statistics are given in parentheses underneath the coefficient estimates. A negative z statistic indicates that the associated variable tends to shorten an episode; if the z statistic is positive, it tends to lengthen an episode. *, **, and *** denote significance at the 10 percent, 5 percent, and 1 percent levels, respectively.

[1]VXO = Chicago Board Options Exchange S&P 100 volatility index.

As seen in the second and third columns of Table 4.1, there is also some evidence that the effects of some variables on the length of expansions have changed over time. To investigate whether the greater resilience observed after 1989 results from changes in the sensitivity of expansions to shocks and policies, we estimate a model in which the effects are allowed to be different before and after 1989.

The sensitivity of expansion duration to shocks has not changed over time. Although the effects of some external shocks is slightly weaker after 1989,

only global uncertainty and U.S. real interest rates have statistically significant effects that differ across these subperiods, and both tend to shorten expansions more after 1989. Domestic shocks also tend to have a weaker effect after 1989, but the difference is not statistically significant.

The effects of policy-related variables and structural characteristics are generally similar across the two subperiods, with a couple of notable exceptions. Income inequality and financial openness shorten expansion only before 1989; after 1989, they have no statistically significant effect.

What Hastens Recoveries?

The three right-hand columns of Table 4.1 show how the various factors affect the speed of recovery. Unfortunately, data limitations require that we drop two of the variables—banking crises and income inequality.

The multivariate results broadly confirm the directional effects from the bivariate analyses, but statistical significance is much weaker. Only a few statistically significant variables are associated with the speed of recoveries.

In general, recoveries accompanied by the large shocks considered in this chapter tend to be slower (the time ratio is larger than 1), but only global uncertainty is statistically significant. Greater policy space helps hasten recoveries, but again with less statistical significance than in the bivariate analyses. Low inflation, low public debt, and high reserves tend to hasten recoveries, but only low public debt has a statistically significant effect. Among the structural characteristics, trade openness significantly hastens recoveries and financial openness significantly slows them, but both effects are comparatively small.

The fifth and sixth columns of Table 4.1 show the estimated effects on the speed of recoveries before and after 1989. Among the external shocks, only the effect of global uncertainty is consistently significant, but it does not appear to have changed over time. Terms-of-trade busts slow recoveries, but are statistically significant only after 1989. Low public debt dramatically hastens recoveries after 1989 (roughly halving the expected duration), but it had no significant effect before 1989. Greater trade openness tends to hasten recoveries more before than after 1989. The estimated effects of the other policy-related variables and structural characteristics were not statistically different between the two subperiods.

Wrapping Up: What Has Contributed to Increased Resilience?

What are the key drivers of the increasing resilience that emerging market and developing economies have demonstrated in recent years? There are a number of potential explanations. One is that the shocks that afflicted them in past decades—credit boom-bust cycles, sudden stops, and financial crises,

to name just a few—have become less frequent, less severe, or both.[25] A second is that although the shocks themselves have not changed, their effects have decreased over time. But, as shown in the previous section, the effects of shocks on the duration of expansions and the speed of recoveries have not lessened since 1989. A third is that emerging market and developing economies have built bigger cushions—in the form of better policy frameworks and enhanced policy space or more diversified production or trade patterns—that help them better weather shocks. We explore each of these possible explanations.

Homegrown shocks seem to have become less frequent in recent years (Figure 4.10, panels 1 and 2). The share of emerging market and developing economies that had a banking crisis, for example, rose during the 1990s but fell during the 2000s. Even with substantial financial spillovers and a much weaker economic environment as a result of the Great Recession, only four of these economies (Latvia, Mongolia, Nigeria, Ukraine) had a systemic banking crisis during 2008–09, and none had one in the past two years. Similarly, the incidence of credit booms fell between the 1990s and the 2000s.[26] Although the number of credit booms was high during 2008–09, it fell back during 2010–11 as economic and credit conditions worsened and as some of these economies tightened macroeconomic and credit policies to rein in rapid credit growth. In addition, the deviation from trend of real credit per capita during recent credit booms has been lower on average than during booms in previous decades (see Figure 4.10, panel 2, red line).

Some external shocks have become more frequent, others less frequent (Figure 4.10, panels 3 through 7). Sudden stops and spikes in global uncertainty have been more common in the past decade. But terms-of-trade busts and advanced economy reces-

---

[25]While it may be tempting to attribute fewer or less severe shocks to good luck, it should be kept in mind that many of these so-called shocks are endogenous to policymaking. For example, less frequent credit boom-bust cycles and banking crises can result from tighter regulation and supervision.

[26]Emerging Europe is a notable exception here—the credit boom-bust cycle that several emerging European countries have gone through is one of the causes of the region's weaker performance in the past decade.

sions declined in frequency between the 1980s and 2000–07. External shocks reemerged with a vengeance amid the 2008–09 global crisis but have receded in the past two years. The continued volatility of capital flows and commodity prices and the weak activity in advanced economies suggest taking a cautious view on the likelihood of such shocks in the future—a point discussed further below.

There has been a broad improvement in policy frameworks and policy space over time, and this has increased the resilience of emerging market and developing economies (Figure 4.11). Inflation has fallen in many of these economies: although half of them had double-digit inflation in the 1970s and 1980s, more than 80 percent now have inflation in the single digits. This may partly reflect the fact that more central banks have adopted inflation targeting. Exchange rate regimes have also become more flexible—there are fewer hard pegs than in the 1970s and 1980s.

The external positions of many of these economies are much improved. More are running current account surpluses, and the median external debt level has fallen from close to 60 percent of GDP in the 1990s to less than 35 percent of GDP today. Most of these economies now have external debt levels below 40 percent of GDP, a threshold that Reinhart, Rogoff, and Savastano (2003) flag as a level beyond which "debt intolerance" increases. And increasing reserves have not been limited to the high-profile Asian emerging markets—the median emerging market and developing economy saw its reserves rise from less than 8 percent of GDP on average in the 1990s to 18 percent of GDP during 2010–11. It should be noted, however, that current account surpluses come at the cost of potentially raising global imbalances, and high reserve holdings can entail a substantial opportunity cost.

Fiscal positions and frameworks have also improved, although fiscal balances have not fully recovered from the effects of the Great Recession. Median public debt has fallen from over 65 percent of GDP in the 1990s to less than 40 percent of GDP in the past two years. The number of countries implementing countercyclical fiscal policies is also on the rise. The share of emerging market and developing economies with fiscal surpluses rose

Figure 4.10. Frequency of Various Types of Domestic and External Shocks to Emerging Market and Developing Economies
(Percent unless noted otherwise)

There is no clear downward trend in the frequency of shocks to these economies. Although domestic shocks (banking crises and credit booms) were less frequent in the 2000–07 period compared with the 1980s, the frequency of external shocks has varied. The frequency of global uncertainty spikes and sudden stops in capital inflows increased between the 1980s and 2000–07, while the frequency of terms-of-trade shocks and advanced economy recessions declined over the same period. Many of these shocks reemerged in 2008–09 but have become less common in the past two years.

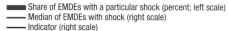

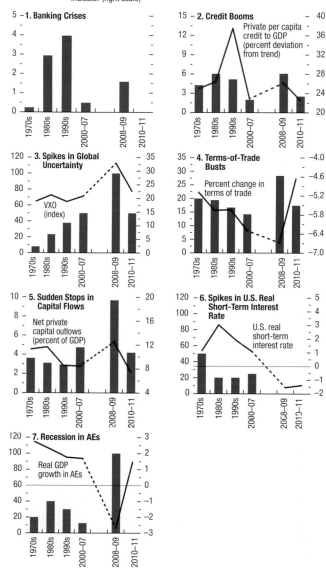

Source: IMF staff calculations.
Note: Economy groups are defined in Table 4.3 of Appendix 4.1. AE = advanced economy; EMDE = emerging market and developing economy; VXO = Chicago Board Options Exchange S&P 100 volatility index. In panels 1, 2, 4, and 5, bars represent the share of EMDEs hit by the shock (banking crises, credit booms, terms-of-trade busts, sudden stops in capital flows) in each subperiod. In panels 3, 6, and 7, bars represent the share of years with shocks (spikes in global uncertainty, spikes in U.S. short-term real interest rate, recessions in AEs) in each subperiod.

Figure 4.11. Policy Frameworks and Policy Space in Emerging Market and Developing Economies
(Percent unless noted otherwise)

Policy frameworks in these economies have improved in the 2000s as more adopted nonpegged exchange rates, inflation targeting, and countercyclical fiscal policy. Policy space also improved: more economies enjoyed single-digit inflation, current account and fiscal surpluses, lower external and public debt, and higher international reserves.

■ Share of EMDEs with characteristic (percent; left scale) ── Median of all EMDEs (right scale)

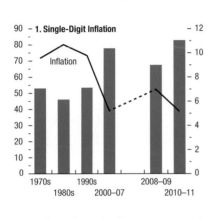

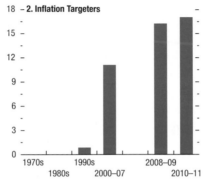

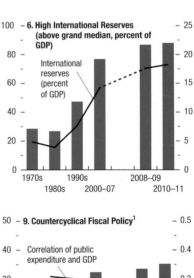

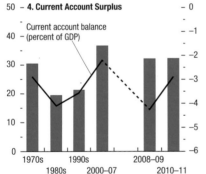

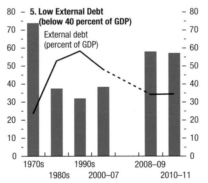

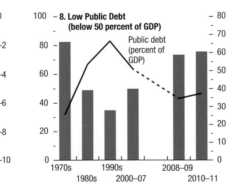

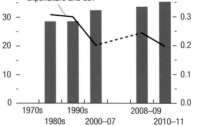

Source: IMF staff calculations.
Note: EMDE = emerging market and developing economy.
[1]The cyclical behavior of fiscal policy is measured as the correlation between the cyclical components of real government expenditure and real GDP (Kaminsky, Reinhart, and Végh, 2004). A negative correlation denotes countercyclical fiscal policy.

steadily from the 1970s to the 1990s. By the early 2000s more than one-quarter had budget surpluses, although that number fell during 2008–09 as many of these economies used this fiscal space to support their economies.

Structural factors—trade openness, financial openness, and income equality—have also mostly moved in the correct direction. The slight downward trend in income inequality—the median Gini coefficient among emerging market and developing economies fell from 42 in the 1990s to less than 40 in 2008–09—may have helped increase expansion duration (Figure 4.12).[27] There has also been a trend toward increased trade among emerging market and developing economies, a greater share of FDI flows, and higher trade and financial integration. But the small and often statistically insignificant effects of these structural characteristics suggest that they are likely not a major factor in explaining these economies' increased resilience.

The Relative Contributions of Shocks, Policies, and Structure to Increased Resilience

The multivariate model from the previous section (see Table 4.1, column 1) can be used to shed light on the relative contributions of these possible explanations to resilience. Such an exercise can only be indicative, because the results will be sensitive to the specific variables that enter the model. Moreover, these contributions should not be given a causal interpretation, because we do not identify the exogenous component of policies (a Herculean task for these economies). Nevertheless, this decomposition can help provide a feel for the importance of the various changes for these economies' performance.

The model suggests that improved policies account for about three-fifths of their increased resilience between the 1980s and 2000–07, and fewer shocks account for the remaining two-fifths; structural characteristics have made a negligible contribution (Figure 4.13, panel 1). As noted above and in Figure 4.10, the frequency of banking crises and credit booms

[27]Country coverage of income inequality data dropped sharply in 2010 and 2011, to fewer than 20 countries, so we exclude it here and in the figure.

Figure 4.12. Structural Characteristics of Emerging Market and Developing Economies
(Percent unless noted otherwise)

Emerging market and developing economies' structural characteristics have improved in the 2000s. There has been a significant increase in trade openness and diversification across trading partners, with a marked increase in intra-EMDE trade. Financial integration has also increased, with a larger share of cross-border flows taking the form of FDI. Income inequality has also fallen, and fewer economies have a high Gini coefficient.

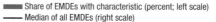

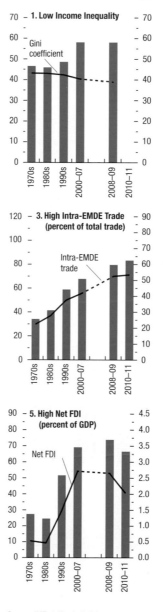

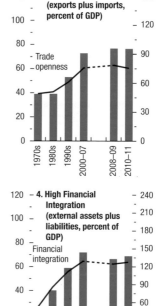

Source: IMF staff calculations.
Note: EMDE = emerging market and developing economy; FDI = foreign direct investment. Bars represent the share of EMDEs with the indicated characteristics either above (high) or below (low) the grand median of the characteristic in the sample (the median across all economies and years in the sample).

Figure 4.13. Contribution of Shocks, Policies, and Structure to the Length of Expansions in Emerging Market and Developing Economies

The expected mean duration of expansion rose steadily from the 1980s to the early 2000s. This increase reflected mostly greater policy space, with more economies achieving lower inflation and building up their international reserve buffers. But fewer and less intense external and domestic shocks also played a part. The expected mean duration of expansions dropped precipitously over 2008–09, with the spike in external shocks coming from advanced economies during the Great Recession. The lack of external shocks over the past two years has helped raise the expected expansion length. However, a sharp rise in advanced economy stresses could largely wipe out these expected gains, reducing the expected expansion length to the level seen during the Great Recession.

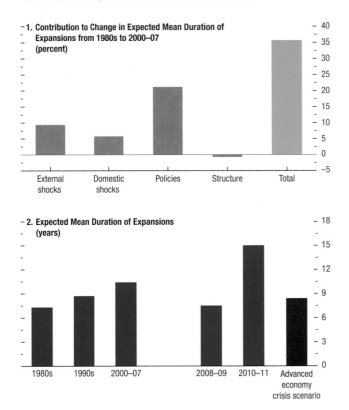

1. Contribution to Change in Expected Mean Duration of Expansions from 1980s to 2000–07 (percent)

2. Expected Mean Duration of Expansions (years)

Source: IMF staff calculations.
Note: Expected mean durations for expansions and the contributions of variables are calculated using the duration model estimates from Table 4.1, column 1, and the average values of the explanatory variables for emerging market and developing economies over the corresponding period. The advanced economy crisis scenario in panel 2 assumes that the external shocks reach the levels experienced by emerging market and developing economies during 2008–09.

declined between 1980 and 2000–07. This reduction in frequency and the estimated impact from the duration model imply that the decline in domestic shocks has improved the expected mean duration of expansions by about 5 percent relative to the 1980s. Similarly, the decline in terms-of-trade busts and advanced economy recessions during 2000–07 relative to the 1980s has more than offset the more frequent spikes in global uncertainty and sudden stops in capital inflows. On the whole, the reduced number of external shocks has improved the expected mean duration of expansions by about 10 percent relative to the 1980s. The largest improvement has been in policies, however, as documented in Figure 4.11; the changes in the policy variables between the 1980s and 2000–07, along with the estimated coefficients, suggest that improved policies have increased the expected mean duration of expansions by about 20 percent during the past two decades.[28]

The relative contributions of shocks, improved policies, and structural characteristics to the increase in resilience are similar across geographic regions and across commodity and noncommodity exporters. Resilience has increased even for heavily indebted poor countries (HIPCs), partly thanks to debt relief they are receiving under the HIPC Initiative but also as a result of the reforms and policy improvements that are a precondition for debt relief (see Box 4.3, and Figure 4.16 in Appendix 4.4).

The past two years (2010–11) were even better than 2000–07 with regard to expected mean duration of expansions (Figure 4.13, panel 2), particularly for external shocks. Despite weak growth in many advanced economies, this was not a period of advanced economy recession. World interest rates were low, which supported global growth and credit conditions and fueled capital flows to emerging market and developing economies. And global uncertainty remained elevated but was actually at the same level on average during 2010–11 as during 2000–07. There have also been no banking crises in emerging market and developing economies in the past two

---

[28]The contribution of policies could be underestimated if the endogenous nature of some of the shocks considered here are taken into account: improved policymaking could lengthen expansions by reducing the incidence of shocks, such as banking crises, credit booms, and sudden stops in capital flows.

years, and policy space has improved. Although fiscal balances declined in the aftermath of the Great Recession, median public debt fell from about 45 percent of GDP during 2000–07 to about 35 percent of GDP during 2010–11, and more of these economies now have low inflation and low public debt. Taken together, these factors have increased the estimated expected mean duration of expansions.

Conclusion

The results of this chapter confirm that emerging market and developing economies are now more resilient than in previous decades. This is not a recent phenomenon—their performance was already noticeably better in the 1990s than during the previous two decades, even with severe downturns such as the Tequila, Asian, and Russian crises. But the recent decade has really been exceptional—for the first time, emerging market and developing economies have performed better than advanced economies as measured by time spent in expansion. The chapter's findings on the explanations for these gains in resilience lend support to an optimistic view that they are not temporary. These economies are doing better now both because the frequency of shocks has fallen and because policymaking has improved. This improvement is evident not only in emerging markets, but also in low-income countries, including countries that are benefiting from the HIPC Initiative.

The caveat, of course, is that the relative calm of the past two years could well be temporary. As highlighted in Chapter 1, there is a significant risk that advanced economies could experience another downturn, as continuing sovereign and banking tensions in Europe and the so-called fiscal cliff in the United States threaten to put the brakes on growth. Terms-of-trade busts in emerging market and developing economies could rise if commodity prices drop. Further spikes in global uncertainty are possible, and sudden stops could emerge once again if greater risk aversion leads to capital outflows. Domestic vulnerabilities could also emerge—as noted in Chapter 1, strong credit growth in some emerging market and developing economies, which likely supported domestic demand, may raise concerns about financial stability.

Should the external environment worsen again, emerging market and developing economies will likely end up recoupling with advanced economies, much as they did during the Great Recession (see Figure 4.13, panel 2, red bar). And even in the absence of an external shock, homegrown shocks could pull down growth further in some key emerging economies, as highlighted in Chapter 1. To guard against such risks, these economies will need to rebuild their buffers to ensure that they have adequate policy space. In response to the global downturn, policy space was rightly used to support activity. These economies will be more resilient to new shocks if recent improvements in their policy frameworks—including greater exchange rate flexibility and more countercyclical macroeconomic policies—are maintained, while policy buffers are being rebuilt.

Appendix 4.1. Data Sources

The primary data sources for this chapter are the IMF's World Economic Outlook (WEO) and International Financial Statistics (IFS) databases and the World Bank's World Development Indicators (WDI) database. All the data sources used in the analysis are listed in Table 4.2. The analytical and regional groupings of economies are presented in Table 4.3.

Data on output per capita at the annual frequency are from the WEO and are extended with series from the WDI and the Penn World Tables 7.0.

External Shocks

Global uncertainty is measured by Bloom's (2009) index of volatility spliced with the Chicago Board Options Exchange S&P 100 volatility index (VXO). Spikes in global uncertainty are periods in which the VXO is above its 75th percentile. *Advanced economy recessions* are defined as in Chapter 1 of the October 2010 issue of the *World Economic Outlook,* with five such recessions during our sample period: 1974–75, 1980–83, 1991–93, 2001, and 2008–09. The *U.S. ex ante real interest rate* is defined as the interest rate on three-month Treasury bills minus projected inflation, which is the percent change in the forecast GDP deflator from the *Survey of Professional*

Table 4.2. Data Sources

Variable	Source
Bank Credit to the Private Sector	International Financial Statistics Database
Banking Crisis Indicators	Laeven and Valencia (2012)
Bilateral Exports	IMF, Direction of Trade Statistics Database
Capital Account Openness	Chinn and Ito (2006), updated to 2010
Consumer Price Inflation	World Economic Outlook Database
Current Account Balance	World Economic Outlook Database
De Facto Exchange Rate Regime	Reinhart and Rogoff (2004); Ilzetzki, Reinhart, and Rogoff (2008), updated to 2010
Export Deflator	World Economic Outlook Database, World Development Indicators Database
Exports of Goods and Services	World Economic Outlook Database, World Development Indicators Database
External Debt to GDP	Lane and Milesi-Ferretti (2007), External Wealth of Nations Mark II Database updated to 2010
Foreign Direct Investment	IMF, Balance of Payments Statistics Database
Foreign Assets	Lane and Milesi-Ferretti (2007), External Wealth of Nations Mark II Database updated to 2010
Foreign Liabilities	Lane and Milesi-Ferretti (2007), External Wealth of Nations Mark II Database updated to 2010
GDP (nominal local currency)	World Economic Outlook Database, World Development Indicators Database
GDP (U.S. dollars)	World Economic Outlook Database, World Development Indicators Database
GDP per Capita (real)	World Economic Outlook Database, World Development Indicators, Penn World Tables 7.0
Gini Coefficient	Solt (2009), Standardized World Income Inequality Database v. 3.1
Global Uncertainty	Bloom (2009) and Chicago Board Options Exchange S&P100 volatility index (VXO)
Government Expenditure	World Economic Outlook Database
Import Deflator	World Economic Outlook Database, World Development Indicators Database
Imports of Goods and Services	World Economic Outlook Database, World Development Indicators Database
Inflation-Targeting Indicator	Roger (2010)
Net Private Capital Flows	IMF, Balance of Payments Statistics Database
Public Debt to GDP	Abbas and others (2010)
Reserves to GDP	Lane and Milesi-Ferretti (2007), External Wealth of Nations Mark II Database updated to 2010
Trade Liberalization Index	Wacziarg and Welch (2008)
U.S. Projected Inflation	*Survey of Professional Forecasters*, Federal Reserve Bank of Philadelphia
U.S. 3-Month Treasury Bill Interest Rate	Global Financial Database

Forecasters. Large increases in the U.S. ex ante real interest rates are those in the top quartile.

Data on net private capital flows are from the IMF Balance of Payments Statistics (BPS) database. Net private capital flows correspond to the sum of net foreign direct investment (FDI) flows (line 4500), net portfolio flows (line 4600), net derivative flows (line 4910), and net other investment flows (line 4700), excluding other investment flows to the general government and monetary authorities. A *sudden stop in capital flows* occurs when the ratio of net private capital flows to GDP falls by at least 5 percentage points from the previous year, and when the level of net private flows is more than 1 standard deviation below its economy-specific mean. The BPS database is also used to obtain the net foreign direct investment flows as a share of GDP.

The trade-weighted terms of trade are constructed using the deflators of exports and imports of goods and services and the series of GDP, exports, and imports of goods and services in nominal terms—all

from the WEO and WDI databases. In particular, the terms-of-trade series is calculated as the percent change in the export price deflator times the share of exports in GDP in the previous period minus the percent change in the import price deflator times the share of imports in GDP in the previous period. *Terms-of-trade busts* are defined as a worsening in the terms of trade of at least 3 percent of GDP.

Domestic Shocks

The *banking crisis* indicator is from Laeven and Valencia (2012). Bank credit to the private nonfinancial sector is taken from the IFS database. Breaks in these data are identified using the IFS Country Notes publications, and data are growth-spliced at these points. We follow Mendoza and Terrones (2008) and define *credit booms* as periods in which the cyclical component of log real private credit per capita is at least 1.65 times its standard deviation above its mean.

Table 4.3. Economy Groups

Advanced Economies (AEs)	Emerging Market and Developing Economies (EMDEs)		
	Emerging Market Economies (EMs)		**Low-Income Countries (LICs)**

Advanced Economies (AEs)	Emerging Market Economies (EMs)		Low-Income Countries (LICs)
Australia	*Asia*	*Latin America*	*Asia*
Austria	China	Argentina	Afghanistan
Belgium	Hong Kong SAR	Brazil	Bangladesh
Canada	India	Chile*	Cambodia
Denmark	Indonesia	Colombia	Lao P.D.R.
Finland	Korea	Costa Rica	Myanmar
France	Malaysia	Dominican Republic	Nepal
Germany	Pakistan	Ecuador*	Papua New Guinea*
Greece	Philippines	El Salvador	Timor-Leste*
Ireland	Singapore	Guatemala	Vietnam
Italy	Sri Lanka	Jamaica	
Japan	Taiwan Province of China	Mexico	*Commonwealth of Independent*
Netherlands	Thailand	Panama	*States (CIS)*
New Zealand		Paraguay	Armenia
Norway	*Commonwealth of*	Peru*	Georgia
Portugal	*Independent States (CIS)*	Trinidad and Tobago*	Kyrgyz Republic
Spain	Azerbaijan*	Uruguay	Moldova
Sweden	Belarus	Venezuela*	Mongolia*
Switzerland	Kazakhstan*		
United Kingdom	Russia*	*Middle East and*	*Latin America*
United States	Ukraine	*North Africa (MENA)*	Bolivia*
		Algeria*	Haiti
	Europe	Egypt	Honduras
	Albania	Iran*	Nicaragua
	Bosnia and Herzegovina	Iraq*	
	Bulgaria	Israel	*Middle East and North Africa (MENA)*
	Croatia	Jordan	Mauritania*
	Czech Republic	Kuwait*	Sudan*
	Estonia	Lebanon	Yemen*
	Hungary	Libya*	
	Latvia	Morocco	*Sub-Saharan Africa (SSA)*
	Lithuania	Oman*	Benin
	Macedonia	Saudi Arabia*	Burkina Faso*
	Poland	Syria	Burundi*
	Romania	Tunisia	Cameroon
	Serbia	United Arab Emirates*	Central African Republic*
	Slovak Republic		Chad*
	Slovenia	*Sub-Saharan Africa (SSA)*	Democratic Republic of the Congo*
	Turkey	Angola*	Republic of Congo*
		Botswana	Côte d'Ivoire
		Namibia	Eritrea
		South Africa	Ethiopia
			Ghana
			Guinea*
			Kenya
			Lesotho
			Liberia
			Madagascar
			Malawi*
			Mali*
			Mozambique*
			Niger
			Nigeria*
			Rwanda
			Senegal
			Sierra Leone*
			Tanzania
			Togo
			Uganda
			Zambia*
			Zimbabwe*

Note: * denotes a primary commodity and/or fuel exporter, as classified in the WEO Statistical Appendix. All economies in the analysis have an average population over the sample period of 1 million inhabitants or more. Some economies currently classified as advanced by the WEO are classified as emerging markets in this chapter, because over the past 60 years these economies were more like emerging markets than advanced economies and because their experience—especially their ability to grow sufficiently to attain advanced economy status—provides valuable lessons.

Policy Frameworks and Policy Space

The dates when countries adopted *inflation target-ing* are from Roger (2010), and *de facto exchange rate regime* data are from Reinhart and Rogoff (2004) and Ilzetzki, Reinhart, and Rogoff (2008). We measure the *cyclicality of fiscal policy* as the correlation between the cyclical component of real government expenditure from the WEO database and the cyclical component of real GDP (similar to Kaminsky, Reinhart, and Végh, 2004). A negative correlation corresponds to a countercyclical fiscal policy, while a positive correlation corresponds to a procyclical fiscal policy. The fiscal balance is calculated as the change in the ratio of public debt to GDP, corrected for nominal GDP growth. *Fiscal surplus* is an indicator equal to 1 if the fiscal balance is positive. Data on *public debt* are from Abbas and others (2010). The low public debt indicator equals 1 if public debt is less than 50 percent of GDP, the level at which Mendoza and Ostry (2008) find that fiscal solvency in emerging markets diminishes.

The External Wealth of Nations Mark II Data-base (see Lane and Milesi-Ferretti, 2007) is used to construct the ratios of *external debt to GDP*, *reserves to GDP*, and *financial integration*, which is defined as the sum of foreign assets and foreign liabilities divided by GDP. The low external debt indicator equals 1 if external debt is less than 40 percent of GDP, a thresh-old that Reinhart, Rogoff, and Savastano (2003) flag as a level beyond which "debt intolerance" increases. The current account balance and consumer price inflation are both taken from the WEO database. The low-inflation indicator equals 1 if inflation is below 10 percent.

Structural Characteristics

Trade openness is measured as the sum of imports and exports of goods and services over GDP. The *trade liberalization* index is from Wacziarg and Welch (2008), and *capital account openness* is from Chinn and Ito (2006). Data on bilateral merchandise imports and exports are from the Direction of Trade Statistics database and are used to construct the *share of exports to emerging market and developing economies*. Finally, *inequality*, as captured in the Gini coefficient of household disposable income, is from Solt (2009).

Appendix 4.2. Characterizing Resilience Using an Autoregressive Process on Growth

To assess the potential drivers of resilience, this appendix characterizes expansions and recoveries for advanced economies and emerging market and developing economies using a first-order autore-gressive—AR(1)— process for growth in real GDP per capita, similar to the one used by Blanchard and Simon (2001). In particular, it explores whether an AR(1) model with time-varying coef-ficients can reproduce the time spent in expansion, median real GDP per capita growth in expansions, and the median amplitude of downturns observed in the data. For that purpose, the following AR(1) process is estimated:

$$g_t = \alpha + \beta g_{t-1} + \varepsilon_t \quad \text{with} \quad \varepsilon_t \sim N(0, \sigma^2), \qquad (4.1)$$

in which g_t is growth in real GDP per capita at time t, α is a constant, β is the first-order autore-gressive coefficient, and ε_t is a mean-zero shock at time t. This equation is estimated for each economy over three subperiods: 1950–69, 1970–89, and 1990–2007. Table 4.4 presents the median estimated coefficients, and interquartile ranges, by economy group and subperiod.

The results for the advanced economies show that steady-state growth and growth variability have fallen. In particular, α and σ have both fallen over time, and β has risen. As a result, steady-state growth, given by $\alpha/(1 - \beta)$, and growth variability, given by $\sigma/\sqrt{1 - \beta^2}$, have fallen. These have countervailing effects on expan-sion duration: lower steady-state growth implies shorter expansions, whereas lower growth variabil-ity implies longer expansions.

The results for emerging market and developing economies show that steady-state growth increased and growth variability fell in 1990–2007 relative to the previous 40 years. In particular, α fell from 1950–69 to 1970–89, but it rose in 1990–2007, while β rose markedly from 1950–69 to 1970–89, remaining constant thereafter. The growth shock's standard deviation σ rose slightly from 1950–69 to 1970–89, but declined during 1990–2007 to levels below that of 1950–69. As a result, steady-state growth rose and growth variability

Table 4.4. AR(1) Median Coefficients and Interquartile Range

		α	β	σ	$\sigma \div ((1 - \beta^2)^{0.5})$	$\alpha \div (1 - \beta)$
Advanced Economies	1950–69	0.032	0.057	0.028	0.028	0.034
	Interquartile Range	(0.025, 0.037)	(−0.043, 0.107)	(0.017, 0.033)	(0.018, 0.034)	(0.027, 0.040)
	1970–89	0.018	0.181	0.023	0.023	0.022
	Interquartile Range	(0.015, 0.022)	(0.124, 0.274)	(0.020, 0.025)	(0.020, 0.025)	(0.021, 0.026)
	1990–2007	0.010	0.428	0.014	0.014	0.019
	Interquartile Range	(0.009, 0.013)	(0.314, 0.531)	(0.012, 0.016)	(0.013, 0.019)	(0.016, 0.023)
Emerging Market and	1950–69	0.019	−0.069	0.041	0.043	0.019
Developing Economies	Interquartile Range	(0.009, 0.035)	(−0.262, 0.228)	(0.031, 0.061)	(0.032, 0.065)	(0.008, 0.035)
	1970–89	0.003	0.232	0.044	0.047	0.004
	Interquartile Range	(−0.004, 0.014)	(0.076, 0.439)	(0.034, 0.063)	(0.038, 0.069)	(−0.005, 0.020)
	1990–2007	0.018	0.272	0.030	0.034	0.027
	Interquartile Range	(0.008, 0.030)	(−0.002, 0.505)	(0.021, 0.046)	(0.025, 0.051)	(0.012, 0.042)
Emerging Market	1950–69	0.027	−0.067	0.040	0.041	0.025
Economies	Interquartile Range	(0.015, 0.038)	(−0.252, 0.175)	(0.029, 0.057)	(0.032, 0.065)	(0.016, 0.041)
	1970–89	0.009	0.232	0.042	0.043	0.015
	Interquartile Range	(0.001, 0.023)	(0.157, 0.471)	(0.031, 0.061)	(0.033, 0.062)	(0.001, 0.029)
	1990–2007	0.022	0.275	0.030	0.032	0.034
	Interquartile Range	(0.012, 0.034)	(0.106, 0.484)	(0.021, 0.041)	(0.025, 0.046)	(0.020, 0.046)
Low-Income Countries	1950–69	0.010	−0.145	0.043	0.045	0.014
	Interquartile Range	(0.004, 0.029)	(−0.323, 0.242)	(0.032, 0.063)	(0.034, 0.066)	(0.004, 0.025)
	1970–89	−0.001	0.230	0.048	0.051	−0.001
	Interquartile Range	(−0.007, 0.005)	(0.029, 0.314)	(0.039, 0.065)	(0.040, 0.070)	(−0.007, 0.006)
	1990–2007	0.012	0.271	0.033	0.037	0.015
	Interquartile Range	(0.003, 0.026)	(−0.058, 0.550)	(0.020, 0.052)	(0.023, 0.055)	(0.003, 0.033)

Source: IMF staff calculations.

Note: Economy groups are defined in Table 4.3 of Appendix 4.1. Standard errors are in parentheses.

fell, resulting in both longer expansions and faster recoveries.[29]

With these estimations in hand, this appendix explores whether the characteristics of expansions and recoveries seen in the data for emerging market and developing economies can be replicated with simulated data based on the median estimated coefficients in Table 4.4 for 1970–89 and 1990–2007. In particular, we use the median coefficients for the emerging market and developing economies in each subperiod to run 1,000 simulations of the growth processes for 50 years each. The Harding-Pagan algorithm is then applied to identify peaks and troughs in the level of simulated GDP per capita. In addition, each coefficient is changed one at a time to assess its impact on resilience. Figure 4.14 presents the results.

The AR(1) model for real GDP growth per capita suggests that the improvement in resilience observed

in emerging market and developing economies during the past 20 years has been mostly a result of an increase in steady-state growth and to a lesser extent of lower output variability. However, as discussed below, these results must be viewed with caution because a linear AR(1) model cannot replicate some of the stylized facts presented in this chapter.

The AR(1) model underestimates the time spent in expansion during 1970–89 and overestimates it during 1990–2007, resulting in a larger rise across periods than in the data (Figure 4.14, panel 1). The increase in time spent in expansion is mostly due to a rise in α. The coefficients β and σ have no impact on the change in time spent in expansion (Figure 4.14, panel 2).

The AR(1) model overestimates growth during expansions during 1970–89 and underestimates growth during 1990–2007, resulting in no change between subperiods, even though the data indicate that there was an increase in the growth rate during this period (Figure 4.14, panel 3). In short, the rise in growth during expansions due to a higher α is fully offset by the fall in growth due to a lower σ

[29]The increase in steady-state growth and the fall in growth variability from 1970–89 to 1990–2007 are both statistically significant.

Figure 4.14. Emerging Market and Developing Economies: Effects of Changing the Autoregressive Model Coefficients

Simulated data from a calibrated AR(1) model with time-varying coefficients broadly replicate the stylized facts of resilience in emerging market and developing economies. However, comparing 1970–89 and 1990–2007 shows that the simulated data overestimate the increase in the time spent in expansion, and underestimate the median real GDP growth during expansions and the amplitude of downturns. Most of the gains in resilience between 1970–89 and 1990–2007 result from an increase in the constant (α) and to a lesser extent from a lower standard deviation of growth innovations (σ).

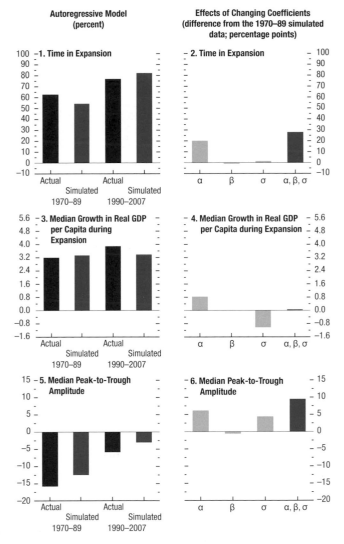

Source: IMF staff estimates.
Note: Peaks and troughs in output per capita are identified using the Harding-Pagan algorithm (Harding and Pagan, 2002). The simulated data are constructed using the median estimated coefficients from Table 4.4 for each period. These coefficients are plugged into an AR(1) equation for GDP growth per capita, and the growth innovations are drawn from a normal distribution with mean zero and variance of σ^2, to run 1,000 simulations of growth processes for 50 years each for each period. The generated series of GDP growth per capita are then used to construct indices of GDP per capita in levels.

(Figure 4.14, panel 4). In addition, the AR(1) model underestimates the amplitude of downturns during both subperiods (Figure 4.14, panel 5). The decline in the downturns' estimated amplitude from 1970–89 to 1990–2007 is mostly due to an increase in α and to a lesser extent to a decline in σ (Figure 4.14, panel 6).

Appendix 4.3. Duration Analysis

As a first step in the analysis of the duration of each episode (expansion or recovery) we map the data from calendar time into analysis time (denoted by t), which counts the time elapsed since the start of an episode ($t = 0$). Duration analysis then involves modeling how the evolution of the episode (as influenced by various explanatory variables) affects the likelihood that the episode will end at a point during the analysis time.

Bivariate Analysis

Figure 4.7 shows the average probability that an episode will end, conditional on whether or not a shock has occurred. The mean is taken over the sample probabilities that an ongoing episode will end at each point in the analysis time. Statistical significance is calculated from a test of the difference between the set of estimated probabilities in which the shock occurs and the set in which it does not.

Figures 4.8 and 4.9 show the average duration of an episode conditional on whether or not the characteristic of interest was present during the episode. These average durations are calculated from the Kaplan-Meier estimated survival curves conditional on the characteristic. Sometimes known as the "product limit estimators of the survival curve," the Kaplan-Meier curve estimation involves (1) calculating the probability that an episode will continue beyond a point in the analysis time, given that it has lasted until that point; and (2) taking the rolling product of these probabilities at each point in analysis time (Kaplan and Meier, 1958). The result is a mapping of analysis time to the probability of continuation, given that an episode has lasted until that point:

$$\bar{S}(t) = \prod_{j|t_j \leq t} \left(\frac{n_j - d_j}{n_j} \right), \tag{4.2}$$

in which j indexes the set of observed episode lengths, $\bar{S}$ represents the estimated survival curve, n_j is the number of episodes at risk of ending at time t_j, given that they have lasted until that time, and d_j is the number of episodes at time t_j that actually ended.

From this curve (using the sample with or without the characteristic of interest), we calculate the expected duration of the episode. Statistical significance is given by a log-rank test of the difference between the two estimated survival curves. The methods used in the bivariate analysis are fundamentally nonparametric, since no specific probability distribution is assumed to govern the data.

Multivariate Analysis

The duration model used in the multivariate analysis is an accelerated-failure-time model, based on the Weibull distribution. The model assumes that the length of episode j, here denoted t_j, can be expressed as the product of a Weibull-distributed random variable τ_j and a scaling proportion that depends on the weighted sum of a set of explanatory variables (denoted by the vector x_{t_j}):

$$t_j = \exp(x_{t_j}'\beta)\tau_j$$
$$= \exp\left(\sum_{k=1}^{K} \beta_k \, x_{k,t_j}\right)\tau_j, \qquad (4.3)$$

in which τ_j has a Weibull distribution with shape parameter γ. The estimated coefficients β_k are the weights applied to each of the explanatory variables in the scaling proportion. As described in the text, we show the exponentiated coefficients in Table 4.1, which may be interpreted as time ratios, indicating how much the baseline expected duration $E(\tau_j)$ would be shortened or lengthened by a one-unit change in a variable. See Cleves and others (2010) for an in-depth description of the approach.

Appendix 4.4. Robustness and Additional Results

We undertook six robustness checks of our baseline model, including (1) accounting for unobserved heterogeneity in episodes across countries by random effects (also known as "frailties"

in the duration analysis literature); (2) an alternative definition of the sudden stop indicator, in which it is interacted with an indicator for spikes in global uncertainty, to capture "systemic" sudden stops; (3) a more stringent cutoff for the low-inflation indicator, in which we consider whether an economy had an inflation rate below 5 percent; (4) accounting for common decade fixed effects; (5) an alternative distributional assumption (the generalized gamma); and (6) using real GDP instead of real GDP per capita to define periods of expansion. The results of these robustness checks are shown in Table 4.5.

It is readily apparent that the point estimates for the time ratios are typically quite similar across the columns (with the baseline specification repeated in column 1 for convenience). The statistical significance of the estimates is also similar across specifications, although it tends to be marginally reduced when frailties are used to account for unobserved heterogeneity.

We also looked at whether our findings for expansions hold for expansions characterized by rapid and sustained growth. To identify these episodes, we removed a 4 percent linear growth trend from real GDP per capita for each economy and applied the Harding-Pagan algorithm to find the turning points in the detrended series. We then undertook our baseline duration analysis for the growth expansions (periods from trough to peak in the detrended series). The results of this analysis are shown in column 8 of Table 4.5. The results are broadly aligned with the findings for the level expansions (column 1)—external and domestic shocks tend to shorten growth expansions, whereas policy space tends to lengthen them. The statistical significance of the estimated results is sometimes reduced, but this appears to be largely a function of the much smaller sample size, given that the point estimates themselves are quite similar to the baseline for level expansions. Thus, the variables associated with longer level expansions are also associated with longer growth expansions.

We investigated whether the stylized facts for emerging market and developing economies' expansions over the past decades were driven by the experience of commodity exporters or by

Table 4.5. What Shortens Expansions? Robustness Checks

Explanatory Variable	Baseline	Baseline with Economy Frailties	Alternative Sudden Stop	Alternative Inflation	Decade Dummies	Alternative Distribution (generalized gamma)	Alternative Output	Growth Expansions
Implied S&P 100 Volatility (VXO)[1]	0.951***	0.951***	0.951***	0.952***	0.944***	0.950***	0.937***	0.967**
	(−4.179)	(−3.688)	(−4.138)	(−3.851)	(−4.624)	(−4.659)	(−4.785)	(−2.191)
U.S. Ex Ante Real Interest Rate	0.956	0.956	0.956	0.944*	0.982	0.939*	0.917**	0.986
	(−1.461)	(−1.170)	(−1.471)	(−1.801)	(−0.494)	(−1.862)	(−2.399)	(−0.328)
Terms-of-Trade Bust Indicator	0.968	0.968	0.969	0.953	0.982	0.926	1.051	0.801
	(−0.214)	(−0.200)	(−0.209)	(−0.298)	(−0.116)	(−0.450)	(0.231)	(−0.826)
Sudden Stop (capital inflows) Indicator	0.590***	0.590**		0.622**	0.590***	0.523***	0.363***	0.657
	(−2.927)	(−2.134)		(−2.536)	(−2.731)	(−2.656)	(−4.946)	(−1.333)
Advanced Economy Recession Indicator	0.642***	0.642**	0.648***	0.608***	0.619***	0.622***	0.685***	0.680***
	(−4.074)	(−2.512)	(−4.016)	(−4.449)	(−3.967)	(−4.091)	(−3.065)	(−2.590)
Credit Boom during Past Three Years	0.616***	0.616***	0.620***	0.617***	0.626***	0.601***	0.596***	0.497***
	(−3.913)	(−2.977)	(−3.843)	(−3.664)	(−3.631)	(−3.373)	(−3.454)	(−3.697)
Banking Crisis Indicator	0.550***	0.550**	0.550***	0.524***	0.567***	0.480***	0.516***	0.451**
	(−3.376)	(−2.392)	(−3.387)	(−3.584)	(−3.180)	(−3.079)	(−3.561)	(−1.977)
Single-Digit Inflation Indicator	1.473***	1.473***	1.475***		1.444***	1.434***	1.604***	1.145
	(3.185)	(2.938)	(3.192)		(2.954)	(2.925)	(3.077)	(0.688)
Low Public Debt to GDP Indicator	1.009	1.009	1.001	1.019	0.989	1.016	0.740*	1.276
	(0.0713)	(0.0651)	(0.0119)	(0.149)	(−0.0811)	(0.127)	(−1.699)	(0.988)
International Reserves to GDP	1.009***	1.009	1.009***	1.009***	1.009***	1.009***	1.010**	1.012*
	(2.866)	(1.584)	(2.887)	(3.099)	(3.037)	(2.620)	(2.122)	(1.893)
Income Inequality (Gini coefficient)	0.986**	0.986**	0.986**	0.986**	0.987**	0.990	0.998	0.990
	(−2.144)	(−1.988)	(−2.154)	(−2.094)	(−2.035)	(−1.327)	(−0.271)	(−0.847)
Trade Openness (exports plus imports to GDP)	0.999	0.999	0.999	1.000	0.999	1.000	0.997*	1.003
	(−0.451)	(−0.317)	(−0.495)	(−0.377)	(−0.468)	(0.0951)	(−1.888)	(1.605)
Financial Openness (external assets plus liabilities to GDP)	0.999***	0.999*	0.999***	0.999***	0.999***	0.999**	1.000	0.998**
	(−3.121)	(−1.766)	(−3.094)	(−3.037)	(−3.577)	(−2.417)	(−0.484)	(−2.324)
Global Uncertainty Spike and Sudden Stop Joint Indicator				0.603***				
				(−2.828)				
Below 5 Percent Inflation Indicator				1.330*				
				(1.729)				
Observations	1,264	1,264	1,264	1,264	1,264	1,264	1,417	452
Weibull Shape Parameter	1.516	1.516	1.519	1.476	1.498		1.401	1.438
Z Statistic of Shape Parameter	6.829	2.653	6.817	5.968	6.411		5.372	3.177
Number of Episodes	188	188	188	188	188	188	163	84
Number of Exits	126	126	126	126	126	126	99	63
Number of Economies	75	75	75	75	75	75	75	54
Log Likelihood	−103.0	−103.0	−103.7	−105.6	−101.0	−99.2	−73.5	−58.0
Model Chi-Squared p Value	0.000	0.000	0.000	0.000	0.000	0.000	0.000	0.000

Source: IMF staff calculations.

Note: Exponentiated coefficients shown are time ratios, which indicate whether the variable tends to shorten (less than 1) or lengthen (greater than 1) the expected time-in-episode. Z statistics are given in parentheses underneath the coefficient estimates. A negative z statistic indicates that the associated variable tends to shorten an episode; if the z statistic is positive, it tends to lengthen an episode. *, **, and *** denote significance at the 10 percent, 5 percent, and 1 percent levels, respectively.

[1]VXO = Chicago Board Options Exchange S&P 100 volatility index.

the largest economies. Figure 4.15 shows that neither of these groups appears to be driving the changes in resilience seen from the 1980s to the 2000s. Commodity exporters and noncommodity exporters follow the same patterns, although at a somewhat different pace. The median commodity exporter was more adversely impacted in the 1980s, whereas the median noncommodity exporter tended to have even stronger growth in the 2000s after a peak. The largest 30 economies also show similar patterns of resilience when compared with the other, smaller economies. The most marked difference is probably the somewhat poorer performance after a peak of smaller economies during the 1980s.

Finally, we examine whether the relative contributions of shocks, policies, and structural characteristics differ across regions, commodity and non–commodity exporters, and for heavily indebted poor countries eligible for debt relief under the Heavily Indebted Poor Country Initiative. We use the same method for decomposing the change in expected duration of expansions as in Figure 4.13. As mentioned in the main text, this decomposition is an accounting exercise, and care should be taken that these contributions not be given a causal interpretation.

As shown in Figure 4.16, our finding that improved policies account for the bulk of the increase in expected duration of expansions from the 1980s to the 2000s holds across all emerging market and developing economy regions and subsamples. Less frequent domestic and external shocks also contributed to improved performance. Structural characteristics had a negligible contribution in almost all subsamples, with the exception of emerging and developing Asia—in that region, financial openness almost doubled between the 1980s and 2000s, resulting in a negative contribution to expected duration of expansions.

Figure 4.15. Emerging Market and Developing Economy Subgroups: Dynamics of Output per Capita following Peaks
(Median output per capita; peak = 100; years on x-axis)

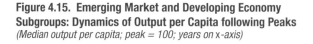

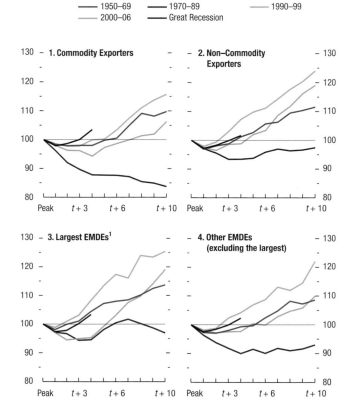

Source: IMF staff calculations.
Note: Economy groups are defined in Table 4.3 of Appendix 4.1. EMDE = emerging market and developing economy. Peaks in output per capita are identified using the Harding-Pagan algorithm (Harding and Pagan, 2002). Output per capita at the peak (*t*) is normalized to 100, and the median output per capita is plotted in years (*t* + 1) through (*t* + 10) for each group.
[1]Refers to the 30 largest emerging market and developing economies based on their average real GDP over the sample period.

Figure 4.16. Emerging Market and Developing Economy Regions: Contributions of Shocks, Policies, and Structure to the Length of Expansions

(Contribution to change in expected mean duration of expansions from 1980s to 2000–07; percent)

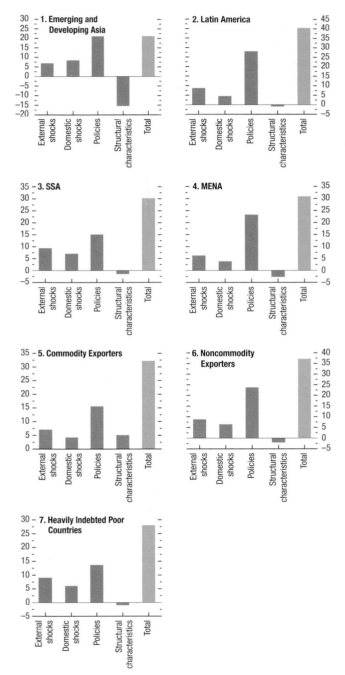

Source: IMF staff calculations.
Note: Economy groups are defined in Table 4.3 of Appendix 4.1. MENA = Middle East and North Africa; SSA = sub-Saharan Africa. Peaks in output per capita are identified using the Harding-Pagan algorithm (Harding and Pagan, 2002).

Box 4.1. Jobs and Growth: Can't Have One without the Other?

Emerging market and developing economies have enjoyed robust growth during the past decade and bounced back quickly from the Great Recession, in marked contrast to the more tepid recovery in advanced economies. These divergent growth trajectories were reflected in their labor markets. For instance, unemployment—both numbers of people unemployed and rates—remained substantially higher in 2011 in advanced economies compared with 2007. In contrast, although unemployment in emerging market and developing economies did go up during the Great Recession, by 2011 it was essentially back to precrisis levels (Figure 4.1.1).

Is the observed correspondence between jobs and growth a surprise, or does it represent a systemic feature of emerging market and developing economies? This box shows that the short-term relationship between labor market developments and output growth has been fairly strong in many of these economies for the past 30 years. Hence, although the emphasis on structural policies to lower long-term unemployment and raise labor force participation remains appropriate, cyclical developments deserve adequate consideration as well. The short-term relationship between jobs and growth suggests that macroeconomic policies to maintain aggregate demand also likely play an important role in labor market outcomes in many of these economies.

Does One Law Fit All?

The short-term relationship between U.S. output and unemployment documented by Okun (1962) has since become famous as "Okun's law." Ball, Leigh, and Loungani (forthcoming) investigate how well Okun's law explains short-term changes in the unemployment rate for the United States since 1960 and for a sample of 20 advanced economies since 1980.

Ball and others (forthcoming) conclude that Okun's law is a strong and stable relationship in most advanced economies. That is, they confirm the view that short-term changes in unemployment

The authors of this box are Davide Furceri and Prakash Loungani. Jair Rodriguez and Hites Ahir provided research assistance.

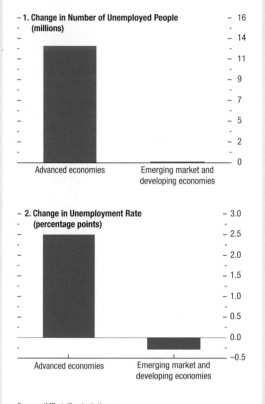

Figure 4.1.1. Diverging Global Labor Market Trends, 2007–11

1. Change in Number of Unemployed People (millions)

2. Change in Unemployment Rate (percentage points)

Source: IMF staff calculations.

are driven by changes in output. On average, a 1 percent deviation of output from potential leads to a reduction in cyclical unemployment of about ½ percentage point. Deviations from Okun's law occur, but they are usually modest in size and short lived.

However, although Okun's law fits the data for most countries, the coefficient in the relationship— the effect of a 1 percent change in output on the unemployment rate—varies across countries, ranging from –0.16 in Japan to –0.85 in Spain.

How well does Okun's law hold in emerging market and developing economies? As in Ball and others (forthcoming), we interpret Okun's law as a relationship between the deviation of unemployment from its natural rate and the deviation of output from its potential:

Box 4.1. *(continued)*

$$u_t - u_t^* = a(y_t - y_t^*) + error_t, \qquad (4.1.1)$$

in which u is the unemployment rate, y is log output, and * indicates a long-term (natural rate or potential) level. The assumption behind equation (4.1.1) is that shifts in aggregate demand cause fluctuations in output, which in turn cause firms to hire and fire workers. The error term captures factors that shift the unemployment-output relationship, such as unusual changes in productivity or in labor force participation. To measure u^*, the natural rate of unemployment, and y^*, potential output, we smooth the series for u and y with the Hodrick-Prescott filter.

We also estimate a version of Okun's law in first differences:

$$u_t - u_{t-1} = c + a(y_t - y_{t-1}) + error_t. \qquad (4.1.2)$$

Here, the change in unemployment depends on the change in output and a constant. This follows from equation (4.1.1) if the natural rate u^* is constant and potential output grows at a constant rate c/a. For many of these economies, these assumptions may not be reasonable because of time variation in u^* and growth accelerations and slowdowns. As noted in the main text of this chapter, output in these economies is often characterized not by "smooth hills" but by "mountains, cliffs, plateaus, and plains." Nevertheless, both the levels and the first-differences specifications show some evidence of the robustness of the results to alternate assumptions about the long-term levels of output and unemployment.[1]

The usefulness of unemployment rates as an indicator of labor market slack in emerging market and developing economies is often questioned.

One argument is that in low-income countries people cannot afford to be unemployed; everyone is in some kind of job, either in the rural sector or in self-employment. Another argument is that many of these economies have large informal sectors, so that neither the unemployment nor the employment statistics have much relevance (Agénor and Montiel, 2008; Singh, Jain-Chandra, and Mohommad, 2012).

To address the first of these issues, we also estimate a version of Okun's law using employment as the dependent variable:

$$e_t - e_{t-1} = c + a(y_t - y_{t-1}) + error_t, \qquad (4.1.3)$$

in which e is log employment. The second issue is addressed later when we look at the relationship between Okun coefficients and the level of informality.

Okun's Law in Emerging Market and Developing Economies: The Evidence[2]

We use data on employment, unemployment, and real GDP for 80 economies between 1980 and 2011, but the length of the time series varies across countries. We also present results for a subset of countries that have at least 30 years of data.

The results confirm the validity of Okun's law for most countries, though the strength of the relationship varies. Figure 4.1.2, panel 1, shows the distribution of Okun coefficients using equation (4.1.2). As shown, the estimates range from small positive values to −0.8, with the majority of the estimates between −0.2 and −0.4. For the group of countries with longer time series, the distribution is quite similar. Estimating the specification in levels (equation 4.1.1 above) yields qualitatively similar results; the rank correlation between the two sets of Okun coefficients is 0.6. Using employment as the dependent variable, the estimates range from small negative values to 0.8 (Figure 4.1.2, panel 2). The rank correlation with the estimates using unemployment as the dependent variable is −0.6.

[1]We carried out other robustness checks as well. In the levels specification—equation (4.1.1)—we tried smoothing parameters for the Hodrick-Prescott filter of 100 and 12 (the latter suggested by Rand and Tarp, 2002, for developing economies). The results are quite similar, so only the ones for the smoothing parameter of 100 are discussed here. In the first-differences specification—equation (4.1.2)—we also tried a version including a time trend and the lag of the change in unemployment. The results of these specifications were very similar to the baseline specification and therefore not reported.

[2]This section draws on ongoing work by Ball and others (forthcoming).

Box 4.1. *(continued)*

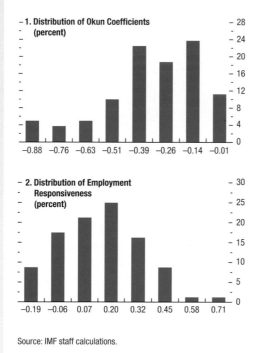

Figure 4.1.2. Distribution of Okun's Law Coefficients and Employment Responsiveness, 2007–11

1. Distribution of Okun Coefficients (percent)

−0.88 −0.76 −0.63 −0.51 −0.39 −0.26 −0.14 −0.01

2. Distribution of Employment Responsiveness (percent)

−0.19 −0.06 0.07 0.20 0.32 0.45 0.58 0.71

Source: IMF staff calculations.

To summarize, regardless of the choice of the three specifications discussed above, there is a significant short-term relationship between output fluctuations and developments in the labor market.

Table 4.1.1 compares the average value of the Okun coefficient and the employment responsiveness in advanced economies with that in emerging market and developing economies. It is evident that on average the short-term relationship between labor market outcomes and output is weaker in emerging market and developing economies than in advanced economies.

Accounting for Cross-Country Differences[3]

We also carry out an investigation of some of the factors that account for the cross-country variation in Okun coefficients. As discussed, many emerging market and developing economies are characterized by large informal sectors. Intuitively, countries with larger informal sectors should have a smaller Okun coefficient—that is, unemployment should respond less to a given change in output (see Figure 4.1.3, panel 1). Ball and others (forthcoming) document a positive relationship for advanced economies between the estimated Okun coefficient and the average level of unemployment: in countries in which unemployment is higher on average, it also fluctuates more in response to output movements. Although the reason for this association is not apparent, we find that a similar correlation holds for emerging market and developing economies as well (Figure 4.1.3, panel 2).

Some recent studies have probed the responsiveness of employment to output (Crivelli, Furceri, and Toujas-Bernaté, forthcoming; Ahmed, Guillaume, and Furceri, 2012). These studies suggest that the responsiveness could depend on features such as labor and product market flexibility. For instance, in discussing hiring and firing regulations in Middle Eastern and North African countries, Ahmed, Guillaume, and Furceri (2012) argue that such regulations can discourage "firms from expanding employment in response to favorable changes in the economic climate." That is, greater employment protection can dampen hiring and firing as output fluctuates, reducing the employment responsiveness.

[3]The data on informality used in this box are from Schneider (2004) and Schneider, Buehn, and Montenegro (2010). The indicators of labor and product market flexibility are described in Crivelli, Furceri, and Toujas-Bernaté (forthcoming).

Table 4.1.1. Short-Term Relationship between Labor Market Outcomes and Growth, by Country Group

	Okun Coefficients (equation 4.1.1)	Okun Coefficients (equation 4.1.2)	Employment Response (equation 4.1.3)
Advanced Economies	−0.39	−0.33	0.49
Emerging Markets and Developing Economies	−0.17	−0.29	0.20

Source: IMF staff calculations.

Box 4.1. *(continued)*

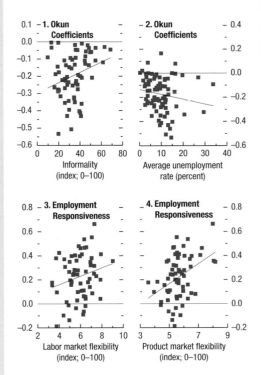

Figure 4.1.3. Okun's Law: Employment and Output in Emerging Market and Developing Economies

1. Okun Coefficients
2. Okun Coefficients
3. Employment Responsiveness
4. Employment Responsiveness

Informality (index; 0–100)
Average unemployment rate (percent)
Labor market flexibility (index; 0–100)
Product market flexibility (index; 0–100)

Source: IMF staff calculations.
Note: The index of informality is taken from Schneider (2004) and Schneider, Buehn, and Montenegro (2010). The indicators of labor and product market flexibility are described in Crivelli, Furceri, and Toujas-Bernaté (forthcoming).

Figure 4.1.3, panels 3 and 4, suggests that greater labor and product market flexibility may indeed be correlated with higher employment responsiveness.

Table 4.1.2 reports weighted-least-squares (WLS) estimates of these determinants of Okun coefficients and employment responsiveness.[4] The results presented in the first two columns confirm that Okun coefficients do depend on the size of the informal sector and the average unemployment rate, as suggested by Figure 4.1.3, panels 1 and 2. The other four regressions in the table examine the determinants of employment responsiveness. Informality influences the responsiveness, but the average unemployment rate does not have a significant impact. Greater labor and product market flexibility each individually raise employment responsiveness. However, when the two are entered in the regression together, only the effects of product market flexibility are statistically significant.[5]

Policy Implications

The structural challenges facing labor markets in emerging market and developing economies deservedly receive a lot of attention. In many of these economies, unemployment rates, particularly youth unemployment rates, remain alarmingly high. Other economies face the challenge of raising labor force participation, particularly among women. The results of this box lend support to a focus on policies to address these structural challenges: the cyclical relationship between jobs and growth is weaker, on average, in emerging market and developing economies than in advanced economies.

At the same time, the finding of a significant relationship in many countries suggests that cyclical considerations should not be ignored. Aggregate demand policies that support output growth in the short term can also help labor markets recover. The results also point to an interaction of cyclical and structural considerations. The strength of the short-term relationship between jobs and growth depends on structural features of the economy such as informality and the degree of product market flexibility. The evidence suggests that as informality is reduced and product markets become more flexible, the short-term relationship between labor market outcomes and growth will become stronger.

[4]Because our dependent variables are based on estimates, the dependent variable is measured with different degrees of precision across countries; hence, we use a WLS estimator. Specifically, the WLS estimator assumes that the errors ε_i are distributed as $\varepsilon_i \sim N(0, \sigma^2 \div s_i)$, in which s_i is the estimated standard deviation of the residual of the Okun coefficients (or employment responsiveness) for each country i, and σ^2 is an unknown parameter that is estimated in the second-stage regression.

[5]We do not find evidence of a significant relationship between labor and product market flexibility and the Okun coefficients, which is similar to the findings of Ball and others (forthcoming) for advanced economies.

Box 4.1. *(continued)*

Table 4.1.2. Determinants of Okun Coefficients and Employment Responsiveness

	Okun Coefficients		Employment Responsiveness			
	Levels Specification	Changes Specification				
	(1)	(2)	(3)	(4)	(5)	(6)
Informality	0.0027***	0.0044**	−0.0034**	−0.0058***	−0.0034***	−0.0044***
	(0.0009)	(0.0021)	(0.0014)	(0.0014)	(0.0013)	(0.0014)
Average Unemployment Rate	−0.0094***	−0.0131***	0.0027	−0.0003	0.0057	0.0031
	(0.0030)	(0.0047)	(0.0049)	(0.0048)	(0.0046)	(0.0047)
Labor Market Flexibility				0.0390**		0.0083
				(0.018)		(0.43)
Product Market Flexibility					0.0727***	0.0747***
					(0.0222)	(0.0250)
R^2	0.20	0.14	0.09	0.28	0.30	0.38
N	67	67	67	56	58	55

Source: IMF staff calculations.

Note: The t-statistics are reported in parentheses; *, **, and *** denote significance at the 10 percent, 5 percent, and 1 percent levels, respectively.

Box 4.2. How Would an Investment Slowdown in China Affect Other Emerging Market and Developing Economies?

This box explores the potential impact of an investment slowdown in China on growth in other emerging market and developing economies. China's growth model has become increasingly dependent on investment during the past decade. Investment contributed about one-half of China's GDP growth in the first decade of the 2000s, with particularly large contributions toward the end of the decade (Figure 4.2.1, panel 1). In part, this reflects the steep increase in infrastructure investment during the 2008–10 stimulus response to the Great Recession. But it appears that other forces are increasingly contributing to investment growth, including the ongoing urbanization process, the more recent emphasis on social housing construction, and capacity building in high-end manufacturing and services.

Associated with these changes are important shifts in China's import basket. As more manufacturing takes place onshore, the share of machinery imports has been gradually declining, whereas mineral and metal imports have grown steadily (Figure 4.2.1, panel 2).

These developments have had a noticeable impact on global trade flows over the past decade as trading partners sent an increasing fraction of their exports to China (Figure 4.2.2, panel 1). The importance of exports to China, when assessed relative to trading partner GDP, shows even sharper increases for several economies. This ratio has, on average, quadrupled during 2001–11 (Figure 4.2.2, panel 2).

The trends suggest that China's rapidly expanding investment may have had a large positive impact on its trading partners' growth. But with investment already close to 50 percent of output and China's continued reliance on investment to drive growth, it is unclear whether the new capacity will be profitable. An abrupt and disorderly end to the investment boom, albeit a tail risk, could have adverse effects on China's trading partners.

To get a sense of the potential magnitude of this dynamic, the spillover from investment activity in China on its trading partners is measured by

The main authors of this box are Ashvin Ahuja and Malhar Nabar. The box draws on Ahuja and Nabar (forthcoming).

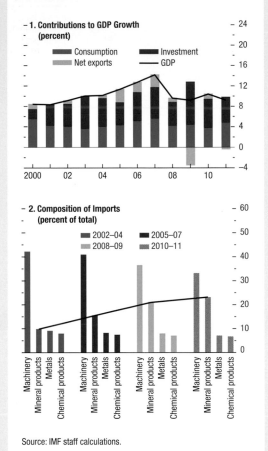

Figure 4.2.1. Composition of China's Growth and Imports

1. Contributions to GDP Growth (percent)
   - Consumption
   - Investment
   - Net exports
   - GDP

2. Composition of Imports (percent of total)
   - 2002–04
   - 2005–07
   - 2008–09
   - 2010–11

Machinery / Mineral products / Metals / Chemical products

Source: IMF staff calculations.

the product of an economy's exports to China (as a share of GDP) and China's fixed investment growth.[1]

[1]More specifically, the spillover is defined as

$$China\ spillover_{j,t} = exCHN_{j,t} \times China\ fixed\ investment\ growth_t, \qquad (4.2.1)$$

in which

$$exCHN_j = \left(\frac{Exports\ to\ China}{GDP} \right)_j,$$

and *China fixed investment growth$_t$* is the annual percent change of real gross fixed capital formation from the national accounts.

Box 4.2. *(continued)*

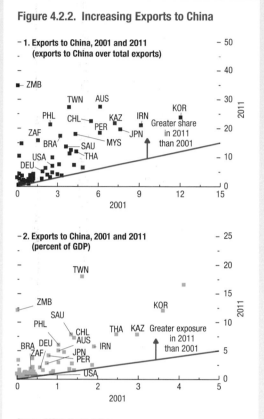

Figure 4.2.2.   Increasing Exports to China

Source: IMF staff calculations.
Note: AUS = Australia; BRA = Brazil; CHL = Chile; DEU = Germany; IRN = Iran; JPN = Japan; KAZ = Kazakhstan; KOR = Korea; MYS = Malaysia; PER = Peru; PHL = Philippines; SAU = Saudi Arabia; THA = Thailand; TWN = Taiwan Province of China; USA = United States; ZAF = South Africa; ZMB = Zambia.

This spillover measure varies across countries based on their export exposure to China and over time based on fluctuations in China's fixed investment growth. By construction, it measures only the influence of Chinese activity on other economies through the direct trade channel; indirect exposure through vertically integrated intermediate economies or through lower commodity prices is not captured.

The effect of the spillover on China's trading partners' growth is estimated by regressing emerging market and developing economies' growth rates on this spillover measure and a number of other controls, including these economies' lagged growth, terms of trade, and output volatility. The

sample covers the period of China's membership in the World Trade Organization (2002–11) and includes the set of emerging market and developing economies classified under the MSCI AC World Index and key commodity producers. The regression is also estimated using different measures of fixed investment growth in China: overall, manufacturing, and nontradables (calculated by applying shares in fixed asset investment data, available beginning in 2003). This breakdown allows for a comparison of spillovers from a slowdown in manufacturing investment with a deceleration concentrated in nontradables.[2]

In line with China's widening footprint on global imports, the effect of China's investment on its trading partners' growth has increased over time. The most heavily exposed emerging market economies are those within the Asian regional supply chain, such as Korea, Malaysia, and Taiwan Province of China. The results suggest that GDP growth in Taiwan Province of China decreases by slightly over nine-tenths percentage point for every 1 percentage point deceleration in investment growth in China (Figure 4.2.3, panel 1).

Among commodity exporters, the impact is largest on mineral ore exporters with relatively less diversified economic structures and higher concentrations of exports to China. In response to a 1 percentage point slowdown in investment growth in China, the estimated effect on Chile's growth is a decrease of close to two-fifths of a percentage point. By contrast, larger commodity exporters with more diversified economies, such as Brazil and Indonesia, experience smaller declines in growth (Figure 4.2.3, panel 2).[3]

[2]The nontradables sector is defined to include utilities, construction, transportation and storage, information technology, wholesale and retail trade, catering, banking and insurance, real estate, leasing and commercial services, education, health care, sports and entertainment, and public administration.

[3]Related to this analysis, a factor-augmented vector autoregression model relating G20 macroeconomic, financial, trade, and global commodity price variables finds that a 1 percent decline in China's fixed asset investment from baseline would, on average, lead to drops of 0.8, 1.0, 1.6, 1.8, 1.8, and 2.2 percent for prices of iron ore, aluminum, copper, lead, nickel, and zinc, respectively, within one year

Box 4.2. *(continued)*

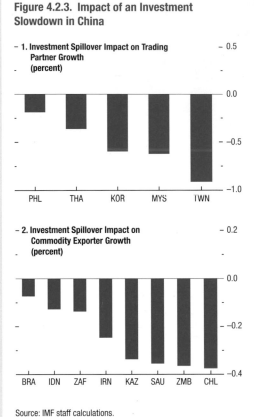

Figure 4.2.3. Impact of an Investment Slowdown in China

1. Investment Spillover Impact on Trading Partner Growth (percent)

2. Investment Spillover Impact on Commodity Exporter Growth (percent)

Source: IMF staff calculations.
Note: BRA = Brazil; CHL = Chile; IDN = Indonesia; IRN = Iran; KAZ = Kazakhstan; KOR = Korea; MYS = Malaysia; PHL = Philippines; SAU = Saudi Arabia; THA = Thailand; TWN = Taiwan Province of China; ZAF = South Africa; ZMB = Zambia. Bars show the effect of a 1 percentage point slowdown in Chinese investment growth.

A decomposition of investment into manufacturing and nontradables shows that spillover effects from China's manufacturing investment reflect the influence of global demand. Once global demand is included as an additional control in the regression, the spillover from manufacturing fixed investment in China no longer has a statistically significant impact on its trading partners' growth (whereas global demand does). By contrast, nontradables investment in China has a significant spillover impact on its trading partners' growth above and beyond the effects of global demand.

The analysis also shows that direct spillover effects from consumption growth on trading partners' growth have been negligible in recent years. China's share in global consumer goods imports has increased at a slower pace than its share in global consumption over the past 15 years. China currently plays a small role as an importer of consumer goods, accounting for only 2 percent of global consumer goods imports.[4] The low import intensity of final consumption in China suggests that if a transition to consumption-based growth takes place in response to the structural reforms envisaged in the 12th Five-Year Plan, the direct benefits to consumer goods exporters are likely to be small. Nevertheless, China's trading partners may still benefit from indirect access to Chinese consumers by selling intermediate goods, parts, and components to Chinese firms that then assemble and customize final products for the local market.

after the shock. For further details, see Ahuja and Nabar (forthcoming).

[4]See IMF (2012) for more details.

Box 4.3. Resilient Growth in Low-Income Countries: Kenya and Tanzania

Kenya and Tanzania are among the group of emerging market and developing economies that showed marked resilience during the Great Recession. Both outpaced earlier advanced economy growth, experienced only a modest growth slowdown during 2008–09, and have charted a subsequent rapid and robust recovery (Figure 4.3.1, panel 1).[1]

A decade of improved macroeconomic stability has helped underpin this resilience. In Tanzania, reforms since the late 1990s liberalized foreign exchange and financial markets and foreign trade, and diminished the role of parastatals. Inflation fell from 20 to 30 percent in the 1990s to 5 percent in the mid-2000s, fiscal revenues increased from 10 to 15 percent of GDP, and gross reserve cover broadly doubled. With the help of the IMF's Heavily Indebted Poor Country/Multilateral Debt Relief Initiative, the debt burden was also halved in relation to GDP. In Kenya, reforms started earlier, with a major program to liberalize price controls, import licensing, and exchange restrictions, as well as steps to privatize parastatals and reduce civil service numbers. As a result of prudent fiscal policy, Kenya's public debt fell from 54 percent of GDP in 2001 to 38 percent in 2008.

Macroeconomic stability and market-friendly policies helped provide a durable growth impetus. As in much of Africa, growth in Kenya and Tanzania has been driven by strong domestic markets, led by a growing middle class. For both countries, an improved investment outlook contributed to a sustained expansion in private sector construction spending. At the same time, the adoption of new technologies has contributed to rapid growth in communications and finance. This engine of growth helped shield both economies from the global downturn, with spending on construction, communications, and finance continuing to grow

The main authors of this box are Nick Gigineishvili, Dimitre Milkov, Armando Morales, and Peter Allum.

[1]In Kenya, growth trends were distorted by domestic factors, with a slowdown in 2008 on account of postelection violence and drought conditions during 2008–09 that undercut agricultural production. Given the latter, panel 1 of Figure 4.3.1 focuses on growth in Kenya's nonagricultural economy.

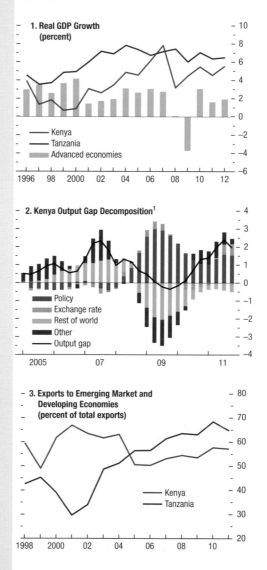

Figure 4.3.1. The Resilience of Kenya and Tanzania

1. Real GDP Growth (percent)
— Kenya
— Tanzania
■ Advanced economies

2. Kenya Output Gap Decomposition[1]
■ Policy
■ Exchange rate
■ Rest of world
■ Other
— Output gap

3. Exports to Emerging Market and Developing Economies (percent of total exports)
— Kenya
— Tanzania

Source: IMF staff estimates.
[1]See Andrle and others (forthcoming) for further details on this output gap decomposition.

Box 4.3. *(continued)*

at a 9 to 10 percent real rate throughout the Great Recession.

Strengthened macroeconomic buffers also provided space for a countercyclical policy response to the global downturn. With modest fiscal deficits and sustainable levels of public debt, both countries allowed government spending to rise between 2006/07 and 2008/09—by 4½ percentage points of GDP in Tanzania and by 2 percentage points in Kenya.[2] This fiscal stimulus helped offset growth spillovers from a less favorable external environment. Monetary policy was also supportive. Tanzania halved its short-term interest rates between 2007 and 2009. And in Kenya, a recent IMF study shows that supportive monetary conditions were successful in offsetting most of the contractionary impact of the Great Recession, which would otherwise have resulted in output falling well below its potential (Figure 4.3.1, panel 2).[3] Under floating exchange rate regimes, both currencies appreciated in real terms against the dollar through 2009, though this did not offset the overall impact of fiscal and monetary easing. Both countries saw quick, albeit temporary, deterioration in their overall balance of payments in 2008, but weathered it readily using their healthy gross reserve buffer (of about four months of imports) and by resorting to new IMF financing.

Diversification of production and export activity may also have helped their resilience. At the product level, Kenya has increased its exports of intermediate nonmanufactured goods while diversifying its tourism market. In Tanzania, a significant decline in traditional agricultural exports was offset by growth in exports of minerals and manufactured goods. At the market level, Kenya's trade with other emerging market and developing economies has

remained broadly stable at slightly more than half of total exports; in Tanzania, sales to these economies doubled to represent two-thirds of exports, helping the country decouple from the advanced economy growth cycle (Figure 4.3.1, panel 3).

Both countries are projected to sustain a robust pace of growth through 2012. The rate of expansion is likely to remain somewhat below the peak rates seen during 2006–07 given steps to gradually reverse the 2008–09 fiscal stimulus and because of the monetary tightening adopted since mid-2011 to bring down food-price-related inflation. Credit growth has decelerated in both countries but remains sufficient to support steady growth. More generally, unlike in some other emerging market and developing economies, growth has been supported by direct investment and capital repatriation, which are less likely to experience sudden stops, and the financial sector remains robust, with low levels of nonperforming loans.

The resilience of Kenya and Tanzania could be tested, however, in the event of an intensified downturn in the global economy. Sustained growth in exports has supported their external performance so far, but a new global downturn, including emerging market and developing economies, would bring new balance of payments pressures. Both countries also have more constrained policy space than at the start of the Great Recession, with higher fiscal deficits and debt levels, higher inflation, and somewhat lower gross reserve cover. Accordingly, both countries are rebuilding macroeconomic buffers under programs supported by the IMF: Kenya's economic program has been supported by a three-year Extended Credit Facility since 2011, and Tanzania recently accessed an 18-month precautionary Standby Credit Facility to complement its preexisting Policy Support Instrument arrangement.

[2]For fiscal years starting July 1.
[3]Andrle and others (forthcoming).

References

Abbas, S. Ali, Nazim Belhocine, Asmaa ElGanainy, and Mark Horton, 2010, "A Historical Public Debt Database," IMF Working Paper No. 10/245 (Washington: International Monetary Fund).

Adler, Gustavo, and Camilo Tovar, 2012, "Riding Global Financial Waves: The Economic Impact of Global Financial Shocks on Emerging Market Economies," IMF Working Paper No. 12/188 (Washington: International Monetary Fund).

Agénor, Pierre-Richard, and Peter J. Montiel, 2008, *Development Macroeconomics* (Princeton, New Jersey: Princeton University Press, 3rd ed.).

Aguiar, Mark, and Gita Gopinath, 2007, "Emerging Market Business Cycles: The Cycle Is the Trend," *Journal of Political Economy*, Vol. 115, No. 1, pp. 69–102.

Ahmed, Masood, Dominique Guillaume, and Davide Furceri, 2012, "Youth Unemployment in the MENA Region: Determinants and Challenges," World Economic Forum, *Addressing the 100 Million Youth Challenge—Perspectives on Youth Employment in the Arab World in 2012* (unpublished; Washington: International Monetary Fund).

Ahuja, Ashvin, and Malhar Shyam Nabar, forthcoming, "Investment-Led Growth in China: Global Spillovers," IMF Working Paper (Washington: International Monetary Fund).

Andrle, Michal, Andrew Berg, Rogelio Morales, Rafael Portillo, and Jan Vlcek, forthcoming, "Forecasting and Policy Analysis Systems in Low-Income Countries: Food and Nonfood Inflation in Kenya," IMF Working Paper (Washington: International Monetary Fund).

Ball, Laurence, Davide Furceri, Daniel Leigh, and Prakash Loungani, forthcoming, "Okun's Law Outside the OECD: Does One Law Fit All?" IMF Working Paper (Washington: International Monetary Fund).

Ball, Laurence, Daniel Leigh, and Prakash Loungani, forthcoming, "Okun's Law: Fit at 50?" IMF Working Paper (Washington: International Monetary Fund).

Becker, Torbjörn, and Paolo Mauro, 2006, "Output Drops and the Shocks That Matter," IMF Working Paper No. 06/172 (Washington: International Monetary Fund).

Berg, Andrew, and Jonathan Ostry, 2011, "Inequality and Unsustainable Growth: Two Sides of the Same Coin?" IMF Staff Discussion Note No. 11/08 (Washington: International Monetary Fund).

Berg, Andrew, Jonathan Ostry, and Jeromin Zettelmeyer, 2012, "What Makes Growth Sustained," *Journal of Development Economics*, Vol. 98, No. 2, pp. 149–66.

Blanchard, Olivier, and John Simon, 2001, "The Long and Large Decline in U.S. Output Volatility," *Brookings Papers on Economic Activity*, Vol. 32, No. 1, pp. 135–74.

Blanchard, Olivier, Hamid Faruqee, and Mitali Das, 2010, "The Initial Impact of the Crisis on Emerging Market Countries," *Brookings Papers on Economic Activity* (Spring), pp. 263–323.

Bloom, Nicholas, 2009, "The Impact of Uncertainty Shocks," *Econometrica*, Vol. 77, No. 3, pp. 623–85.

Cerra, Valerie, and Sweta Saxena, 2008, "Growth Dynamics: The Myth of Economic Recovery," *American Economic Review*, Vol. 98, No. 1, pp. 439–57.

Chang, Roberto, and Andrés Velasco, 2004, "Monetary Policy and the Currency Denomination of Debt: A Tale of Two Equilibria," NBER Working Paper No. 10827 (Cambridge, Massachusetts: National Bureau of Economic Research).

Chinn, Menzie, and Hiro Ito, 2006, "What Matters for Financial Development? Capital Controls, Institutions, and Interactions," *Journal of Development Economics*, Vol. 81, No. 1, pp. 163–92.

Cleves, Mario, William Gould, Roberto G. Gutierrez, and Yulia V. Marchenko, 2010, *An Introduction to Survival Analysis Using Stata* (College Station, Texas: Stata Press, 3rd ed.).

Corbo, Vittorio, Óscar Landerretche, and Klaus Schmidt-Hebbel, 2000, "Does Inflation Targeting Make a Difference?" presented at the Central Bank of Chile Conference *10 Years of Inflation Targeting: Design, Performance, Challenges.*

Crivelli, Ernesto, Davide Furceri, and Joël Toujas-Bernaté, forthcoming, "Can Policies Affect Employment Intensity of Growth? A Cross-Country Analysis," IMF Working Paper (Washington: International Monetary Fund).

de Carvalho Filho, Irineu, 2011, "28 Months Later: How Inflation Targeters Outperformed Their Peers in the Great Recession," *The B.E. Journal of Macroeconomics*, Vol. 11, No. 1, Article 22.

Didier, Tatiana, Constantino Hevia, and Sergio L. Schmukler, 2012, "How Resilient Were Emerging Economies to the Global Crisis," World Bank Policy Research Working Paper No. 5637 (Washington).

Easterly, William, 2001, "The Lost Decades: Developing Countries' Stagnation in Spite of Policy Reform, 1980–1998," *Journal of Economic Growth*, Vol. 6, No. 2, pp. 135–57.

_____, Michael Kremer, Lant Pritchett, and Lawrence Summers, 1993, "Good Policy or Good Luck? Country Growth Performance and Temporary Shocks," *Journal of Monetary Economics*, Vol. 32, No. 3, pp. 459–83.

Engel, James, David Haugh, and Adrian Pagan, 2005, "Some Methods for Assessing the Need for Non-Linear Models in Business Cycle Analysis," *International Journal of Forecasting*, Vol. 21, No. 4, pp. 651–62.

Frankel, Jeffrey, 2012, "Will Emerging Markets Fall in 2012?" *Business & Management Journal*, Vol. 2, No. 2, pp. 119–20.

_____, Carlos Végh, and Guillermo Vuletin, 2011, "On Graduation from Fiscal Procyclicality," NBER Working Paper No. 17619 (Cambridge, Massachusetts: National Bureau of Economic Research).

Harding, Don, and Adrian Pagan, 2002, "Dissecting the Cycle: A Methodological Investigation," *Journal of Monetary Economics*, Vol. 49, No. 2, pp. 365–81.

Hausmann, Ricardo, Lant Pritchett, and Dani Rodrik, 2005, "Growth Accelerations," *Journal of Economic Growth*, Vol. 10, No. 4, pp. 303–29.

Hausmann, Ricardo, Francisco Rodriguez, and Rodrigo Wagner, 2006, "Growth Collapses," Kennedy School of Government Working Paper No. RWP06–046 (Cambridge, Massachusetts: Harvard University).

Ilzetzki, Ethan, Carmen M. Reinhart, and Kenneth S. Rogoff, 2008, "Exchange Rate Arrangements Entering the 21st Century: Which Anchor Will Hold?" (unpublished; Cambridge, Massachusetts: Harvard University).

International Monetary Fund (IMF), 2012, *Consolidated Spillover Report* (Washington).

Kaminsky, Graciela, Carmen Reinhart, and Carlos Végh, 2004, "When it Rains, It Pours: Procyclical Capital Flows and Macroeconomic Policies," *NBER Macroeconomics Annual*, ed. by Mark Gertler and Kenneth Rogoff, pp. 11–79 (Cambridge, Massachusetts: National Bureau of Economic Research).

Kaplan, E. L., and Paul Meier, 1958, "Nonparametric Estimation from Incomplete Observations," *Journal of the American Statistical Association,* Vol. 53, No. 282, pp. 457–81.

Kose, M. Ayhan, 2008, "Seven Questions about Decoupling," *IMF Research Bulletin*, Vol. 9, No. 3, pp. 1–5.

_____, and Eswar Prasad, 2010, *Emerging Markets: Resilience and Growth Amid Global Turmoil* (Washington: Brookings Institution Press).

Laeven, Luc, and Fabián Valencia, 2012, "Systemic Banking Crises Database: An Update," IMF Working Paper No. 12/163 (Washington: International Monetary Fund).

Lane, Philip R., and Gian Maria Milesi-Ferretti, 2007, "The External Wealth of Nations Mark II: Revised and Extended Estimates of Foreign Assets and Liabilities, 1970–2004," *Journal of International Economics*, Vol. 73, No. 2, pp. 223–50.

_____, 2010, "The Cross-Country Incidence of the Global Crisis," IMF Working Paper No. 10/171 (Washington: International Monetary Fund).

Loungani, Prakash, M. Ayhan Kose, and Marco Terrones, 2012, "Divergence of Fortunes in Recoveries" *VoxEU*, April 24. www.voxeu.org/index.php?q=node/7907.

Mendoza, Enrique, and Jonathan Ostry, 2008, "International Evidence on Fiscal Solvency: Is Fiscal Policy 'Responsible'?" *Journal of Monetary Economics*, Vol. 55, No. 6, pp. 1081–93.

Mendoza, Enrique, and Marco Terrones, 2008, "An Anatomy of Credit Booms: Evidence From Macro Aggregates and Micro Data," IMF Working Paper No. 08/226 (Washington: International Monetary Fund).

Okun, Arthur M., 1962, "Potential GNP: Its Measurement and Significance," American Statistical Association, proceedings of the Business and Economics Statistics Section (Alexandria, Virginia: American Statistical Association). Available at http://cowles.econ.yale.edu/P/cp/p01b/p0190.pdf.

Ostry, Jonathan D., Atish R. Ghosh, Jun I. Kim, and Mahvash S. Qureshi, 2010, "Fiscal Space," IMF Staff Position Note No. 10/11 (Washington: International Monetary Fund).

Pagan, Adrian, 1997, "Policy, Theory, and the Cycle," *Oxford Review of Economic Policy*, Vol. 13, No. 3, pp. 19–33.

Pritchett, Lant, 2000, "Understanding Patterns of Economic Growth: Searching for Hills Among Plateaus, Mountains, and Plains," *World Bank Economic Review*, Vol. 14, No. 2, pp. 221–50.

Rand, John, and Finn Tarp, 2002, "Business Cycles in Developing Countries: Are They Different?" *World Development*, Vol. 30, No. 12, pp. 2071–88.

Reinhart, Carmen, and Kenneth S. Rogoff, 2004, "The Modern History of Exchange Rate Arrangements: A Reinterpretation," *Quarterly Journal of Economics*, Vol. 119, No. 1, pp. 1–48.

———, and Miguel Savastano, 2003, "Debt Intolerance," *Brookings Papers on Economic Activity*, Vol. 34, No. 1, pp. 1–74.

Rodrik, Dani, 1999, "Where Did All the Growth Go? External Shocks, Social Conflict, and Growth Collapses," *Journal of Economic Growth*, Vol. 4, No. 4, pp. 385–412.

Roger, Scott, 2010, "Inflation Targeting Turns 20," *Finance and Development*, Vol. 47, No. 1, pp. 46–49.

Rose, Andrew K., and Mark M. Spiegel, 2011, "Cross-Country Causes and Consequences of the Crisis: An Update," *European Economic Review*, Vol. 55, No. 3, pp. 309–24.

Schmidt-Hebbel, Klaus, 2009, "Inflation Targeting Twenty Years on: Where, When, Why, With What Effects, What Lies Ahead?" Economics Institute Working Paper No. 360 (Santiago: Pontifical Catholic University of Chile).

Schneider, Friedrich, 2004, "The Size of the Shadow Economies of 145 Countries All Over the World: First Results over the Period 1999 to 2003," IZA Discussion Paper No. 1431 (Bonn: Institute for the Study of Labor).

———, Andreas Buehn, and Claudio E. Montenegro, 2010, "New Estimates for the Shadow Economies All Over the World," *International Economic Journal*, Vol. 24, No. 4, pp. 443–61.

Singh, Anoop, Sonali Jain-Chandra, and Adil Mohommad, 2012, "Inclusive Growth, Institutions, and the Underground Economy," IMF Working Paper No. 12/47 (Washington: International Monetary Fund).

Solt, Frederick, 2009, "Standardizing the World Income Inequality Database," *Social Science Quarterly*, Vol. 90, No. 2, pp. 231–42.

Végh, Carlos, and Guillermo Vuletin, 2012, "Overcoming the Fear of Free Falling: Monetary Policy Graduation in Emerging Markets," NBER Working Paper No. 18175 (Cambridge, Massachusetts: National Bureau of Economic Research).

Virmani, Arvind, 2012, "Accelerating and Sustaining Growth: Economic and Political Lessons," IMF Working Paper No. 12/185 (Washington: International Monetary Fund).

Wacziarg, Romain, and Karen Horn Welch, 2008, "Trade Liberalization and Growth: New Evidence," *World Bank Economic Review*, Vol. 22, No. 2, pp. 187–231.

IMF EXECUTIVE BOARD DISCUSSION OF THE OUTLOOK, SEPTEMBER 2012

The following remarks were made by the Acting Chair at the conclusion of the Executive Board's discussion of the World Economic Outlook, Global Financial Stability Report, *and* Fiscal Monitor *on September 14, 2012.*

Executive Directors noted that the global economic recovery remains fragile and risks to the global financial system have increased. Growth has slowed recently both in advanced and in emerging market and developing economies, and the outlook remains subdued, largely because policies in major advanced economies have failed to instill lasting confidence. Directors emphasized that clear and credible policies in advanced economies, with improved policy coordination and communication, are of paramount importance to address immediate downside risks. In this regard, ongoing efforts at fiscal consolidation and structural reform, as well as recent policy initiatives in key advanced economies, should help improve financial stability, lower public debt over the medium term, spur growth, and contribute to strengthen market confidence.

Directors agreed that downside risks to the outlook remain considerable. Principal sources of near-term risk are the protracted crisis in the euro area and the "fiscal cliff" and impending "debt ceiling" in the United States. Geopolitical risks that could lead to a disruption of oil supply also remain a concern. Over the medium term, the elevated, though gradually declining, public debt in advanced economies could dampen investor confidence and destabilize global bond markets. Furthermore, stress in key regions could have large spillover effects given cross-border macro-financial and trade linkages.

Directors concurred that resolving the euro area crisis remains the most important policy priority. They welcomed the recent decisions by the European Central Bank to increase liquidity support and safeguard an appropriate monetary policy transmission, particularly through the Outright Monetary Transactions program. They urged timely and accelerated implementation of these and other measures to strengthen the currency union and reduce financial fragmentation. In particular, Directors supported the establishment of a banking union with a unified financial stability framework, as well as further fiscal integration, recapitalization or restructuring of viable banks, and resolution of nonviable banks. It is also imperative to make the euro area firewall sufficiently flexible to help break the adverse feedback loop between sovereigns and banks.

Directors observed that most countries have made progress in reducing fiscal deficits, improving fiscal policy frameworks, and strengthening fiscal governance. Nevertheless, they noted that debt levels remain high and underscored the need for sustained medium-term fiscal consolidation to achieve debt sustainability. The United States and Japan, in particular, urgently need to adopt credible medium-term fiscal adjustment plans to reduce their debt to sustainable levels. Fiscal tightening should be executed in a manner that makes public finances growth friendly and efficient. Most Directors considered that in countries with fiscal space, near-term fiscal adjustment plans should be implemented flexibly, and automatic stabilizers should be allowed to operate fully, as economic conditions warrant. A few Directors, however, stressed the need to preserve the credibility of fiscal policy frameworks by strictly adhering to fiscal targets.

Directors reiterated that fiscal consolidation should be combined with accommodative monetary policies, while respecting the mandate of respective central banks, and with structural reforms to maintain growth and limit the negative social impact of deficit reduction. Most Directors supported further easing of monetary policy to sustain growth, including through unconventional measures if necessary. In that regard, they underscored the importance of the recent announcements by the European Central Bank and the Federal Reserve. A number of Directors noted, however, that prolonged monetary easing could introduce economic and financial distortions, discourage fiscal consolidation, and spur destabilizing capital flows to other regions, while its effectiveness may be limited.

Directors called for faster progress with structural reform. The priorities are to strengthen the financial regulatory framework, improve bank balance sheets and financial health more generally, and reduce household debt. Many countries also need to improve their external competitiveness, which will require reforms to enhance labor and product market flexibility and efficiency. Social safety nets and reforms to reduce long-term unemployment should be strengthened in parallel with fiscal adjustment.

Directors welcomed the steady improvement in the economic performance of emerging market and developing economies, which reflected both good policies and fewer shocks. However, the recent slowdown of growth calls for determined action to mitigate internal and external vulnerabilities, including the use of macroprudential policies as needed. Those countries with stable and low inflation could pause or reverse the monetary policy tightening of the past year to sustain growth. Those with relatively strong fiscal and external positions could also use their fiscal space prudently for this purpose. Others would have to continue to rebuild policy space needed to tackle shocks, with due regard for social and development needs in low-income countries.

Directors agreed that global imbalances and associated risks have diminished, mainly because of weaker demand in external-deficit advanced economies. Lasting resolution of these imbalances is in the self-interest of both deficit and surplus economies. For surplus economies, this will require structural reforms to boost investment and consumption, more market-determined exchange rates, and discontinuation of large-scale official reserve accumulation where appropriate. A few Directors nevertheless emphasized the importance of maintaining adequate reserve buffers against external shocks. Deficit economies will require stronger fiscal positions, higher saving rates, and lower consumption demand.

STATISTICAL APPENDIX

The Statistical Appendix presents historical data as well as projections. It comprises five sections: Assumptions, What's New, Data and Conventions, Classification of Countries, and Statistical Tables.

The assumptions underlying the estimates and projections for 2012–13 and the medium-term scenario for 2014–17 are summarized in the first section. The second section presents a brief description of the changes to the database and statistical tables since the April 2012 issue of the *World Economic Outlook*. The third section provides a general description of the data and the conventions used for calculating country group composites. The classification of countries in the various groups presented in the *World Economic Outlook* is summarized in the fourth section.

The last, and main, section comprises the statistical tables. (Statistical Appendix A is included here; Statistical Appendix B is available online.) Data in these tables have been compiled on the basis of information available through mid-September 2012. The figures for 2012 and beyond are shown with the same degree of precision as the historical figures solely for convenience; because they are projections, the same degree of accuracy is not to be inferred.

Assumptions

Real effective *exchange rates* for the advanced economies are assumed to remain constant at their average levels during the period July 30–August 27, 2012. For 2012 and 2013, these assumptions imply average U.S. dollar/SDR conversion rates of 1.523 and 1.512, U.S. dollar/euro conversion rates of 1.266 and 1.239, and yen/U.S. dollar conversion rates of 79.3 and 79.3, respectively.

It is assumed that the *price of oil* will average $106.18 a barrel in 2012 and $105.10 a barrel in 2013.

Established *policies* of national authorities are assumed to be maintained. The more specific policy assumptions underlying the projections for selected economies are described in Box A1.

With regard to *interest rates,* it is assumed that the London interbank offered rate (LIBOR) on six-month U.S. dollar deposits will average 0.7 percent in 2012 and 0.6 percent in 2013, that three-month euro deposits will average 0.6 percent in 2012 and 0.2 percent in 2013, and that six-month yen deposits will average 0.4 percent in 2012 and 0.3 percent in 2013.

With respect to *introduction of the euro,* on December 31, 1998, the Council of the European Union decided that, effective January 1, 1999, the irrevocably fixed conversion rates between the euro and currencies of the member countries adopting the euro are as follows:

1 euro	=	13.7603	Austrian schillings
	=	40.3399	Belgian francs
	=	0.585274	Cyprus pound[1]
	=	1.95583	Deutsche mark
	=	15.6466	Estonian krooni[2]
	=	5.94573	Finnish markkaa
	=	6.55957	French francs
	=	340.750	Greek drachma[3]
	=	0.787564	Irish pound
	=	1,936.27	Italian lire
	=	40.3399	Luxembourg francs
	=	0.42930	Maltese lira[1]
	=	2.20371	Netherlands guilders
	=	200.482	Portuguese escudos
	=	30.1260	Slovak koruna[4]
	=	239.640	Slovenian tolars[5]
	=	166.386	Spanish pesetas

[1]Established on January 1, 2008.
[2]Established on January 1, 2011.
[3]Established on January 1, 2001.
[4]Established on January 1, 2009.
[5]Established on January 1, 2007.

See Box 5.4 of the October 1998 *World Economic Outlook* for details on how the conversion rates were established.

What's New

- For Cyprus, data reflect a passive scenario based on implementation of approved policies only. It is also assumed that the government will be able to roll over its debt and finance its deficit at a reasonable cost over the medium term and that banks will achieve adequate capitalization without government assistance.
- Data for South Sudan are now included in the sub-Saharan Africa aggregates and classified under those for a country with fuel as the main source of export earnings. Sudan, which remains in the Middle East and North Africa region, is now classified as a country with nonfuel primary products as the main source of export earnings.
- Data for San Marino are now included in the advanced economy classification.
- As in the April 2012 *World Economic Outlook,* data for Syria are excluded for 2011 and later due to the uncertain political situation.
- Starting with the October 2012 *World Economic Outlook,* the label for the Emerging and Developing Economies group is Emerging Market and Developing Economies. The member countries remain unchanged with the exception of South Sudan as a new member of the group.

Data and Conventions

Data and projections for 186 economies form the statistical basis of the *World Economic Outlook* (the WEO database). The data are maintained jointly by the IMF's Research Department and regional departments, with the latter regularly updating country projections based on consistent global assumptions.

Although national statistical agencies are the ultimate providers of historical data and definitions, international organizations are also involved in statistical issues, with the objective of harmonizing methodologies for the compilation of national statistics, including analytical frameworks, concepts, definitions, classifications, and valuation procedures used in the production of economic statistics. The WEO database reflects information from both national source agencies and international organizations.

Most countries' macroeconomic data presented in the *World Economic Outlook* conform broadly to the 1993

version of the *System of National Accounts* (SNA). The IMF's sector statistical standards—the *Balance of Payments and International Investment Position Manual, Sixth Edition* (BPM6), the *Monetary and Financial Statistics Manual* (MFSM 2000), and the *Government Finance Statistics Manual 2001* (GFSM 2001)—have been or are being aligned with the 2008 SNA.[1] These standards reflect the IMF's special interest in countries' external positions, financial sector stability, and public sector fiscal positions. The process of adapting country data to the new standards begins in earnest when the manuals are released. However, full concordance with the manuals is ultimately dependent on the provision by national statistical compilers of revised country data; hence, the *World Economic Outlook* estimates are only partially adapted to these manuals. Nonetheless, for many countries the impact of conversion to the updated standards will be small on major balances and aggregates. Many other countries have partially adopted the latest standards and will continue implementation over a period of years.

Consistent with the recommendations of the *1993 SNA*, several countries have phased out their traditional *fixed-base-year* method of calculating real macroeconomic variable levels and growth by switching to a *chain-weighted* method of computing aggregate growth. The chain-weighted method frequently updates the weights of price and volume indicators. It allows countries to measure GDP growth more accurately by reducing or eliminating the downward biases in volume series built on index numbers that average volume components using weights from a year in the moderately distant past.

Composite data for country groups in the *World Economic Outlook* are either sums or weighted averages of data for individual countries. Unless noted otherwise, multiyear averages of growth rates are expressed as compound annual rates of change.[2] Arithmetically weighted averages are used for all data

[1]Many other countries are implementing the 2008 SNA and will release national accounts data based on the new standard in 2014. A few countries use versions of the SNA older than 1993. A similar adoption pattern is expected for BPM6. While the conceptual standards use the BPM6, the WEO is still using the BPM5 presentation until such a time when a representative number of countries have moved their BOP accounts into the BPM6 framework.

[2]Averages for real GDP and its components, employment, per capita GDP, inflation, factor productivity, trade, and commodity prices, are calculated based on the compound annual rate of

for the emerging market and developing economies group except inflation and money growth, for which geometric averages are used. The following conventions apply.

- Country group composites for exchange rates, interest rates, and growth rates of monetary aggregates are weighted by GDP converted to U.S. dollars at market exchange rates (averaged over the preceding three years) as a share of group GDP.
- Composites for other data relating to the domestic economy, whether growth rates or ratios, are weighted by GDP valued at purchasing power parity (PPP) as a share of total world or group GDP.[3]
- Composites for data relating to the domestic economy for the euro area (17 member countries throughout the entire period unless noted otherwise) are aggregates of national source data using GDP weights. Annual data are not adjusted for calendar-day effects. For data prior to 1999, data aggregations apply 1995 European currency unit exchange rates.
- Composites for fiscal data are sums of individual country data after conversion to U.S. dollars at the average market exchange rates in the years indicated.
- Composite unemployment rates and employment growth are weighted by labor force as a share of group labor force.
- Composites relating to external sector statistics are sums of individual country data after conversion to U.S. dollars at the average market exchange rates in the years indicated for balance of payments data and at end-of-year market exchange rates for debt denominated in currencies other than U.S. dollars.
- Composites of changes in foreign trade volumes and prices, however, are arithmetic averages of percent changes for individual countries weighted by the U.S. dollar value of exports or imports as a share of total world or group exports or imports (in the preceding year).
- Unless noted otherwise, group composites are computed if 90 percent or more of the share of group weights is represented.

Classification of Countries

Summary of the Country Classification

The country classification in the *World Economic Outlook* divides the world into two major groups: advanced economies and emerging market and developing economies.[4] This classification is not based on strict criteria, economic or otherwise, and it has evolved over time. The objective is to facilitate analysis by providing a reasonably meaningful method of organizing data. Table A provides an overview of the country classification, showing the number of countries in each group by region and summarizing some key indicators of their relative size (GDP valued by PPP, total exports of goods and services, and population).

Some countries remain outside the country classification and therefore are not included in the analysis. Anguilla, Cuba, the Democratic People's Republic of Korea, and Montserrat are examples of countries that are not IMF members, and their economies therefore are not monitored by the IMF. The Marshall Islands, the Federated States of Micronesia, Palau, and Somalia are omitted from the emerging market and developing economies group composites because of data limitations.

General Features and Composition of Groups in the *World Economic Outlook* Classification

Advanced Economies

The 35 advanced economies are listed in Table B. The seven largest in terms of GDP—the United

---

change, except for the unemployment rate, which is based on the simple arithmetic average.

[3]See Box A2 of the April 2004 *World Economic Outlook* for a summary of the revised PPP-based weights and Annex IV of the May 1993 *World Economic Outlook*. See also Anne-Marie Gulde and Marianne Schulze-Ghattas, "Purchasing Power Parity Based Weights for the *World Economic Outlook*," in Staff Studies for the *World Economic Outlook* (International Monetary Fund, December 1993), pp. 106–23.

[4]As used here, the terms "country" and "economy" do not always refer to a territorial entity that is a state as understood by international law and practice. Some territorial entities included here are not states, although their statistical data are maintained on a separate and independent basis.

States, Japan, Germany, France, Italy, the United Kingdom, and Canada—constitute the subgroup of *major advanced economies* often referred to as the Group of Seven (G7). The members of the *euro area* and the *newly industrialized Asian economies* are also distinguished as subgroups. Composite data shown in the tables for the euro area cover the current members for all years, even though the membership has increased over time.

Table C lists the member countries of the European Union, not all of which are classified as advanced economies in the *World Economic Outlook*.

Emerging Market and Developing Economies

The group of emerging market and developing economies (151) includes all those that are not classified as advanced economies.

The *regional breakdowns* of emerging market and developing economies are *central and eastern Europe (CEE), Commonwealth of Independent States (CIS), developing Asia, Latin America and the Caribbean (LAC), Middle East and North Africa (MENA),* and *sub-Saharan Africa (SSA)*.

Emerging market and developing economies are also classified according to *analytical criteria*. The analytical criteria reflect the composition of export earnings and other income from abroad; a distinction between net creditor and net debtor economies; and, for the net debtors, financial criteria based on external financing sources and experience with external debt servicing. The detailed composition of emerging market and developing economies in the regional and analytical groups is shown in Tables D and E.

The analytical criterion by *source of export earnings* distinguishes between categories: *fuel* (Standard International Trade Classification—SITC 3) and *nonfuel* and then focuses on *nonfuel primary products* (SITCs 0, 1, 2, 4, and 68). Economies are categorized into one of these groups when their main source of export earnings exceeds 50 percent of total exports on average between 2006 and 2010.

The financial criteria focus on *net creditor economies, net debtor economies,* and *heavily indebted poor countries* (HIPCs). Economies are categorized as net debtors when their current account balance accumulations from 1972 (or earliest data available) to 2010 are negative. Net debtor economies are further differentiated on the basis of two additional financial criteria: *official external financing* and *experience with debt servicing*.[5] Net debtors are placed in the official external financing category when 66 percent or more of their total debt, on average between 2006 and 2010, was financed by official creditors.

The HIPC group comprises the countries that are or have been considered by the IMF and the World Bank for participation in their debt initiative known as the HIPC Initiative, which aims to reduce the external debt burdens of all the eligible HIPCs to a "sustainable" level in a reasonably short period of time.[6] Many of these countries have already benefited from debt relief and have graduated from the initiative.

---

[5] During 2006–10, 40 economies incurred external payments arrears or entered into official or commercial bank debt-rescheduling agreements. This group is referred to as *economies with arrears and/or rescheduling during 2006–10.*

[6] See David Andrews, Anthony R. Boote, Syed S. Rizavi, and Sukwinder Singh, *Debt Relief for Low-Income Countries: The Enhanced HIPC Initiative,* IMF Pamphlet Series No. 51 (Washington: International Monetary Fund, November 1999).

Table A. Classification by *World Economic Outlook* Groups and Their Shares in Aggregate GDP, Exports of Goods and Services, and Population, 2011[1]

(Percent of total for group or world)

	Number of Economies	GDP Advanced Economies	GDP World	Exports of Goods and Services Advanced Economies	Exports of Goods and Services World	Population Advanced Economies	Population World
Advanced Economies	**35**	**100.0**	**51.1**	**100.0**	**62.3**	**100.0**	**15.0**
United States		37.4	19.1	15.2	9.4	30.4	4.5
Euro Area	17	27.9	14.3	41.8	26.0	32.2	4.8
Germany		7.7	3.9	13.1	8.2	8.0	1.2
France		5.5	2.8	6.0	3.7	6.2	0.9
Italy		4.6	2.3	4.5	2.8	5.9	0.9
Spain		3.5	1.8	3.3	2.0	4.5	0.7
Japan		11.0	5.6	6.7	4.2	12.5	1.9
United Kingdom		5.7	2.9	5.7	3.5	6.1	0.9
Canada		3.5	1.8	3.9	2.4	3.4	0.5
Other Advanced Economies	14	14.6	7.4	26.8	16.7	15.5	2.3
Memorandum							
Major Advanced Economies	7	75.3	38.5	55.1	34.3	72.4	10.8
Newly Industrialized Asian Economies	4	7.7	3.9	15.2	9.4	8.3	1.2

	Number of Economies	GDP Emerging Market and Developing Economies	GDP World	Exports of Goods and Services Emerging Market and Developing Economies	Exports of Goods and Services World	Population Emerging Market and Developing Economies	Population World
Emerging Market and Developing Economies	**151**	**100.0**	**48.9**	**100.0**	**37.7**	**100.0**	**85.0**
Regional Groups							
Central and Eastern Europe	14	7.2	3.5	9.1	3.4	3.1	2.6
Commonwealth of Independent States[2]	13	8.8	4.3	10.7	4.0	4.9	4.2
Russia		6.2	3.0	6.9	2.6	2.4	2.1
Developing Asia	27	51.1	25.0	42.6	16.1	61.3	52.1
China		29.3	14.3	24.8	9.4	23.1	19.6
India		11.4	5.6	5.3	2.0	20.7	17.6
Excluding China and India	25	10.4	5.1	12.4	4.7	17.5	14.9
Latin America and the Caribbean	32	17.8	8.7	14.6	5.5	9.9	8.4
Brazil		5.9	2.9	3.5	1.3	3.3	2.8
Mexico		4.3	2.1	4.3	1.6	1.9	1.7
Middle East and North Africa	20	10.0	4.9	17.5	6.6	6.7	5.7
Sub-Saharan Africa	45	5.1	2.5	5.6	2.1	14.2	12.1
Excluding Nigeria and South Africa	43	2.6	1.3	3.1	1.2	10.6	9.0
Analytical Groups							
By Source of Export Earnings							
Fuel	27	17.6	8.6	28.6	10.8	11.1	9.4
Nonfuel	124	82.4	40.3	71.4	26.9	88.9	75.6
Of Which, Primary Products	23	2.7	1.3	2.8	1.1	5.8	4.9
By External Financing Source[3]							
Net Debtor Economies	121	48.1	23.5	39.0	14.7	60.5	51.4
Of Which, Official Financing	29	2.2	1.1	1.5	0.6	8.6	7.3
Net Debtor Economies by Debt-Servicing Experience[3]							
Economies with Arrears and/or Rescheduling during 2006–10	40	4.9	2.4	4.2	1.6	9.4	8.0
Other Net Debtor Economies	81	43.2	21.2	34.8	13.1	51.1	43.4
Other Groups							
Heavily Indebted Poor Countries	38	2.4	1.2	1.9	0.7	10.7	9.1

[1]The GDP shares are based on the purchasing-power-parity valuation of economies' GDP. The number of economies comprising each group reflects those for which data are included in the group aggregates.

[2]Georgia and Mongolia, which are not members of the Commonwealth of Independent States, are included in this group for reasons of geography and similarities in economic structure.

[3]South Sudan in omitted from the external financing group composites for lack of a fully developed database.

Table B. Advanced Economies by Subgroup

Major Currency Areas

United States
Euro Area
Japan

Euro Area

Austria	Germany	Netherlands
Belgium	Greece	Portugal
Cyprus	Ireland	Slovak Republic
Estonia	Italy	Slovenia
Finland	Luxembourg	Spain
France	Malta	

Newly Industrialized Asian Economies

Hong Kong SAR[1]	Singapore
Korea	Taiwan Province of China

Major Advanced Economies

Canada	Italy	United States
France	Japan	
Germany	United Kingdom	

Other Advanced Economies

Australia	Israel	Singapore
Czech Republic	Korea	Sweden
Denmark	New Zealand	Switzerland
Hong Kong SAR[1]	Norway	Taiwan Province of China
Iceland	San Marino	

[1]On July 1, 1997, Hong Kong was returned to the People's Republic of China and became a Special Administrative Region of China.

Table C. European Union

Austria	Germany	Netherlands
Belgium	Greece	Poland
Bulgaria	Hungary	Portugal
Cyprus	Ireland	Romania
Czech Republic	Italy	Slovak Republic
Denmark	Latvia	Slovenia
Estonia	Lithuania	Spain
Finland	Luxembourg	Sweden
France	Malta	United Kingdom

Table D. Emerging Market and Developing Economies by Region and Main Source of Export Earnings

	Fuel	Nonfuel Primary Products
Commonwealth of Independent States[1]		
	Azerbaijan	Mongolia
	Kazakhstan	Uzbekistan
	Russia	
	Turkmenistan	
Developing Asia		
	Brunei Darussalam	Papua New Guinea
	Timor-Leste	Solomon Islands
Latin America and the Caribbean		
	Ecuador	Bolivia
	Trinidad and Tobago	Chile
	Venezuela	Guyana
		Peru
		Suriname
Middle East and North Africa		
	Algeria	Mauritania
	Bahrain	Sudan
	Iran	
	Iraq	
	Kuwait	
	Libya	
	Oman	
	Qatar	
	Saudi Arabia	
	United Arab Emirates	
	Republic of Yemen	
Sub-Saharan Africa		
	Angola	Burkina Faso
	Chad	Burundi
	Republic of Congo	Central African Republic
	Equatorial Guinea	Democratic Republic of the Congo
	Gabon	Guinea
	Nigeria	Guinea-Bissau
	South Sudan	Malawi
		Mali
		Mozambique
		Sierra Leone
		Zambia
		Zimbabwe

[1]Mongolia, which is not a member of the Commonwealth of Independent States, is included in this group for reasons of geography and similarities in economic structure.

Table E. Emerging Market and Developing Economies by Region, Net External Position, and Status as Heavily Indebted Poor Countries

	Net External Position		Heavily Indebted Poor Countries[2]		Net External Position		Heavily Indebted Poor Countries[2]
	Net Creditor	Net Debtor[1]			Net Creditor	Net Debtor[1]	
Central and Eastern Europe				Lao P.D.R.		*	
				Malaysia	*		
Albania		*		Maldives		*	
Bosnia and Herzegovina		*		Myanmar		*	
Bulgaria		*		Nepal		*	
Croatia		*		Pakistan		*	
Hungary		*		Papua New Guinea	*		
Kosovo		*		Philippines		*	
Latvia		*		Samoa		*	
Lithuania		*		Solomon Islands		*	
FYR Macedonia		*		Sri Lanka		*	
Montenegro		*		Thailand	*		
Poland		*		Timor-Leste	*		
Romania		*		Tonga		*	
Serbia		*		Tuvalu		•	
Turkey		*		Vanuatu		*	
Commonwealth of Independent States[3]				Vietnam		*	
Armenia		*		**Latin America and the Caribbean**			
Azerbaijan	*			Antigua and Barbuda		*	
Belarus		*		Argentina		*	
Georgia		*		The Bahamas		*	
Kazakhstan		*		Barbados		*	
Kyrgyz Republic		•		Belize		*	
Moldova		*		Bolivia	*		•
Mongolia		•		Brazil		*	
Russia	*			Chile		*	
Tajikistan		•		Colombia		*	
Turkmenistan	*			Costa Rica		*	
Ukraine		*		Dominica		*	
Uzbekistan	*			Dominican Republic		*	
Developing Asia				Ecuador		•	
Afghanistan		•	•	El Salvador		*	
Bangladesh		•		Grenada		*	
Bhutan		*		Guatemala		*	
Brunei Darussalam	*			Guyana		•	•
Cambodia		*		Haiti		•	•
China	*			Honduras		*	•
Fiji		*		Jamaica		•	
India		*		Mexico		*	
Indonesia	*			Nicaragua		*	•
Kiribati		•		Panama		*	

Table E. *(concluded)*

	Net External Position		Heavily Indebted Poor Countries[2]		Net External Position		Heavily Indebted Poor Countries[2]
	Net Creditor	Net Debtor[1]			Net Creditor	Net Debtor[1]	
Paraguay		*		Central African Republic		•	•
Peru		*		Chad		*	*
St. Kitts and Nevis		*		Comoros		•	*
St. Lucia		*		Democratic Republic of the Congo		•	•
St. Vincent and the Grenadines		•		Republic of Congo		•	•
Suriname		•		Côte d'Ivoire		*	*
Trinidad and Tobago	*			Equatorial Guinea		*	
Uruguay		*		Eritrea		•	*
Venezuela	*			Ethiopia		•	•
Middle East and North Africa				Gabon	*		
Algeria	*			The Gambia		*	•
Bahrain	*			Ghana		•	•
Djibouti		*		Guinea		*	*
Egypt		*		Guinea-Bissau		•	•
Iran	*			Kenya		*	
Iraq	*			Lesotho		*	
Jordan		*		Liberia		*	•
Kuwait	*			Madagascar		*	•
Lebanon		*		Malawi		•	•
Libya	*			Mali		•	•
Mauritania		*	•	Mauritius		*	
Morocco		*		Mozambique		*	•
Oman	*			Namibia	*		
Qatar	*			Niger		*	•
Saudi Arabia	*			Nigeria	*		
Sudan		*	*	Rwanda		•	•
Syria		•		São Tomé and Príncipe		•	•
Tunisia		*		Senegal		*	•
United Arab Emirates	*			Seychelles		*	
Yemen		*		Sierra Leone		*	•
Sub-Saharan Africa				South Africa		*	
Angola	*			South Sudan[4]		...	
Benin		*	•	Swaziland		*	
Botswana	*			Tanzania		*	•
Burkina Faso		•	•	Togo		•	•
Burundi		•	•	Uganda		*	•
Cameroon		*	•	Zambia		*	•
Cape Verde		*		Zimbabwe		*	

[1]Dot instead of star indicates that the net debtor's main external finance source is official financing.

[2]Dot instead of star indicates that the country has reached the completion point.

[3]Georgia and Mongolia, which are not members of the Commonwealth of Independent States, are included in this group for reasons of geography and similarities in economic structure.

[4]South Sudan is omitted from the external financing group composites for lack of a fully developed database.

Box A1. Economic Policy Assumptions Underlying the Projections for Selected Economies

Fiscal Policy Assumptions

The short-term fiscal policy assumptions used in the *World Economic Outlook* (WEO) are based on officially announced budgets, adjusted for differences between the national authorities and the IMF staff regarding macroeconomic assumptions and projected fiscal outturns. The medium-term fiscal projections incorporate policy measures that are judged likely to be implemented. In cases where the IMF staff has insufficient information to assess the authorities' budget intentions and prospects for policy implementation, an unchanged structural primary balance is assumed unless indicated otherwise. Specific assumptions used in some of the advanced economies follow. (See also Tables B5 to B9 in the online section of the Statistical Appendix for data on fiscal net lending/borrowing and structural balances.[1])

Argentina: The 2012 forecasts are based on the 2011 outturn and IMF staff assumptions. For the outer years, the assumed improvement in fiscal balance is predicated on an assumed growth of revenues in the context of a pickup in economic recovery combined with a decline in the growth of expenditures.

Australia: Fiscal projections are based on IMF staff projections and the 2012–13 budget and the Australian Bureau of Statistics.

Austria: Projections take the 2013–16 federal financial framework as well as associated further implementation needs and risks into account.

Belgium: IMF staff projections for 2012 and beyond are based on unchanged policies, as some reform measures remain under discussion.

Brazil: For 2012, the projection is based on the budget, subsequent updates to plans announced by the authorities and the fiscal outturn up to July 2012. In this and outer years, the IMF staff assumes adherence to the announced primary surplus target and further increases in public investment in line with the authorities' intentions.

Canada: Projections use the baseline forecasts in the Economic Action Plan 2012, Jobs, Growth, and Long-Term Prosperity, March 29, 2012 (the fiscal year 2012/13 budget). The IMF staff makes some adjustments to this forecast for differences in macroeconomic projections. The IMF staff forecast also incorporates the most recent data releases from Statistics Canada's Canadian System of National Economic Accounts, including federal, provincial, and territorial budgetary outturns through the end of the second quarter of 2012.

China: For 2012, the government is assumed to slow the pace of fiscal consolidation; the fiscal impulse is assumed to be neutral.

Denmark: Projections for 2012–13 are aligned with the latest official budget estimates and the underlying economic projections, adjusted where appropriate for the IMF staff's macroeconomic assumptions. For 2014–17, the projections incorporate key features of the medium-term fiscal plan as embodied in the authorities' 2011 Convergence Program submitted to the European Union.

France: Estimates for the general government in 2011 reflect the actual outturn. Projections for 2012 and beyond reflect the authorities' 2011–14 multiyear budget, adjusted for fiscal packages and differences in assumptions on macro and financial variables and revenue projections.

Germany: The estimates for 2011 are preliminary estimates from the Federal Statistical Office of Germany. The IMF staff's projections for 2012 and beyond reflect the authorities' adopted core federal government budget plan adjusted for the differences

[1] The output gap is actual minus potential output, as a percent of potential output. Structural balances are expressed as a percent of potential output. The structural balance is the actual net lending/borrowing minus the effects of cyclical output from potential output, corrected for one-time and other factors, such as asset and commodity prices and output composition effects. Changes in the structural balance consequently include effects of temporary fiscal measures, the impact of fluctuations in interest rates and debt-service costs, and other noncyclical fluctuations in net lending/borrowing. The computations of structural balances are based on IMF staff estimates of potential GDP and revenue and expenditure elasticities. (See the October 1993 *World Economic Outlook*, Annex I.) Net debt is defined as gross debt minus financial assets of the general government, which include assets held by the social security insurance system. Estimates of the output gap and of the structural balance are subject to significant margins of uncertainty.

Box A1. *(continued)*

in the IMF staff's macroeconomic framework and staff assumptions about fiscal developments in state and local governments, the social insurance system, and special funds. The projections also incorporate the authorities' plans for a 2013–14 tax reduction. The estimate of gross debt includes portfolios of impaired assets and noncore business transferred to institutions that are winding up as well as other financial sector and EU support operations.

Greece: Macroeconomic, monetary, and fiscal projections for 2012 and the medium term are consistent with the policies discussed between the IMF staff and the authorities in the context of the Extended Fund Facility.

Hong Kong SAR: Projections are based on the authorities' medium-term fiscal projections.

Hungary: Fiscal projections include IMF staff projections of the macroeconomic framework and of the impact of recent legislative measures as well as fiscal policy plans announced at the end of July 2012.

India: Historical data are based on budgetary execution data. Projections are based on available information on the authorities' fiscal plans, with adjustments for IMF staff assumptions. Subnational data are incorporated with a lag of up to two years; general government data are thus finalized well after central government data. IMF and Indian presentations differ, particularly regarding divestment and license auction proceeds, net versus gross recording of revenues in certain minor categories, and some public sector lending.

Indonesia: The 2011 central government deficit was lower than expected (1.1 percent of GDP), reflecting underspending, particularly on public investment. The central government 2012 deficit is estimated at 2.0 percent of GDP, lower than the revised budget estimate of 2.2 percent of GDP. It is assumed that subsidized fuel prices will not be adjusted in 2012. The low projected budget deficit also reflects ongoing budget execution problems. Fiscal projections for 2013–17 are built around key policy reforms needed to support economic growth—namely, enhancing budget implementation to ensure fiscal policy effectiveness, reducing energy subsidies through gradual administrative price increases, and continuous revenue mobilization efforts to increase space for infrastructure development.

Ireland: Fiscal projections are based on the 2012 budget and the Medium-Term Fiscal Statement (published in November 2011), which commits to a €12.4 billion consolidation over 2012–15. The fiscal projections are adjusted for differences between the macroeconomic projections of the IMF staff and those of the Irish authorities.

Italy: Fiscal projections incorporate the impact of the government's announced fiscal adjustment package, as outlined in its April 2012 Documento di Economia e Finanza, modified based on the recent announcement of the government's spending review. The estimates for the 2011 outturn are preliminary. The IMF staff projections are based on the authorities' estimates of the policy scenario and are adjusted mainly for differences in macroeconomic assumptions. After 2015, a zero overall fiscal balance in cyclically adjusted terms is projected, in line with the authorities' fiscal rule.

Japan: The projections include fiscal measures already announced by the government, including consumption tax increases and earthquake reconstruction spending. The medium-term projections assume that expenditure and revenue of the general government are adjusted in line with current underlying demographic and economic trends.

Korea: Fiscal projections assume that fiscal policies will be implemented in 2012 as announced by the government. Projections of expenditure for 2012 are in line with the budget. Revenue projections reflect the IMF staff's macroeconomic assumptions, adjusted for discretionary revenue-raising measures already announced by the government. The medium-term projections assume that the government will continue with its consolidation plans and balance the budget (excluding social security funds) by 2013, consistent with the government's medium-term goal.

Mexico: Fiscal projections for 2012 are broadly in line with the approved budget; projections for 2013 onward assume compliance with the balanced budget rule.

Netherlands: Fiscal projections for the period 2012–17 are based on the authorities' Bureau for Economic Policy Analysis budget projections, after adjusting for differences in macroeconomic assumptions.

Box A1. *(continued)*

New Zealand: Fiscal projections are based on the authorities' 2012 budget and IMF staff estimates. The New Zealand fiscal accounts switched to New Zealand International Financial Reporting Standards in Budget 2007/08. Backdated data have been released back to 1997.

Portugal: Projections reflect the authorities' commitments under the EU- and IMF-supported program for 2012–13 and IMF staff projections thereafter.

Russia: Projections for 2012–14 are based on the non-oil deficit in percent of GDP implied by the 2012–14 medium-term budget, the 2012 supplemental budget, and the IMF staff's revenue projections. The IMF staff assumes an unchanged non-oil federal government balance in percent of GDP during 2015–17.

Saudi Arabia: The authorities base their budget on a conservative assumption for oil prices with adjustments to expenditure allocations considered in the event that revenues exceed budgeted amounts. IMF staff projections of oil revenues are based on WEO baseline oil prices. On the expenditure side, wages are assumed to rise at a natural rate of increase in the medium term with adjustments for recently announced changes in the wage structure. In 2013 and 2016, 13th-month pay is awarded based on the lunar calendar. Capital spending is in line with the priorities established in the authorities' Ninth Development Plan, and recently announced capital spending on housing is assumed to start in 2012 and continue over the medium term.

Singapore: For fiscal year 2012/13, projections are based on budget numbers. For the remainder of the projection period, the IMF staff assumes unchanged policies.

South Africa: Fiscal projections are based on the authorities' 2012 budget and policy intentions stated in the Budget Review, published February 22, 2012.

Spain: For 2012 and beyond, fiscal projections are based on the measures specified in the Stability Program Update 2012–15, the revised fiscal recommendations by the European Council and the subsequent July fiscal package, and the bian-

nual budget plan for 2013–14 announced in August 2012. While the Eurogroup's commitment of up to €100 billion (9.4 percent of GDP) includes an additional safety margin, IMF staff, to be prudent and pending further details on implementation, assumed disbursement of this full amount for its 2012 debt projections. Under the unchanged policies scenario, no additional structural improvement is assumed for the outer years, after the fiscal deficit reaches 3 percent of GDP.

Sweden: Fiscal projections for 2012 are broadly in line with the authorities' projections. The impact of cyclical developments on the fiscal accounts is calculated using the Organization for Economic Cooperation and Development's latest semi-elasticity.

Switzerland: Projections for 2011–17 are based on IMF staff calculations, which incorporate measures to restore balance in the federal accounts and strengthen social security finances.

Turkey: Fiscal projections assume that current expenditures will be in line with the authorities' 2012–14 Medium-Term Program but that capital expenditures will be exceeded given projects initiated in 2011.

United Kingdom: Fiscal projections are based on the authorities' 2012 budget announced in March 2012 and the Economic and Fiscal Outlook by the Office for Budget Responsibility published along with the budget. These projections incorporate the announced medium-term consolidation plans from 2012 onward. The authorities' projections are adjusted for differences between the IMF staff's forecasts of macroeconomic and financial variables (such as GDP growth) and the forecasts of these variables assumed in the authorities' fiscal projections. IMF staff projections also exclude the temporary effects of financial sector interventions and the effect on public sector net investment in 2012–13 of transferring assets from the Royal Mail Pension Plan to the public sector.

United States: Fiscal projections are based on the March 2012 Congressional Budget Office baseline, adjusted for the IMF staff's policy and macro-economic assumptions. The key near-term policy assumptions include an extension of all the Bush

Box A1. *(continued)*

tax cuts and emergency unemployment benefits into 2013 and replacement of automatic spending cuts ("sequestration") with back-loaded consolidation measures. Over the medium term, the IMF staff assumes that Congress will continue to make regular adjustments to the Alternative Minimum Tax parameters and Medicare payments ("Doc Fix") and will extend certain traditional programs (such as the research and development tax credit). It is assumed that the Bush tax cuts for the middle class will be extended permanently, but those for high-income taxpayers will be allowed to expire in 2014 (one year later than planned by the administration). The fiscal projections are adjusted to reflect the IMF staff's forecasts of key macroeconomic and financial variables and different accounting treatment of the financial sector support and are converted to the general government basis.

Monetary Policy Assumptions

Monetary policy assumptions are based on the established policy framework in each country. In most cases, this implies a nonaccommodative stance over the business cycle: official interest rates will increase when economic indicators suggest that inflation will rise above its acceptable rate or range; they will decrease when indicators suggest that prospective inflation will not exceed the acceptable rate or range, that prospective output growth is below its potential rate, and that the margin of slack in the economy is significant. On this basis, the LIBOR on six-month U.S. dollar deposits is assumed to average 0.7 percent in 2012 and 0.6 percent in 2013 (see Table 1.1). The rate on three-month euro deposits is assumed to average 0.6 percent in 2012 and 0.2 percent in 2013. The interest rate on six-month Japanese yen deposits is assumed to average 0.4 percent in 2012 and 0.3 percent in 2013.

Australia: Monetary policy assumptions are in line with market expectations.

Brazil: Monetary policy assumptions are based on current policy and are consistent with the gradual convergence of inflation toward the middle of the target range by the end of 2012.

Canada: Monetary policy assumptions are in line with market expectations.

China: Monetary tightening built into the baseline is consistent with authorities' forecast of 14 percent year-over-year growth for M2 in 2012.

Denmark: The monetary policy is to maintain the peg to the euro.

Euro area: Monetary policy assumptions for euro area member countries are in line with market expectations.

Hong Kong SAR: The IMF staff assumes that the Currency Board system remains intact and projects broad money growth based on the past relationship with nominal GDP.

India: The policy (interest) rate assumption is based on the average of market forecasts.

Indonesia: Bank Indonesia is expected to use a combination of macroprudential measures and policy rate increases.

Japan: The current monetary policy conditions are maintained for the projection period, and no further tightening or loosening is assumed.

Korea: Monetary policy assumptions incorporate resumption of rate normalization over the course of 2013.

Mexico: Monetary assumptions are consistent with attaining the inflation target.

Russia: Monetary projections assume unchanged policies, as indicated in recent statements by the Central Bank of Russia. Specifically, policy rates are assumed to remain at the current levels, with limited interventions in the foreign exchange markets.

Saudi Arabia: Monetary policy projections are based on the continuation of the exchange rate peg to the U.S. dollar.

Singapore: Broad money is projected to grow in line with the projected growth in nominal GDP.

South Africa: Monetary projections are consistent with South Africa's 3 to 6 percent inflation target range.

Sweden: Monetary projections are in line with Riksbank projections.

Switzerland: Monetary policy variables reflect historical data from the national authorities and the market.

Box A1. *(concluded)*

Turkey: Broad money and the long-term bond yield are based on IMF staff projections. The short-term deposit rate is projected to evolve with a constant spread against the interest rate of a similar U.S. instrument.

United Kingdom: On monetary policy, the projections assume no changes to the policy rate or the level of asset purchases through 2014.

United States: Given the outlook for sluggish growth and inflation, the IMF staff expects the federal funds target to remain near zero until late 2014. This assumption is consistent with the Federal Open Market Committee's statement following its January meeting (and reaffirmed in subsequent meetings) that economic conditions are likely to warrant an exceptionally low federal funds rate at least through late 2014.

List of Tables

Table A1. Summary of World Output [1]
(Annual percent change)

	Average 1994–2003	2004	2005	2006	2007	2008	2009	2010	2011	Projections 2012	2013	2017
World	3.4	4.9	4.6	5.3	5.4	2.8	–0.6	5.1	3.8	3.3	3.6	4.6
Advanced Economies	2.8	3.1	2.6	3.0	2.8	0.1	–3.5	3.0	1.6	1.3	1.5	2.6
United States	3.3	3.5	3.1	2.7	1.9	–0.3	–3.1	2.4	1.8	2.2	2.1	3.3
Euro Area	2.2	2.2	1.7	3.2	3.0	0.4	–4.4	2.0	1.4	–0.4	0.2	1.7
Japan	0.9	2.4	1.3	1.7	2.2	–1.0	–5.5	4.5	–0.8	2.2	1.2	1.1
Other Advanced Economies [2]	3.8	4.1	3.6	3.9	4.2	0.9	–2.1	4.5	2.5	1.5	2.4	3.2
Emerging Market and Developing Economies	4.4	7.5	7.3	8.2	8.7	6.1	2.7	7.4	6.2	5.3	5.6	6.2
Regional Groups												
Central and Eastern Europe	3.4	7.3	5.9	6.4	5.4	3.2	–3.6	4.6	5.3	2.0	2.6	3.8
Commonwealth of Independent States [3]	0.6	8.2	6.7	8.8	9.0	5.4	–6.4	4.8	4.9	4.0	4.1	4.1
Developing Asia	7.0	8.5	9.5	10.3	11.4	7.9	7.0	9.5	7.8	6.7	7.2	7.7
Latin America and the Caribbean	2.5	6.0	4.7	5.7	5.8	4.2	–1.5	6.2	4.5	3.2	3.9	4.0
Middle East and North Africa	4.0	6.2	5.3	6.3	5.7	4.5	2.6	5.0	3.3	5.3	3.6	4.5
Sub-Saharan Africa	4.0	7.1	6.2	6.4	7.1	5.6	2.8	5.3	5.1	5.0	5.7	5.8
Memorandum												
European Union	2.6	2.6	2.3	3.6	3.4	0.6	–4.2	2.1	1.6	–0.2	0.5	2.1
Analytical Groups												
By Source of Export Earnings												
Fuel	2.4	8.1	6.7	7.7	7.4	5.0	–1.5	4.7	4.5	5.3	4.2	4.2
Nonfuel	5.0	7.4	7.4	8.4	9.1	6.4	3.7	8.0	6.5	5.3	5.9	6.6
Of Which, Primary Products	4.6	5.7	6.1	6.8	7.3	5.9	2.1	6.7	5.6	4.6	5.3	5.7
By External Financing Source												
Net Debtor Economies	3.6	6.5	6.0	6.8	6.9	4.8	0.8	6.7	5.1	3.6	4.4	5.2
Of Which, Official Financing	3.4	6.4	6.4	6.0	5.9	6.3	5.2	5.5	7.2	5.7	6.1	6.2
Net Debtor Economies by Debt-Servicing Experience												
Economies with Arrears and/or Rescheduling during 2006–10	2.9	7.2	7.5	7.8	7.6	5.8	2.0	6.7	6.1	3.3	4.3	4.9
Memorandum												
Median Growth Rate												
Advanced Economies	3.3	4.1	3.1	3.9	3.8	0.8	–3.7	2.4	1.8	0.9	1.3	2.3
Emerging Market and Developing Economies	4.1	5.4	5.4	5.7	6.3	5.1	1.9	4.5	4.4	4.0	4.1	4.5
Output per Capita												
Advanced Economies	2.1	2.4	1.9	2.3	2.0	–0.7	–4.1	2.4	1.0	0.7	0.9	2.0
Emerging Market and Developing Economies	3.1	6.4	6.0	7.1	7.5	4.9	1.5	6.3	5.2	4.3	4.6	5.2
World Growth Rate Based on Market Exchange	2.9	3.9	3.4	4.0	4.0	1.5	–2.2	4.1	2.8	2.6	2.9	3.9
Value of World Output (billions of U.S. dollars)												
At Market Exchange Rates	31,429	42,178	45,616	49,375	55,718	61,222	57,846	63,180	69,899	71,277	74,149	92,722
At Purchasing Power Parities	39,240	52,741	56,853	61,705	66,835	70,140	70,154	74,684	78,970	82,762	86,836	110,405

[1] Real GDP.
[2] In this table, Other Advanced Economies means advanced economies excluding the United States, Euro Area countries, and Japan.
[3] Georgia and Mongolia, which are not members of the Commonwealth of Independent States, are included in this group for reasons of geography and similarities in economic structure.

Table A2. Advanced Economies: Real GDP and Total Domestic Demand [1]
(Annual percent change)

	Average 1994–2003	2004	2005	2006	2007	2008	2009	2010	2011	Projections 2012	Projections 2013	Projections 2017	Fourth Quarter [2] 2011:Q4	Fourth Quarter [2] Projections 2012:Q4	Fourth Quarter [2] Projections 2013:Q4
Real GDP															
Advanced Economies	**2.8**	**3.1**	**2.6**	**3.0**	**2.8**	**0.1**	**–3.5**	**3.0**	**1.6**	**1.3**	**1.5**	**2.6**	**1.3**	**1.1**	**2.1**
United States	3.3	3.5	3.1	2.7	1.9	–0.3	–3.1	2.4	1.8	2.2	2.1	3.3	2.0	1.7	2.5
Euro Area	2.2	2.2	1.7	3.2	3.0	0.4	–4.4	2.0	1.4	–0.4	0.2	1.7	0.7	–0.5	0.8
Germany	1.5	0.7	0.8	3.9	3.4	0.8	–5.1	4.0	3.1	0.9	0.9	1.3	1.9	0.9	1.4
France	2.2	2.5	1.8	2.5	2.3	–0.1	–3.1	1.7	1.7	0.1	0.4	1.9	1.2	0.0	0.8
Italy	1.7	1.7	0.9	2.2	1.7	–1.2	–5.5	1.8	0.4	–2.3	–0.7	1.4	–0.5	–2.3	0.0
Spain	3.6	3.3	3.6	4.1	3.5	0.9	–3.7	–0.3	0.4	–1.5	–1.3	1.7	0.0	–2.3	0.2
Netherlands	2.9	2.2	2.0	3.4	3.9	1.8	–3.7	1.6	1.1	–0.5	0.4	1.9	–0.4	0.1	0.9
Belgium	2.3	3.3	1.8	2.7	2.9	1.0	–2.8	2.4	1.8	0.0	0.3	1.5	0.9	0.1	0.6
Austria	2.4	2.6	2.4	3.7	3.7	1.4	–3.8	2.1	2.7	0.9	1.1	1.6	1.1	0.6	2.2
Greece	3.5	4.4	2.3	5.5	3.0	–0.2	–3.3	–3.5	–6.9	–6.0	–4.0	3.5	–7.5	–3.6	–2.9
Portugal	2.7	1.6	0.8	1.4	2.4	0.0	–2.9	1.4	–1.7	–3.0	–1.0	1.8	–3.0	–2.7	0.5
Finland	3.8	4.1	2.9	4.4	5.3	0.3	–8.5	3.3	2.7	0.2	1.3	1.9	0.8	–0.1	2.4
Ireland	6.9	4.4	5.9	5.4	5.4	–2.1	–5.5	–0.8	1.4	0.4	1.4	2.9	2.9	0.4	1.0
Slovak Republic	4.4	5.1	6.7	8.3	10.5	5.8	–4.9	4.2	3.3	2.6	2.8	3.6	3.3	2.0	3.7
Slovenia	4.1	4.4	4.0	5.8	7.0	3.4	–7.8	1.2	0.6	–2.2	–0.4	2.3	–2.3	–3.0	3.6
Luxembourg	4.4	4.4	5.4	5.0	6.6	0.8	–5.3	2.7	1.6	0.2	0.7	2.5	1.1	0.3	0.9
Estonia	5.7	6.3	8.9	10.1	7.5	–3.7	–14.3	2.3	7.6	2.4	3.5	3.9	5.1	2.0	4.1
Cyprus	4.3	4.2	3.9	4.1	5.1	3.6	–1.9	1.1	0.5	–2.3	–1.0	2.0	–0.8	–2.8	–0.4
Malta	. . .	–0.5	3.7	3.1	4.4	4.1	–2.6	2.5	2.1	1.2	2.0	2.3	0.1	3.9	0.8
Japan	0.9	2.4	1.3	1.7	2.2	–1.0	–5.5	4.5	–0.8	2.2	1.2	1.1	–0.6	1.6	2.1
United Kingdom	3.5	2.9	2.8	2.6	3.6	–1.0	–4.0	1.8	0.8	–0.4	1.1	2.7	0.6	0.0	1.2
Canada	3.5	3.1	3.0	2.8	2.2	0.7	–2.8	3.2	2.4	1.9	2.0	2.3	2.2	1.7	2.2
Korea	5.7	4.6	4.0	5.2	5.1	2.3	0.3	6.3	3.6	2.7	3.6	4.0	3.4	3.1	3.5
Australia	3.8	4.1	3.1	2.7	4.7	2.5	1.4	2.5	2.1	3.3	3.0	3.2	2.6	2.3	4.4
Taiwan Province of China	4.7	6.2	4.7	5.4	6.0	0.7	–1.8	10.7	4.0	1.3	3.9	5.0	2.0	3.4	3.7
Sweden	3.2	3.7	3.2	4.5	3.4	–0.8	–5.0	5.9	4.0	1.2	2.2	2.4	1.2	0.8	4.7
Hong Kong SAR	2.7	8.5	7.1	7.0	6.4	2.3	–2.6	7.1	5.0	1.8	3.5	4.4	3.0	3.3	2.9
Switzerland	1.3	2.4	2.7	3.8	3.8	2.2	–1.9	3.0	1.9	0.8	1.4	1.9	0.9	0.6	2.3
Singapore	5.4	9.2	7.4	8.8	8.9	1.7	–1.0	14.8	4.9	2.1	2.9	3.9	3.6	2.9	4.0
Czech Republic	. . .	4.7	6.8	7.0	5.7	3.1	–4.7	2.7	1.7	–1.0	0.8	3.4	0.6	–1.0	1.8
Norway	3.2	4.0	2.6	2.4	2.7	0.0	–1.6	0.6	1.5	3.1	2.3	2.0	1.8	0.7	5.2
Israel	4.3	4.8	4.9	5.6	5.5	4.0	0.8	5.7	4.6	2.9	3.2	3.7	3.6	2.6	4.4
Denmark	2.4	2.3	2.4	3.4	1.6	–0.8	–5.8	1.3	0.8	0.5	1.2	1.8	0.1	1.6	0.9
New Zealand	3.6	4.3	3.1	2.3	2.9	–0.2	–2.4	1.8	1.3	2.2	3.1	2.3	1.9	2.9	2.4
Iceland	3.4	7.8	7.2	4.7	6.0	1.3	–6.8	–4.0	3.1	2.9	2.6	3.0	2.7	3.2	2.2
San Marino	. . .	4.6	2.4	3.8	3.5	–3.4	–12.8	–5.2	–2.6	–2.6	0.5	1.3	. . .	. . .	. . .
Memorandum															
Major Advanced Economies	2.6	2.8	2.3	2.6	2.3	–0.4	–3.8	2.8	1.4	1.4	1.5	2.5	1.3	1.1	2.0
Newly Industrialized Asian Economies	5.1	5.9	4.8	5.8	5.9	1.8	–0.7	8.5	4.0	2.1	3.6	4.3	3.0	3.2	3.5
Real Total Domestic Demand															
Advanced Economies	**2.9**	**3.2**	**2.6**	**2.8**	**2.4**	**–0.4**	**–3.8**	**2.9**	**1.3**	**1.1**	**1.3**	**2.6**	**0.9**	**1.1**	**1.6**
United States	3.8	3.9	3.2	2.6	1.2	–1.5	–4.0	2.8	1.7	2.1	2.0	3.5	1.9	1.6	2.5
Euro Area	. . .	1.9	1.8	3.1	2.8	0.3	–3.8	1.3	0.5	–1.7	–0.3	1.4	–0.5	–1.3	0.3
Germany	1.1	0.0	–0.2	2.7	1.9	1.2	–2.5	2.6	2.6	0.1	0.9	1.2	2.2	0.1	1.3
France	2.2	2.8	2.5	2.4	3.2	0.3	–2.6	1.6	1.7	–0.2	0.5	1.5	0.2	0.7	0.8
Italy	1.9	1.4	0.9	2.1	1.4	–1.2	–4.4	2.1	–0.9	–4.6	–0.9	1.2	–3.4	–3.5	–0.1
Spain	3.9	4.8	5.0	5.2	4.1	–0.5	–6.2	–0.6	–1.9	–4.0	–3.3	1.4	–3.1	–4.6	–1.3
Japan	0.9	1.5	1.0	0.9	1.1	–1.3	–4.0	2.8	0.1	2.8	1.1	1.0	0.6	1.8	1.8
United Kingdom	3.7	3.5	2.3	2.2	3.5	–1.8	–5.0	2.3	–0.5	0.3	0.6	2.1	–0.6	0.9	0.4
Canada	3.2	3.9	4.6	4.2	3.8	2.7	–2.9	5.2	3.2	1.9	2.4	1.8	2.3	2.6	2.3
Other Advanced Economies [3]	3.7	4.6	3.4	4.0	4.9	1.5	–2.9	5.6	2.7	2.5	2.8	3.4	1.8	3.7	2.3
Memorandum															
Major Advanced Economies	2.8	2.9	2.3	2.3	1.7	–0.9	–3.8	2.7	1.3	1.3	1.4	2.5	1.1	1.1	1.8
Newly Industrialized Asian Economies	4.1	4.8	2.9	4.2	4.5	1.4	–3.0	7.4	2.3	2.3	3.1	4.2	0.7	4.5	1.5

[1] In this and other tables, when countries are not listed alphabetically, they are ordered on the basis of economic size.
[2] From the fourth quarter of the preceding year.
[3] In this table, Other Advanced Economies means advanced economies excluding the G7 (Canada, France, Germany, Italy, Japan, United Kingdom, United States) and Euro Area countries.

Table A3. Advanced Economies: Components of Real GDP
(Annual percent change)

| | Averages | | 2004 | 2005 | 2006 | 2007 | 2008 | 2009 | 2010 | 2011 | Projections | |
	1994–2003	2004–13									2012	2013
Private Consumer Expenditure												
Advanced Economies	**3.0**	**1.5**	**2.6**	**2.7**	**2.5**	**2.4**	**0.0**	**−1.2**	**2.0**	**1.4**	**1.1**	**1.4**
United States	3.8	1.8	3.3	3.4	2.9	2.3	−0.6	−1.9	1.8	2.5	1.9	2.2
Euro Area	. . .	0.6	1.5	1.8	2.1	1.7	0.4	−1.0	1.0	0.1	−1.1	−0.3
Germany	1.2	0.7	0.4	0.2	1.5	−0.2	0.8	0.1	0.9	1.7	0.7	1.0
France	2.2	1.1	1.7	2.5	2.2	2.4	0.2	0.3	1.5	0.3	−0.2	0.2
Italy	1.7	−0.1	0.7	1.2	1.4	1.1	−0.8	−1.6	1.2	0.2	−3.3	−1.2
Spain	3.3	0.6	4.2	4.1	4.0	3.5	−0.6	−3.8	0.7	−1.0	−2.2	−2.4
Japan	1.1	0.9	1.2	1.5	1.1	0.9	−0.9	−0.7	2.6	0.1	2.5	1.0
United Kingdom	4.1	0.6	3.2	2.5	1.5	2.7	−1.6	−3.1	1.3	−1.0	−0.2	0.9
Canada	3.2	2.8	3.3	3.7	4.2	4.6	3.0	0.4	3.3	2.4	1.7	2.0
Other Advanced Economies [1]	4.0	2.9	3.6	3.5	3.7	4.6	1.3	0.2	3.7	2.7	2.4	2.8
Memorandum												
Major Advanced Economies	2.8	1.3	2.4	2.5	2.3	1.9	−0.4	−1.3	1.8	1.5	1.3	1.4
Newly Industrialized Asian Economies	4.8	3.0	3.0	3.9	4.0	4.8	1.0	0.3	4.7	3.4	2.4	3.2
Public Consumption												
Advanced Economies	**2.1**	**1.1**	**1.7**	**1.2**	**1.6**	**1.8**	**2.1**	**3.3**	**1.3**	**−0.5**	**0.0**	**−1.0**
United States	1.9	0.5	1.4	0.6	1.0	1.3	2.2	4.3	0.9	−2.3	−1.6	−2.4
Euro Area	. . .	1.2	1.6	1.6	2.1	2.2	2.3	2.6	0.8	−0.2	−0.2	−0.6
Germany	1.4	1.3	−0.6	0.3	0.9	1.4	3.2	3.0	1.7	1.0	0.9	0.8
France	1.1	1.4	2.2	1.2	1.4	1.5	1.3	2.5	1.8	0.2	1.4	0.8
Italy	0.9	0.2	2.5	1.9	0.5	1.0	0.6	0.8	−0.6	−0.9	−1.6	−2.0
Spain	3.3	2.2	6.2	5.5	4.6	5.6	5.9	3.7	1.5	−0.5	−4.1	−5.4
Japan	3.0	1.1	1.5	0.8	0.0	1.1	−0.1	2.3	2.2	2.0	1.8	−0.6
United Kingdom	2.2	1.2	3.4	2.0	1.5	0.6	1.6	0.8	0.4	0.1	2.3	−1.1
Canada	1.4	2.1	2.0	1.4	3.0	2.7	4.4	3.6	2.4	0.8	−0.2	0.7
Other Advanced Economies [1]	2.9	2.4	1.8	2.0	2.9	3.1	2.6	3.4	2.6	1.7	2.5	1.8
Memorandum												
Major Advanced Economies	1.9	0.8	1.6	0.8	1.0	1.3	1.8	3.2	1.2	−0.8	−0.3	−1.3
Newly Industrialized Asian Economies	3.6	3.1	2.4	2.4	3.7	3.9	3.2	4.6	3.1	1.9	3.5	2.7
Gross Fixed Capital Formation												
Advanced Economies	**3.6**	**0.8**	**4.4**	**4.1**	**4.1**	**2.4**	**−2.9**	**−12.6**	**1.6**	**2.2**	**2.4**	**3.3**
United States	5.3	0.6	6.3	5.3	2.5	−1.4	−5.1	−15.3	−0.3	3.4	6.2	6.2
Euro Area	. . .	−0.1	2.2	3.2	5.7	4.7	−1.1	−12.8	−0.1	1.4	−3.1	0.2
Germany	0.4	1.5	−0.2	0.8	8.2	4.7	1.3	−11.6	5.9	6.2	−0.7	1.5
France	2.9	1.3	3.3	4.4	4.0	6.3	0.4	−10.6	1.3	3.6	0.7	0.4
Italy	3.0	−1.5	2.0	1.3	3.4	1.8	−3.7	−11.7	2.1	−1.9	−7.8	1.0
Spain	6.0	−2.7	5.1	7.1	7.1	4.5	−4.7	−18.0	−6.2	−5.3	−8.9	−4.1
Japan	−1.0	−0.7	0.4	0.8	1.5	0.3	−4.1	−10.6	0.1	0.8	3.5	1.2
United Kingdom	4.6	0.6	5.0	2.4	6.3	8.2	−4.6	−13.7	3.5	−1.4	0.4	1.6
Canada	5.0	4.0	7.7	9.3	7.0	3.6	2.0	−13.2	10.0	6.6	4.1	4.6
Other Advanced Economies [1]	4.1	3.3	6.3	5.0	5.6	6.6	−0.4	−6.2	7.5	2.5	2.9	3.7
Memorandum												
Major Advanced Economies	3.4	0.6	4.2	3.8	3.6	1.2	−3.5	−13.4	1.4	2.8	3.3	3.9
Newly Industrialized Asian Economies	3.5	2.4	6.2	2.2	3.8	4.4	−3.1	−4.3	11.3	−0.5	1.6	3.4

Table A3. Advanced Economies: Components of Real GDP *(concluded)*
(Annual percent change)

	Averages		2004	2005	2006	2007	2008	2009	2010	2011	Projections	
	1994–2003	2004–13									2012	2013
Final Domestic Demand												
Advanced Economies	**2.9**	**1.3**	**2.8**	**2.7**	**2.7**	**2.3**	**−0.2**	**−2.7**	**1.8**	**1.3**	**1.1**	**1.3**
United States	3.8	1.4	3.5	3.3	2.5	1.4	−1.0	−3.3	1.3	1.8	2.0	2.0
Euro Area	. . .	0.6	1.7	2.0	2.9	2.4	0.5	−2.8	0.7	0.3	−1.3	−0.3
Germany	1.1	1.0	0.1	0.3	2.6	1.1	1.3	−1.6	2.0	2.4	0.5	1.0
France	2.0	1.2	2.1	2.5	2.4	2.9	0.5	−1.4	1.5	0.9	0.4	0.4
Italy	1.8	−0.3	1.3	1.3	1.6	1.2	−1.2	−3.2	1.0	−0.4	−3.8	−1.0
Spain	3.9	0.1	4.8	5.2	5.0	4.1	−0.7	−6.2	−0.8	−1.8	−4.0	−3.4
Japan	0.9	0.6	1.0	1.2	1.0	0.8	−1.6	−2.3	2.1	0.6	2.6	0.7
United Kingdom	3.7	0.7	3.5	2.4	2.2	3.1	−1.4	−4.0	1.4	−0.8	0.5	0.5
Canada	3.1	2.9	3.9	4.4	4.6	4.0	3.0	−2.1	4.5	3.0	1.8	2.3
Other Advanced Economies [1]	3.7	2.9	3.9	3.5	3.9	4.8	1.2	−0.9	4.3	2.5	2.5	2.9
Memorandum												
Major Advanced Economies	2.7	1.1	2.6	2.5	2.3	1.6	−0.6	−2.8	1.7	1.4	1.3	1.4
Newly Industrialized Asian Economies	4.2	2.9	3.7	3.2	3.9	4.6	0.4	−0.2	5.8	2.2	2.4	3.2
Stock Building [2]												
Advanced Economies	**0.0**	**0.0**	**0.4**	**−0.1**	**0.1**	**0.1**	**−0.2**	**−1.1**	**1.0**	**0.0**	**−0.1**	**0.1**
United States	0.0	0.0	0.4	−0.1	0.1	−0.2	−0.5	−0.8	1.5	−0.2	0.2	0.0
Euro Area	. . .	0.0	0.2	−0.2	0.2	0.4	−0.2	−1.0	0.6	0.2	−0.4	0.0
Germany	0.0	0.0	−0.1	−0.4	0.1	0.8	−0.1	−0.7	0.6	0.2	−0.4	−0.1
France	0.2	0.0	0.7	0.0	0.1	0.2	−0.3	−1.3	0.1	0.8	−0.6	0.1
Italy	0.0	−0.1	0.0	−0.4	0.5	0.2	0.0	−1.1	1.1	−0.5	−0.3	0.0
Spain	0.0	0.0	0.0	−0.1	0.3	−0.1	0.1	0.0	0.0	0.1	0.0	0.0
Japan	0.0	0.0	0.5	−0.3	−0.1	0.3	0.2	−1.5	0.7	−0.4	0.0	0.4
United Kingdom	0.1	0.0	0.1	0.0	−0.1	0.4	−0.4	−1.0	0.9	0.3	−0.2	0.1
Canada	0.1	0.0	0.1	0.5	−0.2	−0.1	−0.2	−0.8	0.6	0.2	0.0	0.0
Other Advanced Economies [1]	0.0	0.0	0.6	−0.1	0.1	0.1	0.3	−1.9	1.1	0.2	−0.1	−0.1
Memorandum												
Major Advanced Economies	0.0	0.0	0.3	−0.1	0.1	0.1	−0.3	−1.0	1.1	−0.1	0.0	0.1
Newly Industrialized Asian Economies	−0.1	0.0	0.8	−0.2	0.3	−0.1	0.8	−2.5	1.4	0.1	0.0	−0.1
Foreign Balance [2]												
Advanced Economies	**−0.1**	**0.2**	**−0.1**	**0.0**	**0.2**	**0.4**	**0.5**	**0.3**	**0.2**	**0.4**	**0.2**	**0.2**
United States	−0.5	0.1	−0.7	−0.3	−0.1	0.6	1.2	1.1	−0.5	0.1	0.0	0.0
Euro Area	. . .	0.3	0.4	−0.1	0.2	0.2	0.1	−0.7	0.7	0.9	1.2	0.4
Germany	0.3	0.5	1.1	0.8	1.1	1.5	0.0	−2.9	1.7	0.6	0.7	0.0
France	0.0	−0.3	−0.3	−0.7	0.0	−0.9	−0.3	−0.5	0.0	0.0	0.3	−0.1
Italy	−0.2	0.3	0.3	0.0	0.1	0.3	0.0	−1.2	−0.4	1.4	2.2	0.2
Spain	−0.3	0.6	−1.6	−1.7	−1.5	−0.9	1.5	2.9	0.2	2.4	2.4	1.9
Japan	0.0	0.2	0.8	0.3	0.8	1.0	0.2	−2.0	1.9	−0.8	−0.4	0.1
United Kingdom	−0.4	0.2	−0.8	0.3	0.2	−0.2	0.9	1.1	−0.6	1.2	−0.8	0.4
Canada	0.3	−1.1	−0.8	−1.6	−1.4	−1.5	−2.1	0.2	−2.1	−0.8	0.0	−0.5
Other Advanced Economies [1]	0.4	0.7	0.5	0.9	1.0	0.7	0.3	1.5	0.7	0.7	0.0	0.4
Memorandum												
Major Advanced Economies	−0.2	0.1	−0.2	−0.1	0.2	0.5	0.6	0.0	0.0	0.1	0.1	0.0
Newly Industrialized Asian Economies	0.6	1.5	1.3	2.1	1.9	2.0	0.7	1.9	1.9	2.1	0.1	1.0

[1] In this table, Other Advanced Economies means advanced economies excluding the G7 (Canada, France, Germany, Italy, Japan, United Kingdom, United States) and Euro Area countries.
[2] Changes expressed as percent of GDP in the preceding period.

Table A4. Emerging Market and Developing Economies: Real GDP [1]
(Annual percent change)

	Average 1994–2003	2004	2005	2006	2007	2008	2009	2010	2011	Projections 2012	2013	2017
Central and Eastern Europe [2]	**3.4**	**7.3**	**5.9**	**6.4**	**5.4**	**3.2**	**−3.6**	**4.6**	**5.3**	**2.0**	**2.6**	**3.8**
Albania	6.3	5.7	5.8	5.4	5.9	7.5	3.3	3.5	3.0	0.5	1.7	2.5
Bosnia and Herzegovina	...	6.3	3.9	6.0	6.1	5.6	−2.9	0.7	1.3	0.0	1.0	4.0
Bulgaria	0.6	6.7	6.4	6.5	6.4	6.2	−5.5	0.4	1.7	1.0	1.5	4.5
Croatia	4.3	4.1	4.3	4.9	5.1	2.1	−6.9	−1.4	0.0	−1.1	1.0	2.5
Hungary	3.2	4.8	4.0	3.9	0.1	0.9	−6.8	1.3	1.7	−1.0	0.8	1.8
Kosovo	...	2.6	3.8	3.4	6.3	6.9	2.9	3.9	5.0	3.8	4.1	4.6
Latvia	4.8	8.9	10.1	11.2	9.6	−3.3	−17.7	−0.3	5.5	4.5	3.5	4.0
Lithuania	...	7.4	7.8	7.8	9.8	2.9	−14.8	1.4	5.9	2.7	3.0	3.6
FYR Macedonia	1.1	4.6	4.4	5.0	6.1	5.0	−0.9	2.9	3.1	1.0	2.0	4.0
Montenegro	...	4.4	4.2	8.6	10.7	6.9	−5.7	2.5	2.4	0.2	1.5	2.2
Poland	4.5	5.3	3.6	6.2	6.8	5.1	1.6	3.9	4.3	2.4	2.1	3.6
Romania	2.1	8.5	4.2	7.9	6.3	7.3	−6.6	−1.6	2.5	0.9	2.5	3.5
Serbia	...	9.3	5.4	3.6	5.4	3.8	−3.5	1.0	1.6	−0.5	2.0	2.0
Turkey	2.7	9.4	8.4	6.9	4.7	0.7	−4.8	9.2	8.5	3.0	3.5	4.4
Commonwealth of Independent States [2,3]	**0.6**	**8.2**	**6.7**	**8.8**	**9.0**	**5.4**	**−6.4**	**4.8**	**4.9**	**4.0**	**4.1**	**4.1**
Russia	0.7	7.2	6.4	8.2	8.5	5.2	−7.8	4.3	4.3	3.7	3.8	3.8
Excluding Russia	0.3	10.8	7.6	10.5	10.0	5.6	−3.1	6.0	6.2	4.7	4.8	4.9
Armenia	7.5	10.5	14.1	13.2	13.7	6.9	−14.1	2.1	4.6	3.9	4.0	4.0
Azerbaijan	2.2	10.2	26.4	34.5	25.0	10.8	9.3	5.0	0.1	3.9	2.7	3.1
Belarus	2.3	11.4	9.4	10.0	8.6	10.2	0.2	7.7	5.3	4.3	3.4	4.1
Georgia	...	5.9	9.6	9.4	12.3	2.3	−3.8	6.3	7.0	6.5	5.5	5.5
Kazakhstan	2.1	9.6	9.7	10.7	8.9	3.2	1.2	7.3	7.5	5.5	5.7	6.3
Kyrgyz Republic	1.1	7.0	−0.2	3.1	8.5	7.6	2.9	−0.5	5.7	1.0	8.5	5.0
Moldova	−3.1	7.4	7.5	4.8	3.0	7.8	−6.0	7.1	6.4	3.0	5.0	5.3
Mongolia	3.7	10.6	7.3	8.6	10.2	8.9	−1.3	6.4	17.5	12.7	15.7	9.7
Tajikistan	0.5	10.6	6.7	7.0	7.8	7.9	3.9	6.5	7.4	6.8	6.0	6.0
Turkmenistan	4.3	14.7	13.0	11.0	11.1	14.7	6.1	9.2	14.7	8.0	7.7	8.0
Ukraine	−2.3	12.1	2.7	7.3	7.9	2.3	−14.8	4.1	5.2	3.0	3.5	3.5
Uzbekistan	2.5	7.4	7.0	7.5	9.5	9.0	8.1	8.5	8.3	7.4	6.5	5.5
Developing Asia	**7.0**	**8.5**	**9.5**	**10.3**	**11.4**	**7.9**	**7.0**	**9.5**	**7.8**	**6.7**	**7.2**	**7.7**
Afghanistan	...	1.1	11.2	5.6	13.7	3.6	21.0	8.4	5.8	5.2	6.5	4.2
Bangladesh	5.1	6.1	6.3	6.5	6.3	6.0	5.9	6.4	6.5	6.1	6.1	7.3
Bhutan	6.8	5.9	7.1	6.8	17.9	4.7	6.7	11.8	5.3	9.9	13.5	10.7
Brunei Darussalam	2.4	0.5	0.4	4.4	0.2	−1.9	−1.8	2.6	2.2	2.7	1.5	3.6
Cambodia	7.4	10.3	13.3	10.8	10.2	6.7	0.1	6.1	7.1	6.5	6.7	7.7
China	9.4	10.1	11.3	12.7	14.2	9.6	9.2	10.4	9.2	7.8	8.2	8.5
Fiji	2.7	5.5	2.5	1.9	−0.9	1.4	−1.3	−0.2	2.1	2.0	2.0	2.1
India	6.0	7.6	9.0	9.5	10.0	6.9	5.9	10.1	6.8	4.9	6.0	6.9
Indonesia	3.1	5.0	5.7	5.5	6.3	6.0	4.6	6.2	6.5	6.0	6.3	6.9
Kiribati	3.9	0.2	0.3	1.2	0.5	−2.4	−2.3	1.4	1.8	2.5	2.5	2.0
Lao P.D.R.	6.1	7.0	6.8	8.6	7.8	7.8	7.5	8.1	8.0	8.3	8.0	7.8
Malaysia	5.4	6.8	5.0	5.6	6.3	4.8	−1.5	7.2	5.1	4.4	4.7	5.0
Maldives	8.1	10.4	−8.7	19.6	10.6	12.2	−4.7	5.7	5.8	1.5	2.5	3.4
Myanmar	...	13.6	13.6	13.1	12.0	3.6	5.1	5.3	5.5	6.2	6.3	6.5
Nepal	4.5	4.7	3.5	3.4	3.4	6.1	4.5	4.8	3.9	4.6	3.6	4.0
Pakistan	3.9	7.5	9.0	5.8	6.8	3.7	1.7	3.1	3.0	3.7	3.3	3.5
Papua New Guinea	1.2	0.6	3.9	2.3	7.2	6.6	6.1	7.6	8.9	7.7	4.0	4.9
Philippines	3.8	6.7	4.8	5.2	6.6	4.2	1.1	7.6	3.9	4.8	4.8	5.0
Samoa	4.4	4.2	7.0	2.1	1.8	4.3	−5.1	0.4	2.0	1.5	1.9	2.5
Solomon Islands	−0.1	8.1	12.9	4.0	6.4	7.1	−4.7	7.8	10.7	7.4	4.0	4.0
Sri Lanka	4.4	5.4	6.2	7.7	6.8	6.0	3.5	7.8	8.3	6.7	6.7	6.5
Thailand	3.4	6.3	4.6	5.1	5.1	2.6	−2.3	7.8	0.1	5.6	6.0	5.0
Timor-Leste	...	4.4	6.5	−3.2	11.7	14.6	12.8	9.5	10.6	10.0	10.0	9.0
Tonga	2.1	2.2	0.7	−4.5	−2.4	0.5	0.9	1.6	1.5	1.4	1.5	1.8
Tuvalu	...	−1.4	−3.8	2.6	5.5	7.6	−1.7	−2.9	1.1	1.2	1.3	1.0
Vanuatu	2.0	4.5	5.2	7.4	6.5	6.2	3.5	1.5	2.5	2.6	4.3	4.0
Vietnam	7.4	7.8	8.4	8.2	8.5	6.3	5.3	6.8	5.9	5.1	5.9	7.5

Table A4. Emerging Market and Developing Economies: Real GDP [1] *(continued)*
(Annual percent change)

	Average 1994–2003	2004	2005	2006	2007	2008	2009	2010	2011	Projections 2012	2013	2017
Latin America and the Caribbean	**2.5**	**6.0**	**4.7**	**5.7**	**5.8**	**4.2**	**−1.5**	**6.2**	**4.5**	**3.2**	**3.9**	**4.0**
Antigua and Barbuda	2.9	3.2	7.6	12.8	7.1	1.5	−10.7	−8.5	−5.5	1.0	1.5	3.5
Argentina [4]	0.8	8.9	9.2	8.5	8.7	6.8	0.9	9.2	8.9	2.6	3.1	4.0
The Bahamas	4.2	0.9	3.4	2.5	1.4	−2.3	−4.9	0.2	1.6	2.5	2.7	2.5
Barbados	1.9	1.4	4.0	5.7	1.7	0.3	−4.1	0.2	0.6	0.7	1.0	2.5
Belize	5.0	4.6	3.0	4.7	1.3	3.5	0.0	2.7	2.0	2.3	2.5	2.5
Bolivia	3.4	2.7	6.8	2.8	5.3	6.1	3.4	4.1	5.2	5.0	5.0	5.0
Brazil	2.5	5.7	3.2	4.0	6.1	5.2	−0.3	7.5	2.7	1.5	4.0	4.1
Chile	4.6	6.8	6.3	5.8	5.2	3.1	−0.9	6.1	5.9	5.0	4.4	4.6
Colombia	2.3	5.3	4.7	6.7	6.9	3.5	1.7	4.0	5.9	4.3	4.4	4.5
Costa Rica	4.4	4.3	5.9	8.8	7.9	2.7	−1.0	4.7	4.2	4.8	4.3	4.5
Dominica	2.0	3.3	−0.5	4.5	6.0	7.9	−1.3	1.2	1.0	0.4	1.3	2.0
Dominican Republic	4.9	1.3	9.3	10.7	8.5	5.3	3.5	7.8	4.5	4.0	4.5	5.0
Ecuador	2.4	8.8	5.7	4.8	2.0	7.2	0.4	3.6	7.8	4.0	4.1	3.4
El Salvador	3.4	1.9	3.6	3.9	3.8	1.3	−3.1	1.4	1.4	1.5	2.0	3.0
Grenada	5.2	0.1	12.5	−4.4	6.3	1.7	−5.7	−1.3	0.4	0.5	0.5	2.5
Guatemala	3.4	3.2	3.3	5.4	6.3	3.3	0.5	2.9	3.9	3.1	3.2	3.5
Guyana	3.0	1.6	−1.9	5.1	7.0	2.0	3.3	4.4	5.4	3.7	5.5	3.3
Haiti	0.9	−3.5	1.8	2.2	3.3	0.8	2.9	−5.4	5.6	4.5	6.5	5.3
Honduras	2.9	6.2	6.1	6.6	6.2	4.1	−2.1	2.8	3.6	3.8	3.6	4.0
Jamaica	0.9	1.3	0.9	2.9	1.4	−0.8	−3.5	−1.5	1.3	0.9	1.0	1.5
Mexico	2.6	4.0	3.2	5.1	3.2	1.2	−6.0	5.6	3.9	3.8	3.5	3.3
Nicaragua	4.2	5.3	4.3	4.2	3.6	2.8	−1.5	4.5	4.7	3.7	4.0	4.0
Panama	3.9	7.5	7.2	8.5	12.1	10.1	3.9	7.6	10.6	8.5	7.5	6.0
Paraguay	1.7	4.1	2.1	4.8	5.4	6.4	−4.0	13.1	4.3	−1.5	11.0	4.7
Peru	4.3	5.0	6.8	7.7	8.9	9.8	0.9	8.8	6.9	6.0	5.8	6.0
St. Kitts and Nevis	3.6	3.8	9.2	3.5	5.0	4.0	−5.6	−2.7	−2.0	0.0	1.8	4.2
St. Lucia	1.4	8.4	−1.9	9.3	1.5	5.3	0.1	0.4	1.3	0.7	1.3	2.3
St. Vincent and the Grenadines	3.5	4.6	3.0	6.0	3.1	−0.6	−2.3	−1.8	0.0	1.2	1.5	3.0
Suriname	2.6	7.3	4.9	5.8	5.1	4.1	3.0	4.1	4.2	4.0	4.5	5.0
Trinidad and Tobago	7.2	7.9	6.2	13.2	4.8	2.7	−3.3	0.0	−1.5	0.7	2.2	3.0
Uruguay	0.7	4.6	6.8	4.1	6.5	7.2	2.4	8.9	5.7	3.5	4.0	4.0
Venezuela	−0.9	18.3	10.3	9.9	8.8	5.3	−3.2	−1.5	4.2	5.7	3.3	2.5
Middle East and North Africa	**4.0**	**6.2**	**5.3**	**6.3**	**5.7**	**4.5**	**2.6**	**5.0**	**3.3**	**5.3**	**3.6**	**4.5**
Algeria	3.2	5.2	5.1	2.0	3.0	2.4	2.4	3.3	2.4	2.6	3.4	4.0
Bahrain	4.2	5.6	7.9	6.7	8.4	6.3	3.2	4.7	2.1	2.0	2.8	2.8
Djibouti	0.2	3.0	3.2	4.8	5.1	5.8	5.0	3.5	4.5	4.8	5.0	5.8
Egypt	4.8	4.1	4.5	6.8	7.1	7.2	4.7	5.1	1.8	2.0	3.0	6.5
Iran	4.2	6.1	4.7	6.2	6.4	0.6	3.9	5.9	2.0	−0.9	0.8	2.0
Iraq	. . .	. . .	−0.7	6.2	1.5	9.5	2.9	3.0	8.9	10.2	14.7	9.4
Jordan	4.2	8.6	8.1	8.1	8.2	7.2	5.5	2.3	2.6	3.0	3.5	4.5
Kuwait	3.9	10.8	10.1	8.1	6.5	4.2	−7.8	2.5	8.2	6.3	1.9	3.9
Lebanon	3.6	7.5	1.0	0.6	7.5	9.3	8.5	7.0	1.5	2.0	2.5	4.0
Libya	0.4	4.5	11.9	6.5	6.4	2.4	−1.4	3.7	−59.7	121.9	16.7	3.9
Mauritania	2.9	5.2	5.4	11.4	1.0	3.5	−1.2	5.1	4.0	5.3	6.9	5.5
Morocco	3.9	4.8	3.0	7.8	2.7	5.6	4.9	3.7	4.9	2.9	5.5	5.9
Oman	3.2	3.4	4.0	5.5	6.7	13.1	3.9	5.0	5.4	5.0	3.9	3.7
Qatar	8.1	17.7	7.5	26.2	18.0	17.7	12.0	16.7	14.1	6.3	4.9	7.3
Saudi Arabia	2.2	5.3	5.6	3.2	2.0	4.2	0.1	5.1	7.1	6.0	4.2	4.2
Sudan [5]	14.3	6.5	3.7	11.9	12.2	2.3	4.6	2.2	−4.5	−11.2	0.0	5.0
Syria [6]	2.5	6.9	6.2	5.0	5.7	4.5	5.9	3.4	. . .	. . .	. . .	. . .
Tunisia	4.5	6.0	4.0	5.7	6.3	4.5	3.1	3.1	−1.8	2.7	3.3	6.0
United Arab Emirates	6.1	10.1	8.6	8.8	6.5	5.3	−4.8	1.3	5.2	4.0	2.6	3.6
Yemen	5.0	4.0	5.6	3.2	3.3	3.6	3.9	7.7	−10.5	−1.9	4.1	4.8

Table A4. Emerging Market and Developing Economies: Real GDP [1] (concluded)
(Annual percent change)

	Average 1994–2003	2004	2005	2006	2007	2008	2009	2010	2011	Projections 2012	2013	2017
Sub-Saharan Africa	**4.0**	**7.1**	**6.2**	**6.4**	**7.1**	**5.6**	**2.8**	**5.3**	**5.1**	**5.0**	**5.7**	**5.8**
Angola	6.7	11.2	20.6	20.7	22.6	13.8	2.4	3.4	3.9	6.8	5.5	5.3
Benin	4.7	3.1	2.9	3.8	4.6	5.0	2.7	2.6	3.5	3.5	3.8	4.5
Botswana	6.6	6.0	1.6	5.1	4.8	3.0	−4.7	7.0	5.1	3.8	4.1	4.7
Burkina Faso	5.9	4.5	8.7	6.3	4.1	5.8	3.0	7.9	4.2	7.0	7.0	6.8
Burundi	−1.1	3.8	4.4	5.4	4.8	5.0	3.5	3.8	4.2	4.2	4.5	5.9
Cameroon [7]	3.7	3.7	2.3	3.2	3.4	2.6	2.0	2.9	4.2	4.7	5.0	5.5
Cape Verde	7.2	4.3	6.5	10.1	8.6	6.2	3.7	5.2	5.0	4.3	4.4	5.0
Central African Republic	0.9	1.0	2.4	3.8	3.7	2.0	1.7	3.0	3.3	4.1	4.2	5.7
Chad	5.2	33.6	7.9	0.2	0.2	1.7	−1.2	13.0	1.8	7.3	2.4	2.8
Comoros	1.5	−0.2	4.2	1.2	0.5	1.0	1.8	2.1	2.2	2.5	3.5	4.0
Democratic Republic of the Congo	−1.6	6.6	7.8	5.6	6.3	6.2	2.8	7.2	6.9	7.1	8.2	7.9
Republic of Congo	1.9	3.5	7.8	6.2	−1.6	5.6	7.5	8.8	3.4	4.9	5.3	5.8
Côte d'Ivoire	1.7	1.6	1.9	0.7	1.6	2.3	3.7	2.4	−4.7	8.1	7.0	7.8
Equatorial Guinea	37.0	38.0	9.7	1.3	21.4	10.7	4.6	−0.5	7.8	5.7	6.1	3.7
Eritrea	3.6	1.5	2.6	−1.0	1.4	−9.8	3.9	2.2	8.7	7.5	3.4	−3.2
Ethiopia	4.0	11.7	12.6	11.5	11.8	11.2	10.0	8.0	7.5	7.0	6.5	6.5
Gabon	1.4	1.4	3.0	1.2	5.6	2.3	−1.4	6.6	6.6	6.1	2.0	2.3
The Gambia	3.9	7.0	−0.3	0.8	4.0	6.5	6.7	5.5	3.3	−1.6	9.7	5.6
Ghana	4.6	5.3	6.0	6.1	6.5	8.4	4.0	8.0	14.4	8.2	7.8	7.3
Guinea	4.0	2.3	3.0	2.5	1.8	4.9	−0.3	1.9	3.9	4.8	5.0	14.3
Guinea-Bissau	0.2	2.8	4.3	2.1	3.2	3.2	3.0	3.5	5.3	−2.8	5.7	4.5
Kenya	2.5	4.6	6.0	6.3	7.0	1.5	2.7	5.8	4.4	5.1	5.6	5.9
Lesotho	3.6	2.8	2.9	4.1	4.8	4.8	3.8	5.2	4.9	4.3	4.7	3.9
Liberia	...	4.1	5.9	9.0	13.2	6.2	5.3	6.1	8.2	9.0	7.9	5.7
Madagascar	2.2	5.3	4.6	5.0	6.2	7.1	−4.1	0.4	1.8	1.9	2.6	5.0
Malawi	2.6	5.5	2.6	2.1	9.5	8.3	9.0	6.5	4.3	4.3	5.7	6.7
Mali	4.9	2.3	6.1	5.3	4.3	5.0	4.5	5.8	2.7	−4.5	3.0	5.8
Mauritius	4.2	5.5	1.5	4.5	5.9	5.5	3.0	4.2	4.1	3.4	3.7	4.6
Mozambique	8.3	7.9	8.4	8.7	7.3	6.8	6.3	7.1	7.3	7.5	8.4	7.8
Namibia	3.6	12.3	2.5	7.1	5.4	3.4	−0.4	6.6	4.9	4.0	4.1	4.2
Niger	3.3	−0.8	8.4	5.8	3.1	9.6	−0.9	8.0	2.3	14.5	6.6	5.5
Nigeria	5.5	10.6	5.4	6.2	7.0	6.0	7.0	8.0	7.4	7.1	6.7	6.7
Rwanda	3.5	7.4	9.4	9.2	5.5	11.2	4.1	7.2	8.6	7.7	7.5	7.0
São Tomé and Príncipe	2.4	4.5	1.6	12.6	2.0	9.1	4.0	4.5	4.9	4.5	5.5	10.9
Senegal	3.8	5.9	5.6	2.4	5.0	3.7	2.1	4.1	2.6	3.7	4.3	5.6
Seychelles	2.1	−2.9	8.0	8.9	9.9	−1.0	0.5	6.7	5.1	3.0	3.5	3.8
Sierra Leone	−1.1	6.5	4.4	4.4	8.0	5.4	3.2	5.3	6.0	21.3	7.5	5.0
South Africa	3.0	4.6	5.3	5.6	5.5	3.6	−1.5	2.9	3.1	2.6	3.0	4.1
South Sudan	...	...	...	...	...	...	...	...	1.4	−55.0	69.6	6.1
Swaziland	2.8	2.3	2.2	2.9	2.8	3.1	1.2	2.0	0.3	−2.9	−1.0	0.2
Tanzania	4.5	7.8	7.4	6.7	7.1	7.4	6.0	7.0	6.4	6.5	6.8	7.0
Togo	3.3	2.1	1.2	4.1	2.3	2.4	3.5	4.0	4.9	5.0	5.3	5.8
Uganda	7.1	6.6	8.6	9.5	8.6	7.7	7.0	6.1	5.1	4.2	5.7	7.0
Zambia	1.0	5.4	5.3	6.2	6.2	5.7	6.4	7.6	6.6	6.5	8.2	7.7
Zimbabwe [8]	...	−6.0	−5.5	−3.5	−3.8	−18.3	6.3	9.6	9.4	5.0	6.0	4.0

[1] For many countries, figures for recent years are IMF staff estimates. Data for some countries are for fiscal years.
[2] Data for some countries refer to real net material product (NMP) or are estimates based on NMP. For many countries, figures for recent years are IMF staff estimates. The figures should be interpreted only as indicative of broad orders of magnitude because reliable, comparable data are not generally available. In particular, the growth of output of new private enterprises of the informal economy is not fully reflected in the recent figures.
[3] Georgia and Mongolia, which are not members of the Commonwealth of Independent States, are included in this group for reasons of geography and similarities in economic structure.
[4] Figures are based on Argentina's official GDP data. The IMF has called on Argentina to adopt remedial measures to address the quality of these data. The IMF staff is also using alternative measures of GDP growth for macroeconomic surveillance, including data produced by private analysts, which have shown significantly lower real GDP growth than the official data since 2008.
[5] Data for 2011 exclude South Sudan after July 9. Data for 2012 and onward pertain to the current Sudan.
[6] Data for Syria are excluded for 2011 onward due to the uncertain political situation.
[7] The percent changes in 2002 are calculated over a period of 18 months, reflecting a change in the fiscal year cycle (from July–June to January–December).
[8] The Zimbabwe dollar ceased circulating in early 2009. Data are based on IMF staff estimates of price and exchange rate developments in U.S. dollars. IMF staff estimates of U.S. dollar values may differ from authorities' estimates. Real GDP is in constant 2009 prices.

Table A5. Summary of Inflation
(Percent)

	Average 1994–2003	2004	2005	2006	2007	2008	2009	2010	2011	Projections 2012	2013	2017
GDP Deflators												
Advanced Economies	**1.7**	**2.0**	**2.1**	**2.1**	**2.2**	**2.0**	**0.7**	**1.1**	**1.4**	**1.4**	**1.3**	**1.9**
United States	1.9	2.8	3.3	3.2	2.9	2.2	0.9	1.3	2.1	1.6	1.3	2.1
Euro Area	2.0	1.9	1.9	1.8	2.4	2.0	1.0	0.8	1.2	1.5	1.4	1.7
Japan	−0.8	−1.4	−1.3	−1.1	−0.9	−1.3	−0.5	−2.2	−2.1	−0.8	−1.0	0.7
Other Advanced Economies [1]	2.2	2.4	2.0	2.1	2.5	3.0	0.8	2.4	2.0	1.9	2.2	2.2
Consumer Prices												
Advanced Economies	**2.1**	**2.0**	**2.3**	**2.3**	**2.2**	**3.4**	**0.1**	**1.5**	**2.7**	**1.9**	**1.6**	**1.9**
United States	2.4	2.7	3.4	3.2	2.9	3.8	−0.3	1.6	3.1	2.0	1.8	2.1
Euro Area [2]	2.0	2.2	2.2	2.2	2.1	3.3	0.3	1.6	2.7	2.3	1.6	1.7
Japan	0.0	0.0	−0.3	0.2	0.1	1.4	−1.3	−0.7	−0.3	0.0	−0.2	1.0
Other Advanced Economies [1]	2.3	1.7	2.1	2.1	2.1	3.8	1.4	2.4	3.4	2.3	2.2	2.2
Emerging Market and Developing Economies	**19.8**	**5.9**	**5.8**	**5.6**	**6.5**	**9.3**	**5.1**	**6.1**	**7.2**	**6.1**	**5.8**	**4.6**
Regional Groups												
Central and Eastern Europe	37.7	6.6	5.9	5.9	6.0	8.1	4.7	5.3	5.3	5.6	4.4	3.6
Commonwealth of Independent States [3]	62.9	10.4	12.1	9.4	9.7	15.6	11.2	7.2	10.1	6.8	7.7	6.8
Developing Asia	6.1	4.1	3.7	4.2	5.4	7.4	3.0	5.7	6.5	5.0	4.9	3.8
Latin America and the Caribbean	25.6	6.6	6.3	5.3	5.4	7.9	6.0	6.0	6.6	6.0	5.9	5.4
Middle East and North Africa	8.0	6.6	6.5	7.7	10.2	13.5	6.6	6.9	9.7	10.4	9.1	6.6
Sub-Saharan Africa	20.2	7.4	9.0	7.0	7.0	12.6	9.4	7.5	9.7	9.1	7.1	5.6
Memorandum												
European Union	4.2	2.3	2.3	2.3	2.4	3.6	0.9	2.0	3.1	2.5	1.8	1.9
Analytical Groups												
By Source of Export Earnings												
Fuel	32.9	9.8	10.0	9.1	10.2	15.0	9.3	8.1	10.2	9.1	9.0	7.6
Nonfuel	16.6	5.0	4.8	4.7	5.6	7.9	4.2	5.6	6.6	5.5	5.1	4.0
Of Which, Primary Products	19.9	4.4	5.5	5.4	5.6	9.7	5.7	4.7	6.9	7.0	5.5	4.2
By External Financing Source												
Net Debtor Economies	22.0	5.6	5.9	5.9	6.2	9.1	7.3	7.2	7.6	7.3	6.7	4.9
Of Which, Official Financing	19.8	6.2	8.2	7.7	8.1	15.2	6.7	7.0	11.2	9.3	7.3	5.6
Net Debtor Economies by Debt-Servicing Experience												
Economies with Arrears and/or Rescheduling during 2006–10	18.7	7.9	8.1	8.9	8.3	11.5	6.6	7.9	11.8	11.9	9.3	7.3
Memorandum												
Median Inflation Rate												
Advanced Economies	2.2	2.0	2.1	2.2	2.2	3.9	0.6	2.0	3.1	2.4	2.0	2.0
Emerging Market and Developing Economies	6.7	4.4	5.6	6.1	6.3	10.3	4.1	4.3	5.8	5.1	5.0	4.0

[1] In this table, Other Advanced Economies means advanced economies excluding the United States, Euro Area countries, and Japan.
[2] Based on Eurostat's harmonized index of consumer prices.
[3] Georgia and Mongolia, which are not members of the Commonwealth of Independent States, are included in this group for reasons of geography and similarities in economic structure.

Table A6. Advanced Economies: Consumer Prices
(Annual percent change)

	Average 1994–2003	2004	2005	2006	2007	2008	2009	2010	2011	Projections 2012	2013	2017	End of Period [1] 2011	Projections 2012	2013
Advanced Economies	**2.1**	**2.0**	**2.3**	**2.3**	**2.2**	**3.4**	**0.1**	**1.5**	**2.7**	**1.9**	**1.6**	**1.9**	**2.5**	**1.7**	**1.7**
United States	2.4	2.7	3.4	3.2	2.9	3.8	−0.3	1.6	3.1	2.0	1.8	2.1	3.1	1.6	1.8
Euro Area [2]	2.0	2.2	2.2	2.2	2.1	3.3	0.3	1.6	2.7	2.3	1.6	1.7	2.7	2.1	1.7
Germany	1.4	1.8	1.9	1.8	2.3	2.8	0.2	1.2	2.5	2.2	1.9	2.1	2.3	2.2	1.9
France	1.5	2.1	1.8	1.7	1.5	2.8	0.1	1.5	2.1	1.9	1.0	1.9	2.1	1.9	1.0
Italy	2.9	2.3	2.2	2.2	2.0	3.5	0.8	1.6	2.9	3.0	1.8	1.4	3.7	1.5	2.9
Spain	3.2	3.1	3.4	3.6	2.8	4.1	−0.2	2.0	3.1	2.4	2.4	1.4	2.4	3.3	1.4
Netherlands	2.5	1.4	1.5	1.7	1.6	2.2	1.0	0.9	2.5	2.2	1.8	2.1	2.3	2.0	1.8
Belgium	1.7	1.9	2.5	2.3	1.8	4.5	0.0	2.3	3.5	2.8	1.9	1.2	3.2	2.6	1.5
Austria	1.6	2.0	2.1	1.7	2.2	3.2	0.4	1.7	3.6	2.3	1.9	1.9	3.4	1.9	1.9
Greece	5.4	2.9	3.5	3.2	2.9	4.2	1.2	4.7	3.3	0.9	−1.1	0.6	2.2	0.4	−0.7
Portugal	3.2	2.5	2.1	3.0	2.4	2.7	−0.9	1.4	3.6	2.8	0.7	1.5	3.5	2.3	0.2
Finland	1.6	0.1	0.8	1.3	1.6	3.9	1.6	1.7	3.3	2.9	2.3	2.0	2.6	2.6	2.3
Ireland	3.1	2.3	2.2	2.7	2.9	3.1	−1.7	−1.6	1.2	1.4	1.0	1.8	1.4	1.2	1.0
Slovak Republic	8.3	7.5	2.8	4.3	1.9	3.9	0.9	0.7	4.1	3.6	2.3	2.3	4.7	2.5	2.6
Slovenia	9.6	3.6	2.5	2.5	3.6	5.7	0.9	1.8	1.8	2.2	1.5	2.1	2.1	1.7	1.4
Luxembourg	1.9	3.2	3.8	3.0	2.7	4.1	0.0	2.8	3.7	2.5	2.3	2.3	3.4	1.8	2.3
Estonia	12.9	3.0	4.1	4.4	6.6	10.4	−0.1	2.9	5.1	4.4	3.2	2.8	4.1	5.0	3.2
Cyprus	3.0	1.9	2.0	2.2	2.2	4.4	0.2	2.6	3.5	3.1	2.2	2.0	4.2	2.7	2.2
Malta	3.0	2.7	2.5	2.6	0.7	4.7	1.8	2.0	2.5	3.5	2.2	2.2	1.5	3.5	2.6
Japan	0.0	0.0	−0.3	0.2	0.1	1.4	−1.3	−0.7	−0.3	0.0	−0.2	1.0	−0.3	−0.2	0.3
United Kingdom [2]	1.7	1.3	2.0	2.3	2.3	3.6	2.1	3.3	4.5	2.7	1.9	1.9	4.7	2.2	1.7
Canada	1.8	1.8	2.2	2.0	2.1	2.4	0.3	1.8	2.9	1.8	2.0	2.0	2.7	1.7	2.0
Korea	4.1	3.6	2.8	2.2	2.5	4.7	2.8	2.9	4.0	2.2	2.7	3.0	4.2	2.2	3.0
Australia	2.6	2.3	2.7	3.5	2.3	4.4	1.8	2.8	3.4	2.0	2.6	2.4	3.1	3.3	1.0
Taiwan Province of China	1.4	1.6	2.3	0.6	1.8	3.5	−0.9	1.0	1.4	2.5	2.0	2.0	−3.4	2.5	2.0
Sweden	1.3	0.4	0.5	1.4	2.2	3.4	−0.5	1.2	3.0	1.4	2.0	2.0	0.4	0.9	2.0
Hong Kong SAR	1.7	−0.4	0.9	2.0	2.0	4.3	0.6	2.3	5.3	3.8	3.0	3.0	5.7	3.8	3.0
Switzerland	0.9	0.8	1.2	1.1	0.7	2.4	−0.5	0.7	0.2	−0.5	0.5	1.0	−0.7	−0.5	0.5
Singapore	1.0	1.7	0.5	1.0	2.1	6.6	0.6	2.8	5.2	4.5	4.3	2.5	5.5	3.8	4.9
Czech Republic	...	2.8	1.8	2.5	2.9	6.3	1.0	1.5	1.9	3.4	2.1	2.0	2.4	3.1	2.2
Norway	2.2	0.5	1.5	2.3	0.7	3.8	2.2	2.4	1.3	1.0	2.2	2.5	0.2	1.7	1.8
Israel	6.1	−0.4	1.3	2.1	0.5	4.6	3.3	2.7	3.4	1.7	2.1	2.0	2.2	2.0	2.0
Denmark	2.1	1.2	1.8	1.9	1.7	3.4	1.3	2.3	2.8	2.6	2.0	1.8	2.5	2.7	2.1
New Zealand	2.0	2.3	3.0	3.4	2.4	4.0	2.1	2.3	4.0	1.9	2.4	2.0	1.8	2.4	2.5
Iceland	3.1	3.2	4.0	6.8	5.0	12.4	12.0	5.4	4.0	5.6	4.4	2.5	5.3	5.3	3.7
San Marino	...	1.4	1.7	2.1	2.5	4.1	2.4	2.6	2.0	3.0	2.1	1.4	2.0	1.9	1.8
Memorandum															
Major Advanced Economies	1.8	2.0	2.3	2.3	2.2	3.2	−0.1	1.4	2.6	1.8	1.5	1.9	2.6	1.5	1.6
Newly Industrialized Asian Economies	2.8	2.4	2.2	1.6	2.2	4.5	1.3	2.3	3.6	2.7	2.7	2.7	2.3	2.6	2.9

[1] December–December changes. Several countries report Q4–Q4 changes.
[2] Based on Eurostat's harmonized index of consumer prices.

Table A7. Emerging Market and Developing Economies: Consumer Prices [1]
(Annual percent change)

	Average 1994–2003	2004	2005	2006	2007	2008	2009	2010	2011	Projections 2012	Projections 2013	Projections 2017	End of Period [2] 2011	End of Period [2] Projections 2012	End of Period [2] Projections 2013
Central and Eastern Europe [3]	**37.7**	**6.6**	**5.9**	**5.9**	**6.0**	**8.1**	**4.7**	**5.3**	**5.3**	**5.6**	**4.4**	**3.6**	**6.4**	**4.8**	**4.0**
Albania	10.3	2.9	2.4	2.4	2.9	3.4	2.2	3.6	3.4	2.0	3.0	3.0	1.7	3.0	3.0
Bosnia and Herzegovina	...	0.3	3.6	6.1	1.5	7.4	−0.4	2.1	3.7	2.2	2.1	2.4	2.7	2.2	2.1
Bulgaria	62.5	6.1	6.0	7.4	7.6	12.0	2.5	3.0	3.4	1.9	2.3	3.0	2.0	2.1	2.5
Croatia	10.4	2.0	3.3	3.2	2.9	6.1	2.4	1.0	2.3	3.0	3.0	3.0	2.0	3.7	3.0
Hungary	14.0	6.8	3.6	3.9	7.9	6.1	4.2	4.9	3.9	5.6	3.5	3.0	4.1	5.4	3.5
Kosovo	...	−1.1	−1.4	0.6	4.4	9.4	−2.4	3.5	7.3	0.6	1.2	1.3	3.6	1.0	1.9
Latvia	9.8	6.2	6.9	6.6	10.1	15.3	3.3	−1.2	4.2	2.4	2.2	2.2	3.9	2.1	2.0
Lithuania	...	1.2	2.7	3.8	5.8	11.1	4.2	1.2	4.1	3.2	2.4	2.4	3.5	3.4	2.3
FYR Macedonia	12.4	−0.4	0.5	3.2	2.3	8.4	−0.8	1.5	3.9	2.0	2.0	2.0	2.8	2.0	2.0
Montenegro	...	3.1	3.4	2.1	3.5	9.0	3.6	0.7	3.1	3.4	3.0	3.4	2.8	3.8	2.9
Poland	12.8	3.5	2.1	1.0	2.5	4.2	3.5	2.5	4.3	3.9	2.7	2.5	4.6	3.2	2.5
Romania	53.2	11.9	9.0	6.6	4.8	7.8	5.6	6.1	5.8	2.9	3.2	2.6	3.1	3.6	3.2
Serbia	...	10.6	16.2	10.7	6.9	12.4	8.1	6.2	11.1	5.9	7.5	3.7	7.0	8.6	5.0
Turkey	67.3	8.6	8.2	9.6	8.8	10.4	6.3	8.6	6.5	8.7	6.5	5.0	10.4	6.5	5.7
Commonwealth of Independent States [3,4]	**62.9**	**10.4**	**12.1**	**9.4**	**9.7**	**15.6**	**11.2**	**7.2**	**10.1**	**6.8**	**7.7**	**6.8**	**9.2**	**7.4**	**7.4**
Russia	57.5	10.9	12.7	9.7	9.0	14.1	11.7	6.9	8.4	5.1	6.6	6.5	6.1	6.7	6.5
Excluding Russia	79.1	9.1	10.6	8.8	11.6	19.5	10.1	7.9	14.0	10.8	10.2	7.6	17.0	9.2	9.6
Armenia	72.9	7.0	0.6	3.0	4.6	9.0	3.5	7.3	7.7	2.8	4.2	4.0	4.7	2.8	4.0
Azerbaijan	62.4	6.7	9.7	8.4	16.6	20.8	1.6	5.7	7.9	3.0	6.0	5.0	5.6	6.5	5.5
Belarus	175.7	18.1	10.3	7.0	8.4	14.8	13.0	7.7	53.2	60.2	30.6	17.4	108.7	27.6	29.8
Georgia	...	5.7	8.2	9.2	9.2	10.0	1.7	7.1	8.5	0.2	5.5	6.0	2.0	3.0	6.0
Kazakhstan	59.9	6.9	7.5	8.6	10.8	17.1	7.3	7.1	8.3	5.0	6.6	6.0	7.4	5.7	6.6
Kyrgyz Republic	29.4	4.1	4.3	5.6	10.2	24.5	6.8	7.8	16.6	2.9	9.4	5.9	5.7	8.0	7.5
Moldova	34.6	12.4	11.9	12.7	12.4	12.7	0.0	7.4	7.6	5.1	5.0	5.0	7.8	5.0	5.0
Mongolia	24.2	7.9	12.5	4.5	8.2	26.8	6.3	10.2	7.7	14.1	11.7	7.0	9.4	12.9	10.4
Tajikistan	105.9	7.2	7.3	10.0	13.2	20.4	6.5	6.5	12.4	6.0	8.1	7.0	9.3	6.5	8.0
Turkmenistan	146.2	5.9	10.7	8.2	6.3	14.5	−2.7	4.4	5.3	4.3	6.0	7.0	5.6	5.0	7.0
Ukraine	70.2	9.0	13.5	9.1	12.8	25.2	15.9	9.4	8.0	2.0	7.4	5.0	4.6	6.0	5.9
Uzbekistan	91.6	6.6	10.0	14.2	12.3	12.7	14.1	9.4	12.8	12.9	10.7	11.0	13.3	11.0	11.0
Developing Asia	**6.1**	**4.1**	**3.7**	**4.2**	**5.4**	**7.4**	**3.0**	**5.7**	**6.5**	**5.0**	**4.9**	**3.8**	**5.1**	**5.5**	**4.8**
Afghanistan	...	13.2	12.3	5.1	13.0	26.8	−12.2	7.7	11.8	6.6	6.7	5.0	11.3	5.9	5.4
Bangladesh	5.2	6.1	7.0	6.8	9.1	8.9	5.4	8.1	10.7	8.5	6.7	5.5	10.6	6.9	6.4
Bhutan	6.1	4.6	5.3	5.0	5.2	8.3	4.4	7.0	8.9	9.4	7.8	6.4	6.5	10.5	6.7
Brunei Darussalam	1.1	0.9	1.1	0.2	1.0	2.1	1.0	0.4	2.0	1.7	1.4	1.3	1.8	1.6	1.4
Cambodia	5.3	3.9	6.3	6.1	7.7	25.0	−0.7	4.0	5.5	3.6	4.4	3.0	4.9	4.6	4.6
China	4.9	3.9	1.8	1.5	4.8	5.9	−0.7	3.3	5.4	3.0	3.0	3.0	4.1	2.8	3.1
Fiji	2.7	2.8	2.3	2.5	4.8	7.7	3.7	5.5	8.7	4.7	4.5	3.5	7.8	4.5	4.5
India	7.0	3.9	4.0	6.3	6.4	8.3	10.9	12.0	8.9	10.2	9.6	5.0	6.5	13.0	9.3
Indonesia	13.7	6.1	10.5	13.1	6.7	9.8	4.8	5.1	5.4	4.4	5.1	4.0	3.8	5.0	5.1
Kiribati	2.5	−0.9	−0.3	−1.5	4.2	11.0	8.8	−2.8	2.8	2.5	3.0	2.5	2.8	2.5	3.0
Lao P.D.R.	29.7	10.5	7.2	6.8	4.5	7.6	0.0	6.0	7.6	5.1	6.8	4.2	7.7	5.3	6.2
Malaysia	2.7	1.4	3.0	3.6	2.0	5.4	0.6	1.7	3.2	2.0	2.4	2.5	3.0	2.0	2.4
Maldives	2.1	6.3	2.5	3.5	7.4	12.3	4.0	4.7	14.1	12.3	8.3	3.0	20.8	8.0	8.0
Myanmar	...	3.8	10.7	26.3	32.9	22.5	8.2	8.2	4.0	5.8	6.5	5.0	5.0	5.6	5.3
Nepal	6.5	4.0	4.5	8.0	6.2	6.7	12.6	9.5	9.6	8.3	8.0	6.5	9.7	11.5	7.3
Pakistan	7.3	4.0	9.3	8.0	7.8	10.8	17.6	10.1	13.7	11.0	10.4	13.0	13.3	11.3	11.8
Papua New Guinea	11.5	2.1	1.8	2.4	0.9	10.8	6.9	6.0	8.4	6.8	6.7	6.5	6.9	6.8	6.7
Philippines	6.3	4.8	6.6	5.5	2.9	8.2	4.2	3.8	4.7	3.5	4.5	4.0	4.2	4.6	4.0
Samoa	4.0	7.8	7.8	3.5	4.7	6.3	14.6	−0.2	2.9	6.2	2.0	4.0	2.9	5.5	4.0
Solomon Islands	9.7	6.9	7.5	11.2	7.7	17.3	7.1	0.9	7.4	6.6	3.3	4.3	9.4	4.6	4.5
Sri Lanka	9.4	9.0	11.0	10.0	15.8	22.4	3.5	6.2	6.7	7.9	8.0	6.0	4.9	10.1	7.2
Thailand	3.6	2.8	4.5	4.6	2.2	5.5	−0.8	3.3	3.8	3.2	3.3	2.7	3.5	4.7	1.9
Timor-Leste	...	3.2	1.1	3.9	10.3	9.0	0.7	6.8	13.5	12.0	8.0	8.0	17.4	9.0	8.0
Tonga	5.1	10.8	8.5	6.1	7.4	7.4	3.5	3.9	5.3	4.5	5.3	6.0	5.4	4.5	6.0
Tuvalu	...	2.4	3.2	4.2	2.3	10.4	−0.3	−1.9	0.5	2.6	2.7	2.7	...	...	...
Vanuatu	2.5	1.4	1.2	2.0	3.9	4.8	4.3	2.8	0.9	2.0	3.0	3.0	1.2	2.2	3.0
Vietnam	5.1	7.9	8.4	7.5	8.3	23.1	6.7	9.2	18.7	8.1	6.2	5.0	18.1	4.5	5.6

Table A7. Emerging Market and Developing Economies: Consumer Prices [1] (continued)
(Annual percent change)

	Average 1994–2003	2004	2005	2006	2007	2008	2009	2010	2011	Projections 2012	Projections 2013	Projections 2017	End of Period [2] 2011	Projections 2012	Projections 2013
Latin America and the Caribbean	**25.6**	**6.6**	**6.3**	**5.3**	**5.4**	**7.9**	**6.0**	**6.0**	**6.6**	**6.0**	**5.9**	**5.4**	**6.8**	**5.8**	**5.9**
Antigua and Barbuda	2.2	2.0	2.1	1.8	1.4	5.3	−0.6	3.4	3.5	3.8	3.0	2.4	4.0	3.0	3.1
Argentina [5]	4.2	4.4	9.6	10.9	8.8	8.6	6.3	10.5	9.8	9.9	9.7	9.8	9.5	9.9	9.9
The Bahamas	1.7	1.2	2.0	1.8	2.5	4.4	2.1	1.0	2.5	2.0	2.0	2.0	4.0	1.5	2.0
Barbados	1.8	1.4	6.1	7.3	4.0	8.1	3.7	5.8	9.4	8.2	4.8	4.5	9.5	6.4	4.5
Belize	1.7	3.1	3.7	4.2	2.3	6.4	−1.1	0.9	1.5	2.2	2.2	2.5	2.5	1.9	2.5
Bolivia	5.5	8.1	5.2	4.1	8.7	10.3	6.5	2.5	9.9	4.8	4.7	4.0	6.9	5.0	4.5
Brazil	52.7	6.6	6.9	4.2	3.6	5.7	4.9	5.0	6.6	5.2	4.9	4.5	6.5	5.0	5.1
Chile	5.4	1.1	3.1	3.4	4.4	8.7	1.5	1.4	3.3	3.1	3.0	3.0	4.4	2.5	3.0
Colombia	14.2	5.9	5.0	4.3	5.5	7.0	4.2	2.3	3.4	3.2	2.8	3.0	3.7	2.7	3.0
Costa Rica	12.9	12.3	13.8	11.5	9.4	13.4	7.8	5.7	4.9	4.6	5.0	4.0	4.7	5.0	5.0
Dominica	1.2	2.4	1.6	2.6	3.2	6.4	0.0	2.8	1.4	2.3	2.3	2.0	2.0	3.6	1.5
Dominican Republic	9.3	51.5	4.2	7.6	6.1	10.6	1.4	6.3	8.5	4.1	4.8	4.0	7.8	4.5	5.0
Ecuador	33.0	2.7	2.1	3.3	2.3	8.4	5.2	3.6	4.5	5.1	4.3	3.0	5.4	4.6	4.5
El Salvador	4.4	4.5	4.7	4.0	4.6	7.3	0.4	1.2	3.6	4.0	2.9	2.8	5.1	3.0	2.8
Grenada	1.6	2.3	3.5	4.3	3.9	8.0	−0.3	3.4	3.0	3.2	2.2	2.0	3.5	2.4	2.2
Guatemala	8.0	7.6	9.1	6.6	6.8	11.4	1.9	3.9	6.2	3.9	4.1	4.0	6.2	4.1	4.0
Guyana	6.7	4.7	6.9	6.7	12.2	8.1	3.0	3.7	5.0	3.0	5.6	4.0	3.3	4.6	6.0
Haiti	19.0	28.3	16.8	14.2	9.0	14.4	3.4	4.1	7.4	6.7	5.9	3.4	10.4	6.0	5.0
Honduras	15.4	8.1	8.8	5.6	6.9	11.4	5.5	4.7	6.8	5.8	6.7	5.9	5.6	6.5	6.5
Jamaica	13.4	13.5	15.1	8.5	9.3	22.0	9.6	12.6	7.5	7.3	8.2	6.4	6.0	7.2	8.0
Mexico	15.0	4.7	4.0	3.6	4.0	5.1	5.3	4.2	3.4	4.0	3.5	3.0	3.8	4.0	3.3
Nicaragua	8.2	8.5	9.6	9.7	9.3	16.8	11.6	3.0	7.4	8.2	8.3	6.9	8.0	8.0	7.5
Panama	1.0	0.5	2.9	2.5	4.2	8.8	2.4	3.5	5.9	6.0	5.5	4.0	6.3	6.2	5.5
Paraguay	10.9	4.3	6.8	9.6	8.1	10.2	2.6	4.7	6.6	5.0	5.0	4.1	4.9	5.0	5.0
Peru	7.2	3.7	1.6	2.0	1.8	5.8	2.9	1.5	3.4	3.7	2.5	2.0	4.7	3.0	2.0
St. Kitts and Nevis	3.1	2.2	3.4	8.5	4.5	5.3	2.1	0.6	7.1	2.5	2.5	2.5	2.9	1.9	2.5
St. Lucia	2.6	1.5	3.9	3.6	2.8	5.5	−0.2	3.3	2.8	3.2	2.8	3.0	4.8	2.2	2.9
St. Vincent and the Grenadines	1.3	2.9	3.4	3.0	7.0	10.1	0.4	0.8	3.2	2.6	1.7	2.5	4.7	0.8	2.6
Suriname	62.0	9.1	9.6	11.1	6.6	15.0	0.0	6.9	17.7	6.2	5.5	4.0	15.3	5.7	5.0
Trinidad and Tobago	4.2	3.7	6.9	8.3	7.9	12.0	7.0	10.5	5.1	10.0	6.5	4.0	5.3	9.0	4.0
Uruguay	18.6	9.2	4.7	6.4	8.1	7.9	7.1	6.7	8.1	7.9	7.6	6.0	8.6	8.0	7.3
Venezuela	39.1	21.7	16.0	13.7	18.7	30.4	27.1	28.2	26.1	23.2	28.8	27.3	27.6	22.0	29.2
Middle East and North Africa	**8.0**	**6.6**	**6.5**	**7.7**	**10.2**	**13.5**	**6.6**	**6.9**	**9.7**	**10.4**	**9.1**	**6.6**	**10.1**	**9.2**	**8.9**
Algeria	9.4	3.6	1.6	2.3	3.6	4.9	5.7	3.9	4.5	8.4	5.0	4.0	5.2	6.3	5.0
Bahrain	0.9	2.2	2.6	2.0	3.3	3.5	2.8	2.0	−0.4	0.6	2.0	2.0	0.2	3.0	2.0
Djibouti	2.5	3.1	3.1	3.5	5.0	12.0	1.7	4.0	5.1	4.7	2.4	2.4	7.6	2.4	1.3
Egypt	5.1	8.1	8.8	4.2	11.0	11.7	16.2	11.7	11.1	8.6	10.7	6.5	11.8	7.3	12.3
Iran	21.4	15.3	10.4	11.9	18.4	25.4	10.8	12.4	21.5	25.2	21.8	15.5	21.8	22.0	20.3
Iraq	...	...	37.0	53.2	30.8	2.7	−2.2	2.4	5.6	6.0	5.5	4.0	6.0	6.0	5.5
Jordan	2.5	3.4	3.5	6.3	4.7	13.9	−0.7	5.0	4.4	4.5	3.9	3.0	3.3	4.4	4.2
Kuwait	1.7	1.3	4.1	3.1	5.5	10.6	4.0	4.0	4.7	4.3	4.1	4.1	4.7	4.3	4.1
Lebanon	4.1	1.7	−0.7	5.6	4.1	10.8	1.2	4.5	5.0	6.5	5.7	2.0	3.1	10.1	2.0
Libya	0.7	1.3	2.7	1.5	6.2	10.4	2.4	2.5	15.9	10.0	0.9	4.0	26.6	−1.7	3.1
Mauritania	4.9	10.4	12.1	6.2	7.3	7.5	2.1	6.3	5.7	5.9	6.1	5.1	5.5	6.0	6.3
Morocco	2.5	1.5	1.0	3.3	2.0	3.9	1.0	1.0	0.9	2.2	2.5	2.6	0.9	2.5	2.5
Oman	−0.3	0.7	1.9	3.4	5.9	12.6	3.5	3.3	4.0	3.2	3.0	3.3	3.3	4.7	3.0
Qatar	2.5	6.8	8.8	11.8	13.8	15.0	−4.9	−2.4	1.9	2.0	3.0	4.0	1.9	2.0	3.0
Saudi Arabia	0.4	0.4	0.6	2.3	4.1	9.9	5.1	5.4	5.0	4.9	4.6	4.0	5.3	4.7	4.0
Sudan [6]	36.4	8.4	8.5	7.2	8.0	14.3	11.3	13.0	18.3	28.6	17.0	6.8	18.9	28.6	17.0
Syria [7]	3.2	4.4	7.2	10.4	4.7	15.2	2.8	4.4	...	...	...	...	...	...	...
Tunisia	3.5	3.6	2.0	4.1	3.4	4.9	3.5	4.4	3.5	5.0	4.0	3.5	3.5	5.0	4.0
United Arab Emirates	3.0	5.0	6.2	9.3	11.1	12.3	1.6	0.9	0.9	0.7	1.6	2.1	0.8	1.1	1.7
Yemen	22.6	12.5	9.9	10.8	7.9	19.0	3.7	11.2	19.5	15.0	12.7	7.1	23.2	14.0	11.5

Table A7. Emerging Market and Developing Economies: Consumer Prices [1] *(concluded)*
(Annual percent change)

	Average 1994–2003	2004	2005	2006	2007	2008	2009	2010	2011	Projections 2012	2013	2017	End of Period [2] 2011	Projections 2012	2013
Sub-Saharan Africa	**20.2**	**7.4**	**9.0**	**7.0**	**7.0**	**12.6**	**9.4**	**7.5**	**9.7**	**9.1**	**7.1**	**5.6**	**10.6**	**8.2**	**6.8**
Angola	413.6	43.6	23.0	13.3	12.2	12.5	13.7	14.5	13.5	10.8	8.6	7.4	11.4	9.6	7.5
Benin	7.5	0.9	5.4	3.8	1.3	7.4	0.9	2.1	2.7	6.9	3.3	2.8	1.8	7.2	3.3
Botswana	8.7	7.0	8.6	11.6	7.1	12.6	8.1	6.9	8.5	7.5	6.2	5.4	9.2	6.4	6.0
Burkina Faso	5.2	−0.4	6.4	2.4	−0.2	10.7	2.6	−0.6	2.7	3.0	2.0	2.0	5.1	3.0	2.0
Burundi	14.6	11.8	1.2	9.1	14.4	26.0	4.6	4.1	14.9	14.7	8.4	5.5	14.9	14.7	8.4
Cameroon [8]	6.1	0.3	2.0	4.9	1.1	5.3	3.0	1.3	2.9	3.0	3.0	2.5	2.7	3.0	3.0
Cape Verde	3.9	−1.9	0.4	4.8	4.4	6.8	1.0	2.1	4.5	2.1	2.0	2.0	3.6	2.3	2.3
Central African Republic	5.6	−2.2	2.9	6.7	0.9	9.3	3.5	1.5	1.2	6.8	1.6	1.8	4.3	2.9	2.3
Chad	7.3	−4.8	3.7	7.7	−7.4	8.3	10.1	−2.1	1.9	5.5	3.0	3.0	10.8	5.5	3.0
Comoros	5.0	4.5	3.0	3.4	4.5	4.8	4.8	3.9	6.8	5.6	3.1	3.4	7.0	4.3	2.0
Democratic Republic of the Congo	382.7	4.0	21.4	13.2	16.7	18.0	46.2	23.5	15.5	10.4	9.5	7.2	15.4	9.9	9.0
Republic of Congo	7.7	3.7	2.5	4.7	2.6	6.0	4.3	5.0	1.8	5.1	4.5	2.7	1.8	5.3	4.1
Côte d'Ivoire	6.3	1.5	3.9	2.5	1.9	6.3	1.0	1.4	4.9	2.0	2.5	2.5	1.9	1.5	2.5
Equatorial Guinea	9.3	4.2	5.6	4.5	2.8	4.7	8.3	6.1	6.3	5.4	7.0	6.9	6.5	7.0	7.0
Eritrea	13.0	25.1	12.5	15.1	9.3	19.9	33.0	12.7	13.3	12.3	12.3	12.3	12.3	12.3	12.3
Ethiopia	3.2	3.2	11.7	13.6	17.2	44.4	8.5	8.1	33.1	22.9	10.2	9.0	35.9	16.6	9.0
Gabon	5.0	0.4	1.2	−1.4	5.0	5.3	1.9	1.4	1.3	2.3	2.6	3.0	2.3	2.3	2.6
The Gambia	4.7	14.3	5.0	2.1	5.4	4.5	4.6	5.0	4.8	4.7	5.5	5.0	4.4	5.0	6.0
Ghana	27.8	12.6	15.1	10.2	10.7	16.5	19.3	10.7	8.7	9.8	10.9	7.5	8.6	11.5	9.5
Guinea	5.0	17.5	31.4	34.7	22.9	18.4	4.7	15.5	21.4	14.7	10.3	5.9	19.0	12.0	8.7
Guinea-Bissau	13.6	0.8	3.2	0.7	4.6	10.4	−1.6	1.1	5.0	5.0	2.5	2.0	3.3	3.3	1.7
Kenya	8.9	11.8	9.9	6.0	4.3	15.1	10.6	4.1	14.0	10.0	5.8	5.0	18.6	7.0	7.0
Lesotho	8.4	5.0	3.4	6.1	8.0	10.7	7.4	3.6	5.6	5.3	4.9	4.2	7.7	4.3	5.5
Liberia	...	3.6	6.9	7.2	13.7	17.5	7.4	7.3	8.5	6.6	5.4	5.0	11.4	4.9	4.7
Madagascar	15.0	14.0	18.4	10.8	10.4	9.2	9.0	9.3	10.0	6.5	7.0	5.0	7.5	7.7	7.0
Malawi	30.1	11.5	15.4	13.9	8.0	8.7	8.4	7.4	7.6	17.7	16.2	5.6	9.8	22.6	11.8
Mali	5.0	−3.1	6.4	1.5	1.5	9.1	2.2	1.3	3.1	7.2	6.2	3.5	5.3	6.4	7.6
Mauritius	6.0	4.7	4.9	8.7	8.6	9.7	2.5	2.9	6.5	4.5	5.2	4.4	4.9	4.8	5.1
Mozambique	20.6	12.6	6.4	13.2	8.2	10.3	3.3	12.7	10.4	3.0	8.6	5.6	5.5	5.5	8.2
Namibia	8.9	4.1	2.3	5.1	6.7	10.4	8.8	4.5	5.8	6.7	5.9	4.5	7.2	6.2	5.7
Niger	6.0	0.4	7.8	0.1	0.1	10.5	1.1	0.9	2.9	4.5	2.0	2.0	1.4	4.5	2.0
Nigeria	22.0	15.0	17.9	8.2	5.4	11.6	12.5	13.7	10.8	11.4	9.5	7.0	10.3	11.0	9.5
Rwanda	13.0	12.0	9.1	8.8	9.1	15.4	10.3	2.3	5.7	7.0	6.1	5.0	8.3	6.3	5.9
São Tomé and Príncipe	27.6	13.3	17.2	23.1	18.6	32.0	17.0	13.3	14.3	10.5	6.2	3.0	11.9	8.3	6.0
Senegal	4.9	0.5	1.7	2.1	5.9	5.8	−1.7	1.2	3.4	2.3	2.1	2.1	2.7	2.2	2.1
Seychelles	2.5	3.9	0.6	−1.9	5.3	37.0	31.7	−2.4	2.6	7.5	4.5	3.1	5.5	7.0	3.1
Sierra Leone	15.5	14.2	12.0	9.5	11.6	14.8	9.2	17.8	18.5	13.7	7.0	5.4	16.9	11.0	7.5
South Africa	7.2	1.4	3.4	4.7	7.1	11.5	7.1	4.3	5.0	5.6	5.2	4.7	6.1	5.3	5.3
South Sudan	...	...	...	...	...	...	...	...	47.3	54.8	22.2	5.0	65.6	60.4	−5.9
Swaziland	8.6	3.4	4.9	5.2	8.1	12.7	7.4	4.5	6.1	7.8	6.9	5.2	7.8	3.1	14.3
Tanzania	13.4	4.1	4.4	7.3	7.0	10.3	12.1	7.2	12.7	15.6	9.8	6.3	19.8	11.1	9.6
Togo	6.5	0.4	6.8	2.2	0.9	8.7	1.9	3.2	3.6	2.5	4.2	4.3	1.5	1.0	12.0
Uganda	4.8	3.7	8.6	7.2	6.1	12.0	13.1	4.0	18.7	14.6	6.1	5.0	27.0	7.1	5.0
Zambia	29.5	18.0	18.3	9.0	10.7	12.4	13.4	8.5	8.7	6.4	6.2	5.0	7.2	6.7	6.1
Zimbabwe [9]	...	...	...	...	...	...	6.2	3.0	3.5	5.0	5.7	4.6	4.9	6.5	4.3

[1] In accordance with standard practice in the *World Economic Outlook*, movements in consumer prices are indicated as annual averages rather than as December–December changes during the year, as is the practice in some countries. For many countries, figures for recent years are IMF staff estimates. Data for some countries are for fiscal years.
[2] December–December changes. Several countries report Q4–Q4 changes.
[3] For many countries, inflation for the earlier years is measured on the basis of a retail price index. Consumer price index (CPI) inflation data with broader and more up-to-date coverage are typically used for more recent years.
[4] Georgia and Mongolia, which are not members of the Commonwealth of Independent States, are included in this group for reasons of geography and similarities in economic structure.
[5] Figures are based on Argentina's official consumer price index (CPI-GBA) data. The IMF has called on Argentina to adopt remedial measures to address the quality of these data. The IMF staff is also using alternative measures of inflation for macroeconomic surveillance, including data produced by provincial statistical offices and private analysts, which have shown considerably higher inflation figures than the official data since 2007.
[6] Data for 2011 exclude South Sudan after July 9. Data for 2012 and onward pertain to the current Sudan.
[7] Data for Syria are excluded for 2011 onward due to the uncertain political situation.
[8] The percent changes in 2002 are calculated over a period of 18 months, reflecting a change in the fiscal year cycle (from July–June to January–December).
[9] The Zimbabwe dollar ceased circulating in early 2009. Data are based on IMF staff estimates of price and exchange rate developments in U.S. dollars. IMF staff estimates of U.S. dollar values may differ from authorities' estimates.

Table A8. Major Advanced Economies: General Government Fiscal Balances and Debt [1]
(Percent of GDP unless noted otherwise)

	Average 1996–2005	2006	2007	2008	2009	2010	2011	Projections 2012	2013	2017
Major Advanced Economies										
Net Lending/Borrowing	. . .	−2.3	−2.1	−4.5	−10.1	−9.0	−7.8	−7.2	−6.1	−3.3
Output Gap [2]	0.7	1.3	1.6	−0.3	−5.1	−3.5	−3.3	−3.2	−3.1	−0.3
Structural Balance [2]	. . .	−2.9	−2.9	−4.2	−6.6	−7.0	−6.3	−5.6	−4.6	−3.1
United States										
Net Lending/Borrowing	. . .	−2.0	−2.7	−6.7	−13.3	−11.2	−10.1	−8.7	−7.3	−4.4
Output Gap [2]	1.6	1.8	1.4	−0.9	−5.6	−4.5	−4.4	−4.1	−4.0	−0.2
Structural Balance [2]	. . .	−2.7	−3.3	−5.5	−8.4	−8.7	−7.9	−6.8	−5.5	−4.2
Net Debt	43.4	48.6	48.2	53.8	65.8	73.2	80.3	83.8	87.7	89.4
Gross Debt	62.7	66.6	67.2	76.1	89.7	98.6	102.9	107.2	111.7	114.0
Euro Area										
Net Lending/Borrowing	−2.4	−1.3	−0.7	−2.1	−6.4	−6.2	−4.1	−3.3	−2.6	−0.8
Output Gap [2]	0.0	1.4	2.7	1.7	−3.5	−2.3	−1.4	−2.4	−2.7	−0.4
Structural Balance [2]	−2.6	−2.4	−2.3	−2.9	−4.4	−4.2	−3.4	−2.1	−1.0	−0.5
Net Debt	55.3	54.3	52.0	54.1	62.4	65.5	68.0	73.4	74.8	71.9
Gross Debt	70.6	68.6	66.4	70.2	80.0	85.4	88.0	93.6	94.9	89.5
Germany [3]										
Net Lending/Borrowing	−2.6	−1.6	0.2	−0.1	−3.2	−4.1	−0.8	−0.4	−0.4	0.0
Output Gap [2]	−0.6	1.0	2.7	2.3	−3.7	−1.2	0.6	0.2	−0.2	0.0
Structural Balance [2,4]	−2.5	−2.3	−1.1	−0.9	−1.2	−2.3	−0.9	−0.5	−0.3	0.0
Net Debt	45.2	53.0	50.5	50.2	57.0	56.2	55.3	58.4	57.5	56.2
Gross Debt	61.9	67.9	65.4	66.9	74.7	82.4	80.6	83.0	81.5	73.7
France										
Net Lending/Borrowing	−2.9	−2.4	−2.8	−3.3	−7.6	−7.1	−5.2	−4.7	−3.5	0.0
Output Gap [2]	0.0	0.0	0.7	−0.6	−4.6	−3.8	−2.7	−3.0	−3.3	−0.6
Structural Balance [2,4]	−2.8	−2.2	−3.0	−3.0	−4.7	−4.6	−3.5	−2.8	−1.4	0.4
Net Debt	53.9	59.6	59.6	62.3	72.0	76.1	78.8	83.7	85.9	80.2
Gross Debt	60.4	64.1	64.2	68.2	79.2	82.3	86.0	90.0	92.1	86.5
Italy										
Net Lending/Borrowing	−3.4	−3.4	−1.6	−2.7	−5.4	−4.5	−3.8	−2.7	−1.8	−0.7
Output Gap [2]	0.6	2.0	2.8	1.0	−4.5	−2.9	−2.3	−4.2	−4.9	−1.4
Structural Balance [2,5]	−4.4	−4.1	−3.3	−3.5	−3.6	−3.3	−3.4	−0.6	0.6	0.0
Net Debt	94.8	89.3	86.9	88.8	97.2	99.1	99.6	103.1	103.9	98.7
Gross Debt	110.0	106.1	103.1	105.7	116.0	118.6	120.1	126.3	127.8	120.6
Japan										
Net Lending/Borrowing	−6.4	−3.7	−2.1	−4.1	−10.4	−9.4	−9.8	−10.0	−9.1	−5.8
Output Gap [2]	−0.9	−0.5	0.5	−1.3	−7.0	−3.0	−4.0	−2.2	−1.5	0.0
Structural Balance [2]	−6.2	−3.5	−2.2	−3.5	−7.4	−7.9	−8.3	−9.1	−8.6	−5.8
Net Debt	60.3	81.0	80.5	95.3	106.2	112.8	126.4	135.4	144.7	158.7
Gross Debt [6]	144.9	186.0	183.0	191.8	210.2	215.3	229.6	236.6	245.0	250.3
United Kingdom										
Net Lending/Borrowing	−1.4	−2.7	−2.8	−5.1	−10.4	−9.9	−8.5	−8.2	−7.3	−1.7
Output Gap [2]	1.1	2.6	3.6	1.7	−2.1	−1.8	−2.6	−4.2	−4.4	−1.4
Structural Balance [2]	−2.0	−4.7	−5.2	−7.2	−9.7	−8.5	−6.6	−5.4	−4.0	−0.5
Net Debt	37.2	37.8	38.0	45.8	60.6	71.0	76.6	83.7	88.2	88.7
Gross Debt	42.3	43.0	43.7	52.2	68.0	75.0	81.8	88.7	93.3	93.7
Canada										
Net Lending/Borrowing	0.5	1.6	1.4	−0.4	−4.9	−5.6	−4.4	−3.8	−3.0	−0.7
Output Gap [2]	0.5	1.7	1.7	0.2	−4.0	−2.4	−1.7	−1.7	−1.6	0.0
Structural Balance [2]	0.3	0.8	0.5	−0.6	−2.5	−4.1	−3.4	−2.9	−2.1	−0.7
Net Debt	48.9	26.3	22.9	22.4	28.3	30.4	33.1	35.8	37.5	36.3
Gross Debt	85.1	70.3	66.5	71.3	83.3	85.1	85.4	87.5	87.8	78.1

Note: The methodology and specific assumptions for each country are discussed in Box A1. The country group composites for fiscal data are calculated as the sum of the U.S. dollar values for the relevant individual countries.
[1] Debt data refer to the end of the year. Debt data are not always comparable across countries.
[2] Percent of potential GDP.
[3] Beginning in 1995, the debt and debt-services obligations of the Treuhandanstalt (and of various other agencies) were taken over by the general government. This debt is equivalent to 8 percent of GDP, and the associated debt service to 0.5 to 1 percent of GDP.
[4] Excludes sizable one-time receipts from the sale of assets, including licenses.
[5] Excludes one-time measures based on the authorities' data and, in the absence of the latter, receipts from the sale of assets.
[6] Includes equity shares.

Table A9. Summary of World Trade Volumes and Prices
(Annual percent change)

	Averages		2004	2005	2006	2007	2008	2009	2010	2011	Projections	
	1994–2003	2004–13									2012	2013
Trade in Goods and Services												
World Trade [1]												
Volume	6.9	5.2	10.7	7.7	9.2	7.8	3.0	−10.4	12.6	5.8	3.2	4.5
Price Deflator												
In U.S. Dollars	0.2	4.1	9.6	5.3	5.3	7.7	11.3	−10.8	5.6	11.2	−1.9	−0.5
In SDRs	0.2	3.3	3.7	5.6	5.8	3.5	7.8	−8.5	6.8	7.5	1.7	0.2
Volume of Trade												
Exports												
Advanced Economies	6.2	4.3	9.4	6.3	8.7	6.7	2.2	−11.3	12.0	5.3	2.2	3.6
Emerging Market and Developing Economies	8.4	7.0	13.4	11.3	11.0	9.9	3.9	−7.6	13.7	6.5	4.0	5.7
Imports												
Advanced Economies	7.0	3.7	9.3	6.4	7.7	5.3	1.0	−11.9	11.4	4.4	1.7	3.3
Emerging Market and Developing Economies	7.2	9.1	16.1	12.1	12.3	14.9	8.6	−8.3	14.9	8.8	7.0	6.6
Terms of Trade												
Advanced Economies	0.2	−0.5	−0.4	−1.5	−1.1	0.4	−1.8	2.4	−0.9	−1.6	−0.8	0.1
Emerging Market and Developing Economies	0.7	1.8	3.5	5.5	3.4	1.7	3.3	−4.8	2.3	3.5	0.5	−0.4
Trade in Goods												
World Trade [1]												
Volume	7.1	5.2	10.6	7.7	9.1	7.2	2.5	−11.5	14.1	6.3	3.4	4.6
Price Deflator												
In U.S. Dollars	0.2	4.3	9.5	5.8	5.9	7.9	12.1	−12.0	6.6	12.6	−2.1	−0.7
In SDRs	0.2	3.5	3.5	6.0	6.4	3.8	8.6	−9.8	7.8	8.8	1.5	0.0
World Trade Prices in U.S. Dollars [2]												
Manufactures	0.0	2.3	4.8	2.8	2.5	5.6	6.2	−6.6	2.7	6.5	−0.5	−0.3
Oil	5.6	13.8	30.7	41.3	20.5	10.7	36.4	−36.3	27.9	31.6	2.1	−1.0
Nonfuel Primary Commodities	−0.3	7.4	15.2	6.1	23.2	14.1	7.5	−15.7	26.3	17.8	−9.5	−2.9
Food	−0.8	6.9	14.0	−0.9	10.5	15.2	23.4	−14.7	11.5	19.7	−1.1	−2.0
Beverages	1.2	6.3	−0.9	18.1	8.4	13.8	23.3	1.6	14.1	16.6	−20.1	−4.4
Agricultural Raw Materials	−1.0	3.2	4.1	0.5	8.8	5.0	−0.8	−17.0	33.2	22.7	−12.9	−2.1
Metal	1.4	11.7	34.6	22.4	56.2	17.4	−7.8	−19.2	48.2	13.5	−16.5	−4.5
World Trade Prices in SDRs [2]												
Manufactures	0.0	1.5	−0.9	3.0	2.9	1.5	2.8	−4.3	3.8	3.0	3.2	0.5
Oil	5.5	12.9	23.6	41.6	21.0	6.4	32.1	−34.8	29.3	27.2	5.8	−0.3
Nonfuel Primary Commodities	−0.4	6.6	9.0	6.3	23.8	9.6	4.1	−13.6	27.7	13.8	−6.2	−2.2
Food	−0.9	6.1	7.8	−0.7	11.0	10.7	19.5	−12.6	12.7	15.7	2.6	−1.3
Beverages	1.2	5.5	−6.3	18.3	8.8	9.4	19.4	4.1	15.4	12.7	−17.2	−3.7
Agricultural Raw Materials	−1.1	2.4	−1.6	0.8	9.3	0.9	−3.9	−14.9	34.7	18.6	−9.7	−1.4
Metal	1.4	10.8	27.3	22.7	56.9	12.8	−10.7	−17.2	49.8	9.7	−13.4	−3.8
World Trade Prices in Euros [2]												
Manufactures	0.3	1.4	−4.7	2.6	1.7	−3.2	−1.1	−1.3	7.8	1.6	9.4	1.9
Oil	6.0	12.8	18.9	41.0	19.5	1.4	27.1	−32.7	34.3	25.5	12.2	1.2
Nonfuel Primary Commodities	0.0	6.4	4.8	5.9	22.3	4.5	0.1	−10.9	32.6	12.3	−0.5	−0.8
Food	−0.5	6.0	3.7	−1.1	9.6	5.6	14.9	−9.8	17.0	14.1	8.7	0.2
Beverages	1.6	5.3	−9.9	17.8	7.5	4.2	14.8	7.3	19.8	11.2	−12.2	−2.3
Agricultural Raw Materials	−0.7	2.3	−5.3	0.3	8.0	−3.8	−7.6	−12.3	39.9	17.0	−4.3	0.1
Metal	1.8	10.7	22.4	22.2	55.0	7.5	−14.1	−14.6	55.5	8.3	−8.2	−2.4

Table A9. Summary of World Trade Volumes and Prices *(concluded)*
(Annual percent change)

	Averages		2004	2005	2006	2007	2008	2009	2010	2011	Projections	
	1994–2003	2004–13									2012	2013
Trade in Goods												
Volume of Trade												
Exports												
Advanced Economies	6.4	4.1	9.0	5.8	8.6	5.8	1.7	−13.2	14.1	5.7	2.4	3.5
Emerging Market and Developing Economies	8.6	6.7	12.4	11.2	10.5	9.0	3.8	−8.0	14.0	6.6	4.0	5.6
Fuel Exporters	3.8	3.4	10.5	6.7	3.9	4.3	3.1	−6.8	4.4	3.6	2.8	2.7
Nonfuel Exporters	10.4	8.0	13.1	12.8	13.3	11.1	4.0	−8.6	17.7	7.7	4.6	6.9
Imports												
Advanced Economies	7.2	3.8	9.6	6.7	7.9	4.9	0.4	−12.9	13.4	4.9	1.7	3.7
Emerging Market and Developing Economies	7.3	9.0	16.4	11.9	11.6	14.4	8.1	−9.5	15.6	9.8	7.4	6.9
Fuel Exporters	4.7	10.0	16.3	15.4	12.5	23.4	14.6	−12.4	8.0	9.9	9.6	6.3
Nonfuel Exporters	8.0	8.8	16.5	11.2	11.5	12.5	6.6	−8.8	17.5	9.8	6.9	7.1
Price Deflators in SDRs												
Exports												
Advanced Economies	−0.2	2.2	2.1	3.5	4.3	3.7	5.3	−7.0	4.7	6.5	−0.4	−0.1
Emerging Market and Developing Economies	2.0	6.7	8.6	13.8	11.4	5.4	14.4	−14.0	13.8	13.3	4.0	−0.1
Fuel Exporters	5.0	11.0	15.7	31.3	19.0	7.8	25.5	−26.4	23.4	23.9	4.2	−1.1
Nonfuel Exporters	0.9	5.0	6.1	7.3	8.1	4.3	9.7	−8.0	10.0	9.1	3.9	0.4
Imports												
Advanced Economies	−0.3	2.7	2.8	5.1	5.6	3.0	7.7	−10.4	5.8	8.4	0.6	−0.2
Emerging Market and Developing Economies	1.2	4.7	4.3	6.9	7.6	3.7	11.0	−9.0	10.9	8.6	3.5	0.7
Fuel Exporters	0.5	4.4	3.1	7.8	8.4	4.3	8.9	−5.1	7.7	6.3	2.8	0.2
Nonfuel Exporters	1.4	4.7	4.6	6.7	7.4	3.5	11.5	−10.0	11.7	9.1	3.6	0.8
Terms of Trade												
Advanced Economies	0.1	−0.5	−0.7	−1.5	−1.3	0.7	−2.2	3.8	−1.1	−1.8	−1.0	0.2
Emerging Market and Developing Economies	0.8	2.0	4.1	6.5	3.5	1.6	3.0	−5.5	2.6	4.3	0.5	−0.8
Regional Groups												
Central and Eastern Europe	0.6	−0.1	1.1	−0.1	−4.0	1.6	−2.8	2.4	−2.0	−1.3	4.9	0.0
Commonwealth of Independent States [3]	2.7	5.4	11.9	14.8	8.7	2.4	14.5	−19.0	12.8	11.9	1.6	−0.5
Developing Asia	−1.3	−0.6	0.7	−0.6	−0.1	0.6	−3.2	4.7	−6.0	−1.8	0.6	−0.3
Latin America and the Caribbean	1.1	2.8	6.0	5.2	6.7	1.8	3.5	−7.9	10.7	7.8	−3.1	−0.8
Middle East and North Africa	4.2	5.7	9.1	22.8	7.5	2.2	12.7	−18.9	12.6	15.0	1.5	−1.6
Sub-Saharan Africa	...	3.5	4.4	10.0	7.3	4.8	9.1	−13.0	10.1	9.4	−2.8	−1.8
Analytical Groups												
By Source of Export Earnings												
Fuel Exporters	4.4	6.4	12.3	21.8	9.7	3.4	15.2	−22.4	14.6	16.6	1.3	−1.3
Nonfuel Exporters	−0.4	0.2	1.5	0.6	0.6	0.7	−1.6	2.2	−1.5	0.0	0.3	−0.4
Memorandum												
World Exports in Billions of U.S. Dollars												
Goods and Services	7,227	17,926	11,401	12,951	14,924	17,376	19,870	15,888	18,899	22,231	22,419	23,303
Goods	5,830	14,490	9,148	10,433	12,069	13,984	16,053	12,499	15,207	18,177	18,329	18,999
Average Oil Price [4]	5.6	13.8	30.7	41.3	20.5	10.7	36.4	−36.3	27.9	31.6	2.1	−1.0
In U.S. Dollars a Barrel	21.03	77.96	37.76	53.35	64.27	71.13	97.04	61.78	79.03	104.01	106.18	105.10
Export Unit Value of Manufactures [5]	0.0	2.3	4.8	2.8	2.5	5.6	6.2	−6.6	2.7	6.5	−0.5	−0.3

[1] Average of annual percent change for world exports and imports.
[2] As represented, respectively, by the export unit value index for manufactures of the advanced economies and accounting for 83 percent of the advanced economies' trade (export of goods) weights; the average of U.K. Brent, Dubai, and West Texas Intermediate crude oil prices; and the average of world market prices for nonfuel primary commodities weighted by their 2002–04 shares in world commodity exports.
[3] Georgia and Mongolia, which are not members of the Commonwealth of Independent States, are included in this group for reasons of geography and similarities in economic structure.
[4] Percent change of average of U.K. Brent, Dubai, and West Texas Intermediate crude oil prices.
[5] Percent change for manufactures exported by the advanced economies.

Table A10. Summary of Balances on Current Account
(Billions of U.S. Dollars)

	2004	2005	2006	2007	2008	2009	2010	2011	Projections 2012	Projections 2013	Projections 2017
Advanced Economies	**−209.6**	**−383.8**	**−426.1**	**−317.7**	**−482.1**	**−71.1**	**−20.5**	**−93.3**	**−165.0**	**−130.4**	**−185.1**
United States	−628.5	−745.8	−800.6	−710.3	−677.1	−381.9	−442.0	−465.9	−486.5	−499.2	−687.9
Euro Area [1,2]	121.7	51.4	53.7	45.6	−99.8	18.2	48.8	56.6	136.0	151.7	237.4
Japan	172.1	166.1	170.9	212.1	159.9	146.6	204.0	119.3	95.4	137.8	127.6
Other Advanced Economies [3]	125.1	144.5	149.9	134.9	135.0	146.1	168.6	196.8	90.1	79.3	137.7
Memorandum											
Newly Industrialized Asian Economies	87.1	83.2	99.0	128.3	86.5	123.8	137.2	138.0	121.0	123.3	136.0
Emerging Market and Developing Economies	**206.4**	**416.9**	**639.5**	**629.6**	**673.7**	**291.8**	**336.2**	**481.2**	**361.8**	**310.1**	**258.3**
Regional Groups											
Central and Eastern Europe	−55.1	−61.3	−89.0	−136.3	−159.9	−49.5	−81.4	−116.6	−90.6	−94.6	−145.9
Commonwealth of Independent States [4]	63.5	87.6	96.3	71.5	107.7	41.6	71.9	111.8	110.4	82.5	−31.4
Developing Asia	92.4	141.2	268.3	399.9	405.8	296.9	233.6	188.2	118.6	149.6	466.9
Latin America and the Caribbean	22.1	35.9	48.7	13.2	−32.2	−21.9	−57.4	−73.7	−97.1	−111.2	−180.7
Middle East and North Africa	91.7	214.9	286.7	270.4	354.8	52.9	182.5	392.1	361.4	329.5	219.6
Sub-Saharan Africa	−8.2	−1.4	28.5	10.8	−2.5	−28.3	−13.1	−20.6	−41.0	−45.7	−70.4
Memorandum											
European Union	66.8	7.9	−27.5	−61.7	−171.6	−0.2	5.7	34.5	82.4	111.0	232.5
Analytical Groups											
By Source of Export Earnings											
Fuel	175.5	354.7	482.1	435.8	596.4	148.3	331.4	612.4	577.6	515.1	250.3
Nonfuel	30.9	62.3	157.4	193.8	77.3	143.4	4.8	−131.1	−215.8	−205.1	8.0
Of Which, Primary Products	−1.2	−3.2	6.5	5.2	−17.0	−8.7	−8.7	−22.6	−35.5	−33.5	−25.9
By External Financing Source											
Net Debtor Economies	−61.2	−89.6	−119.2	−229.2	−375.8	−190.7	−282.2	−364.8	−399.3	−417.8	−539.7
Of Which, Official Financing	−5.2	−6.0	−3.5	−5.1	−12.3	−9.0	−11.0	−13.0	−18.1	−14.8	−19.2
Net Debtor Economies by Debt-Servicing Experience											
Economies with Arrears and/or Rescheduling during 2006–10	−3.7	−5.4	−4.1	−14.1	−27.4	−23.5	−33.5	−42.8	−50.5	−48.2	−60.5
World [1]	**−3.2**	**33.2**	**213.4**	**311.9**	**191.6**	**220.7**	**315.7**	**387.9**	**196.8**	**179.6**	**73.1**

Table A10. Summary of Balances on Current Account (concluded)

(Percent of GDP)

	2004	2005	2006	2007	2008	2009	2010	2011	Projections 2012	Projections 2013	Projections 2017
Advanced Economies	**−0.6**	**−1.1**	**−1.2**	**−0.8**	**−1.1**	**−0.2**	**0.0**	**−0.2**	**−0.4**	**−0.3**	**−0.4**
United States	−5.3	−5.9	−6.0	−5.1	−4.7	−2.7	−3.0	−3.1	−3.1	−3.1	−3.5
Euro Area [1,2]	1.2	0.5	0.5	0.4	−0.7	0.1	0.4	0.4	1.1	1.3	1.8
Japan	3.7	3.6	3.9	4.9	3.3	2.9	3.7	2.0	1.6	2.3	1.9
Other Advanced Economies [3]	1.8	2.0	1.9	1.5	1.4	1.8	1.8	1.9	0.9	0.7	1.1
Memorandum											
Newly Industrialized Asian economies	6.5	5.5	5.9	7.0	5.0	7.7	7.2	6.6	5.6	5.5	4.6
Emerging Market and Developing Economies	**2.3**	**3.8**	**5.0**	**4.0**	**3.5**	**1.6**	**1.5**	**1.9**	**1.3**	**1.1**	**0.6**
Regional Groups											
Central and Eastern Europe	−5.6	−5.2	−6.8	−8.3	−8.3	−3.1	−4.7	−6.1	−5.0	−4.9	−5.8
Commonwealth of Independent States [4]	8.2	8.7	7.4	4.2	4.9	2.5	3.6	4.6	4.2	2.9	−0.8
Developing Asia	2.6	3.5	5.6	6.6	5.4	3.7	2.4	1.6	0.9	1.1	2.3
Latin America and the Caribbean	1.0	1.4	1.6	0.4	−0.7	−0.5	−1.2	−1.3	−1.7	−1.9	−2.4
Middle East and North Africa	8.3	16.0	18.0	14.5	15.3	2.6	7.7	14.2	12.2	10.6	5.8
Sub-Saharan Africa	−1.5	−0.2	4.0	1.3	−0.3	−3.2	−1.2	−1.7	−3.2	−3.3	−3.9
Memorandum											
European Union	0.5	0.1	−0.2	−0.4	−0.9	0.0	0.0	0.2	0.5	0.7	1.2
Analytical Groups											
By Source of Export Earnings											
Fuel	9.7	15.4	16.8	12.4	13.3	4.0	7.7	11.7	10.3	8.6	3.2
Nonfuel	0.4	0.7	1.6	1.6	0.5	1.0	0.0	−0.6	−1.0	−0.9	0.0
Of Which, Primary Products	−0.4	−1.0	1.7	1.2	−3.4	−1.7	−1.4	−3.3	−4.8	−4.2	−2.4
By External Financing Source											
Net Debtor Economies	−1.3	−1.5	−1.8	−2.8	−4.0	−2.2	−2.7	−3.1	−3.4	−3.3	−3.2
Of Which, Official Financing	−2.6	−2.6	−1.4	−1.7	−3.4	−2.4	−2.7	−3.3	−4.3	−3.2	−3.0
Net Debtor Economies by Debt-Servicing Experience											
Economies with Arrears and/or Rescheduling during 2006–10	−0.9	−1.1	−0.7	−2.0	−3.2	−2.9	−3.5	−4.0	−4.4	−4.0	−4.0
World [1]	**0.0**	**0.1**	**0.4**	**0.6**	**0.3**	**0.4**	**0.5**	**0.6**	**0.3**	**0.2**	**0.1**
Memorandum											
In Percent of Total World Current Account Transactions	0.0	0.1	0.7	0.9	0.5	0.7	0.8	0.9	0.4	0.4	0.1
In Percent of World GDP	0.0	0.1	0.4	0.6	0.3	0.4	0.5	0.6	0.3	0.2	0.1

[1] Reflects errors, omissions, and asymmetries in balance of payments statistics on current account, as well as the exclusion of data for international organizations and a limited number of countries. See "Classification of Countries" in the introduction to this Statistical Appendix.
[2] Calculated as the sum of the balances of individual Euro Area countries.
[3] In this table, Other Advanced Economies means advanced economies excluding the United States, Euro Area countries, and Japan.
[4] Georgia and Mongolia, which are not members of the Commonwealth of Independent States, are included in this group for reasons of geography and similarities in economic structure.

Table A11. Advanced Economies: Balance on Current Account
(Percent of GDP)

	2004	2005	2006	2007	2008	2009	2010	2011	Projections 2012	2013	2017
Advanced Economies	**−0.6**	**−1.1**	**−1.2**	**−0.8**	**−1.1**	**−0.2**	**0.0**	**−0.2**	**−0.4**	**−0.3**	**−0.4**
United States	−5.3	−5.9	−6.0	−5.1	−4.7	−2.7	−3.0	−3.1	−3.1	−3.1	−3.5
Euro Area [1]	1.2	0.5	0.5	0.4	−0.7	0.1	0.4	0.4	1.1	1.3	1.8
Germany	4.7	5.1	6.3	7.4	6.2	5.9	6.0	5.7	5.4	4.7	4.2
France	0.5	−0.5	−0.6	−1.0	−1.7	−1.3	−1.6	−1.9	−1.7	−1.7	−0.3
Italy	−0.3	−0.8	−1.5	−1.2	−2.9	−2.1	−3.6	−3.3	−1.5	−1.4	−1.0
Spain	−5.2	−7.4	−9.0	−10.0	−9.6	−4.8	−4.5	−3.5	−2.0	−0.1	2.2
Netherlands	7.6	7.4	9.3	6.7	4.3	4.1	7.0	8.5	8.2	8.2	6.5
Belgium	3.2	2.0	1.9	1.6	−1.6	−1.6	1.4	−1.0	−0.1	0.3	1.4
Austria	2.2	2.2	2.8	3.5	4.9	2.7	3.0	1.9	1.9	1.6	1.1
Greece	−5.8	−7.6	−11.4	−14.6	−14.9	−11.1	−10.1	−9.8	−5.8	−2.9	0.5
Portugal	−8.3	−10.3	−10.7	−10.1	−12.6	−10.9	−10.0	−6.4	−2.9	−1.7	0.7
Finland	6.2	3.4	4.2	4.3	2.6	1.8	1.4	−1.2	−1.6	−1.7	−1.4
Ireland	−0.6	−3.5	−3.5	−5.4	−5.7	−2.3	1.1	1.1	1.8	2.7	3.8
Slovak Republic	−7.8	−8.5	−7.8	−5.3	−6.6	−2.6	−2.5	0.1	0.8	0.3	0.3
Slovenia	−2.6	−1.7	−2.5	−4.8	−6.2	−0.7	−0.6	0.0	1.1	1.0	0.5
Luxembourg	11.9	11.5	10.4	10.1	5.1	6.5	7.7	7.1	7.3	7.1	6.7
Estonia	−11.3	−10.0	−15.3	−15.9	−9.1	3.4	2.9	2.1	0.7	−0.1	−2.6
Cyprus	−5.0	−5.9	−7.0	−11.8	−15.6	−10.7	−9.9	−10.4	−3.5	−2.0	−2.8
Malta	−5.9	−8.7	−9.9	−4.5	−5.0	−7.5	−5.8	−1.3	−1.5	−1.6	−2.1
Japan	3.7	3.6	3.9	4.9	3.3	2.9	3.7	2.0	1.6	2.3	1.9
United Kingdom	−2.1	−2.1	−2.9	−2.3	−1.0	−1.3	−2.5	−1.9	−3.3	−2.7	−0.7
Canada	2.3	1.9	1.4	0.8	0.3	−3.0	−3.1	−2.8	−3.4	−3.7	−3.0
Korea	4.5	2.2	1.5	2.1	0.3	3.9	2.9	2.4	1.9	1.7	0.7
Australia	−6.1	−5.7	−5.3	−6.2	−4.4	−4.2	−2.9	−2.3	−4.1	−5.5	−5.6
Taiwan Province of China	5.8	4.8	7.0	8.9	6.9	11.4	9.3	8.9	6.9	7.3	7.4
Sweden	6.5	6.7	8.3	9.1	8.7	7.0	6.8	6.9	7.2	7.8	7.5
Hong Kong SAR	9.5	11.4	12.1	12.3	13.7	8.6	5.5	5.3	4.1	3.8	6.5
Switzerland	13.0	13.6	14.4	8.6	2.1	10.6	14.3	10.5	10.1	10.0	9.4
Singapore	17.1	21.4	24.5	25.8	13.9	16.2	24.4	21.9	21.0	20.7	16.3
Czech Republic	−5.0	−0.9	−2.1	−4.4	−2.1	−2.5	−3.8	−3.0	−2.4	−2.2	−2.0
Norway	12.6	16.1	16.4	12.5	16.0	10.8	12.4	14.5	15.2	15.6	13.4
Israel	1.7	3.1	4.8	2.7	0.9	3.8	3.8	0.8	−2.1	−1.3	1.2
Denmark	3.0	4.3	3.0	1.4	2.9	3.3	5.5	6.7	5.0	4.6	4.7
New Zealand	−5.7	−7.9	−8.3	−8.1	−8.8	−2.6	−3.5	−4.2	−5.4	−5.9	−6.9
Iceland	−9.8	−16.1	−25.6	−15.7	−28.4	−11.8	−8.5	−6.2	−2.7	−2.1	−2.8
San Marino	...	...	...	...	...	...	...	...	...	...	...
Memorandum											
Major Advanced Economies	−1.3	−1.8	−1.9	−1.2	−1.3	−0.6	−0.8	−1.1	−1.3	−1.2	−1.3
Euro Area [2]	0.8	0.1	−0.1	0.1	−1.6	−0.2	−0.1	0.0	1.1	1.3	1.8
Newly Industrialized Asian Economies	6.5	5.5	5.9	7.0	5.0	7.7	7.2	6.6	5.6	5.5	4.6

[1] Calculated as the sum of the balances of individual Euro Area countries.
[2] Corrected for reporting discrepancies in intra-area transactions.

Table A12. Emerging Market and Developing Economies: Balance on Current Account
(Percent of GDP)

	2004	2005	2006	2007	2008	2009	2010	2011	Projections 2012	Projections 2013	Projections 2017
Central and Eastern Europe	**−5.6**	**−5.2**	**−6.8**	**−8.3**	**−8.3**	**−3.1**	**−4.7**	**−6.1**	**−5.0**	**−4.9**	**−5.8**
Albania	−4.0	−6.1	−5.6	−10.4	−15.1	−14.0	−11.4	−12.3	−11.8	−11.5	−8.2
Bosnia and Herzegovina	−16.2	−17.1	−7.9	−10.7	−14.1	−6.3	−5.7	−8.8	−8.0	−7.7	−4.6
Bulgaria	−6.4	−11.6	−17.6	−25.2	−23.0	−8.9	−1.0	0.9	−0.3	−1.5	−4.1
Croatia	−4.1	−5.3	−6.7	−7.3	−9.0	−5.1	−1.1	−1.0	−1.2	−1.3	−2.9
Hungary	−8.4	−7.5	−7.4	−7.3	−7.4	−0.2	1.2	1.4	2.6	2.7	−2.2
Kosovo	−8.4	−7.4	−6.7	−8.3	−15.3	−15.4	−17.4	−20.3	−18.3	−18.2	−13.8
Latvia	−12.9	−12.6	−22.6	−22.4	−13.2	8.7	3.0	−1.2	−1.6	−2.8	−3.8
Lithuania	−7.6	−7.0	−10.6	−14.5	−13.3	4.7	1.5	−1.5	−1.1	−1.4	−3.3
FYR Macedonia	−8.1	−2.5	−0.4	−7.1	−12.8	−6.8	−2.1	−2.7	−4.0	−6.0	−4.9
Montenegro	−7.2	−16.6	−31.3	−39.5	−50.6	−29.6	−24.6	−19.5	−20.0	−19.8	−15.6
Poland	−5.2	−2.4	−3.8	−6.2	−6.6	−4.0	−4.7	−4.3	−3.7	−3.8	−3.5
Romania	−8.4	−8.6	−10.4	−13.4	−11.6	−4.2	−4.5	−4.4	−3.7	−3.8	−4.4
Serbia	−12.2	−8.8	−10.2	−16.1	−21.5	−7.1	−7.4	−9.5	−11.5	−12.6	−11.6
Turkey	−3.7	−4.6	−6.1	−5.9	−5.7	−2.2	−6.4	−10.0	−7.5	−7.1	−7.9
Commonwealth of Independent States [1]	**8.2**	**8.7**	**7.4**	**4.2**	**4.9**	**2.5**	**3.6**	**4.6**	**4.2**	**2.9**	**−0.8**
Russia	10.1	11.1	9.5	5.9	6.2	4.0	4.7	5.3	5.2	3.8	−1.1
Excluding Russia	2.2	1.3	0.6	−1.3	0.8	−1.9	0.4	2.2	1.3	0.2	0.1
Armenia	−0.5	−1.0	−1.8	−6.4	−11.8	−15.8	−14.7	−10.9	−9.8	−9.3	−6.4
Azerbaijan	−29.8	1.3	17.6	27.3	35.5	23.0	28.4	26.5	20.4	16.1	6.0
Belarus	−5.3	1.4	−3.9	−6.7	−8.2	−12.6	−15.0	−10.5	−3.6	−5.8	−4.9
Georgia	−6.9	−11.1	−15.1	−19.7	−21.9	−10.6	−10.3	−11.8	−12.6	−11.2	−6.7
Kazakhstan	0.8	−1.8	−2.5	−8.1	4.7	−3.6	1.6	7.6	6.2	4.5	2.9
Kyrgyz Republic	4.9	2.8	−3.1	−6.2	−15.5	−2.5	−6.4	−6.3	−12.8	−6.2	−2.8
Moldova	−1.8	−7.6	−11.3	−15.2	−16.2	−8.6	−7.9	−11.5	−11.4	−10.7	−8.8
Mongolia	1.2	1.2	6.5	6.3	−12.9	−9.0	−14.9	−31.8	−31.4	−10.1	4.4
Tajikistan	−3.9	−1.7	−2.8	−8.6	−7.6	−5.9	−0.3	0.6	−0.4	−1.5	−1.5
Turkmenistan	0.6	5.1	15.7	15.5	16.5	−14.7	−10.6	2.0	−1.5	−1.6	5.3
Ukraine	10.6	2.9	−1.5	−3.7	−7.1	−1.5	−2.2	−5.5	−5.6	−6.6	−5.5
Uzbekistan	7.2	7.7	9.1	7.3	8.7	2.2	6.2	5.8	4.7	3.3	1.0
Developing Asia	**2.6**	**3.5**	**5.6**	**6.6**	**5.4**	**3.7**	**2.4**	**1.6**	**0.9**	**1.1**	**2.3**
Afghanistan	−0.3	3.1	−1.1	5.8	5.1	1.6	3.9	3.3	2.1	0.5	−3.8
Bangladesh	−0.3	0.0	1.2	0.8	1.4	2.8	1.6	0.0	−0.3	−0.3	0.2
Bhutan	−32.6	−4.8	14.8	−2.5	−2.3	−10.6	−22.9	−25.4	−31.4	−28.7	−16.4
Brunei Darussalam	42.2	47.3	50.1	47.8	48.9	40.2	45.5	48.5	49.1	50.3	61.6
Cambodia	−2.2	−3.8	−0.6	−1.9	−5.7	−4.5	−3.9	−8.1	−9.7	−9.1	−5.4
China	3.6	5.9	8.6	10.1	9.1	5.2	4.0	2.8	2.3	2.5	4.3
Fiji	−12.6	−8.6	−17.5	−12.8	−18.1	−7.6	−11.3	−10.1	−9.8	−16.4	−7.7
India	0.1	−1.3	−1.0	−0.7	−2.5	−2.0	−3.2	−3.4	−3.8	−3.3	−2.3
Indonesia	0.6	0.1	3.0	2.4	0.0	2.0	0.7	0.2	−2.1	−2.4	−2.9
Kiribati	−25.2	−34.4	−17.6	−19.3	−16.8	−26.6	−15.4	−22.9	−24.0	−20.2	−21.2
Lao P.D.R.	−17.9	−18.1	−9.9	−15.7	−18.5	−21.0	−18.3	−21.4	−21.9	−24.0	−15.2
Malaysia	12.1	14.4	16.1	15.4	17.1	15.5	11.1	11.0	7.5	6.9	5.8
Maldives	−11.4	−27.5	−23.2	−28.4	−34.2	−21.0	−17.3	−15.7	−29.1	−29.3	−31.1
Myanmar	2.4	3.7	7.1	−0.5	−3.3	−2.8	−1.3	−2.6	−4.4	−4.0	−4.0
Nepal	2.7	2.0	2.1	−0.1	2.7	4.2	−2.4	−1.0	4.4	−0.2	−0.4
Pakistan	1.8	−1.4	−3.9	−4.8	−8.5	−5.7	−2.2	0.1	−2.0	−1.7	−3.5
Papua New Guinea	0.4	13.9	−1.7	4.0	8.4	−16.4	−25.6	−36.4	−28.4	−20.2	8.3
Philippines	1.8	1.9	4.4	4.8	2.1	5.6	4.5	3.1	3.0	2.6	1.8
Samoa	−8.4	−9.6	−10.2	−15.5	−6.5	−3.1	−7.2	−8.6	−11.4	−12.3	−10.1
Solomon Islands	16.8	−6.7	−9.1	−15.7	−20.5	−21.4	−30.8	−6.7	−7.8	−10.7	−7.0
Sri Lanka	−3.1	−2.5	−5.3	−4.3	−9.5	−0.5	−2.2	−7.7	−5.4	−4.7	−3.3
Thailand	1.7	−4.3	1.1	6.3	0.8	8.3	4.1	3.4	−0.2	0.1	1.0
Timor-Leste	11.4	32.2	50.0	65.1	66.7	51.7	48.1	57.2	45.4	37.9	28.7
Tonga	0.4	−5.0	−5.5	−5.5	−8.1	−7.8	−3.9	−4.0	−4.2	−3.1	−3.3
Tuvalu	5.9	24.7	27.2	14.2	−13.2	27.8	−3.8	−29.2	−8.5	−3.3	4.2
Vanuatu	−6.2	−8.8	4.8	3.4	8.5	−6.3	−5.1	−6.5	−6.1	−10.2	−9.9
Vietnam	−3.5	−1.1	−0.3	−9.8	−11.9	−6.6	−4.1	0.2	0.3	−0.9	−1.5

Table A12. Emerging Market and Developing Economies: Balance on Current Account *(continued)*
(Percent of GDP)

	2004	2005	2006	2007	2008	2009	2010	2011	Projections 2012	2013	2017
Latin America and the Caribbean	**1.0**	**1.4**	**1.6**	**0.4**	**−0.7**	**−0.5**	**−1.2**	**−1.3**	**−1.7**	**−1.9**	**−2.4**
Antigua and Barbuda	−13.1	−18.8	−27.8	−30.9	−27.2	−19.3	−13.1	−10.7	−11.4	−12.3	−16.2
Argentina [2]	1.8	2.6	3.4	2.6	1.8	2.5	0.7	−0.1	0.3	−0.1	−1.9
The Bahamas	−2.4	−8.4	−17.7	−11.5	−10.6	−10.5	−10.5	−14.0	−16.0	−16.8	−8.9
Barbados	−7.6	−7.5	−4.8	−2.7	−9.6	−5.6	−8.2	−8.7	−7.9	−7.1	−3.8
Belize	−14.7	−13.6	−2.1	−4.1	−10.6	−5.9	−2.9	−2.6	−2.3	−4.4	−5.9
Bolivia	3.7	5.9	11.2	11.3	12.0	4.3	4.9	2.2	1.8	1.1	0.0
Brazil	1.8	1.6	1.3	0.1	−1.7	−1.5	−2.2	−2.1	−2.6	−2.8	−3.3
Chile	2.6	1.5	4.6	4.1	−3.2	2.0	1.5	−1.3	−3.2	−3.0	−2.7
Colombia	−0.8	−1.3	−1.9	−2.8	−2.8	−2.1	−3.1	−3.0	−2.9	−2.9	−2.4
Costa Rica	−4.3	−4.9	−4.5	−6.3	−9.3	−2.0	−3.5	−5.3	−5.5	−5.3	−5.5
Dominica	−16.0	−21.0	−12.9	−20.8	−27.1	−21.0	−16.0	−12.7	−13.3	−13.7	−15.6
Dominican Republic	4.8	−1.4	−3.6	−5.3	−9.9	−5.0	−8.6	−8.1	−7.5	−7.3	−5.8
Ecuador	−1.5	1.3	4.2	4.3	3.0	0.3	−2.8	−0.3	−0.3	3.0	−2.6
El Salvador	−4.1	−3.6	−4.1	−6.1	−7.1	−1.5	−3.1	−5.4	−5.0	−4.3	−3.0
Grenada	−2.9	−22.1	−26.3	−27.8	−25.7	−23.9	−25.2	−24.6	−22.3	−23.2	−15.4
Guatemala	−4.9	−4.6	−5.0	−5.2	−4.3	0.0	−1.5	−3.1	−3.5	−3.6	−3.6
Guyana	−6.7	−10.1	−13.1	−11.1	−13.2	−9.1	−9.9	−13.6	−14.0	−17.6	−12.2
Haiti	−1.6	0.7	−1.5	−1.5	−4.4	−3.5	−2.5	−4.6	−4.3	−5.3	−4.0
Honduras	−7.7	−3.0	−3.7	−9.0	−15.4	−3.6	−6.2	−8.7	−9.8	−9.6	−6.8
Jamaica	−6.3	−9.3	−10.2	−16.9	−18.4	−11.1	−8.8	−11.7	−11.7	−11.1	−6.9
Mexico	−0.7	−0.7	−0.6	−1.1	−1.6	−0.6	−0.4	−1.0	−0.9	−1.1	−1.1
Nicaragua	−14.5	−14.3	−13.4	−17.8	−23.8	−12.2	−14.4	−18.0	−20.5	−18.1	−14.1
Panama	−7.5	−4.9	−3.1	−7.9	−10.9	−0.7	−10.8	−12.8	−12.1	−11.8	−9.5
Paraguay	1.8	0.2	1.2	1.3	−1.7	0.4	−3.1	−1.0	−1.1	−0.4	−1.3
Peru	0.1	1.5	3.2	1.4	−4.2	−0.5	−2.5	−1.9	−3.0	−3.0	−2.4
St. Kitts and Nevis	−16.2	−14.9	−14.1	−16.7	−24.3	−27.3	−22.1	−15.2	−17.1	−16.4	−14.9
St. Lucia	−10.6	−14.3	−30.4	−30.4	−28.9	−11.9	−15.1	−23.1	−24.0	−20.5	−17.9
St. Vincent and the Grenadines	−19.6	−18.0	−19.3	−28.0	−32.9	−29.4	−31.6	−30.2	−27.3	−25.7	−16.6
Suriname	−8.2	−11.7	4.5	8.1	6.6	−0.5	6.4	5.5	−0.1	−2.1	3.1
Trinidad and Tobago	12.4	22.5	39.6	23.9	30.5	8.3	20.0	7.1	8.1	7.6	6.7
Uruguay	0.0	0.2	−2.0	−0.9	−5.7	−1.5	−2.2	−3.1	−3.0	−1.9	−1.9
Venezuela	13.8	17.7	14.8	8.7	11.9	2.6	4.9	8.6	6.7	5.6	2.7
Middle East and North Africa	**8.3**	**16.0**	**18.0**	**14.5**	**15.3**	**2.6**	**7.7**	**14.2**	**12.2**	**10.6**	**5.8**
Algeria	13.0	20.5	24.7	22.8	20.1	0.3	7.5	10.0	6.2	6.1	3.5
Bahrain	4.2	11.0	13.8	15.7	10.2	2.9	3.6	12.6	9.9	10.5	6.2
Djibouti	−1.3	−3.2	−11.5	−21.4	−24.3	−9.1	−5.8	−12.6	−12.2	−12.5	−8.2
Egypt	4.3	3.2	1.6	1.7	0.5	−2.3	−2.0	−2.6	−3.4	−3.3	−1.9
Iran	0.5	7.6	8.5	10.6	6.5	2.6	6.0	12.5	3.4	1.3	−0.4
Iraq	−43.2	5.7	18.1	11.5	18.8	−13.4	−3.0	8.3	0.3	6.1	9.8
Jordan	0.1	−5.1	−11.5	−17.2	−9.3	−4.9	−7.1	−12.0	−14.1	−9.9	−4.3
Kuwait	26.2	37.2	44.6	36.8	40.9	26.7	31.9	44.0	44.1	39.2	29.4
Lebanon	−15.3	−13.4	−5.3	−6.8	−9.2	−9.8	−9.6	−14.0	−16.2	−15.6	−10.8
Libya	21.1	36.5	50.7	43.8	42.3	14.7	19.8	1.3	21.8	10.3	−0.4
Mauritania	−34.6	−47.2	−1.3	−17.2	−14.8	−10.7	−8.7	−7.5	−23.6	−13.9	−6.4
Morocco	1.7	1.8	2.2	−0.1	−5.2	−5.4	−4.3	−8.0	−7.9	−5.4	−3.4
Oman	4.5	16.8	15.4	5.9	8.3	−1.2	8.6	16.7	14.0	10.0	−5.7
Qatar	22.4	29.9	25.1	25.4	28.7	10.2	26.7	30.2	29.6	26.8	11.5
Saudi Arabia	20.7	28.5	27.8	24.3	27.8	5.6	14.6	26.5	26.1	22.7	12.8
Sudan [3]	−4.9	−10.0	−8.8	−5.9	−2.0	−10.0	−2.1	−0.5	−7.8	−6.6	−4.6
Syria [4]	−3.1	−2.2	1.4	−0.2	−1.3	−3.6	−3.3	...	...	...	...
Tunisia	−2.4	−0.9	−1.8	−2.4	−3.8	−2.8	−4.8	−7.3	−7.9	−7.7	−5.6
United Arab Emirates	6.1	12.4	16.3	6.9	7.9	3.5	3.2	9.7	9.3	10.1	9.7
Yemen	1.6	3.8	1.1	−7.0	−4.6	−10.2	−4.4	−3.0	−2.7	−4.0	−6.0

Table A12. Emerging Market and Developing Economies: Balance on Current Account *(concluded)*
(Percent of GDP)

	2004	2005	2006	2007	2008	2009	2010	2011	Projections 2012	Projections 2013	Projections 2017
Sub-Saharan Africa	**−1.5**	**−0.2**	**4.0**	**1.3**	**−0.3**	**−3.2**	**−1.2**	**−1.7**	**−3.2**	**−3.3**	**−3.9**
Angola	3.8	18.2	25.6	19.9	10.3	−9.9	9.0	9.6	8.5	6.6	−2.7
Benin	−7.0	−6.3	−5.3	−10.2	−8.1	−8.9	−7.3	−10.0	−9.3	−9.1	−7.7
Botswana	3.5	15.2	17.2	15.0	6.9	−5.2	−2.0	1.6	3.9	3.4	2.4
Burkina Faso	−11.0	−11.6	−9.5	−8.3	−11.5	−4.7	−2.3	−1.1	−4.2	−3.2	−4.0
Burundi	−6.3	−4.9	−21.5	−5.4	−1.0	1.8	−9.4	−11.4	−11.4	−10.7	−6.3
Cameroon	−3.4	−3.4	1.6	1.4	−1.2	−3.6	−3.0	−4.1	−4.1	−3.8	−2.7
Cape Verde	−14.3	−3.5	−5.4	−14.7	−15.7	−15.6	−12.5	−12.5	−11.5	−8.9	−7.4
Central African Republic	−1.8	−6.5	−3.0	−6.2	−10.0	−9.2	−10.2	−8.7	−7.6	−6.3	−4.6
Chad	−17.1	1.2	5.9	11.6	9.0	−4.0	−3.5	2.0	−1.9	−2.0	−5.4
Comoros	−4.6	−7.4	−6.0	−5.7	−10.9	−7.8	−7.0	−9.5	−10.4	−9.6	−7.5
Democratic Republic of the Congo	−3.0	−13.3	−2.7	−1.1	−17.5	−10.5	−8.1	−11.5	−12.5	−14.3	−8.4
Republic of Congo	−5.7	3.7	3.6	−6.5	2.3	−7.4	5.1	0.8	−0.6	−0.4	−11.9
Côte d'Ivoire	1.6	0.2	2.8	−0.7	1.9	7.0	1.1	6.7	−3.1	−1.6	−4.7
Equatorial Guinea	−21.6	−6.2	7.7	4.0	−2.3	−17.7	−20.5	−6.0	−7.7	−7.7	−8.3
Eritrea	−0.7	0.3	−3.6	−6.1	−5.5	−7.6	−5.6	0.5	2.1	2.0	−3.0
Ethiopia	−1.4	−6.3	−9.1	−4.5	−5.6	−5.0	−4.0	0.6	−6.1	−7.7	−5.9
Gabon	11.2	22.9	15.6	17.0	24.2	6.3	9.1	10.6	9.1	4.1	1.9
The Gambia	−4.5	−10.3	−6.9	−8.3	−12.1	−12.3	−15.7	−14.2	−15.9	−14.2	−12.0
Ghana	−4.7	−7.0	−8.2	−8.7	−11.9	−5.4	−8.4	−9.2	−9.1	−7.0	−4.7
Guinea	−2.5	−1.0	−4.6	−11.7	−10.3	−9.9	−12.4	−16.3	−38.8	−39.2	0.2
Guinea-Bissau	1.4	−2.1	−5.6	−3.5	−4.9	−6.4	−8.3	−6.4	−3.5	−2.9	−1.6
Kenya	0.1	−1.5	−2.3	−4.0	−6.6	−5.8	−6.5	−10.6	−8.5	−8.6	−5.6
Lesotho	8.1	1.4	11.5	8.2	10.0	0.2	−12.1	−17.3	−11.2	−10.6	2.9
Liberia	−16.3	−30.3	−11.2	−22.4	−43.7	−29.2	−33.2	−34.6	−55.8	−71.0	−36.6
Madagascar	−10.6	−11.6	−9.9	−12.7	−20.6	−21.1	−9.7	−6.9	−7.9	−8.0	2.4
Malawi	−11.2	−11.9	−11.3	1.0	−9.7	−4.8	−1.3	−5.9	−4.1	−1.4	−2.8
Mali	−7.9	−8.5	−4.1	−6.9	−12.2	−7.3	−12.6	−10.2	−5.4	−4.8	−8.6
Mauritius	−1.8	−5.0	−9.1	−5.4	−10.1	−7.4	−8.2	−10.3	−10.5	−9.1	−6.7
Mozambique	−10.7	−11.6	−10.7	−9.7	−11.9	−12.2	−11.7	−12.8	−11.6	−12.4	−8.8
Namibia	7.0	4.7	13.8	9.1	2.8	−0.3	0.3	−1.7	−3.8	−4.5	0.8
Niger	−7.3	−8.9	−8.6	−8.2	−13.0	−25.0	−21.1	−25.9	−26.3	−20.7	−11.8
Nigeria	5.7	8.9	25.3	16.8	14.1	8.3	5.9	3.6	3.5	3.1	0.9
Rwanda	1.8	1.0	−4.3	−2.2	−4.9	−7.3	−5.9	−7.3	−9.8	−9.9	−5.6
São Tomé and Príncipe	−16.0	−11.0	−25.8	−30.1	−22.0	−25.5	−27.6	−25.4	−22.8	−24.5	14.9
Senegal	−6.9	−8.9	−9.2	−11.6	−14.1	−6.7	−4.4	−6.4	−8.5	−6.9	−6.3
Seychelles	−9.1	−22.2	−15.8	−15.3	−20.2	−9.8	−20.1	−21.5	−19.8	−19.5	−10.1
Sierra Leone	−4.4	−5.3	−4.3	−4.3	−9.1	−6.5	−19.3	−52.3	−13.1	−9.3	−6.6
South Africa	−3.0	−3.5	−5.3	−7.0	−7.2	−4.0	−2.8	−3.3	−5.5	−5.8	−5.9
South Sudan	...	...	...	...	...	...	4.8	21.6	−12.6	5.8	−4.1
Swaziland	3.1	−4.1	−7.4	−2.2	−8.2	−14.0	−10.5	−9.1	0.1	−5.4	−4.0
Tanzania	−2.3	−6.6	−9.6	−11.0	−10.2	−9.8	−9.3	−13.7	−15.4	−13.4	−8.4
Togo	−10.0	−9.9	−8.4	−8.7	−6.8	−6.6	−6.7	−7.2	−8.8	−9.1	−7.2
Uganda	0.1	−1.3	−3.1	−2.9	−5.7	−9.4	−10.2	−11.4	−11.0	−11.7	−8.7
Zambia	−10.4	−8.5	−0.4	−6.5	−7.2	4.2	7.1	1.2	−1.8	−1.1	1.8
Zimbabwe [5]	−8.0	−10.3	−8.0	−6.7	−21.6	−22.2	−28.8	−36.2	−20.4	−20.0	−18.4

[1] Georgia and Mongolia, which are not members of the Commonwealth of Independent States, are included in this group for reasons of geography and similarities in economic structure.
[2] Calculations are based on Argentina's official GDP data. See footnote to Table A4.
[3] Data for 2011 exclude South Sudan after July 9. Data for 2012 and onward pertain to the current Sudan.
[4] Data for Syria are excluded for 2011 onward due to the uncertain political situation.
[5] The Zimbabwe dollar ceased circulating in early 2009. Data are based on IMF staff estimates of price and exchange rate developments in U.S. dollars. IMF staff estimates of U.S. dollar values may differ from authorities' estimates.

Table A13. Emerging Market and Developing Economies: Net Financial Flows [1]
(Billions of U.S. dollars)

	Average 2001–03	2004	2005	2006	2007	2008	2009	2010	2011	Projections 2012	2013
Emerging Market and Developing Economies											
Private Financial Flows, Net	113.0	267.7	316.0	314.7	694.4	264.5	337.1	604.7	503.0	268.3	399.6
Private Direct Investment, Net	157.1	191.9	293.2	303.7	440.8	484.8	317.0	392.0	462.4	393.8	409.0
Private Portfolio Flows, Net	−11.9	68.8	38.0	−28.5	108.6	−61.9	124.8	240.8	129.7	133.0	150.9
Other Private Financial Flows, Net	−32.2	7.0	−15.2	39.5	145.0	−158.4	−104.7	−28.1	−89.1	−258.6	−160.2
Official Financial Flows, Net [2]	−14.6	−94.5	−88.2	−188.8	−84.3	−104.2	100.6	62.8	−108.3	−51.8	−89.2
Change in Reserves [3]	−182.3	−422.4	−592.8	−756.0	−1,210.2	−723.4	−522.7	−862.9	−765.3	−565.7	−632.3
Memorandum											
Current Account [4]	93.0	206.4	416.9	639.5	629.6	673.7	291.8	336.2	481.2	361.8	310.1
Central and Eastern Europe											
Private Financial Flows, Net	23.5	49.4	102.1	117.4	182.5	153.5	25.6	78.9	88.9	79.6	82.7
Private Direct Investment, Net	14.4	30.6	37.8	64.1	74.7	67.5	30.7	21.4	35.6	33.1	39.0
Private Portfolio Flows, Net	2.4	15.6	20.8	0.8	−4.1	−10.4	8.5	26.8	30.8	19.9	22.7
Other Private Financial Flows, Net	6.8	3.2	43.5	52.5	111.8	96.4	−13.7	30.7	22.5	26.6	21.0
Official Flows, Net [2]	5.5	9.9	3.3	5.2	−6.2	20.5	48.8	35.6	26.9	10.5	4.8
Change in Reserves [3]	−6.9	−12.8	−43.6	−32.3	−36.4	−4.1	−29.0	−36.8	−14.7	−13.0	−1.0
Commonwealth of Independent States [5]											
Private Financial Flows, Net	6.8	5.6	29.1	51.6	129.7	−97.8	−62.9	−22.8	−64.4	−55.9	−39.5
Private Direct Investment, Net	5.1	13.2	11.7	21.4	28.3	50.6	16.2	10.3	17.6	7.9	10.4
Private Portfolio Flows, Net	1.6	4.7	3.9	4.9	19.5	−31.7	−9.3	10.1	−29.0	−5.5	−3.3
Other Private Financial Flows, Net	0.0	−12.3	13.5	25.4	82.0	−116.8	−69.8	−43.2	−53.0	−58.3	−46.5
Official Flows, Net [2]	−1.3	−10.1	−18.3	−25.4	−5.9	−19.0	42.4	0.4	−16.5	−19.7	−20.6
Change in Reserves [3]	−20.7	−54.9	−77.1	−127.9	−168.0	27.0	−7.9	−53.0	−24.7	−29.3	−19.2
Developing Asia											
Private Financial Flows, Net	53.6	161.3	128.4	94.4	205.0	80.4	192.3	407.4	302.6	113.3	182.5
Private Direct Investment, Net	55.0	68.3	131.9	131.6	175.3	169.6	104.0	223.7	217.9	166.9	162.8
Private Portfolio Flows, Net	−2.9	38.7	16.0	−45.1	68.4	9.7	57.8	101.2	41.6	42.4	52.3
Other Private Financial Flows, Net	1.5	54.2	−19.5	7.9	−38.7	−98.9	30.5	82.6	43.2	−96.0	−32.6
Official Flows, Net [2]	−9.2	−18.2	−1.7	3.5	6.3	−5.7	24.5	23.1	14.9	7.6	7.7
Change in Reserves [3]	−120.7	−245.8	−281.4	−360.9	−611.2	−492.5	−467.1	−573.9	−452.6	−241.8	−352.5
Latin America and the Caribbean											
Private Financial Flows, Net	26.4	7.9	40.3	30.1	85.8	79.5	74.3	126.2	186.4	131.0	125.3
Private Direct Investment, Net	53.6	50.5	57.4	33.0	91.2	98.7	69.9	76.1	128.2	122.5	121.6
Private Portfolio Flows, Net	−8.7	−15.9	0.8	8.6	32.7	−5.3	33.4	59.4	49.9	16.6	22.2
Other Private Financial Flows, Net	−18.5	−26.8	−17.9	−11.5	−38.2	−13.9	−29.1	−9.2	8.3	−8.1	−18.6
Official Flows, Net [2]	16.7	−2.2	−35.6	−49.4	1.4	−4.7	40.2	48.1	21.2	62.9	55.5
Change in Reserves [3]	−10.3	−24.5	−36.0	−53.2	−134.9	−50.8	−50.4	−104.8	−119.7	−70.0	−54.2
Middle East and North Africa											
Private Financial Flows, Net	1.2	32.7	−2.3	13.4	72.3	38.4	90.3	28.2	−16.8	−22.3	13.4
Private Direct Investment, Net	15.4	17.6	35.9	45.0	48.9	59.4	64.0	37.7	26.7	29.3	33.6
Private Portfolio Flows, Net	−0.3	23.2	−3.5	−3.9	−8.3	3.8	37.4	44.6	45.1	53.6	50.9
Other Private Financial Flows, Net	−14.0	−8.1	−34.7	−27.8	31.6	−24.8	−11.1	−54.0	−88.6	−105.2	−71.1
Official Flows, Net [2]	−26.8	−73.6	−30.5	−88.8	−79.2	−106.7	−68.6	−73.7	−182.6	−143.9	−163.4
Change in Reserves [3]	−23.2	−65.8	−131.4	−152.6	−231.0	−186.1	23.6	−91.5	−131.6	−194.9	−183.9
Sub-Saharan Africa											
Private Financial Flows, Net	1.5	10.9	18.4	7.7	19.0	10.6	17.5	−13.2	6.2	22.6	35.2
Private Direct Investment, Net	13.6	11.7	18.5	8.6	22.3	39.0	32.1	22.9	36.5	34.1	41.6
Private Portfolio Flows, Net	−4.0	2.5	0.0	6.2	0.3	−28.1	−3.1	−1.3	−8.7	6.0	6.2
Other Private Financial Flows, Net	−8.1	−3.3	−0.2	−7.1	−3.6	−0.3	−11.5	−34.8	−21.6	−17.6	−12.5
Official Flows, Net [2]	0.6	−0.4	−5.3	−33.9	−0.8	11.3	13.2	29.4	27.9	30.7	26.8
Change in Reserves [3]	−0.4	−18.6	−23.4	−29.2	−28.6	−17.0	7.9	−2.8	−22.2	−16.7	−21.6
Memorandum											
Fuel Exporting Countries											
Private Financial Flows, Net	−2.7	26.6	−3.6	25.4	124.0	−142.9	−30.3	−73.5	−142.6	−161.2	−108.1
Other Countries											
Private Financial Flows, Net	115.7	241.1	319.6	289.4	570.4	407.4	367.4	678.2	645.7	429.5	507.7

[1] Net financial flows comprise net direct investment, net portfolio investment, other net official and private financial flows, and changes in reserves.
[2] Excludes grants and includes transactions in external assets and liabilities of official agencies.
[3] A minus sign indicates an increase.
[4] The sum of the current account balance, net private financial flows, net official flows, and the change in reserves equals, with the opposite sign, the sum of the capital account and errors and omissions.
[5] Georgia and Mongolia, which are not members of the Commonwealth of Independent States, are included in this group for reasons of geography and similarities in economic structure.

Table A14. Emerging Market and Developing Economies: Private Financial Flows [1]

(Billions of U.S. dollars)

	Average 2001–03	2004	2005	2006	2007	2008	2009	2010	2011	Projections 2012	2013
Emerging Market and Developing Economies											
Private Financial Flows, Net	113.0	267.7	316.0	314.7	694.4	264.5	337.1	604.7	503.0	268.3	399.6
Assets	–100.0	–258.7	–343.6	–616.5	–823.4	–582.3	–287.2	–610.7	–624.2	–680.9	–610.5
Liabilities	212.6	525.5	652.9	927.9	1,511.8	848.3	623.5	1,213.5	1,126.7	948.9	1,008.4
Central and Eastern Europe											
Private Financial Flows, Net	23.5	49.4	102.1	117.4	182.5	153.5	25.6	78.9	88.9	79.6	82.7
Assets	–6.9	–30.0	–17.8	–56.4	–44.5	–29.3	–10.3	–6.9	8.3	3.7	5.2
Liabilities	30.5	79.4	119.8	173.5	226.1	182.0	36.5	86.0	80.9	76.1	77.8
Commonwealth of Independent States [2]											
Private Financial Flows, Net	6.8	5.6	29.1	51.6	129.7	–97.8	–62.9	–22.8	–64.4	–55.9	–39.5
Assets	–20.6	–53.1	–80.5	–100.3	–160.8	–265.2	–73.9	–104.0	–170.4	–171.8	–162.8
Liabilities	27.4	58.5	109.4	152.0	290.4	167.5	11.2	81.1	105.9	115.9	123.3
Developing Asia											
Private Financial Flows, Net	53.6	161.3	128.4	94.4	205.0	80.4	192.3	407.4	302.6	113.3	182.5
Assets	–18.9	–54.8	–121.4	–224.6	–254.0	–167.5	–96.3	–253.5	–281.3	–377.9	–311.4
Liabilities	72.6	215.1	244.3	315.8	453.4	251.3	287.3	659.6	584.3	491.9	493.6
Latin America and the Caribbean											
Private Financial Flows, Net	26.4	7.9	40.3	30.1	85.8	79.5	74.3	126.2	186.4	131.0	125.3
Assets	–31.5	–45.3	–50.1	–91.4	–114.5	–74.5	–98.3	–167.1	–113.3	–84.7	–82.2
Liabilities	57.0	53.0	89.3	121.5	200.4	153.0	172.3	292.3	299.2	214.7	206.5
Middle East and North Africa											
Private Financial Flows, Net	1.2	32.7	–2.3	13.4	72.3	38.4	90.3	28.2	–16.8	–22.3	13.4
Assets	–13.4	–64.0	–57.8	–115.7	–215.8	–27.8	6.7	–50.9	–42.5	–22.1	–28.4
Liabilities	14.5	96.7	55.5	129.1	288.1	66.2	83.6	79.1	25.7	–0.2	41.8
Sub-Saharan Africa											
Private Financial Flows, Net	1.5	10.9	18.4	7.7	19.0	10.6	17.5	–13.2	6.2	22.6	35.2
Assets	–8.7	–11.5	–15.9	–28.1	–33.9	–18.0	–15.0	–28.2	–25.0	–28.0	–30.9
Liabilities	10.5	22.7	34.6	36.0	53.3	28.4	32.7	15.2	30.7	50.5	65.5

[1] Private financial flows comprise direct investment, portfolio investment, and other long- and short-term investment flows.
[2] Georgia and Mongolia, which are not members of the Commonwealth of Independent States, are included in this group for reasons of geography and similarities in economic structure.

Table A15. Summary of Sources and Uses of World Savings
(Percent of GDP)

| | Averages | | | | | | | | Projections | | Average |
	1990–97	1998–2005	2006	2007	2008	2009	2010	2011	2012	2013	2014–17
World											
Savings	22.1	21.7	24.0	24.3	24.2	21.8	23.1	23.9	24.0	24.6	25.5
Investment	22.9	21.9	23.2	23.8	23.8	21.7	22.7	23.4	23.9	24.4	25.4
Advanced Economies											
Savings	21.7	20.5	20.9	20.8	19.8	17.1	18.1	18.2	18.3	18.7	19.6
Investment	22.2	21.1	21.6	21.6	21.0	17.7	18.4	18.7	18.8	19.1	20.1
Net Lending	–0.5	–0.6	–0.7	–0.9	–1.2	–0.6	–0.3	–0.4	–0.5	–0.4	–0.4
Current Transfers	–0.4	–0.6	–0.7	–0.8	–0.8	–0.9	–0.9	–0.9	–0.8	–0.8	–0.8
Factor Income	–0.5	0.4	1.1	0.5	0.6	0.2	0.7	0.8	0.7	0.7	0.6
Resource Balance	0.5	–0.3	–1.0	–0.5	–0.8	0.1	0.0	–0.2	–0.3	–0.2	–0.2
United States											
Savings	16.0	16.3	16.4	14.6	13.4	11.1	12.2	12.2	13.1	13.7	15.5
Investment	18.3	19.8	20.6	19.6	18.1	14.7	15.5	15.5	16.2	16.8	18.8
Net Lending	–2.3	–3.5	–4.2	–5.0	–4.7	–3.6	–3.3	–3.3	–3.1	–3.1	–3.3
Current Transfers	–0.5	–0.6	–0.7	–0.8	–0.9	–0.9	–0.9	–0.9	–0.8	–0.8	–0.7
Factor Income	–0.7	1.0	2.2	0.8	1.0	0.0	1.1	1.3	1.4	1.4	1.3
Resource Balance	–1.1	–3.9	–5.6	–5.0	–4.9	–2.7	–3.4	–3.7	–3.7	–3.7	–3.8
Euro Area											
Savings	...	21.5	22.4	23.0	21.5	19.0	19.6	20.0	19.9	20.0	20.6
Investment	...	21.0	21.9	22.6	22.2	18.8	19.2	19.5	18.7	18.7	19.0
Net Lending	...	0.5	0.5	0.4	–0.7	0.2	0.4	0.5	1.2	1.3	1.6
Current Transfers [1]	–0.6	–0.8	–1.0	–1.1	–1.1	–1.2	–1.3	–1.2	–1.1	–1.1	–1.1
Factor Income [1]	–0.6	–0.4	0.3	–0.2	–0.6	–0.1	0.2	0.1	–0.2	–0.4	–0.5
Resource Balance [1]	1.2	1.7	1.2	1.6	1.0	1.5	1.5	1.6	2.5	2.8	3.2
Germany											
Savings	21.9	20.9	24.4	26.7	25.5	22.4	23.5	23.9	23.4	22.5	22.1
Investment	22.8	19.6	18.1	19.3	19.3	16.5	17.5	18.3	18.0	17.9	17.8
Net Lending	–0.9	1.2	6.3	7.4	6.2	5.9	6.0	5.7	5.4	4.7	4.3
Current Transfers	–1.6	–1.3	–1.2	–1.3	–1.3	–1.4	–1.5	–1.3	–1.4	–1.4	–1.4
Factor Income	0.0	–0.2	1.9	1.8	1.3	2.4	2.0	1.9	1.5	1.0	0.8
Resource Balance	0.6	2.7	5.6	7.0	6.2	4.9	5.6	5.1	5.4	5.1	4.9
France											
Savings	19.1	20.5	20.3	21.0	20.2	17.6	17.7	18.7	18.5	18.4	19.5
Investment	18.5	19.1	20.9	22.0	21.9	19.0	19.3	20.6	20.2	20.1	20.4
Net Lending	0.6	1.4	–0.6	–1.0	–1.7	–1.3	–1.6	–1.9	–1.7	–1.7	–0.9
Current Transfers	–0.7	–1.0	–1.2	–1.2	–1.3	–1.8	–1.7	–1.8	–1.4	–1.4	–1.4
Factor Income	–0.3	1.1	1.6	1.7	1.7	1.7	2.1	2.1	1.5	1.5	1.5
Resource Balance	1.6	1.3	–1.0	–1.4	–2.2	–1.3	–1.9	–2.2	–1.8	–1.7	–1.0
Italy											
Savings	20.8	20.8	20.3	20.9	18.7	16.8	16.7	16.4	16.9	17.4	18.6
Investment	20.6	20.7	21.8	22.1	21.6	18.9	20.2	19.6	18.4	18.8	19.7
Net Lending	0.2	0.1	–1.5	–1.2	–2.9	–2.1	–3.6	–3.3	–1.5	–1.4	–1.1
Current Transfers	–0.5	–0.5	–0.9	–0.9	–1.0	–0.9	–1.1	–1.0	–1.0	–1.0	–1.0
Factor Income	–1.7	–0.6	0.2	–0.1	–1.2	–0.7	–0.5	–0.8	–0.7	–0.7	–0.8
Resource Balance	2.5	1.2	–0.8	–0.3	–0.7	–0.5	–1.9	–1.5	0.2	0.4	0.7
Japan											
Savings	31.7	26.7	26.6	27.8	26.3	22.6	23.5	21.9	21.9	22.9	23.0
Investment	29.7	23.8	22.7	22.9	23.0	19.7	19.8	19.9	20.3	20.6	20.7
Net Lending	2.0	2.9	3.9	4.9	3.3	2.9	3.7	2.0	1.6	2.3	2.2
Current Transfers	–0.2	–0.2	–0.2	–0.3	–0.3	–0.2	–0.2	–0.2	–0.2	–0.2	–0.1
Factor Income	0.8	1.6	2.7	3.2	3.2	2.7	2.6	3.0	2.9	2.9	2.8
Resource Balance	1.4	1.5	1.4	1.9	0.4	0.5	1.4	–0.7	–1.2	–0.4	–0.4
United Kingdom											
Savings	15.8	15.4	14.5	16.0	16.1	12.9	12.5	12.9	11.4	12.1	14.7
Investment	17.1	17.4	17.4	18.3	17.1	14.1	15.0	14.8	14.7	14.9	16.1
Net Lending	–1.2	–2.0	–2.9	–2.3	–1.0	–1.3	–2.5	–1.9	–3.3	–2.7	–1.4
Current Transfers	–0.7	–0.9	–0.9	–1.0	–1.0	–1.1	–1.4	–1.5	–1.5	–1.5	–1.5
Factor Income	–0.4	0.9	0.6	1.3	2.2	1.3	1.0	1.1	0.6	0.6	0.6
Resource Balance	–0.1	–2.1	–2.6	–2.7	–2.3	–1.5	–2.1	–1.6	–2.4	–1.8	–0.5

Table A15. Summary of Sources and Uses of World Savings *(continued)*
(Percent of GDP)

| | Averages | | | | | | | | Projections | | |
	1990–97	1998–2005	2006	2007	2008	2009	2010	2011	2012	2013	Average 2014–17
Canada											
Savings	16.5	21.7	24.4	24.1	23.6	17.9	19.1	20.0	20.3	20.7	21.4
Investment	19.0	20.3	23.0	23.2	23.2	20.9	22.2	22.8	23.7	24.4	24.8
Net Lending	−2.5	1.4	1.4	0.8	0.3	−3.0	−3.1	−2.8	−3.4	−3.7	−3.4
Current Transfers	−0.1	0.0	−0.1	−0.1	−0.1	−0.2	−0.2	−0.2	−0.2	−0.2	−0.2
Factor Income	−3.6	−2.7	−0.9	−0.9	−1.1	−1.0	−1.0	−1.3	−1.2	−1.2	−1.7
Resource Balance	1.1	4.1	2.4	1.9	1.5	−1.8	−2.0	−1.3	−2.0	−2.4	−1.5
Newly Industrialized Asian Economies											
Savings	34.6	32.2	32.5	33.4	32.6	31.2	33.7	32.6	31.5	31.5	30.7
Investment	32.7	26.5	26.4	26.2	27.6	23.5	26.4	25.9	25.8	26.0	25.9
Net Lending	1.9	5.7	6.1	7.2	4.9	7.7	7.3	6.6	5.6	5.5	4.8
Current Transfers	−0.1	−0.5	−0.7	−0.7	−0.6	−0.6	−0.8	−0.8	−0.9	−0.9	−0.8
Factor Income	0.8	0.4	0.6	0.7	0.9	0.7	0.8	0.8	0.8	0.8	0.9
Resource Balance	1.2	5.9	6.2	7.2	4.7	7.7	7.2	6.6	5.7	5.5	4.7
Emerging Market and Developing Economies											
Savings	23.7	26.3	32.8	33.3	33.7	32.0	32.5	33.7	33.3	33.6	33.6
Investment	26.2	25.1	27.9	29.2	30.1	30.5	31.0	31.8	32.1	32.6	32.9
Net Lending	−1.9	1.2	4.9	4.1	3.5	1.6	1.5	1.8	1.3	1.0	0.6
Current Transfers	0.6	1.3	1.8	1.6	1.5	1.4	1.3	1.1	1.1	1.0	1.1
Factor Income	−1.7	−2.0	−1.8	−1.5	−1.5	−1.6	−1.8	−1.8	−1.6	−1.5	−1.1
Resource Balance	−0.8	1.8	5.1	4.0	3.6	1.7	2.1	2.6	1.8	1.5	0.7
Memorandum											
Acquisition of Foreign Assets	1.7	4.8	10.5	12.6	6.9	5.0	7.0	6.0	4.4	3.9	3.5
Change in Reserves	1.1	2.5	5.9	7.7	3.8	2.9	4.0	3.0	2.1	2.2	2.2
Regional Groups											
Central and Eastern Europe											
Savings	20.3	17.3	16.2	17.3	17.5	15.3	15.4	17.1	16.0	16.5	16.7
Investment	22.0	21.0	23.4	24.7	25.0	18.9	20.5	23.1	21.1	21.5	22.2
Net Lending	−1.6	−3.7	−7.2	−7.4	−7.5	−3.6	−5.2	−6.0	−5.2	−5.0	−5.6
Current Transfers	1.8	2.0	1.8	1.6	1.5	1.7	1.5	1.6	1.6	1.6	1.4
Factor Income	−1.2	−1.4	−2.7	−1.9	−1.6	−2.9	−2.8	−2.4	−2.6	−2.4	−2.3
Resource Balance	−2.3	−4.5	−6.3	−7.1	−7.5	−2.6	−4.0	−5.3	−4.3	−4.3	−4.7
Memorandum											
Acquisition of Foreign Assets	0.9	2.7	6.1	4.8	1.7	1.7	2.7	−0.2	0.7	0.1	0.4
Change in Reserves	0.4	1.4	2.5	2.2	0.2	1.8	2.1	0.8	0.7	0.1	0.4
Commonwealth of Independent States [2]											
Savings	...	27.1	30.2	30.7	30.1	21.9	25.7	28.2	27.9	28.3	25.7
Investment	...	20.2	23.0	26.7	25.2	19.1	21.9	23.6	23.6	25.3	25.3
Net Lending	...	6.9	7.3	4.0	4.8	2.8	3.8	4.6	4.3	3.0	0.3
Current Transfers	...	0.6	0.4	0.3	0.4	0.4	0.3	0.3	0.3	0.3	0.4
Factor Income	...	−3.0	−3.3	−2.9	−3.4	−3.6	−3.7	−4.0	−3.3	−3.1	−2.3
Resource Balance	...	9.2	10.3	6.8	8.0	5.7	7.1	8.3	7.4	5.8	2.4
Memorandum											
Acquisition of Foreign Assets	...	9.3	14.9	17.5	10.0	1.5	6.1	6.2	5.5	4.2	3.2
Change in Reserves	...	4.0	9.8	9.8	−1.2	0.5	2.7	1.0	1.1	0.7	0.4
Developing Asia											
Savings	31.6	34.3	42.6	43.6	43.8	45.2	43.9	43.6	43.0	43.1	43.3
Investment	33.6	32.0	37.0	36.9	38.3	41.4	41.4	41.9	42.1	42.0	41.5
Net Lending	−2.0	2.4	5.5	6.6	5.4	3.7	2.4	1.6	0.9	1.0	1.8
Current Transfers	1.0	1.8	2.2	2.2	2.1	1.9	1.7	1.5	1.4	1.4	1.7
Factor Income	−1.7	−1.5	−0.9	−0.5	−0.3	−0.5	−1.0	−0.7	−0.7	−0.5	−0.4
Resource Balance	−1.3	2.1	4.3	4.9	3.7	2.4	1.7	0.9	0.2	0.1	0.5
Memorandum											
Acquisition of Foreign Assets	3.2	5.4	11.1	13.4	7.6	6.9	8.7	6.2	4.1	3.9	4.0
Change in Reserves	1.8	3.8	7.5	10.1	6.6	5.9	6.0	3.9	1.9	2.5	3.1

Table A15. Summary of Sources and Uses of World Savings *(continued)*
(Percent of GDP)

	Averages 1990–97	Averages 1998–2005	2006	2007	2008	2009	2010	2011	Projections 2012	Projections 2013	Projections Average 2014–17
Latin America and the Caribbean											
Savings	18.8	19.1	23.3	23.0	22.9	20.0	20.5	21.0	20.5	20.7	20.8
Investment	21.0	20.5	21.7	22.6	23.8	20.6	21.8	22.6	22.4	22.7	23.2
Net Lending	–2.2	–1.4	1.6	0.4	–0.9	–0.5	–1.3	–1.6	–1.9	–2.0	–2.4
Current Transfers	0.9	1.5	2.1	1.8	1.6	1.4	1.3	1.1	1.1	1.1	1.1
Factor Income	–2.5	–3.0	–3.1	–2.7	–2.7	–2.5	–2.6	–2.8	–2.5	–2.6	–2.5
Resource Balance	–0.5	0.1	2.6	1.3	0.2	0.5	0.0	0.1	–0.5	–0.6	–1.1
Memorandum											
Acquisition of Foreign Assets	1.3	2.3	3.1	5.7	2.3	4.6	5.3	4.7	2.6	1.8	1.0
Change in Reserves	0.9	0.5	1.7	3.6	1.2	1.3	2.1	2.1	1.2	0.9	0.4
Middle East and North Africa											
Savings	22.4	29.9	41.0	40.9	43.0	31.4	35.4	40.7	38.3	37.5	34.9
Investment	24.4	23.4	22.9	26.7	27.6	29.0	27.7	26.6	26.1	27.0	27.5
Net Lending	–2.0	6.6	18.3	14.6	15.1	3.0	8.1	14.5	12.8	10.8	7.4
Current Transfers	–2.5	–1.0	–0.4	–0.9	–0.8	–1.5	–1.3	–1.5	–1.5	–1.8	–2.0
Factor Income	1.1	0.1	0.9	1.0	0.6	0.1	–0.3	–0.3	–0.1	0.0	1.2
Resource Balance	–0.6	7.3	18.1	14.6	15.6	3.9	9.4	16.1	14.0	12.4	8.2
Memorandum											
Acquisition of Foreign Assets	–0.2	9.2	23.9	28.0	15.8	4.7	9.3	13.1	10.8	10.5	7.7
Change in Reserves	0.8	3.6	9.6	12.4	8.0	–1.1	3.8	4.8	6.6	5.9	4.2
Sub-Saharan Africa											
Savings	15.5	16.8	24.8	23.4	21.9	19.3	20.2	19.2	18.8	18.9	18.9
Investment	16.8	19.0	20.6	21.9	22.0	22.4	21.4	21.1	22.0	22.2	22.8
Net Lending	–1.4	–2.2	4.1	1.5	0.0	–3.1	–1.2	–1.8	–3.2	–3.2	–3.9
Current Transfers	1.9	2.3	4.6	4.6	4.6	4.7	4.2	4.0	3.7	3.5	3.3
Factor Income	–3.1	–4.8	–4.0	–5.4	–6.1	–4.5	–4.8	–5.5	–5.3	–5.4	–4.7
Resource Balance	0.0	0.3	3.5	2.3	1.3	–3.4	–0.1	0.0	–1.5	–1.2	–2.5
Memorandum											
Acquisition of Foreign Assets	1.1	2.3	8.3	7.5	3.8	2.5	3.3	2.6	3.1	3.6	3.5
Change in Reserves	0.9	1.2	4.1	3.4	1.8	–0.9	0.3	1.8	1.3	1.6	1.1
Analytical Groups											
By Source of Export Earnings											
Fuel Exporters											
Savings	22.9	30.4	39.5	38.5	38.9	28.7	32.2	36.4	35.0	34.4	30.7
Investment	26.0	22.7	22.7	26.5	25.6	24.7	24.5	24.7	24.7	25.8	25.8
Net Lending	–1.2	7.7	16.8	12.2	13.0	4.3	7.8	11.7	10.5	8.6	4.7
Current Transfers	–3.5	–1.6	–0.4	–0.7	–0.6	–1.0	–1.0	–1.0	–1.1	–1.2	–1.2
Factor Income	–0.2	–1.9	–1.7	–1.6	–2.2	–2.2	–2.5	–2.9	–2.5	–2.3	–1.1
Resource Balance	2.6	11.2	19.1	14.6	16.1	7.2	11.3	15.7	13.9	12.1	7.3
Memorandum											
Acquisition of Foreign Assets	0.3	10.0	21.0	23.5	14.2	3.7	8.0	11.0	9.3	8.3	5.6
Change in Reserves	0.2	3.7	10.2	10.9	3.7	–1.5	3.0	3.5	4.6	3.7	2.3
Nonfuel Exporters											
Savings	23.8	25.4	30.9	31.8	32.1	32.9	32.6	33.0	32.9	33.4	34.3
Investment	25.9	25.7	29.3	30.0	31.5	31.9	32.6	33.6	34.0	34.3	34.6
Net Lending	–2.1	–0.3	1.6	1.8	0.7	1.0	0.0	–0.7	–1.1	–0.9	–0.4
Current Transfers	1.4	1.9	2.4	2.3	2.2	2.0	1.8	1.6	1.6	1.6	1.7
Factor Income	–2.0	–2.0	–1.9	–1.5	–1.3	–1.4	–1.7	–1.5	–1.4	–1.3	–1.1
Resource Balance	–1.5	–0.2	1.1	1.0	–0.2	0.3	–0.2	–0.8	–1.3	–1.3	–0.9
Memorandum											
Acquisition of Foreign Assets	1.9	3.7	7.4	9.4	4.6	5.3	6.8	4.7	3.1	2.8	2.9
Change in Reserves	1.3	2.2	4.6	6.7	3.8	4.0	4.2	2.9	1.4	1.8	2.1

Table A15. Summary of Sources and Uses of World Savings *(concluded)*
(Percent of GDP)

	Averages								Projections		Average
	1990–97	1998–2005	2006	2007	2008	2009	2010	2011	2012	2013	2014–17
By External Financing Source											
Net Debtor Economies											
Savings	19.2	19.4	22.4	22.9	21.9	20.8	21.2	21.4	21.0	21.4	22.3
Investment	21.5	21.4	24.1	25.5	25.7	23.1	24.0	24.5	24.5	24.8	25.7
Net Lending	–2.3	–2.0	–1.8	–2.6	–3.9	–2.3	–2.8	–3.2	–3.5	–3.4	–3.3
Current Transfers	1.8	2.6	3.0	2.9	2.9	2.9	2.6	2.5	2.6	2.6	2.5
Factor Income	–2.0	–2.3	–2.6	–2.3	–2.3	–2.3	–2.4	–2.5	–2.4	–2.4	–2.4
Resource Balance	–2.1	–2.3	–2.2	–3.2	–4.5	–2.9	–3.1	–3.3	–3.7	–3.6	–3.5
Memorandum											
Acquisition of Foreign Assets	1.1	2.3	4.2	5.8	1.5	2.9	3.9	2.5	1.5	1.2	1.2
Change in Reserves	0.9	1.1	2.5	3.9	0.7	1.5	2.0	1.2	0.5	0.5	0.7
Official Financing											
Savings	17.3	19.3	22.9	23.5	21.7	21.7	22.3	22.6	22.1	22.7	22.7
Investment	19.9	21.6	23.6	23.6	24.0	23.4	24.2	25.1	26.0	26.0	26.3
Net Lending	–2.6	–2.4	–0.7	–0.1	–2.4	–1.6	–1.9	–2.4	–3.9	–3.3	–3.6
Current Transfers	4.7	7.5	10.6	11.4	11.1	11.0	11.0	11.9	11.8	11.5	10.5
Factor Income	–2.8	–3.0	–2.6	–1.1	–1.6	–1.7	–1.6	–2.1	–2.6	–3.2	–3.6
Resource Balance	–4.6	–7.0	–8.7	–10.3	–11.7	–10.9	–11.2	–12.2	–13.1	–11.7	–10.5
Memorandum											
Acquisition of Foreign Assets	1.4	1.6	0.6	3.8	1.6	2.8	2.7	2.8	0.9	1.8	1.4
Change in Reserves	1.4	1.2	1.0	2.1	0.9	1.9	2.0	1.1	0.1	1.4	1.5
Net Debtor Economies by Debt-Servicing Experience											
Economies with Arrears and/or Rescheduling during 2006–10											
Savings	15.0	17.0	22.7	22.1	21.1	18.9	19.4	19.4	18.9	19.6	19.8
Investment	18.9	19.0	23.1	24.0	24.7	21.7	23.7	24.6	24.5	24.5	24.5
Net Lending	–3.8	–2.0	–0.4	–1.9	–3.6	–2.9	–4.3	–5.2	–5.6	–4.9	–4.7
Current Transfers	1.7	3.9	5.6	5.0	4.6	4.7	4.4	3.8	3.7	3.6	3.4
Factor Income	–3.5	–4.1	–3.0	–2.9	–3.4	–3.2	–3.9	–4.1	–4.0	–3.8	–3.5
Resource Balance	–2.1	–1.9	–3.1	–4.1	–4.9	–4.5	–4.8	–4.9	–5.3	–4.7	–4.6
Memorandum											
Acquisition of Foreign Assets	2.8	2.7	3.5	6.0	1.3	1.4	3.0	3.0	0.8	1.0	0.5
Change in Reserves	0.8	0.7	2.0	3.9	0.6	1.8	1.4	0.2	–0.2	0.5	0.5

Note: The estimates in this table are based on individual countries' national accounts and balance of payments statistics. Country group composites are calculated as the sum of the U.S. dollar values for the relevant individual countries. This differs from the calculations in the April 2005 and earlier issues of the *World Economic Outlook*, where the composites were weighted by GDP valued at purchasing power parities as a share of total world GDP. For many countries, the estimates of national savings are built up from national accounts data on gross domestic investment and from balance-of-payments-based data on net foreign investment. The latter, which is equivalent to the current account balance, comprises three components: current transfers, net factor income, and the resource balance. The mixing of data sources, which is dictated by availability, implies that the estimates for national savings that are derived incorporate the statistical discrepancies. Furthermore, errors, omissions, and asymmetries in balance of payments statistics affect the estimates for net lending; at the global level, net lending, which in theory would be zero, equals the world current account discrepancy. Despite these statistical shortcomings, flow of funds estimates, such as those presented in these tables, provide a useful framework for analyzing development in savings and investment, both over time and across regions and countries.
[1] Calculated from the data of individual Euro Area countries.
[2] Georgia and Mongolia, which are not members of the Commonwealth of Independent States, are included in this group for reasons of geography and similarities in economic structure.

Table A16. Summary of World Medium-Term Baseline Scenario

	Averages 1994–2001	Averages 2002–09	2010	2011	Projections 2012	2013	Averages 2010–13	Averages 2014–17
			Annual Percent Change					
World Real GDP	**3.5**	**3.6**	**5.1**	**3.8**	**3.3**	**3.6**	**4.0**	**4.4**
Advanced Economies	3.1	1.5	3.0	1.6	1.3	1.5	1.9	2.5
Emerging Market and Developing Economies	4.2	6.4	7.4	6.2	5.3	5.6	6.1	6.1
Memorandum								
Potential Output								
Major Advanced Economies	2.5	1.9	1.0	1.2	1.3	1.4	1.3	1.7
World Trade, Volume [1]	**7.4**	**4.5**	**12.6**	**5.8**	**3.2**	**4.5**	**6.5**	**6.1**
Imports								
Advanced Economies	7.8	2.9	11.4	4.4	1.7	3.3	5.1	5.1
Emerging Market and Developing Economies	6.9	8.8	14.9	8.8	7.0	6.6	9.3	7.8
Exports								
Advanced Economies	7.0	3.4	12.0	5.3	2.2	3.6	5.7	5.2
Emerging Market and Developing Economies	8.3	7.2	13.7	6.5	4.0	5.7	7.4	7.5
Terms of Trade								
Advanced Economies	0.0	0.0	−0.9	−1.6	−0.8	0.1	−0.8	−0.1
Emerging Market and Developing Economies	0.7	1.7	2.3	3.5	0.5	−0.4	1.4	−0.6
World Prices in U.S. Dollars								
Manufactures	−0.8	2.7	2.7	6.5	−0.5	−0.3	2.1	0.3
Oil	4.7	12.4	27.9	31.6	2.1	−1.0	14.2	−4.1
Nonfuel Primary Commodities	−1.4	6.7	26.3	17.8	−9.5	−2.9	6.9	−2.5
Consumer Prices								
Advanced Economies	2.1	2.0	1.5	2.7	1.9	1.6	1.9	1.9
Emerging Market and Developing Economies	23.3	6.5	6.1	7.2	6.1	5.8	6.3	4.9
Interest Rates			*Percent*					
Real Six-Month LIBOR [2]	3.7	0.5	−0.8	−1.6	−1.0	−0.8	−1.1	0.4
World Real Long-Term Interest Rate [3]	3.5	1.9	1.6	0.3	0.3	1.0	0.8	2.1
Balances on Current Account			*Percent of GDP*					
Advanced Economies	−0.2	−0.8	0.0	−0.2	−0.4	−0.3	−0.2	−0.3
Emerging Market and Developing Economies	−0.6	2.9	1.5	1.9	1.3	1.1	1.5	0.7
Total External Debt								
Emerging Market and Developing Economies	37.0	30.2	25.4	24.0	24.4	24.1	24.5	23.1
Debt Service								
Emerging Market and Developing Economies	8.8	9.9	8.0	8.1	8.3	8.6	8.3	8.5

[1] Data refer to trade in goods and services.
[2] London interbank offered rate on U.S. dollar deposits minus percent change in U.S. GDP deflator.
[3] GDP-weighted average of 10-year (or nearest maturity) government bond rates for Canada, France, Germany, Italy, Japan, United Kingdom, and United States.

WORLD ECONOMIC OUTLOOK
SELECTED TOPICS

World Economic Outlook Archives

I. Methodology—Aggregation, Modeling, and Forecasting

II. Historical Surveys

III. Economic Growth—Sources and Patterns

IV. Inflation and Deflation, and Commodity Markets

VII. Labor Markets, Poverty, and Inequality

VIII. Exchange Rate Issues

IX. External Payments, Trade, Capital Movements, and Foreign Debt

X. Regional Issues

XI. Country-Specific Analyses

XII. Special Topics

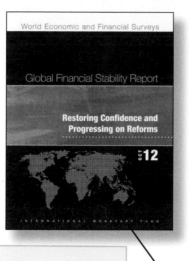
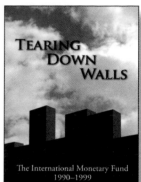
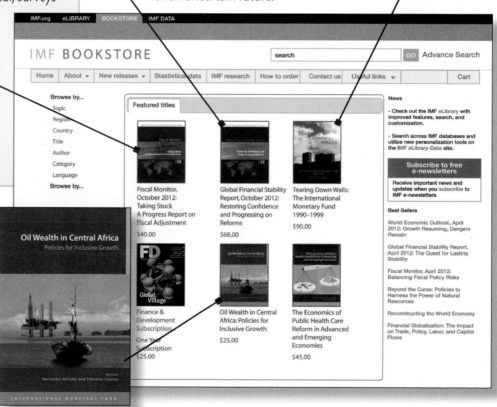